T0093157

Transformation in Healthcare with Emerging Technologies

Transformation in Healthcare with Emerging Technologies

Edited by

Pushpa Singh

Divya Mishra

Kirti Seth

CRC Press
Taylor & Francis Group
Boca Raton London New York

CRC Press is an imprint of the
Taylor & Francis Group, an **Informa** business

A CHAPMAN & HALL BOOK

First edition published 2022
by CRC Press
6000 Broken Sound Parkway NW, Suite 300, Boca Raton, FL 33487-2742

and by CRC Press
2 Park Square, Milton Park, Abingdon, Oxon, OX14 4RN

CRC Press is an imprint of Taylor & Francis Group, LLC

© 2022 selection and editorial matter, [Pushpa Singh, Divya Mishra, Kirti Seth]; individual chapters, the contributors

Reasonable efforts have been made to publish reliable data and information, but the author and publisher cannot assume responsibility for the validity of all materials or the consequences of their use. The authors and publishers have attempted to trace the copyright holders of all material reproduced in this publication and apologize to copyright holders if permission to publish in this form has not been obtained. If any copyright material has not been acknowledged please write and let us know so we may rectify in any future reprint.

Except as permitted under U.S. Copyright Law, no part of this book may be reprinted, reproduced, transmitted, or utilized in any form by any electronic, mechanical, or other means, now known or hereafter invented, including photocopying, microfilming, and recording, or in any information storage or retrieval system, without written permission from the publishers.

For permission to photocopy or use material electronically from this work, access www.copyright.com or contact the Copyright Clearance Center, Inc. (CCC), 222 Rosewood Drive, Danvers, MA 01923, 978-750-8400. For works that are not available on CCC please contact mpkbookspermissions@tandf.co.uk

Trademark notice: Product or corporate names may be trademarks or registered trademarks and are used only for identification and explanation without intent to infringe.

Library of Congress Cataloging-in-Publication Data
Names: Singh, Pushpa, editor. | Mishra, Divya, editor. | Seth, Kirti, 1966- editor.
Title: Transformation in healthcare with emerging technologies / edited by Pushpa Singh, Divya Mishra, Kirti Seth.
Description: First edition. | Boca Raton : Chapman & Hall/CRC Press, 2022. | Includes bibliographical references and index. | Summary: "The book, Transformation in Healthcare with Emerging Technologies, presents healthcare industrial revolution based on service aggregation and virtualisation that can transform the healthcare sector with the aid of technologies such as Artificial Intelligence (AI), Internet of Things (IoT), Bigdata and Blockchain. These technologies offer fast communication between doctors and patients, protected transactions, safe data storage and analysis, immutable data records, transparent data flow service, transaction validation process, and secure data exchanges between organizations. Features: Discusses the Integration of AI, IoT, big data and blockchain in healthcare industry Highlights the security and privacy aspect of AI, IoT, big data and blockchain in healthcare industry Talks about challenges and issues of AI, IoT, big data and blockchain in healthcare industry Includes several case studies It is primarily aimed at graduates and researchers in computer science and IT who are doing collaborative research with the medical industry. Industry professionals will also find it useful"-- Provided by publisher.
Identifiers: LCCN 2021048205 (print) | LCCN 2021048206 (ebook) | ISBN 9781032063416 (hardback) | ISBN 9781032063706 (paperback) | ISBN 9781003201960 (ebook)
Subjects: LCSH: Bioinformatics. | Medical care--Technological innovations.
Classification: LCC R855.3 .T728 2022 (print) | LCC R855.3 (ebook) | DDC 610.285--dc23/eng/20211112
LC record available at https://lccn.loc.gov/2021048205
LC ebook record available at https://lccn.loc.gov/2021048206

ISBN: 978-1-032-06341-6 (hbk)
ISBN: 978-1-032-06370-6 (pbk)
ISBN: 978-1-003-20196-0 (ebk)

DOI: 10.1201/9781003201960

Typeset in Palatino
by SPi Technologies India Pvt Ltd (Straive)

Contents

Preface

Analyzing human civilization advancement includes the development and progression of healthcare and associated disciplines. If you look back at how modern healthcare systems are designed, there are many important milestones. Primary medical civilizations include Egypt, China, India, and Babylon. The concept of medical practice was born when the Hippocratic Oath started the first school of medicine and documented this profession's ethics.

From the fifth to fifteen centuries BCE, advancements in healthcare were limited, and it was the era with epidemic and infectious diseases. By the eighteenth century, the existence of microorganisms was discovered and the first vaccine (smallpox, based on cowpox) was created. The nineteenth century, especially the latter half of it, saw the development of surgical techniques and recognition of the importance of aseptic environment in healthcare practice. The twentieth century saw advancements that radically changed the face of medicine, from effective antiinfectives, advanced vaccination campaigns that made diseases like polio into a global retreat, and continuous refinement of surgical procedures to the invention of microtechnology and fiber-optics to perform surgeries on the previously unimaginable micro scale.

In the twenty-first century, healthcare is considered the highest priority by most countries with advancements in computing and data storage capacities and the involvement of multidisciplinary talents in the healthcare industry. The global reaction to the COVID-19 pandemic, particularly rapid development of treatments and vaccines, is the evidence that the momentum of healthcare evolution is significant and will continue at high pace throughout the century. It likely will mark a new milestone in healthcare history and drive the rapid development of data applications in this industry.

Healthcare industry and digital technologies are at a convergence point where significant changes are taking place almost on a daily basis. The past two decades saw a giant leap in machine learning, artificial intelligence (AI), data mining, and wearable technologies that manage, process, and share large quantities of data. Advances in AI, IoT, Big Data, and Blockchain technologies, and their intersections within various industries, opens a future for leveraging advanced technologies within the healthcare industry.

This book presents the healthcare industrial revolution based on service aggregation and virtualization that can transform the healthcare sector with the aid of technologies such as AI, Internet of Things (IoT), Big Data, and Blockchain. Its main objective is to demonstrate the benefits of Industry 4.0 with the latest technologies in the healthcare industry and to endorse various frameworks for supporting the technical implementation. Key topics include foundation and architecture of AI and IoT to help Healthcare 4.0; the role of Big Data and Blockchain architecture in transforming the healthcare industry; integration of AI, IoT, Big Data, and Blockchain with medical practice along with their security and privacy aspects; various cases of AI, IoT, Big Data, and Blockchain convergence; various government policies and practices to implement emerging technology in the healthcare industry; and the future of healthcare within Industry 4.0 as a whole.

This book provides a detailed look at smart healthcare systems, as well as describes the primary role of IoT, AI, and Big Data in the healthcare industry. It posits that the Blockchain architecture's main advantage is in the facilitation of faster, seamless interoperability, fault tolerance, data encryption, data recovery, and cryptography technologies in the healthcare industries. This book explores the use of Blockchain for electronic health research (EHR) and the creation of Healthcare Big Data. It also introduces the integration aspects and challenges of these emerging technologies in the smart healthcare industry, as well as discusses the impact of accepting these technologies in the healthcare industry. It provides a look at diverse functioning to create and develop a better prediction model for Big Data analytics's continuing progress within the healthcare industry.

This book is a product of the transforming healthcare, with contributions from authors around the globe. Contributors' expertise ranges from healthcare experts and data scientists to academics and digital healthcare entrepreneurs. For readers with a basic understanding of the healthcare industry and data technologies and interested in the future of AI, IoT, Big Data, and Blockchain in healthcare, the chapters in this book will provide a wealth of insights into the healthcare's new landscape.

Editors

Dr. Pushpa Singh is an Associate Professor of CSIT Department at the KIET Group of Institutions, Delhi-NCR, Ghaziabad, India. She has more than 17 years of experience teaching B.Tech and MCA students. Dr. Singh has acquired MCA, M.Tech (CSE), and Ph.D. (CSE) in Wireless Networks from AKTU Lucknow. Her current areas of research include performance evaluation of heterogeneous wireless networks, machine learning, and cryptography. She has published 45 papers in reputed international journals and conference proceedings. She has published four books and contributed six book chapters in international publication. She is one of active reviewers of IGI, Springer, and other conference proceedings and journals. She has been invited to serve on various technical program committees.

Dr. Divya Mishra is working as a full-time academician for last 13+ years. She is presently an Professor and Head of the Department of Computer Science & Engineering Department at the ABES Engineering College, Ghaziabad. She has a Ph.D. (Engineering) from Amity University Uttar Pradesh and an M.Tech (Information Security) from Guru Gobind Singh Indraprastha University, New Delhi. She also holds a B.Tech (Computer Science & Engineering) from Sant Longowal Institute of Engineering & Technology, IKJPTU, Punjab. She has published many research papers in reputed international journals and conference proceedings with Scopus & SCI indexing. She was also recognized by the IEEE Sensors Council for her paper, "Application of Non-Linear Gaussian Regression-Based Adaptive Clock Synchronization Technique for Wireless Sensor Network in Agriculture" (*IEEE Sensors Journal*, Vol. 18, No. 10, May 2018), being one of the 25 most downloaded *Sensors Journal* papers in the month of February 2019. She is an active member of international societies such as IEEE, IAENG, and organizing committees for many international conferences, workshops, and seminars to enhance the teaching–learning process. She is also associated with a project on Cloud Computing Security funded by the International Bilateral Cooperation Division, Department of Science and Technology, MS&T, Government of India. She has guided more than M.Tech 15 students through their degree work. Her research areas include networking, cloud computing, information security, and IoT.

Dr. Kirti Seth is a consultant, researcher and teacher. She is presently an Associate Professor at the School of Computer and Information Engineering, INHA University, Tashkent. She holds a Ph.D. (Computer Science) from Dr. APJ Abdul Kalam Technical University, Lucknow, and an M.Tech (Computer Science and Engineering) from Banasthali University, India. She also holds an M.Sc in Computer Science. She has published many research papers in reputed journals and authored five books. She is an active member of international societies such as IEEE, CSI, IACSIT, IAENG, and many workshops to enhance the teaching–learning process. She also conducted many training programs for students, researchers, and faculty members to bridge the gap between industry and academics. She also serves as an editor, reviewer, and evaluator for some journals. She shares her knowledge and offers guidance to students through various online forums; her educational channel on YouTube provides video lectures on various areas of computer science.

Contributors

Shivani Agarwal
Apex Institute of Technology
Chandigarh University
Chandigarh, India

Shubham Bansal
Amity University
Greater Noida, India

Devendra Bharadwaj
Harman Connected Services
Bengaluru, India

Shreya Dhapke
Mechanical Department
Yeshwantrao Chavan College of
    Engineering
Nagpur, India

Saru Dhir
Amity University
Greater Noida, India

Jayant Giri
Mechanical Department
Yeshwantrao Chavan College of
    Engineering
Nagpur, India

Sanjeev Gour
Career College
Bhopal, India

A. Sri Krishna Govind
School of Electrical Engineering
Vellore Institute of Technology
Chennai, India

Pratima Guatam
RNTU University
Bhopal, India

Deepa Gupta
GL Bajaj Institute of Management and
    Research
Greater Noida, India

Mukul Gupta
GL Bajaj Institute of Management
Greater Noida, India

Deena Nath Gupta
Research Laboratory, Department of
    Computer Science, JMI
New Delhi, India

Madhurima Hooda
Amity University
Greater Noida, India

Apoorva Joshi
Career College
Bhopal, India

Upasna Joshi
Delhi Technical Campus
Greater Noida, India

Ashwani Kumar
Department of Computer Science and
    Engineering
United College of Engineering &
    Research
Greater Noida, India

Rajendra Kumar
Research Laboratory
Department of Computer Science, JMI
New Delhi, India

Divya Mishra
ABES Engineering College
Ghaziabad, India

Dhananjay Mutyarapwar
Mechanical Department
Yeshwantrao Chavan College of
    Engineering
Nagpur, India

R. Nivedhithaa
School of Electrical Engineering
Vellore Institute of Technology
Chennai, India

Medhavi Pandey
Delhi Technical Campus
Greater Noida, India

Shreyaa Parvath Rajkumar
School of Electrical Engineering
Vellore Institute of Technology
Chennai, India

Navneet Rajpoot
Amity University
Greater Noida, India

Priti Rani Rajvanshi
GL Bajaj Institute of Management
Greater Noida, India

Shradha Sapra
Amity University
Greater Noida, India

Ambrish Kumar Sharma
NRI College
Bhopal, India

Nidhi Sharma
Delhi Technical Campus
Greater Noida, India

Murari Kumar Singh
Department of Computer Science and
    Engineering
Sharda University, School of Engineering
    and Technology
Greater Noida, India

Narendra Singh
Department of Management Studies
GL Bajaj Institute of Management and
    Research
Greater Noida, India

Pushpa Singh
KIET Group of Institutions, Delhi-NCR
Ghaziabad, India

Rajnesh Singh
GL Bajaj Institute of Technology and
    Management
Greater Noida, India

Taranjeet Singh
GL Bajaj Institute of Management
Greater Noida, India

P. Sriramalakshmi
School of Electrical Engineering
Vellore Institute of Technology
Chennai, India

Gautam Srivastava
GL Bajaj Institute of Management and
    Research
Greater Noida, India

Ranjit Varma
Delhi Technical Campus
Greater Noida, India

Srimathnath Thejasvi Vondivillu
School of Electrical Engineering
Vellore Institute of Technology
Chennai, India

1

AI- and IoT-Based Architecture in Healthcare

Divya Mishra
ABES Engineering College, Ghaziabad, India

Pushpa Singh
KIET Group of Institutions, Delhi-NCR, Ghaziabad, India

Shivani Agarwal
Apex Institute of Technology Chandigarh University, Chandigarh, Punjab, India

CONTENTS

DOI: 10.1201/9781003201960-1

1.1 Introduction

With the continual advancement in digitized healthcare data acquisition, learning algorithms, and computing infrastructure, emerging technology like AI, IoT, and Cloud computing bring revolutionary changes in the healthcare industry. IoT provides an environment to connect multiple different devices using a common platform to communicate through a computer network (Hameed et al., 2020; Whitemore et al., 2015). IoT connects worldwide networks to share information through various related and dependent sensors. IoT helps connect physical entities with the Internet and provides opportunities for developing devices based on multiple tools and technologies such as wireless network sensors (WSN) and near field communication (NFC).

Artificial intelligence (AI) is a wide-ranging branch of computer science concerned with building smart machines capable of performing tasks that typically require human intelligence. AI entails utilizing a computer system to execute and automate tasks usually performed by a human being. This automation opens a large marketplace for AI and IoT tools for automation and Big Data solutions. AI is recognized as the most groundbreaking and extensively researched technology of the twenty-first century. It has brought a revolutionary change to the digital world. AI is an interdisciplinary science with multiple approaches, but advancements in machine learning (ML) and deep learning (DL) are creating a paradigm shift in virtually every tech industry sector.

AI has transformed several areas of human life, and the health care industry has advanced through it as well. It ensures the invention and innovation in the health care industry for a safer and better delivery of care and disease prevention. AI algorithms will support the doctors to increase efficiency in disease diagnosis, make better data-driven decisions, integrate patients and disease information effectively, reduce unnecessary visits to hospitals, and produce time-saving administrative responsibilities (Singh et al., 2021a, 2021b). On the other hand, IoT creates devices for examining and analyzing health (Ray, 2014). Health-related data can be collected and accessed using IoT-connected sensors. These IoT devices can even send user's health information to a health care provider or other health professional in real time. A smart healthcare system can be deployed to improve the health industry and help diagnose and treat diseases using a joint AI- and IoT-based health architecture (Hameed et al., 2020; Pradhan et al., 2021; Singh and Singh, 2020).

As health-related complications are becoming better and more regularly diagnosed, especially with the COVID-19–exacerbated issues for many patients, various health-monitoring devices are deployed using different technologies such as expert systems, wearable sensors, and portable remote health systems using wireless communication, in order to diagnose ailments and suggest specific treatments (Cao et al., 2020; Vaishya et al., 2020). The advantages of leveraging AI and IoT in healthcare have tremendously impacted patients and facilities. Several clinical and healthcare AI and IoT applications have already positively impacted healthcare practices by reducing pressure on healthcare staff, reducing costs, and improving patient outcomes (Bohr and Memarzadeh, 2020). According to a survey conducted by Tractica, the market for the healthcare industry implemented using AI tools is expected to surpass USD 34 billion by 2025, powered by the need to provide deeper insight and automate critical tasks. (Tractica is an intelligence market firm with a focus on technologies related to human–machine interaction. Their survey is based on an in-depth assessment of significant companies and start-ups specializing in healthcare and healthcare-related AI.

This chapter focuses on AI- and IoT-based architecture frameworks for the healthcare industry which make for a "smart" healthcare system. IoT-based medical devices connect all basic entities in the smart healthcare system through the high-speed mobile network. The application of AI can offer optimized, significant improvements in all areas of healthcare, from diagnostics to treatment.

The rest of the chapter is organized as follows. Section 1.2 presents an overview of IoMT devices and their deployable types. Section 1.3 presents components of IoMT devices, and Section 1.4 discusses the basic learning techniques of AI. Section 1.5 discusses the AI- and IoT-based architecture framework within the healthcare system. Section 1.6 presents the application of AI- and IoT-based healthcare management. The impact of the convergence of AI and IoT on the healthcare industry is discussed in Section 1.7. Section 1.8 introduces the possible limitations, and Section 1.9 offers a conclusion.

1.2 Overview of IoMT Devices

Emerging technologies continue to transform activities of daily life, connecting people of various fields and providing intelligent solutions. In healthcare, AI and IoT offer smart medical facilities capable of monitoring patients remotely, connecting the specialized providers remotely, and managing the medical equipment smartly and efficiently. Remote patient monitoring is possible through the power of IoT that enables patients to communicate with their medical experts by transmitting the medical data in a secure environment. These data are generated by medical devices/equipment connecting the patient with medical experts, and is generally referred to as the Internet of Medical Things, or IoMT. IoMT opens up a new era of possibilities and redefines how we get medical data are collected, analyzed, and transmitted across the distributed geographical locations using emerging technology (Rubi et al., 2019). It can connect digital (such as heart monitors) and nondigital (such as patient beds) devices to the Internet. IoMT is changing the existing healthcare industry by providing innovative digital solutions, particularly noticeable – and impactful – during the ongoing COVID-19 pandemic.

IoMT devices help monitor a patient from a remote location when the patient is unable to visit the doctor regularly. If these devices are equipped with AI mechanisms, they can send reminders or alerts based on prediction and updated medical plans to patients based on the data collected. IoMT is turning the type of remote healthcare that was the subject of science fiction – the one eliminating the need for physical proximity of the patient and provider – into reality.

IoMT can be deployed in the following ways: IoMT as home devices, IoMT as wearable devices, IoMT as community devices, and IoMT as hospital devices. Deployable types of IoMT devices are shown in Figure 1.1.

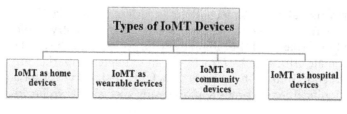

FIGURE 1.1
Types of IoMT devices.

1.2.1 IoMT as Home Devices

IoMT as a home device permits people to transfer medical information from their home to a hospital in real time. It is of prime importance nowadays, during the COVID-19 pandemic. As hospitals are being overloaded and running out of beds, providers have been forced to find ways to get treatment for sick patients at home. IoMT-enabled home device is used to monitor the patient remotely, and hence plays a vital role here by communicating the critical indicators of patient health, such as blood pressure level, oxygen saturation, pulse rate, heartbeat, etc., to the hospitals/providers in real time. This can significantly reduce the pressure on healthcare staff and hospitals and further reduce the chances of spreading infection. This IoMT model is also very useful and efficient in keeping track of health indicators of critically ill patients after they are discharged from the hospital.

1.2.2 IoMT as Wearable Devices

IoMT wearable technologies comprise devices enabled to collect user's personal health and exercise regime data while the user is wearing them. Consumers can monitor their vital signs such as heart rate, temperature, oxygen level, blood pressure, blood sugar level, etc., anywhere, anytime. Commonly available wearable devices include smart bands, smartwatches, biosensors, ECG monitors and blood pressure monitors, etc. (Dias and Cunha, 2018). Wearable IoMT devices can be used both for self-monitoring and for sharing information with healthcare providers. For instance, continuous glucose monitoring (CGM) via glucometer is crucial for individuals affected with diabetes. Glucose sensors worn by a person thus afflicted alert the wearer immediately of blood glucose level fluctuations. CGM can be personal and professional (continuous glucose monitoring, mobile technology, and biomarkers of glycemic control). Most of the CGMs have three components: a monitor to display information; blood glucose level sensor and a transmitter that communicates the sensor data to the monitor; and a smartphone, either the patient's or the provider's (or both), to which data is transmitted.

In addition to tracking a standard metric, such as heart rate, these devices can also detect early warning signs for more serious health conditions. For example, the Apple Watch is capable of warning users about irregular heart rhythms.

1.2.3 IoMT as Hospital Devices

IoMT devices are also assisting hospitals in managing the quality medical records of patients and hospitals entities. Healthcare professionals use IoMT sensors and other tracking systems to track and understand the facility's supply chain management interactions.

IoMT, as hospitals devices, can manage assets, patient flow, inventory, and hospitals staffs as listed below:

- Asset management monitors and tracks the IoMT-equipped devices such as infusion pumps and wheelchairs, Zoll's wearable defibrillator, etc.
- IoMT devices enhance patient flow management and reduce bottlenecks and enhance the patient experience, such as monitoring patient arrival times from an operating room to post-care to a wardroom.
- IoMT devices are also used to manage or systematize hospital inventory. It keeps records of orders, stores, hospital supplies, consumables, pharmaceuticals, and medical devices to reduce inventory costs and improve staff efficiency.

1.2.4 IoMT as Community Devices

IoMT devices deployable throughout a large geographical area are known as IoMT community devices. These types of IoMT devices are used to provide mobility and emergency services to their user; for example, patients can be tracked while transiting in an ambulance or vehicle. Similarly, paramedics and first responders use emergency response intelligence systems to track patient metrics outside of the hospital setting. Healthcare vendors and suppliers can also use IoMT devices in logistics to help transport medical devices.

1.3 Components of IoMT System

Early and timely diagnostics of disease can save lives. IoMT has the potential for early diagnostics with minimum error. IoMT allows sending vital health data to the user or their healthcare provider. IoMT devices can sense and collect the health data, process it, and transmit it via wireless connectivity. Components of the IoMT system are shown in a layered approach, as shown in Figure 1.2.

1.3.1 IoMT Device Component

IoMT component layer denotes various types of smart IoT-based medical devices such as smart pills, Fitbits, smartwatches, point-of-testing devices, clinical devices, smart wheelchairs, and remote patient monitoring systems, among others. A smart pill is an electronic device designed in the shape of pharmaceutical capsules. Smart pills provide highly advanced functions such as sensing, imaging, and drug delivery. They may include biosensors or images as well as pH and other chemical sensors. Smart pills replace the traditional method of endoscopy. POC diagnostic devices are used to test glucose and cholesterol levels, perform electrolyte and enzyme analysis, test for drugs of abuse and for infectious diseases, and conduct pregnancy testing. POC devices are used in doctors' offices, hospitals, and patients' homes, as POC provides quicker feedback on many types of medical tests.

1.3.2 Network and Processing Component

This layer consists of components related to the high-speed network infrastructure, cloud storage, and AI tools. High-speed infrastructure such as 5G provides a best-connected

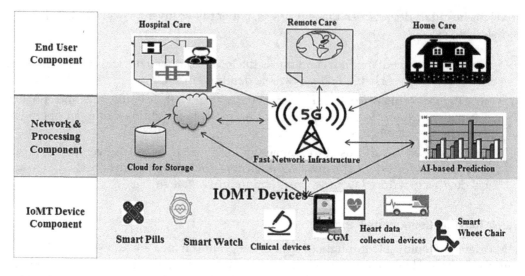

FIGURE 1.2
Component of IoMT devices.

channel for real-time application (Singh and Agrawal, 2018). 5G networks are expected to provide intelligent healthcare applications that can fulfill requirements such as ultra-low latency, high bandwidth, ultra-high reliability, high density, and high energy efficiency (Ahad et al., 2020). Furthermore, IoMT devices have built-in sensors that collect and transmit massive data every time a user/patient performs physical activities. This enormous data is stored and processed by using the cloud. AI tools are used to generate medical analytics of patients and any emergency or medication required, and then transmit an alert to the end-user component.

1.3.3 End-User Components

These components are intelligent electronic devices that are connected to the IoMT devices through the high-speed network. Each device user, such as professional care, remote care and home care user, can view data analytics, reporting, and device control opportunities.

1.4 Artificial Intelligence in Healthcare

Health practices involve gathering all kinds of patient information that can help a physician better diagnose a patient's health. These data can be simple symptoms identified by the subject, initial diagnostic tests, or detailed test results from the laboratory. After that, this information is analyzed by a healthcare practitioner who then diagnoses the disease using medical technology. In this digitized era, the ever-growing availability of healthcare data has paved the way for AI analytics techniques to assist healthcare professionals in better and more effective disease diagnoses and predictions. What differentiates AI from traditional clinical methods is the ability to use advanced algorithms to analyze huge amounts of healthcare data and produce real-time health outcome prediction and

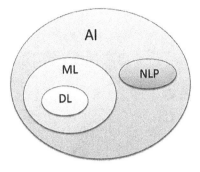

FIGURE 1.3
Approaches of AI techniques used in healthcare.

inferences for health risk alert. Primarily three AI approaches – machine learning (ML), deep learning (DL), and Natural Language Processing (NLP) – have been instrumental in healthcare applications, as shown in Figure 1.3.

1.4.1 Conventional Machine Learning Approaches

ML incorporates data analytical algorithms or procedures to obtain features from data. Patient attributes and sometimes medical outcomes of interest are inputted into ML algorithms for training. Baseline information about the patient, such as age, height, gender, disease history, diagnostic images, physical examination records, clinical symptoms, medication, etc., is considered input attributes for the ML algorithm. At the same time, patients' medical outcomes such as disease indicators, patient's survival times, and quantitative disease levels such as tumor sizes and blockage percentages are considered the targeted output of ML datasets. ML techniques are categorized into two prime types based on the inclusion of outcomes: supervised and unsupervised learning, as shown in Figure 1.4. Many times a hybrid approach called semi-supervised learning is also used.

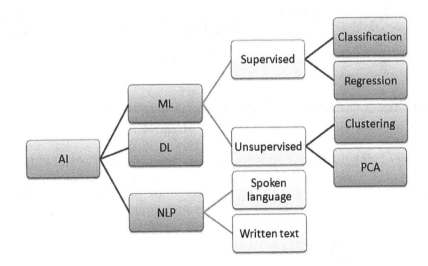

FIGURE 1.4
Hierarchical diagram showing various approaches of AI.

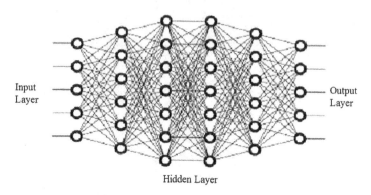

FIGURE 1.5
Deep learning neural network with four hidden layers.

Supervised learning uses training and testing datasets to train models to produce the desired output. This dataset, consisting of input values (independent variables) and correct outputs (dependent variable), is fed to the model, enabling it to learn over time. The accuracy of the supervised learning algorithms is measured by computing minimum squared error. This learning mechanism works by first finding the correlation among the input variables (patient's attributes) and the output variable (outcome of interest) and then uses this correlation for predictive analysis. This approach can further be categorized as classification and regression.

Unsupervised learning (works on unlabeled data) includes the algorithms that analyze and cluster unlabeled data to identify patterns by grouping similar features together. Two main approaches of unsupervised learnings are principal component analysis (PCA) and clustering algorithms. PCA is a dimensionality reduction method generally used to reduce the dimension of data given without losing much useful information.

1.4.2 Deep Learning Approach

Deep learning can be considered a subset of machine learning incorporating neural network techniques. In this learning mechanism, deep refers to the use of a three-layered (or deeper) neural network architecture, as shown in Figure 1.5.

Deep learning is gaining popularity over its classical machine learning version due to following two prime reasons:

- Capability of handling huge volume of complex data
- Ability to extract more intricate, nonlinear (arbitrary) patterns from the datasets

Deep learning's ability to interpret medical imaging like CT scans, x-rays, MRI scans, etc. has made it easy to analyze patient's test result and health data. This learning mechanism and machine learning are used to maintain smart electronic health records, proactively predict upcoming health risks, and provide necessary prescriptions and treatment to patients.

1.4.3 Natural Language Processing (NLP)

Natural language processing is a branch of AI that enables machines or computers to comprehend written text and spoken words almost like human beings can. NLP in the healthcare industry can be applied in two scenarios: (1) to comprehend human speech by extracting the meaning and (2) to map and interpret unstructured data available in handwritten prescriptions and health records to extract essential values and concepts automatically. NLP ability to handle unstructured data comes in handy to extract useful clinical information from narrative text such as laboratory reports, discharge summaries, physical examination records, etc. Rule-based systems and statistical methods used by machine learning models are two prime approaches to NLP.

1.5 AI- and IoT-Based Architecture Framework of Smart Healthcare System

Smart healthcare systems effectively overcome the shortcomings of the current treatment problems, diagnosis, patient monitoring, and maintenance of hospital records in electronic format. AI- and IoT-based framework, leveraged with recent emerging technology, achieves a profound positive impact on the current methods followed in the hospital environment. A dataset is the base of all AI-based applications and environments. These data are collected from the EHR data, genomic data, clinical data, patient data, disease symptoms records, and IoT data in the healthcare system. IoT data include data from mobile software applications, voice assistants, and wearable devices such as smartwatches, smart pills, etc. (CODE, 2019). In a smart healthcare system, data are primarily collected from IoMT devices. Healthcare data are preprocessed and stored in cloud for further analysis. Various AI-based learning model and techniques are applied for disease diagnosis and prediction. The result of the model is presented to the patient and provider. The overall framework is presented in Figure 1.6.

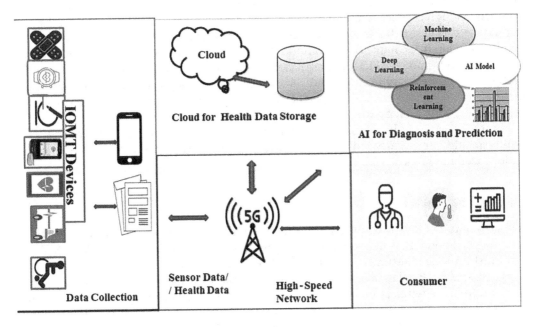

FIGURE 1.6
AI–IoT-based architecture framework for the smart healthcare system.

1.5.1 Sensor-Based Data Collection Methods

Billions of healthcare devices such as fitness tracking devices, clinical-grade wearables, remote patient monitoring (RPM) devices, clinical monitoring setups, smart drugs, and hospital devices generate enormous amounts data. These devices incorporate sensors that generate data by sensing the changes in their environment. The sensor networks of IoMT devices possess an adequate number of base stations that transmit the data to the main server or data center. Data collection is the core of any AI-IoMT system, as it provides the ground to produce insightful results or improve decision-making capability. The collection of huge volumes of sensor-based data from such a wide network produces various issues and concerns. Specialized algorithms such as highly concurrent and massive data (HCMD) collection algorithm, clustering-based algorithm, and privacy-preserving based data collection (P2DC) algorithm are being employed to deal with data collection failures.

1.5.2 AI-Based Disease Diagnosis and Prediction

AI-based planning and prediction algorithm has proved its significance in the field of disease diagnosis and prediction. Nowadays, all the advanced diagnosis devices and applications are used to detect chronic diseases such as diabetes, cardiovascular ailments, and cancer. Availability of lots of good-quality, digitized healthcare data has enabled AI to create automated disease prediction models. AI provides its capability to diagnose the disease at the preliminary stage.

However, recognizing a disease in its initial stage is a very challenging task. AI-based data-processing algorithms can be used to perceive data from ECG sensors, smart pills, smart bands, such as wristbands, and track footsteps, heart rate, blood pressure, calories, etc. (Paul et al., 2021). Figure 1.7 presents the steps involved during AI disease diagnosis and prediction methods. It includes data preprocessing, classifications, and applying AI algorithms for final disease diagnosis and predictions. AI algorithms/techniques are powerful enough to process huge amounts of data from multiple sources in real time; these techniques can assist doctors in predicting or diagnosing disease more accurately and timely. Decision trees, naïve Bayes, random forest, SVM, and artificial neural network are some of the well-known AI techniques (Jackins et al., 2021; Singh and Singh, 2020). Different performance metrics are used to assess and evaluate the classification algorithms. These metrics are accuracy, sensitivity, specificity, and F1-score. These metrics are calculated based on the confusion matrix (Tharwat, 2020).

Figure 1.8 shows the various commercially applicable learning algorithms in the healthcare industry, clearly indicating that artificial neural networks and SVM are the most widely used methods.

1.5.3 High-Speed Network

A huge amount of data is being generated every minute through numerous IoMT devices. A high-speed network is necessary to make proper use of this valuable data. An IoMT system must provide real-time connectivity and performance, since the healthcare system is a very time critical: delay in few seconds could cost a life. Establishing high-speed, adaptable, and reliable wireless connectivity is one of the most challenging factors in creating a connected healthcare ecosystem. Various communication technologies such as cellular networks, GPS, Wifi, Bluetooth, radiofrequency identification (RFID), 4G and 5G network, near-field communications (NFC), and LoWPAN are being used to connect IoMT devices

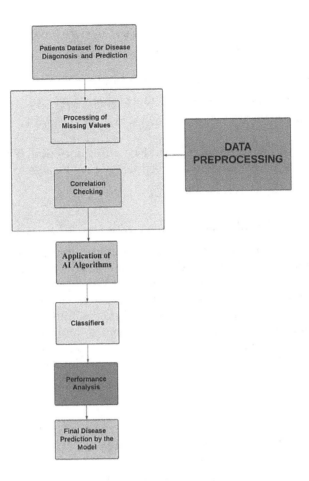

FIGURE 1.7
Steps in disease diagnosis and prediction using AI.

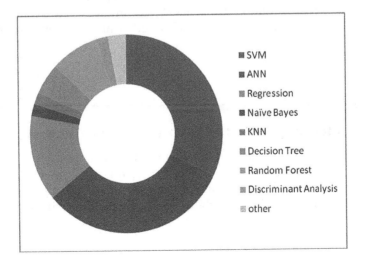

FIGURE 1.8
AI techniques used in healthcare industry.

(Ahad et al., 2020). IoMT comprises diverse kinds of devices having different connectivity requirements. These distinctive requirements of the IoMT can be outlined based on:

- Communication range, i.e., long range vs. short range
- Rate of data transfer, i.e., low vs. moderate vs. high data rate
- Latency tolerance, i.e., ultra-low latency vs. low latency

No single communication technology would be sufficient enough to cater to all these issues. However, fifth-generation wireless technology may be able to provide the solution in the near future.

1.5.4 Cloud Storage for Health Data

IoMT is a network of healthcare devices, software applications, and hardware infrastructure connected through the Internet, and these numerous devices produce a huge amount of data. The huge volume and sensitive nature of healthcare data make cloud storage the most viable option, as it provides a scalable, robust, and secure storage infrastructure. Cloud storage can be seen as the on-demand accessibility of virtual storage through data centers over the Internet. Cloud storage systems or applications are providing effective solutions for secure data storage, systematic service allocation, and scalability (Sivan and Zukarnain, 2021). IoMT technology unified with the cloud enriches the efficiency and delivery of healthcare services.

1.5.5 Consumer or End-User

AI–IoMT is revolutionizing the healthcare industry beyond imagination by providing real-time, inexpensive, remotely accessible healthcare services to patients. End-users such as hospitals, doctors, healthcare staff, administration, patients, and patients' families benefit immensely from this technology. Doctors and physicians can collaborate in real time, have access to sophisticated AI analyzed reports, access vital health attributes information like blood pressure, temperature, glucose level, etc., minute by minute, and share data with each other. Healthcate facilities use IoMT for efficient management of recourses and inventory.

1.6 Artificial Intelligence and IoT in Healthcare Management

IoMT devices generate a tremendous amount of sensor data that needs to be processed or analyzed to make a significant and intelligent decision for the benefit of the healthcare industry. IoT can work at its full potential if it is integrated with AI algorithms. The prominent use cases of AI-enabled IoT in healthcare management are shown in Figure 1.9.

1.6.1 Inventory, Staff, and Patients Management

Healthcare inventory management is a type of supply chain management (SCM) that can keep track of your health system's inventory, purchases, orders, payments, and more. With

FIGURE 1.9
AI and IoT in healthcare management.

RFID and IoT, the inventory manager does not require to devote time to manual tracking and reporting of medical equipment. Each equipment or device can be tracked, and the data are recorded automatically. IoT- and AI-based technology helps monitor medical staff, availability of experts, operation of instruments, and biological samples. AI and ML techniques predict daily demand and classification of the product. Support vector machine, regression, deep learning algorithm, and time series algorithm ensure significant demand forecasting process accuracy (Kilimci et al., 2019). IoT devices used to monitor critical patients allow round-the-clock observation by providers and other medical staff. The patient's state and disease status are more precisely defined, supporting developing a personalized treatment plan (Tian et al., 2019).

1.6.2 Chronic Disease Management

IoT with AI algorithm is used to manage chronic diseases such as diabetes, cardiovascular afflictions, Alzheimer, cancer, and COVID-19. Chronic disease management comprises combining sensors, data, and algorithms along with medical specialists in a four-step program (Agarwal et al., 2021):

a) IoMT sensor device can capture biological signals in the hospital and at home.
b) Data are collected from several sources to offer a holistic picture of the patient's health and create a patient profile.
c) Patient profile is analyzed using AI techniques to perceive the presence and evolution of chronic diseases.
d) Patient profile is monitored to manage their health.

1.6.3 Drug Management

AI–IoT technology is bringing innovative solutions in drug management. The conception of smart pills allows monitoring of a patient's internal health via wirelessly transmitting critical health data. Smart pills are tiny tablets or capsules containing nanoscopic sensors, which, once ingested, can wirelessly transmit data to connected devices. Smart pills also enable physicians to verify whether the medication has been ingested and in what amount. Various IoMT drug tracking software applications and devices, such as Wisepill dispensers, allow patients to track their drug intake.

1.6.4 Emergency Healthcare Management

Emergency healthcare management is defined as providing life-saving measures in life-threatening situations. According to a WHO report, road accidents are one of the major causes of death worldwide. Over 1.2 million individuals die each year on the road. The efficacy of emergency care and medical treatment in ICU crucially depends on the timely and accurate information received during the emergency call and essential data collected during the emergency transportation. AI–IoMT provides various prospects for enhancing emergency medical care at every step, from first responders' initial assessment of the victim, during transportation, and to the admission of the patient to the emergency room. Advanced wireless technologies such as wireless sensor wearable network (WSWN), multihop transmition, and multiple input multiple output (MIMO) are used to gather vital health parameters along with screening electronic media records (EMR) of patients to gain patient-centric data. An IoT-based calling system is an innovative tool as it embeds the patient's emergency data, place of casuality, geographical data, and information about the caller in an emergency response that is further passed on to the emergency doctor and emergency transportation unit. AI–IoMT convergence is enhancing emergency care management by providing continuous monitoring and real-time actionable information resulting in enhanced trauma care and reduced death rate.

1.6.5 Remote Healthcare Management

AI–IoT technology has revolutionized remote monitoring in the healthcare industry. IoT-enabled tools equip health care professionals to provide efficient remote care and long-term care to chronically ill patients. Various innovative wearable devices and home-installed devices are used to track heart rate, blood sugar, calorie counts, blood pressure, etc. This allows providers and other health care professionals to track patient health remotely and identify new symptoms before they advance and create more serious health emergencies. Telemedicine and teleconsultation improve the lives of older patients and those who live alone with a health condition. Remote patient monitoring (RPM) uses alert mechanisms to send signals to family members and healthcare providers if routines change.

1.6.6 Pharma Management

IoT has transformed pharmaceutical manufacturing by covering almost every aspect of the process, be it drug discovery, manufacturing, transportation, or even distribution. IoT plays a tremendous role in the digitization and automation of pharmaceutical manufacturing processes and, thus, is being adopted by top pharma manufacturers in their manufacturing plants to optimize and enhance process efficiency. It also enables standardization of manufacturing plants by seamlessly connecting networks, equipment, and systems across the plant, which previously has been considered a significant challenge because of different data formats, data access, and interpretation. As AI–IoT technology is capable of generating, handling, processing, and analyzing a massive amount of data seamlessly, it has brought tremendous technological advancement in automating the pharma industry.

1.6.7 COVID-19 Management

The COVID-19 virus outbreak has not just threatened public health but also severely disrupted the economic and social well-being of people. Since late 2019, the world has been struggling with the pandemic and looking for cost-effective and practical solutions to mitigate the effects, and IoMT has come forward as an effective technology to manage the COVID-19 situations, as it is able to provide solutions for tackling COVID-19 in all three main phases: early detection and diagnosis, during quarantine, and after recovery. The use of the IoMT technology is expanding the reachability to the patients through tele-assistance, telemedicine, and remote patient monitoring, thus demonstrating its utility in assisting patients, healthcare professional, and administrative authorities. Numerous IoMT devices and applications such as wearable tech, IoT buttons, drones, robots, and smartphone applications are utilized to combat COVID-19.

1.7 Impact of AI–IoT Convergence for the Healthcare Industry

The smart IoT healthcare management system includes many stakeholders such as patients, doctors, hospitals, and AI model support software and research centers. It covers various fields including disease monitoring and prevention, analysis, diagnosis and treatment, intelligent hospital management, medical decision-making, and health research. Innovative healthcare industries make extensive use of this technology in all aspects of their operations. From a patient's point of view, various wearable devices are used to monitor their health, seek out online health services using user-friendly programs, and use remote hospitals to perform remote health services. From a provider's perspective, various programs to support therapeutic decisions help analyze, assist, and monitor the diagnosis. AI techniques such as machine learning, deep learning, and NLP, among others, are capable of handling both structured as well as unstructured data generated in healthcare processes, and thus is able to analyze x-rays, mammography, CT scans, ultrasound images, MRI, etc. with higher accuracy and in less time.

Industry 4.0 basically revolves around the integration of IoT and AI. Therefore, AI–IoT convergence has a positive impact on the healthcare industry. The healthcare and pharmacological industries rapidly realize that emerging technology could also be the key to providing better care to patients, better diagnostic tools to providers, and better facilities to the hospital system. Scientific researchers use machine learning methods and in-depth learning methods instead of manual drug testing and obtain relevant studies using extensive data tools. AI-powered robots and machine learning tools perform very precise surgery. In hospitals, AIoT has enabled RFID techniques that assist in procurement management and personnel through integrated collection management and decision-making platform. The complementary healthcare system will improve the patient's knowledge. These technologies will reduce risk and lead to fewer treatment procedures

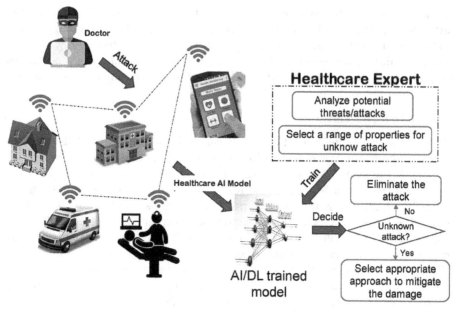

FIGURE 1.10
Architectural flowchart for convergence of AI–IoT in health care management system.

and will also improve resource utilization and promote cooperation and exchange in various regions. It will also improve telemedicine and self-care healthcare and eventually make select healthcare facilities ubiquitous.

Figure 1.10 presents the architectural flowchart for convergence of AI–IoT in healthcare management systems. A healthcare AI model is trained using AI and deep learning algorithms to analyze potential threats and attacks. These models are trained on the previously collected records of patients. These models are then used to analyze and eliminate the impact of illness on new patients. These expert systems also recommend the providers select the appropriate approach to mitigate the damage to patients' health.

1.8 Current Limitation of AI- and IoT-Based Healthcare Industry

The convergence of AI–IoT in the healthcare industry improves disease diagnosis and prediction and allows healthcare professionals to provide better healthcare services. But still, there exist some challenges that impede the commercial viability of AI- and IoT-based healthcare solutions. Availability of sound internet connectivity in rural areas poses another limitation, as the quality of IoMT solely depends on it. Cybersecurity is one of the most crucial challenges, as patient information is very sensitive and requires fail-proof storing and handling mechanisms. Other significant issues include data privacy, too much data, inexplicable BlackBox Deep Learning models, outdated infrastructure, etc. There should be a requirement for designing strict testing procedures to prevent diagnostic errors and efficient disease prediction.

1.9 Conclusion

This chapter presented the AI- and IoT-based architectural framework for smart healthcare systems. The framework consists of IoMT devices, a high-speed network, a cloud for storage, AI for model evaluation, and end-user components. IoMT devices such as home devices, hospital devices, wearable devices, and community devices are used to collect patient's health data. Patient health data is stored in the cloud for analysis and prediction. AI-based learning techniques such as supervised, unsupervised, and reinforcement learning are applied to train the model. The result of the model is presented to the end-user devices. High-speed networks such as 5G-based wireless networks transmit the sensor data, cloud data, and end-user data from different stakeholders (providers, patients, and hospitals) of the healthcare system. AI, ML, and DL techniques play an important role, and their execution involves computational capacity that is presented only by means of cloud services. The chapter revealed that AI and IoT convergence positively impacts the healthcare industry, referred to as Industry 4.0.

References

Agarwal, Neha, Pushpa Singh, Narendra Singh, Krishna Kant Singh, and Rohit Jain. "Machine learning applications for IoT healthcare." In *Machine Learning Approaches for Convergence of IoT and Blockchain*, pp. 129–144. Scrivener Publishing LLC, 2021.

Ahad, Abdul, Mohammad Tahir, Muhammad Aman Sheikh, Kazi Istiaque Ahmed, Amna Mughees, and Abdullah Numani. "Technologies trend towards 5G network for smart healthcare using IoT: A review." *Sensors* 20, no. 14 (2020): 4047.

Bohr, Adam, and Kaveh Memarzadeh. "The rise of artificial intelligence in healthcare applications." In *Artificial Intelligence in Healthcare*, pp. 25–60. Academic Press, 2020.

CODE. "Sharing and utilizing health data for AI applications." *Roundtable Report* (2019): 1–26. Accessed from: https://www.hhs.gov/sites/default/files/sharing-and-utilizing-health-data-for-ai-applications.pdf.

Dias, Duarte, and João Paulo Silva Cunha. "Wearable health devices—Vital sign monitoring, systems and technologies." *Sensors* 18, no. 8 (2018): 2414.

Jackins, V., S. Vimal, M. Kaliappan, and M. Y. Lee. "AI-based smart prediction of clinical disease using random forest classifier and Naive Bayes." *The Journal of Supercomputing* 77, no. 5 (2021): 5198–5219.

Hameed, Kashif, Imran Sarwar Bajwa, Shabana Ramzan, Waheed Anwar, and Akmal Khan. "An intelligent IoT based healthcare system using fuzzy neural networks." *Scientific Programming*, vol. 2020, article ID 8836927, 15 pages, 2020.

Cao, Keyan, Haoli Liu, Yefan Liu, Gongjie Meng, Si Ji, and Gui Li. "Efficient data collection method in sensor networks." *Complexity*, vol. 2020, article ID 6467891, 17 pages, 2020. doi:10.1155/2020/6467891.

Kilimci, Zeynep Hilal, A. Okay Akyuz, Mitat Uysal, Selim Akyokus, M. Ozan Uysal, Berna Atak Bulbul, and Mehmet Ali Ekmis. "An improved demand forecasting model using deep learning approach and proposed decision integration strategy for supply chain." *Complexity* 2019 (2019).

Paul, Shuva, Muhtasim Riffat, Abrar Yasir, Mir Nusrat Mahim, Bushra Yasmin Sharnali, Intisar Tahmid Naheen, Akhlaqur Rahman, and Ambarish Kulkarni. "Industry 4.0 applications for medical/healthcare services." *Journal of Sensor and Actuator Networks* 10, no. 3 (2021): 43.

Pradhan, Bikash, Saugat Bhattacharyya, and Kunal Pal. "IoT-based applications in healthcare devices." *Journal of Healthcare Engineering* 2021 (2021).

Ray, Partha P. "Home Health Hub Internet of Things (H 3 IoT): An architectural framework for monitoring health of elderly people." In *2014 International Conference on Science Engineering and Management Research (ICSEMR)*, pp. 1–3. IEEE, 2014.

Singh, Pushpa, and Rajeev Agrawal. "A customer centric best connected channel model for heterogeneous and IoT networks." *Journal of Organizational and End User Computing (JOEUC)* 30, no. 4 (2018): 32–50.

Singh, Pushpa, and Narendra Singh. "Blockchain with IoT and AI: A review of agriculture and healthcare." *International Journal of Applied Evolutionary Computation (IJAEC)* 11, no. 4 (2020): 13–27.

Singh, Pushpa, Narendra Singh, and Ganesh Chandra Deka. "Prospects of machine learning with blockchain in healthcare and agriculture." In *Multidisciplinary Functions of Blockchain Technology in AI and IoT Applications*, pp. 178–208. IGI Global, 2021a.

Singh, Pushpa, Narendra Singh, Krishna Kant Singh, and Akansha Singh. "Diagnosing of disease using machine learning." In *Machine Learning and the Internet of Medical Things in Healthcare*, pp. 89–111. Academic Press, 2021b.

Sivan, Remya, and Zuriati Ahmad Zukarnain. "Security and privacy in cloud-based e-health system." *Symmetry* 13, no. 5 (2021): 742.

Rubí, S., N. Jesús, and Paulo R. L. Gondim. "Iomt platform for pervasive healthcare data aggregation, processing, and sharing based on onem2m and openehr." *Sensors* 19, no. 19 (2019): 4283.

Tharwat, Alaa. "Classification assessment methods." In *Applied Computing and Informatics*. Emerald Insight, 2020.

Tian, Shuo, Wenbo Yang, Jehane Michael Le Grange, Peng Wang, Wei Huang, and Zhewei Ye. "Smart healthcare: Making medical care more intelligent." *Global SHealth Journal* 3, no. 3 (2019): 62–65.

Vaishya, Raju, Mohd Javaid, Ibrahim Haleem Khan, and Abid Haleem. "Artificial Intelligence (AI) applications for COVID-19 pandemic." *Diabetes & Metabolic Syndrome: Clinical Research & Reviews* 14, no. 4 (2020): 337–339.

Whitemore, Andrew, Anurag Agarwal, and Li Da Xu. "The Internet of Things—A survey of topics and trends." *Information Systems Frontiers* 17, no. 2 (2015): 261–274.

2

Role of IoT, AI, and Big Data Analytics in Healthcare Industry

P. Sriramalakshmi, Srimathnath Thejasvi Vondivillu, and A. Sri Krishna Govind

Vellore Institute of Technology, Chennai, India

CONTENTS

2.1 Introduction

With the increase in population around the world along with the rise of chronic diseases, it is a need of the hour to develop efficient healthcare systems that manage and deliver the diverse healthcare services with less expense, as discussed by Nguyen et al.[1] In order to maintain healthcare services for elderly individuals or people with chronic diseases, remote healthcare monitoring is playing a key role in reducing hospitalization and increasing healthy lifestyle habits. The healthcare industry is one of the fastest-growing industries and is expected to reach 10 trillion dollars USD by 2022. In statista,[2] it is mentioned that during 2016, healthcare in India was a 140 billion dollar USD industry and is projected to reach 372 billion dollars USD in 2022. This rapid growth is due to key driving factors such as rapid development in medical procedures, growth of the pharmaceutical industry, and a shift to a patient-centric model. The Internet of Things (IoT) technologies are the most enabling communication paradigm that make collecting, recording, and analyzing the patients' data more accurate and improvie sharing of knowledge among the healthcare providers.[3,4] With its use on the rise, IoT has the potential to provide healthcare access to millions. The massive amount of diverse data from the IoT devices creates a need for various data extraction methodologies. Data sources include patient record data; visit patterns; prescriptions; data on various scans such as computerized axial tomography (CAT) scan and magnetic resonance imaging (MRI); data of vital signs from wearable technologies; etc. The digitalization in processing of the massive amounts of data is needed to provide better-quality healthcare, diagnostics, and prediction of chronic conditions, improve patient's health management, and reduce medical expenses of the patient and operating costs for healthcare services. Extracting information from the various and diverse data sources allows for higher quality of healthcare, identifying the best and most cost-effective clinical treatment for a patient, licensing patient data for research applications, suggesting lifestyle changes, identifying potential risks using predictive modeling, lowering costs, predicting patterns, and making more sound business decisions. Having access to vast amounts of data can help reduce insurance fraud by checking the legitimacy of claims and the necessity of healthcare services offered to the patient.

At present, artificial intelligence has progressed far enough to reduce a lot of inefficiencies in the healthcare industry and diagnose a handful of diseases as well. The artificial intelligence blanket in healthcare is an overarching terminology used to describe various algorithms and techniques to mimic or assimilate human cognition in diagnosis, analysis and comprehension of the various medical processes. This technology should be robust enough to diagnose with high confidence based solely on the input data from the patient. Though AI in healthcare is relatively new, it is quickly putting down roots in different industries. For example, the vehicle industry uses GPS data from the car to send the location to a nearby ambulance in case of an accident or using the sensor data from a crash to predict the type and location of injuries. Current research in dermatology, radiology, psychiatry, tele-medicine, screening technology, primary care, and drug interaction and creation has seen astronomical growth and development. These technologies have the potential to drastically change each sector of the industry after gaining approval from governmental agencies, after going through rigorous testing.

The healthcare industry comprises hospitals, medical professionals, health insurance companies, rehabilitation facilities, pharmaceutical companies, and the consumers. The ongoing increase in demand for healthcare services calls for the development in technology to process patient data and to provide better diagnostics, improve quality of service, and reduce costs for the patient as well as operating costs for the healthcare facility. IoT systems can assist the providers in monitoring their patients remotely and managing their consultation time accordingly. Patients can also improve the level of self-care and reduce the risk of redundant and inappropriate healthcare from the hospitals or the clinics.[5] This can improve the healthcare and safety of the patients with the reduction in overall costs for care. The automation of the smart healthcare monitoring systems reduces the risk of human error, which is beneficial to both patients and providers.[6]

This chapter reviews the role of IoT, AI, and Big Data analytics in the healthcare industry. The organization of the chapter is as follows: Section 2.2 discusses issues with the current healthcare system, and Section 2.3 presents the architecture of IoT-based smart healthcare system and procedure for IoT solution deployment. The role of Big Data analytics, ML, and AI in the healthcare industry is discussed in Section 2.4. Applications of AI, ML, and Big Data analytics in the healthcare industry are elaborated in Section 2.5. Sections 2.6 and 2.7 present the cloud storage technology in IoT and cloud computing in IoT, respectively. Section 2.8 details the edge devices and computing in IoT. Fog computing in IoT is elaborated in Section 2.9. Applications of IoT in smart healthcare systems are presented in Section 2.10. Challenges and drawbacks of IoT devices are discussed in Section 2.11. The chapter is concluded with a summary and the future scope of research concerning the discussed topics.

2.2 Issues with Current Healthcare System

The disproportionate distribution of healthcare services across countries/areas is a very basic issue. Lack of basic healthcare in rural areas and lack of modern techniques and facilities are the major issues. There is lack of highly skilled medical professionals to provide efficient healthcare services in many area, and the problem is exacerbated by the fact that many people avoid accessing healthcare services because they can't afford them.

Technological innovation and new methodologies are needed to cater to ensure more equitable healthcare accessibility. The Internet of Things (IoT) in the healthcare sector has huge untapped potential. IoT has enabled remote monitoring, personal care, digitization of records, Big Data analytics, and better diagnosis.[7,8,9] Healthcare monitoring systems have become more and more common. Their spread is seen as an industry-wide evolution that enables better healthcare facilities worldwide. IoT in the healthcare sector had a market size valued at USD72.5 billion in 2020 and is expected to grow to USD180.2 billion by 2025.[10] This growth is attributed to the development in technological advancements, investments in healthcare start-ups, and increasing adoption of digital technologies by health centers. The growth of IoT in the healthcare industry is depicted in Figure 2.1.

IoT in healthcare enables doctors to monitor patients remotely and to receive alerts in case of emergencies; it also allows for more streamlined scheduling of face-to-face visits. This also enables doctors to cater to multiple patients' needs at once.[7] Patients are monitored in real time, which reduces the number of face-to-face checkups and saves the patient money.[11] Using Bid Data analytics (BDA) and usage statistics, hospitals can optimize requirements, and digitizing records can save operating costs.[9] Medicines can be monitored to track the usage and to ensure proper dosages.[12] Another growing technological development is using BDA, machine learning, and Artificial Intelligence algorithms to predict diseases and overall to give a better and faster diagnosis.[13] The use of technologies such as smart watches are effectively used to monitor heart rate, blood oxygen levels, temperature, and other patient health stats is on the rise, which is especially during global pandemics like the COVID-19 outbreak, gripping the world since early 2020.[14] With the consent of the patients, their data can be used in medical research, saving millions of dollars annually.[15]

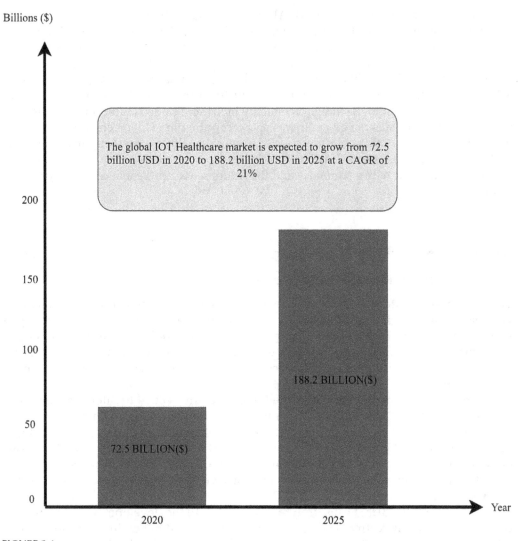

FIGURE 2.1
Growth of IoT in the healthcare industry.

Source: https://www.marketsandmarkets.com/Market-Reports/iot-healthcare-market-160082804.html

2.3 Architecture of IoT-Based Smart Healthcare System and Procedure for IoT Solution Deployment

There are four steps involved in deployment of IoT solutions. The first step involves the deployment of devices that contain sensors, monitors, transducers, cameras, etc., which generate data.[11] This includes getting sensory data from all the devices, which are converted to digital form. Data are aggregated and preprocessed, and moved to cloud or data centers.[11] Data are managed and extensively analyzed, and then presented to make business decisions based on that analysis.[11] Figure 2.2 depicts the various stages of IoT

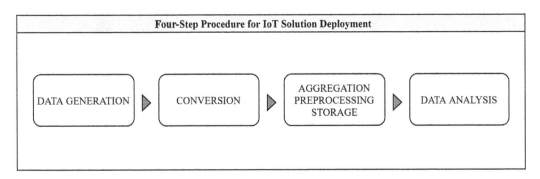

FIGURE 2.2
Stages of IoT solution deployment.[11]

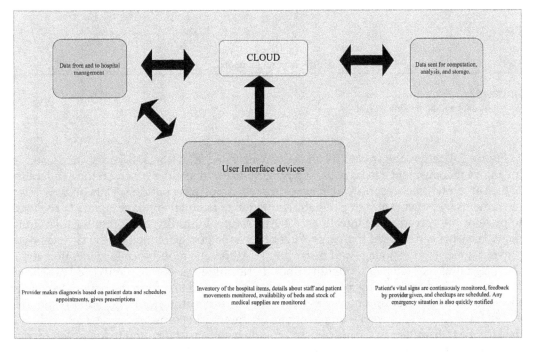

FIGURE 2.3
Architecture of IoT-based smart healthcare system.

solution deployment; the architecture of an IoT-based smart healthcare system is shown in Figure 2.3.

IoT in hospitals can be used for a wide variety of applications from the optimization of management, to inventory management, to keeping track of patients, providers, nurses, patient health monitoring, etc.[16] An example of inventory management is using radiofrequency identification (RFID) tags on hospital items. Medication boxes, bottles, and surgical tools can be equipped with RFID tags enabling smart resource management and preventing bottlenecks.[17] Another example is using indoor GPS for hospitals and using RFID technologies to track the movements of patients and staff members.[17]

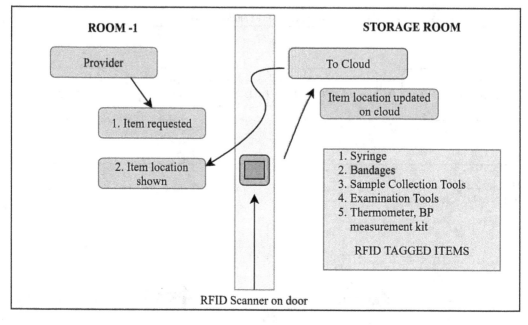

FIGURE 2.4
Inventory management using RFID tags.[17]

Figure 2.4 shows the inventory management using RFID tags. Sensory data used in inventory management can be used to place orders for medicines based on the availability of the same, and sales records can be used to predict purchase patterns. Data on unwanted movements by patients and tracking the sanitation of hospital appliances can also be used to prevent the spreading of infections.[12] Temperature, humidity, and other such environmental sensors can be used to maintain conditions for storage of medicine and vaccines to prevent unnecessary spoilage and discarding.[12] Automatic reports can be generated about the hospital usage statistics to identify underperforming assets.[11] To avoid pressure ulcers by staying in bed for too long, pressure sensors can be used to inform the patient to change the side he/she is resting on, thereby preventing ulcers from forming.[8] First-responder ambulances can be equipped with patient health monitoring sensors, from which real-time data can be transmitted to the hospital to provide better assistance and to make emergency room staff better prepared for appropriate type and level of care.[12] A new area of growth is the use of drones, which have a wide variety of applications, such as delivering blood vaccines, antidotes, first aid kits, food, and water. Countries such as Sweden and Canada are working on drones that can deliver defibrillators, as the time from cardiac arrest to the administration of a defibrillator is crucial to reduce mortality. An example of this is the TU Delft Ambulance Drone, which has been designed as a prototype containing a cardiac defibrillator and a two-way communication radio and video capabilities.[18] Emergency drone services are presented in Figure 2.5.

IoT for providers plays a similar role as IoT in hospitals. Providers can monitor patients in real time and track any anomaly and give the necessary treatment when needed.[11,14,19] Having access to patients' data can help the provider decide on the most optimal treatment for a particular patient.[7,13] Companies such as DocsApp and Medibuddy have come up with subscription-based unlimited consultations, online booking of tests, booking of

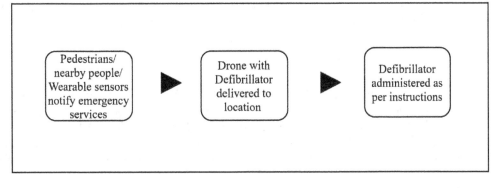

FIGURE 2.5
Emergency drone services.[18]

appointments, etc.[15,20] This allows a single doctor to cater to the needs of multiple patients. Digitizing hospital records and patient records helps in immediate consultation and quick diagnosis. IoT implementation in the form of sensors to monitor patients' vital signs for patients on bed rest at home is crucial to avoid any complications. These data can be sent to the hospital to schedule checkups or address any emergency.[7,12,13] The development of technologies such as wearable smart devices, which monitor a persons' heart rate, blood pressure, calories expended, skin moisture, and temperature, can help the user improve lifestyle choices.[12,14,19] The development of mobile applications to schedule appointments and visits, and to book medicines as per requirements, has made healthcare more convenient and accessible, and the digitalization of medical records has made diagnosis easier.[13,15]

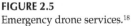

2.4 Role of Big Data Analytics, ML, and AI in Healthcare Industry

BDA is the process of handling and processing large amounts of data, in the form of large datasets, which cannot be done via manual methods, to extract vital information, patterns, market trends, preferences of customers, and predict markets, diseases, etc.[21,22,23,24] With the rapid growth of technological advancement over the last 50 years, huge amounts of data are generated on a daily basis, which needs to be processed, thus giving rise to BDA. Enterprises and institutions that use BDA and can reduce operational costs, predict sales or profits, come up with new innovations, etc.

The 7 V's of BDA are as follows[22,24,25]:

Volume: This refers to the amount of data available/generated and stored.

Velocity: This refers to how fast data are obtained and how quickly data can be used.

Variety: This refers to the nature of the data, namely whether it is unstructured, semistructured, or structured.

Variability: This refers to the variation of the data, such as different formats, sources, learning to non-homogeneity.

Veracity: This refers to the trustworthiness or reliability of the given data.

Visualization: Visual representation of the data can give an easier understanding of the scenario and lead to better decision-making within an organization.

Value: This refers to the ultimate worth of information or insights that can be obtained from processing of the given data.

The numerous algorithms used to detect faces, objects, build models for various medical conditions, and cleaning of data are all handled by a separate vast branch called data science, which employs various techniques to efficiently process data. A few of the more popular algorithms are decision tree, K-nearest neighbors (KNN), clustering, linear regression, support vector machine (SVM), time series analysis, anomaly detection, and neural networks.[26]

The data obtained from previous records and data entries are never perfect and always have flaws or unusable data. The higher the complexity of the diagnosis, the more data need to be stored, processed, and retrieved due to the sheer volume and variability. There are many data-cleansing methods available.[27,28,29,30]

There are a lot of propositions to use AI and ML to diagnose diseases and prescribe medicine. This reduces the time wasted by booking an appointment, traveling, and explaining the medical condition and medical history.[29,30] This streamlined method, for some, maybe more damaging than the current system. This is evident by looking at the homeopathy industry.[31] It is said that the success of this industry is mostly due to the increase in time between patient and doctor. Thus this group of people will most definitely oppose the change to a more streamlined relationship with the healthcare industry. Therefore this will be yet another hurdle to overcome.

2.5 Applications of AI, ML, and Big Data Analytics in Healthcare Industry

AI and ML technology has shown exponential growth over the years by solving the need for the human variable. In doing so, AI and ML have been ingrained into many industries and made a few of them practically devoid of any human operators. There has been a rise in the number of new software developed to diagnose certain medical conditions using facial recognition and object detection.[26] A promising area of application of BDA is in the healthcare industry. The healthcare industry generates vast amounts of data in the form of patient records, records of scans, reports, prescriptions, pharmaceutical data, data on trials conducted for new drugs, data on insurance claims, patient behavior, and visits scheduled.[32,33,34] Other sources include data from health-monitoring systems such as wearable devices and mobile applications.[33] "A single 3D CAT scan takes up about 1 GB of data, and a single human genome can take up 3GB of data."[33] BDA applications in healthcare industry include analyzing previous history of a patient and comparing with other patients' data to evaluate and identify the best treatment, provide cost-effective treatments,[34] detection of early warning signs for any ailment and manage overall population health,[34] and development of newer solutions to enable remote health monitoring of patients.[34] Smartphone-based IoT healthcare with AI and BDA is depicted in Figure 2.6.

Several applications of BDA in healthcare are discussed below.

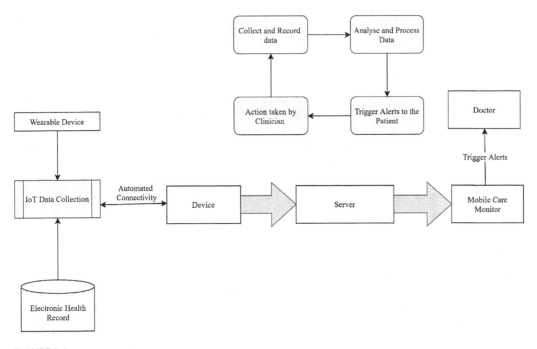

FIGURE 2.6
Smartphone-based IoT health care with AI and Big Data analytics.

2.5.1 Disease Diagnosis, Prediction, and Screening

With the help of electronic health records, several organizations can identify individuals of high risk by creating risk scores. Big Data analytics can be further used to manage overall population health, and can help in identifying groups that need immediate attention, such as during the COVID-19 pandemic. A program called Face2Gene has been developed to diagnose genetic disorders and various birth defects using facial recognition. It only provides a certain probability of that particular genetic disorder, but it shows the tremendous opportunity to innovate and improve. There are so many different skin composition and color variations that an accurate result cannot be declared with high confidence. But BDA seems to be one of the few ways of getting past this hurdle.[27]

Data on previous history of patients, in the form of medical records, scans, and past history on medication use, can be utilized for research into pharmaceuticals, development of new drugs, analysis of side effects, development of new medicinal procedures, etc.[34] A Philadelphia-based healthcare system known as Penn Medicine has created a program that uses machine learning algorithms to develop various scoring models and determine the patient's condition for the following 6 months.[35,36] A software model to differentiate between various types of lymphoma was developed by researchers from Massachusetts Hospital and Massachusets Institute of Technology.[37] In the context of predictive analytics in the field of medical imaging, CheXNeXt is an AI algorithm developed by a team at Stanford University, with the capability to screen chest x-rays to detect various pathologies.[35,38] University of Pennsylvania has developed a machine learning tool to identify patients at risk for septic shock up to 12 hours before it is actually to occur.[39]

Cardiovascular diseases can be predicted using neural networks, which consider risk factors such as age, previous history of disease in the family, cholesterol, diabetes, obesity, etc.[40] SVM classification model gives predicted survival rate and chances of disease relapse for breast cancer patients with high accuracy and minimal error rate.[40]

2.5.2 Genetic Screening and Testing

Patients' genetic information can be used to predict their response to a specific dosage of drugs and can allow a more individualistic development for pharmaceutical companies, and cater to the needs of patients on an individual basis.[41,42] The data can further be incorporated into electronic medical records of the patient, and can be used by providers and other healthcare professionals for individual and population health control.[42]

Counsyl is a company that offers DNA screening for men, women, children, and for couples, on the basis of which it determines the probability of an unborn child inheriting any disease.[43]

2.5.3 Resource Management and Financial Claims

Big Data analytics can also be used to predict the needs of resources, staff required based on previous history, to be better equipped to handle unforeseen situations, allocate resources judiciously during peak hours, and reduce the burden among healthcare workers.[39] Databases and logging systems can be used in laboratories, to better keep track of samples and quicker processing, and can also be used to better keep track of purchases by patients, insurance companies, inventories, etc.[42] As discussed in the previous sections, RFID-tagged important hospital resources, such as ventilators, and various other equipment can be tracked through the hospital to better manage resources. The same can be done for high-risk patients, elderly patients, and for preventing disease spreading via contagious patients.[42] Data on insurance payments and claims can be used for identifying duplicate claims, any unfair charging, and identifying fraudulent claims by finding any anomalies within the data.[44]

2.5.4 Readmission

Big Data analytics can be used to identify patients at high risk of readmission to the hospital, and can be used to schedule discharges and follow-up with providers accordingly.[39] Intel and Cloudera have used predictive analytics to prevent readmission of 6,000 people, saving a potential of $4 million in Medicare penalties and around $72 million in medical service costs.[44]

2.5.5 Analysis of Biosignals

Several biological signals such as heart rate, brain waves, and gastrointestinal system can be measured by various sensors, and require heavy processing, filtering, and making decisions based on proper anomaly detection.[45] Acquisition and analysis of data from patients in ICU before and after surgery can be used for future reference, and alerting the medical staff is of great importance.[46]

Anomalous activity can be detected using procedures such as electrocardiogram (ECG), and wavelet transform along with the Bayesian network classifier model is proposed to detect any premature atrial contraction or myocardial infarction.[47] Similarly, any anomalous activity in brain neurons can be observed by taking a power spectrum analysis of the brain signals.[48]

2.6 Cloud Storage Technology in IoT

It has been mentioned before that modern tracking technologies create a colossal amount of data that needs to be processed and analyzed to derive suitable conclusions. To realize the true immensity of the data generated, let's look at some projections and surveys. It has been estimated that by 2025, there will be 65 billion IoT devices plugged into the global IoT network,[49] compared to 8.4 billion in 2017.[50] The true impact of this growth follows with the sea of data it brings in. The data generated has grown from 0.1 zettabytes in 2013 to 4.4 zettabytes in 2020.[51] Research in this field predicts that the cloud service industry can reach $260 billion in 2021.[52] BDA and AI technologies solve only a fraction of the problem; the heavy lifting is taken care of by cloud storage technologies.

First, let's understand what cloud storage is. Cloud storage is a type of data storage in which the data is stored in "the cloud," which is composed of multiple servers, sometimes over multiple locations, where the physical environment is owned and managed by a "hosting company." The hosting company is responsible for the data stored and is required to keep the data available, accessible, and protected. Most people and organizations that use this service often buy or lease a certain amount of storage capacity.[53] Some of the hosting companies also offer a pay-as-you-go model (e.g., Amazon Web Service [AWS] and Microsoft Azure) to incentivize smaller businesses or individuals.[54]

So why use cloud storage? It is impossible to reliably store data from the IoT devices in local storage, i.e., on smartphones or the IoT device itself. Even if it becomes economical to have high-capacity storage inside the IoT device, it still imposes high complexity. Rather, having servers that perform storage operatio, allows a streamlined process of data collection, processing, and analysis. Cloud storage is made up of many distributed storages but still acts as a centralized unit either in a federated or a cooperative storage architecture. It has high fault tolerance and high durability through the creation of versioned copies.[53] It has an added benefit of having a superior support system and infrastructure that allows greater data security and higher chance of successful data recovery in case of failure of an IoT device in the IoT network.

Cloud storage enables IoT development with portability and interoperability across the network. This means the intercloud solutions utilizing software development kits (SDKs) can be used to develop applications and software without having too much concern over the back-end processes.[55]

Cloud storage has branched off from just object storage service and broadened to various other types of data storage service, block storage being one of them. Block storage is a type of data storage approach in which each storage volume has a unique address acting as an individual hard drive. In this storage model, the volumes of data are stored in fixed-sized chunks called blocks. The address of each block is the only metadata assigned. A software manages these blocks and decides where they are placed and how they are organized across the storage devices in servers. These blocks are controlled using server-based operating system and usually accessed by iSCSI (Internet Small Computer System Interface, a transport layer protocol that works on top of a standard transport layer protocol, also known as TCP) and fiber channel communications (also known as fiber channel over ethernet [FCoE]) protocols. The main use cases for block storage services are for "mission-critical" applications requiring low latency and consistent input/output (I/O) operations and performance in storage area network (SAN) environments. It also plays a critical role in enterprise applications, and some cloud service vendors offer block storage in addition to object storage service.[56]

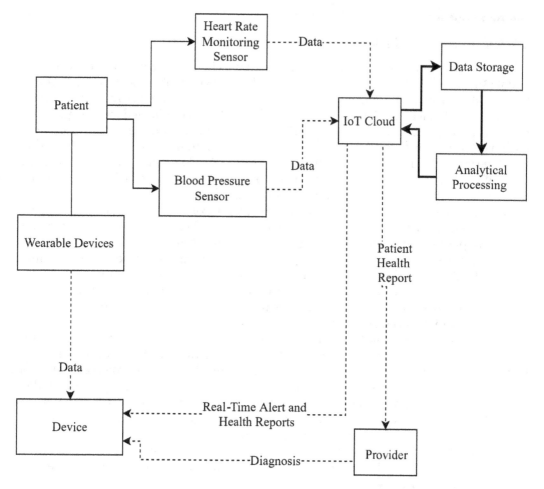

FIGURE 2.7
Integration of cloud storage and IoT healthcare.

Figure 2.7 presents the integration of cloud storage and IoT healthcare. Companies using cloud storage need to pay for the amount of data actually being stored; usually it is the average consumption during that specific month. This does not mean that cloud storage is less expensive than other types of storage, but it only incurs operating costs. Thus it allows small businesses with less capital funding to use cloud storage technologies. Due to growing awareness of climate change, there has been a recent move of big companies focusing on converting their businesses to "go green," and cloud storage is being adopted rapidly due to an increase in savings of up to 70%.[57] Organizations often choose a mixture of on-site and off-site storage options, considering the security (HIPAA, PII, SARBOX, IA/CND), continuity of operations (COOP), disaster recovery (DR), and regulations pertaining to the government.[58] Cloud storage can also be used to back up important data to protect from natural disasters by creating copies in servers located in different parts of the globe.

Creating backups of data and moving data around frequently dramatically increase the likelihood of unauthorized data access. The disposal of old drives, reuse of hard drives and reallocation of storage space can also lead to unauthorized data access. Crypto-shredding is a technology that can be used to safely dispose of data in hard drives. Longevity of the data stored and hosting company are of potential concern, because the longer the data are stored, the higher the risk that the hosting company may go out of business, change its business focus, or be acquired by another entity, sometimes a foreign one, with different privacy policies.[59]

2.7 Cloud Computing in IoT

Similar to cloud storage, cloud computing is the ability to use on-demand computing services over the internet. Cloud computing and cloud storage are heavily intertwined, and the terms are often used interchangeably. The cloud computing service can be public or private. The public cloud service can be used in places like railway stations, bus stops, and cafes to allow high accessibility and ease of use. The private cloud service, on the other hand, allocates computing resources to individual companies or to a group of individuals, meaning that the data being processed has less chance of being leaked or handled without the necessary authority. There has been a recent emergence of hybrid models that combine public and private cloud services to increase efficiency and profit.[60] Companies need not buy and set up computing infrastructure, and thus do not incur the initial capital cost. In turn, cloud computing services benefit by having a wider reach of the customer base and thus significantly increase profits with help of economies of scale.[52] Cloud computing "as a service" revenue increase from 2016 to 2021 is presented in Figure 2.8.

Cloud computing is more like a system than a single technology. This system comprises infrastructure-as-a-service (IaaS), platform-as-a-service (PaaS), and software-as-a-service (SaaS).

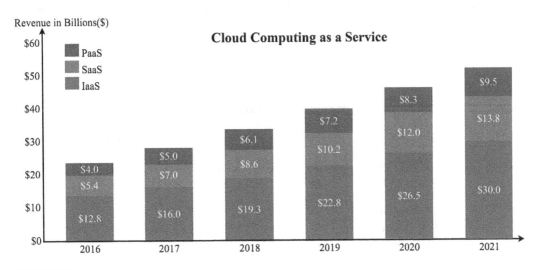

FIGURE 2.8
Cloud computing "as a service" revenue – 19% increase from 2016 to 2021.[52]

2.7.1 Software-as-a-Service (SaaS)

This is the most basic and most used category of the cloud computing service.[52,61] A license of the software is sold as a service in this type of system.[60] This can also be referred to as applications-as-a-service (SaaS). Here, the actual hardware and operating system (OS) are relevant, as the consumer will use the service via the application or web browser, and it is often bought on "per user" basis. In addition, SaaS can run the application in a web browser and not require installation of the software, updating or maintaining the software, allow access to the data from anywhere in the world, and help in mobilizing the workforce effectively.[62] SaaS remains the dominant cloud computing system, dropping in global use only slightly from 66% in 2017 to 60% in 2021.[52] Examples of this system used are Microsoft's Office 365 and Google docs. In the healthcare industry, in the clinical information system, it can be used in picture archiving and communication system (PACS), electronic health record (EHR), and telehealth; in nonclinical information systems, it can be used in billing, revenue cycle management (RCM), and supply chain.[63,64,65,66,67]

2.7.2 Infrastructure-as-a-Service (IaaS)

This is the fundamental building block of the three cloud computing models. Here, the rented services (physical or virtual servers, storages, and networking) attract companies wanting to start from the ground up.[52] Companies can avoid purchasing expensive servers and software and instead purchase resources on an on-demand basis. In addition, IaaS can help in cases of disaster recovery, business continuity, rapid ideation and development, improve stability, reliability, supportability, and security.[68] Examples of IaaS systems include Microsoft Azure, and IBM cloud; in the field of healthcare industry it can manage availability of resources, improve security of sensitive data, and scale infrastructure depending on the throughput of data.[60,69]

2.7.3 Platform-as-a-Service (PaaS)

This system is considered to be the most complex of the cloud computing services. Similar to SaaS, PaaS delivers a platform in which software can be developed, created, tested, deployed, managed, and delivered via the internet. PaaS is widely used to create web or mobile apps quickly, without the need to set up the hardware components like servers,

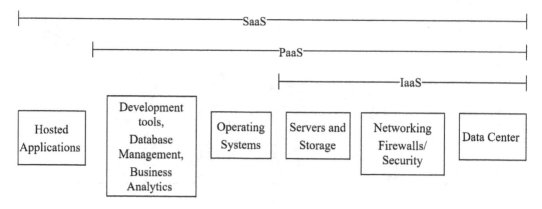

FIGURE 2.9
Cloud computing services.[70]

storage, and network required for development.[60,61] PaaS can help cut time to code, add new development capabilities without the need to employ more skilled individuals, work with development teams across the globe, manage an application lifecycle efficiently, and develop multiple platforms more easily.[70] Examples of this system include platforms like Heroku and Salesforce.[60]

New models are introduced to solve various problems that arise in the integration of cloud-based computing and IoT. Some of them are Sensing as a Service, Ethernet as a Service, Sensing and Actuation as a Service, Identity and Policy Management as a Service, Database as a Service, Sensor Event as a Service, and Data as a Service.[70]

2.8 Edge Devices and Computing in IoT

As discussed earlier, devices in the IoT network collect and send data to the cloud where it is processed further. Sometimes it is crucial for the data to be processed at the data collection point. Cloud computing will not be suitable for these time-critical applications; this is solved by edge devices and edge computing. In the edge computing framework, processing happens at the device level, which reduces latency and improves performance and bandwidth availability.[71,72] The architecture of the edge computing model brings the computing and other related infrastructure closer to the user (device where the data are generated). This is a decentralized model and is typically accompanied by cellular networks (4G, 5G). The goal of edge computing is not to replace cloud computing; rather, it puts certain applications closer to the end-user. In this hybrid model, data do not have to shuffle around, which saves time when it comes to data processing.[72,73,74,75]

With the rise of 5G technology, edge computing can be transformed to multi-access edge computing (MEC) having ultra low latency with gigabits-per-second (Gbps) throughput. Applications of this technology in the healthcare industry are as follows:

Autonomous ambulance: A single autonomous vehicle can produce 30 terabytes (TB) of data per day and thus requires MEC to process all the data with low latency to quickly make decisions while driving.

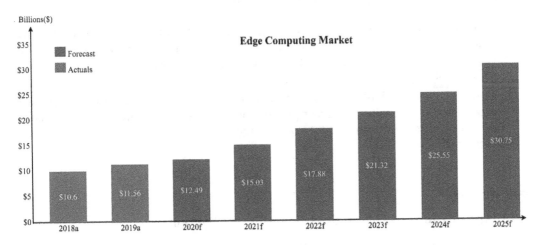

FIGURE 2.10
Global intelligent industrial edge computing market size ($B).[88]

(i) Virtual, mixed, extended, and augmented reality: Using augmented reality, surgeons can perform surgery with better visualization. Using virtual, mixed, and extended reality, demonstrations can be performed to practice surgery. MEC can provide low-latency VR, AR, MR, and XR to greatly improve the realistic component.

(ii) Connected ambulance: In the current ambulances, only primary data about the patient is available to the emergency room healthcare provider. This can hinder the process and delay the treatment for the patient. Thus moving to a system where more critical information can be transmitted in real time can help the provider guide the first responder and can also help in the transfer of the patient from the ambulance.

(iii) Patient monitoring system: In current monitoring systems, most sensors are either underutilized or not used at all due to the extremely large amount of data generated. MEC can provide real-time data processing with richer datasets and reduce the load on the cloud network. Examples include Google DeepMind, CareAI, and AWS outposts.

(iv) Remote monitoring and care: This can help patients that physically cannot move or go to a hospital. Remote health-monitoring devices are extremely important in these conditions, especially for elderly people. Examples include Intel and Flex, Diabetacare, and TELUS health home monitoring (HMM).

2.9 Fog Computing in IoT

Fog computing is another layer in the distributed network that perfectly bridges the edge layer and the cloud layer and executes application-specific logic.[76,77] Often, Fog and Edge computing are incorrectly used or thought to be the same, but Fog is actually a subset of edge computing.[78] In Fog computing the data are often processed on nodes called Fog nodes or IoT gateway, whereas edge computing takes place solely on the device level and typically is not processed further on other layers.[79] Placing the computing component in the network closer to the end-user reduces latency and improves energy efficiency.[77] The advantages of Fog in the healthcare industry are similar to those of edge computing: an application-specific layer or node is chosen to process the data, thereby creating a richer dataset. Applications of Fog in healthcare system include:

I. Remote health monitoring system: with the help of Fog computing, features like fall detection and patient activity (using movement patterns) can be analyzed to determine possible health issues and alert the necessary healthcare personnel, especially for the elderly.[77,80]

II. Connected health: Utilizing Fog, the patient or user is able to view, access, and modify data (according to preset permissions), similar to mobile electronic health records. This system can also take advantage of block chain technology to improve security.[81]

2.10 Applications of IoT in Smart Healthcare System

It is claimed that the next milestone humanity will cross in the realm of healthcare will be proactive personal health or mobile health.[82] As wearable IoT technology has become more refined over the years, the ability to collect reliable and constant data of one's health

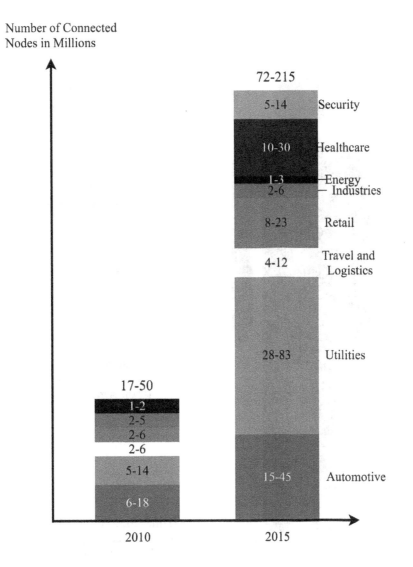

Number of Connected
Nodes in Millions

72-215

5-14	Security
10-30	Healthcare
1-3	Energy
2-6	Industries
8-23	Retail
4-12	Travel and Logistics
28-83	Utilities
15-45	Automotive

17-50

1-2	
2-5	
2-6	
2-6	
5-14	
6-18	

2010   2015

FIGURE 2.11
Infographic depicts the growing interconnectedness of different sectors/industries.[82]

through affordable and compact biosensors has become more than just a dream. But the enormous volumes of data beaming at the cloud servers need to be churned up into sophisticated datasets to help in drawing unmitigated analysis. Due to the recent boom in AI and BDA, the ability to process and predict using abundant data has become more accurate and reliable by using various machine learning algorithms and models to simulate even the edge case scenarios.[83]

Innovations in IoT bring tremendous opportunity in unobtrusive monitoring scenarios for proactive personal healthcare. The tech giant Apple is already equipping its latest watches with ECG capabilities that can detect heart attacks and even call or alert healthcare personnel to arrive at the location swiftly. Though currently very expensive, these are only the first generation of such a high-end wearable device. Various other companies and even technologically adept individuals have made affordable wearable devices that obtain pedometer and heart rate data to help improve people's general lifestyle.[83,7]

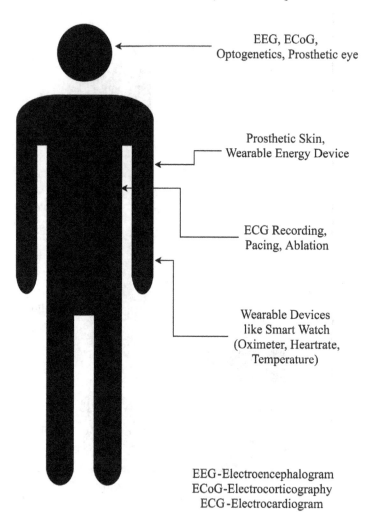

FIGURE 2.12
Application of a minimally invasive device, implanted device, and wearable IoT device to closely monitor the vital conditions of patients/users.[84]

The application of a minimally invasive implanted device, a wearable IoT device to closely monitor the vital conditions of patients/users, is presented in Figure 2.12. Zio Patch is another example of a device that measures heart rate and ECG and has also got approval from the US Food and Drug Administration (FDA). GlaxoSmithKlein, a pharmaceutical company, has announced that their current investments are funneled into bio-electrical drugs that stimulate nerves to achieve better treatment. In the field of automated surgery robots, Google, Johnson & Johnson, and Philips have collaborated to design new robots and wearable devices. Blood glucose measuring sensors are being worked on by Google and Novartis. HealthCare+ is a new mobile application that assesses coronary heart conditions (it uses the Framingham Scoring Model to classify the patients into low, moderate, or high risk) and uses the same platform to connect with nearby physicians, especially in rural areas. A couple of other similar apps are SleepBot and myDario. Smart clothing sensors are also coming into the market to provide a seamless experience while using an array of different sensors to monitor vital conditions continuously.[82]

Intelligent biomedical sensors are used to detect several chronic diseases. A list of sensors available or in development is given below:

I. Cardiovascular heart diseases: sensors strapped to the chest and smartwatches are used for heart rate detection. The electrical activity of the heart is recorded by electrocardiography. Using BlueTooth or onboard wifi, the data is transferred to the device or the cloud for further processing.

II. Asthma: Smartwatches with ECG sensors in addition to carbon monoxide, nitrogen dioxide, and other environmental conditions are monitored and alert medical personnel in case of emergencies.

III. Alzheimer's, autism, dementia, or other cognitive disorders: GPS Smart Soles are motion sensors used to alert the caretaker or medical professional in case of abnormal situations. Smart Soles work by using geofenced location: if the patient leaves the boundaries, a signal is sent to the necessary personnel. In case of low battery or out-of-service situations, the last recorded location can be configured to be sent to the necessary personnel. These sensors usually work using the ZigBee protocol or GSM to provide real-time information.

The previously discussed applications are noninvasive wearable IoT devices, but some companies have been working on invasive devices as a permanent and comprehensive solution.[85] A few companies have products to help with the management of Parkinson's disease.[86] Videos of patients using this product are almost mind-boggling to witness: as the device is switched on, there is a clear reduction in parkinsonian tremors. Neurolink is a popular company, with Tesla's Elon Musk as one of the large investors, whose products aim at eliminating nervous system disorders by physically connecting the human brain to the IoT.[83] Ingestible sensors are an emerging technology that detects irregularities in the body in a minimally invasive way; instead of a probe, the patient ingests a pill-sized device equipped with various sensors that record and transmit the data wirelessly to a corresponding smartphone app.[87]

2.11 Challenges and Drawbacks of IoT Devices

IoT platforms for healthcare are designed to allow a better understanding of the patient, to gain insight, and to provide interoperability. The requirements listed below are essential for the wide-scale adoption of IoT in healthcare, but can be challenging to meet.[82]

I. Providing a simple dashboard to connect various IoT devices in the IoT network and allow easy access to data through cloud-based services.

II. Providing a robust service to be able to manage these devices (e.g., subscription plans, increase throughput and reduce maintenance cost).

III. Intelligent data storage between the local and cloud services.

IV. Analysis of information on Big Data in real time to gain insight and construct better decisions.

V. Provide a robust platform to redirect users to medical professionals in case of an unknown disease or low confidence prediction.

VI. Provide a robust platform with up-to-date firewalls and sophisticated measures to prevent a data breach or isolate compromised devices from the IoT network.

Further, a few steps can be taken to mitigate data breaches and privacy issues.[84,87] Key points are listed below.

I. Erasing sensitive information from a device after the session has ended or the product is disposed of.

II. Blocking third-party interfering applications (e.g., data collection or commercial advertisements).

III. Using two-step authentication to secure data stored in the device/cloud.

IV. End-to-end encryption to be used while communicating with healthcare workers, etc.

V. Secure Socket Layer / Transport Layer Security (SSL/TLS) protocol communication between IoT devices, apps, and other systems.

Regardless of how advanced and sophisticated the technology is, the public needs to consciously make a move to add these IoT devices into their daily life. This requires a complete overhaul of the present infrastructure and updates of the laws of the governing bodies to better suit this changing industry. This could also bring various challenges in international coverage/usage. A standardized set of laws need to be put in place to regulate such devices.

2.12 Conclusion and Future Scope

The healthcare sector is one of the most important and vital parts of a community in terms of revenue as well as the quality of service it provides. Over the years, the quality of service has risen due to new innovative methods to cure diseases and to treat them, but so has the cost. This increase in cost can be reduced by using IoT, AI, ML, and Big Data analytics in the healthcare industry. As more and more houses convert into smart homes and embrace the IoT tech in their life, the future of remote surgery, AI-based health monitoring, and nanobots that can cure cancer becomes more than just a dream. This chapter discussed the roles of AI, IoT, and ML in various healthcare applications. It presented a clear picture about the challenges in implementation of AI- and IoT-based smart healthcare systems. Healthcare in the future will be synonymous with IoT, AI, and ML healthcare, as they would be playing a substantial role in this industry.

References

1. H. H. Nguyen, F. Mirza, M. A. Naeem, and M. Nguyen. "A review on IoT healthcare monitoring applications and a vision for transforming sensor data into real-time clinical feedback." In *2017 IEEE 21st International Conference on Computer Supported Cooperative Work in Design (CSCWD)*, 2017, pp. 257–262. doi:10.1109/CSCWD.2017.8066704.
2. https://www.statista.com/statistics/701556/healthcare-sector-size-india/ (accessed June 2021).
3. M. Saranya, R. Preethi, M. Rupasri, and V. Sundareswaran. "A survey on health monitoring system by using IoT." *Int. J. Res. Appl. Sci. Eng. Technol* 6 (2018). doi:10.22214/ijraset.2018.3124.
4. A. Abdul-Jabbar Mohammed, M. A. Burhanuddin, and H. Basiron. "Key enablers of IoT strategies in the context of smart city innovation." *Journal of Advanced Research in Dynamical and Control Systems* 10, no. 4 (2018): 582–589.
5. P. P. D. Prof and P. R. I. Prof. "IoT based smart health care kit: A review." *International Journal for Scientific Research and Development*, vol. 4, no. 11 (2017): 573–575.
6. Naveen, R. K. Sharma, and A. R. Nair. "IoT-based secure healthcare monitoring system." In *2019 IEEE International Conference on Electrical, Computer and Communication Technologies (ICECCT)*, 2019, pp. 1–6. doi:10.1109/ICECCT.2019.8868984.
7. B. Pradhan, S. Bhattacharyya, and K. Pal. "IoT-based applications in healthcare devices." *Journal of Healthcare Engineering*, vol. 2021, 18 pages, 2021. doi:10.1155/2021/6632599.
8. A Tal, Z Shinar, D Shaki, S Codish, and A Goldbart "Validation of contact-free sleep monitoring device with comparison to polysomnography." *J Clin Sleep Med* 13, no. 3 (2017): 517–522. Published March 15, 2017. doi:10.5664/jcsm.6514.
9. S. M. R. Islam, D. Kwak, M. H. Kabir, M. Hossain, and K. Kwak. "The Internet of Things for health care: A comprehensive survey." *IEEE Access* 3 (2015): 678–708. doi:10.1109/ACCESS.2015.2437951.
10. https://www.marketsandmarkets.com/Market-Reports/iot-healthcare-market-160082804.html (accessed June 2021).
11. P. Sethi and Smruti R. Sarangi. "Internet of Things: Architectures, protocols, and applications." *Journal of Electrical and Computer Engineering*, vol. 2017, article ID 9324035, 25 pages, 2017. doi:10.1155/2017/9324035.
12. S. P. Dash. "The Impact of IoT in healthcare: Global technological change & the roadmap to a networked architecture in India." *J Indian Inst Sci* 100 (2020): 773–785. doi:10.1007/s41745-020-00208-y.
13. M. Elhoseny, G. Ramírez-González, O. M. Abu-Elnasr, S. A. Shawkat, N. Arunkumar, and A. Farouk. "Secure medical data transmission model for IoT-based healthcare systems." *IEEE Access* 6 (2018): 20596–20608. doi:10.1109/ACCESS.2018.2817615.
14. R. Kumbhar. "Health monitoring using fitness band and IoT." *IOSR: Journal of Computer Engineering (IOSR-JCE)* (2017), e-ISSN: 2278-0661, p-ISSN: 2278-8727, pp. 41–46. www.iosrjournals.org. National Conference on Advances in Computational Biology, Communication, and Data Analytics 41 | Page (ACBCDA 2017).
15. Laplante PA, Kassab M, Laplante NL, and Voas JM. "Building caring healthcare systems in the Internet of Things." *IEEE Syst J* 12, no. 3 (2018). doi:10.1109/JSYST.2017.2662602.
16. Goodridge D and Marciniuk D. "Rural and remote care: Overcoming the challenges of distance." *Chron Respir Dis* 13, no. 2 (2016): 192–203. doi:10.1177/1479972316633414.
17. Vaibhav Thakare and Gauri Khire. "Role of emerging technology for building smart hospital information system." *Procedia Economics and Finance* 11 (2014): 583–588. doi:10.1016/S2212-5671(14)00223-8. ISSN: 2212-5671.
18. Mackle C, Bond R, Torney H, et al. "A data-driven simulator for the strategic positioning of aerial ambulance drones reaching out-of-hospital cardiac arrests: A genetic algorithmic approach." *IEEE J Transl Eng Health Med* 8 (2020): 1900410. Published 2020 Apr 21. doi:10.1109/JTEHM.2020.2987008.

19. Jorge Gómez, Byron Oviedo, Emilio Zhuma. "Patient monitoring system based on Internet of Things." *Procedia Computer Science* 83 (2016): 90–97. ISSN: 1877-0509. doi:10.1016/j.procs.2016.04.103.

20. Yoo, S., Kim, S., Kim, E., et al. "Real-time location system-based asset tracking in the healthcare field: Lessons learned from a feasibility study." *BMC Med Inform Decis Mak* 18, no. 80 (2018). doi:10.1186/s12911-018-0656-0.

21. Prableen Kaur, Manik Sharma, and Mamta Mittal. "Big data and machine learning based secure healthcare framework." *Procedia Computer Science* 132 (2018): 1049–1059. ISSN: 1877-0509. doi:10.1016/j.procs.2018.05.020.

22. Amir Gandomi and Murtaza Haider. "Beyond the hype: Big data concepts, methods, and analytics." *International Journal of Information Management* 35, no. 2 (2015): 137–144. ISSN: 0268-4012. doi:10.1016/j.ijinfomgt.2014.10.007.

23. Uthayasankar Sivarajah, Muhammad Mustafa Kamal, Zahir Irani, and Vishanth Weerakkody. "Critical analysis of big data challenges and analytical methods." *Journal of Business Research* 70 (2017): 263–286. ISSN: 0148-2963. doi:10.1016/j.jbusres.2016.08.001.

24. Khan, M., Uddin, Muhammad, and Gupta, Navarun. "Seven V's of big data understanding big data to extract value." (2014): 1–5. doi:10.1109/ASEEZone1.2014.6820689.

25. Hiba, Jasim, Hadi, Hiba Hameed, Shnain, Ammar, Hadishaheed, Sarah, and Haji, Azizahbt. "Big data and five V's characteristics." (2015): 2393–2835.

26. Yadav V., Kundra P., Verma D. (2021) Role of IoT and Big Data Support in Healthcare. In: Gao X.Z., Tiwari S., Trivedi M., Mishra K. (eds) Advances in Computational Intelligence and Communication Technology. Advances in Intelligent Systems and Computing, vol 1086. Springer, Singapore. https://doi.org/10.1007/978-981-15-1275-9_36

27. Martinez-Martin, Nicole. "What are important ethical implications of using facial recognition technology in health care?" *AMA Journal of Ethics* 21, no. 2 (2019): E180–187. February 1, 2019. doi:10.1001/amajethics.2019.180.

28. Dash, S., Shakyawar, S. K., Sharma, M., et al. "Big data in healthcare: Management, analysis and future prospects." *J Big Data* 6, no. 54 (2019). doi:10.1186/s40537-019-0217-0.

29. Z. Faizal Khan and Sultan Refa Alotaibi. "Applications of artificial intelligence and big data analytics in m-health: A healthcare system perspective." *Journal of Healthcare Engineering*, vol. 2020, article ID 8894694, 15 pages, 2020. doi:10.1155/2020/8894694.

30. Syed L., Jabeen S., Manimala S., Elsayed H.A. (2019) Data Science Algorithms and Techniques for Smart Healthcare Using IoT and Big Data Analytics. In: Mishra M., Mishra B., Patel Y., Misra R. (eds) Smart Techniques for a Smarter Planet. Studies in Fuzziness and Soft Computing, vol 374. Springer, Cham. https://doi.org/10.1007/978-3-030-03131-2_11

31. Andrea Basili, Francesco Lagona, Paolo Roberti di Sarsina, Corallina Basili, and Teresa Valeria Paterna. "Allopathic versus homeopathic strategies and the recurrence of prescriptions: Results from a pharmacoeconomic study in Italy." *Evidence-Based Complementary and Alternative Medicine*, vol. 2011, article ID 969343, 6 pages, 2011. doi:10.1093/ecam/nep023.

32. Sayantan Khanra, Amandeep Dhir, A. K. M. Najmul Islam, and Matti Mäntymäki. "Big data analytics in healthcare: A systematic literature review." *Enterprise Information Systems* 14, no. 7 (2020): 878–912. doi:10.1080/17517575.2020.1812005.

33. Kankanhalli, A., Hahn, J., Tan, S., et al. "Big data and analytics in healthcare: Introduction to the special section." *Inf Syst Front* 18 (2016): 233–235. doi:10.1007/s10796-016-9641-2.

34. Raghupathi, W., and Raghupathi, V. "Big data analytics in healthcare: Promise and potential." *Health Inf Sci Syst* 2, no. 3 (2014). doi:10.1186/2047-2501-2-3.

35. Boukenze, Basma, Mousannif, Hajar, and Haqiq, Abdelkrim. "Predictive analytics in healthcare system using data mining techniques." *Computer Science & Information Technology* 6 (2016): 1–9. doi:10.5121/csit.2016.60501.

36. Terwiesch, C, Mehta, SJ, and Volpp, KG. "Innovating in health delivery: The Penn medicine innovation tournament." *Healthcare* 1 (2013): 37–41. doi:10.1016/j.hjdsi.2013.05.003.

37. MIT Spectrum. *Big Data + Machine Learning = More Accurate Cancer Diagnosis*, 2015.

38. Rajpurkar P, Irvin J, Ball RL, Zhu K, Yang B, Mehta H, et al. "Deep learning for chest radiograph diagnosis: A retrospective comparison of the CheXNeXt algorithm to practicing radiologists." *PLoS Med* 15, no. 11 (2018): E1002686. doi:10.1371/journal.pmed.1002686.

39. Bates, David, Saria, Suchi, Ohno-Machado, Lucila, and Shah, Anand. "Big data in health care: Using analytics to identify and manage high-risk and high-cost patients." *Health Affairs (Project Hope)* 33 (2014): 1123–1131. doi:10.1377/hlthaff.2014.0041.

40. B. Nithya and V. Ilango. "Predictive analytics in health care using machine learning tools and techniques." In *2017 International Conference on Intelligent Computing and Control Systems (ICICCS)*, Madurai, India, 2017, pp. 492–499. doi:10.1109/ICCONS.2017.8250771.

41. Meiliana, Anna, Dewi, Nurrani, and Wijaya, Andi. "Personalized medicine: The future of health care." *The Indonesian Biomedical Journal* 8 (2016). doi:10.18585/inabj.v8i3.271.

42. Ward, M. J., Marsolo, K. A., and Froehle, C. M. "Applications of business analytics in healthcare." *Business Horizons* 57, no. 5 (2014): 571–582. doi:10.1016/j.bushor.2014.06.003.

43. Gamma, Alex. "The role of genetic information in personalized medicine." *Perspectives in Biology and Medicine* 56 (2013): 485–512. doi:10.1353/pbm.2013.0040.

44. Intel. "Intel and cloudera use predictive analytics to help a large hospital group reduce read-mission rates." 2015. https://api.semanticscholar.org/CorpusID:6729087

45. A. Ukil, S. Bandyoapdhyay, C. Puri, and A. Pal. "IoT healthcare analytics: The importance of anomaly detection." In *2016 IEEE 30th International Conference on Advanced Information Networking and Applications (AINA)*, Crans-Montana, Switzerland AG, 2016, pp. 994–997. doi:10.1109/AINA.2016.158.

46. H. Han, H. C. Ryoo, and H. Patrick. "An infrastructure of stream data mining, fusion and management for monitored patients." In *Proceedings of the 19th IEEE International Symposium on Computer-Based Medical Systems (CBMS '06)*, Salt Lake City, Utah, USA, pp. 461–468. IEEE, June 2006.

47. M. Hadjem, O. Salem, and F. Nait-Abdesselam. "An ECG monitoring system for prediction of cardiac anomalies using WBAN." In *IEEE 16th International Conference on e-Health Networking, Applications and Services (Healthcom)*, pp. 441–446, 2014.

48. T. Musha, H. Matsuzaki, Y. Kobayashi, Y. Okamoto, M. Tanaka, and T. Asada. "EEG markers for characterizing anomalous activities of cerebral neurons in NAT (neuronal activity topography) method." *IEEE Transactions on Biomedical Engineering* 60, no. 8 (August 2013): 2332–2338.

49. Sharma N., Shamkuwar M., Singh I. (2019) The History, Present and Future with IoT. In: Balas V., Solanki V., Kumar R., Khari M. (eds) Internet of Things and Big Data Analytics for Smart Generation. Intelligent Systems Reference Library, vol 154. Springer, Cham. https://doi.org/10.1007/978-3-030-04203-5_3

50. Dean, Andrew, and Opoku Agyeman Michael. "A study of the advances in IoT security." (2018): 1–5. doi:10.1145/3284557.3284560.

51. Yang, Yang, Xianghan Zheng, Wenzhong Guo, Ximeng Liu, and Victor Chang. "Privacy-preserving smart IoT-based healthcare big data storage and self-adaptive access control system." *Information Sciences* 479 (2019): 567–592.

52. Ahuja, Sanjay P., Sindhu Mani, and Jesus Zambrano. "A survey of the state of cloud computing in healthcare." *Network and Communication Technologies* 1, no. 2 (2012): 12.

53. Liu, Kun, and Dong, Long-jiang. "Research on cloud data storage technology and its architecture implementation." *Procedia Engineering* 29 (2012): 133–137. doi:10.1016/j.proeng.2011.12.682.

54. Zhang, Bang, Xingwei Wang, and Min Huang. "A data replica placement scheme for cloud storage under healthcare IoT environment." In *2014 11th International Conference on Fuzzy Systems and Knowledge Discovery (FSKD)*, pp. 542–547. IEEE, 2014.

55. Miah, Shah J., Edwin Camilleri, and H. Quan Vu. "Big data in healthcare research: A survey study." *Journal of Computer Information Systems* (2021): 1–13.

56. Tahir, Adnan, Fei Chen, Habib Ullah Khan, Zhong Ming, Arshad Ahmad, Shah Nazir, and Muhammad Shafiq. "A systematic review on cloud storage mechanisms concerning e-health-care systems." *Sensors* 20, no. 18 (2020): 5392.

57. Gupta, Prashant, Arumugam Seetharaman, and John Rudolph Raj. "The usage and adoption of cloud computing by small and medium businesses." *International Journal of Information Management* 33, no. 5 (2013): 861–874.
58. Liang, Xueping, Juan Zhao, Sachin Shetty, Jihong Liu, and Danyi Li. "Integrating blockchain for data sharing and collaboration in mobile healthcare applications." In *2017 IEEE 28th Annual International Symposium on Personal, Indoor, and Mobile Radio Communications (PIMRC)*, pp. 1–5. IEEE, 2017.
59. Haque, Shah Ahsanul, Syed Mahfuzul Aziz, and Mustafizur Rahman. "Review of cyber-physical system in healthcare." *International Journal of Distributed Sensor Networks* 10, no. 4 (2014): 217415.
60. Simmon, Eric, Kyoung-Sook Kim, Eswaran Subrahmanian, Ryong Lee, Frederic De Vaulx, Yohei Murakami, Koji Zettsu, and Ram D. Sriram. *A Vision of Cyber-Physical Cloud Computing for Smart Networked Systems*. Gaithersburg, Maryland: US Department of Commerce, National Institute of Standards and Technology, 2013.
61. Calabrese, Barbara, and Mario Cannataro. "Cloud computing in healthcare and biomedicine." *Scalable Computing: Practice and Experience* 16, no. 1 (2015): 1–18.
62. Asija, Ruchika, and Rajarathnam Nallusamy. "Healthcare SaaS based on a data model with built-in security and privacy." *International Journal of Cloud Applications and Computing (IJCAC)* 6, no. 3 (2016): 1–14.
63. Oh, Sungyoung, Jieun Cha, Myungkyu Ji, Hyekyung Kang, Seok Kim, Eunyoung Heo, Jong Soo Han, et al. "Architecture design of healthcare software-as-a-service platform for cloud-based clinical decision support service." *Healthcare Informatics Research* 21, no. 2 (2015): 102.
64. Bryan, Stirling, G. C. Weatherburn, J. R. Watkins, and Martin J. Buxton. "The benefits of hospital-wide picture archiving and communication systems: A survey of clinical users of radiology services." *The British Journal of Radiology* 72, no. 857 (1999): 469–478.
65. LaPointe, J. (2016). What is healthcare revenue cycle management? Retrieved from https://revcycleintelligence.com/features/what-is-healthcare-revenue-cyclemanagement
66. Bracci, Fabio, Antonio Corradi, and Luca Foschini. "Database security management for healthcare SaaS in the Amazon AWS Cloud." In *2012 IEEE Symposium on Computers and Communications (ISCC)*, pp. 000812–000819. IEEE, 2012.
67. Menachemi, Nir, and Taleah H. Collum. "Benefits and drawbacks of electronic health record systems." *Risk Management and Healthcare Policy* 4 (2011): 47.
68. Prasad, Vivek Kumar, and Madhuri D. Bhavsar. "Monitoring IaaS cloud for healthcare systems: Healthcare information management and cloud resources utilization." *International Journal of E-Health and Medical Communications (IJEHMC)* 11, no. 3 (2020): 54–70.
69. Ghoneim, Ahmed, Ghulam Muhammad, Syed Umar Amin, and Brij Gupta. "Medical image forgery detection for smart healthcare." *IEEE Communications Magazine* 56, no. 4 (2018): 33–37.
70. Doukas, Charalampos, and Ilias Maglogiannis. "Bringing IoT and cloud computing towards pervasive healthcare." In *2012 Sixth International Conference on Innovative Mobile and Internet Services in Ubiquitous Computing*, pp. 922–926. IEEE, 2012.
71. Soldani, David, Fabio Fadini, Heikki Rasanen, Jose Duran, Tuomas Niemela, Devaki Chandramouli, Tom Hoglund, et al. "5G mobile systems for healthcare." In *2017 IEEE 85th Vehicular Technology Conference (VTC Spring)*, pp. 1–5. IEEE, 2017.
72. Taleb, Tarik, Konstantinos Samdanis, Badr Mada, Hannu Flinck, Sunny Dutta, and Dario Sabella. "On multi-access edge computing: A survey of the emerging 5G network edge cloud architecture and orchestration." *IEEE Communications Surveys & Tutorials* 19, no. 3 (2017): 1657–1681.
73. Hu, Yun Chao, Milan Patel, Dario Sabella, Nurit Sprecher, and Valerie Young. "Mobile edge computing—A key technology towards 5G." *ETSI White Paper* 11, no. 11 (2015): 1–16.
74. Dong, Peiran, Zhaolong Ning, Mohammad S. Obaidat, Xin Jiang, Yi Guo, Xiping Hu, Bin Hu, and Balqies Sadoun. "Edge computing based healthcare systems: Enabling decentralized health monitoring in Internet of medical Things." *IEEE Network* 34, no. 5 (2020): 254–261.
75. Subahi, Ahmad F. "Edge-based IoT medical record system: Requirements, recommendations and conceptual design." *IEEE Access* 7 (2019): 94150–94159.

76. Krishnan, Y. Navaneeth, Chandan N. Bhagwat, and Aparajit P. Utpat. "Fog computing—Network based cloud computing." In *2015 2nd International Conference on Electronics and Communication Systems (ICECS)*, pp. 250–251. IEEE, 2015.

77. Kraemer, Frank Alexander, Anders Eivind Braten, Nattachart Tamkittikhun, and David Palma. "Fog computing in healthcare – A review and discussion." *IEEE Access* 5 (2017): 9206–9222.

78. Andriopoulou, Foteini, Tasos Dagiuklas, and Theofanis Orphanoudakis. "Integrating IoT and fog computing for healthcare service delivery." In *Components and Services for IoT Platforms*, pp. 213–232. Springer, Cham, 2017.

79. Hartmann, Morghan, Umair Sajid Hashmi, and Ali Imran. "Edge computing in smart health care systems: Review, challenges, and research directions." *Transactions on Emerging Telecommunications Technologies* (2019): e3710.

80. Engineer, Margi, Razma Tusha, Ankit Shah, and Kinjal Adhvaryu. "Insight into the importance of fog computing in Internet of Medical Things (IoMT)." In *2019 International Conference on Recent Advances in Energy-efficient Computing and Communication (ICRAECC)*, pp. 1–7. IEEE, 2019.

81. Paul, Anand, Hameed Pinjari, Won-Hwa Hong, Hyun Cheol Seo, and Seungmin Rho. "Fog computing-based IoT for health monitoring system." *Journal of Sensors* 2018 (2018).

82. Syed, Liyakathunisa, Saima Jabeen, S. Manimala, and Hoda A. Elsayed. "Data science algorithms and techniques for smart healthcare using IoT and big data analytics." In *Smart Techniques for a Smarter Planet*, pp. 211–241. Springer, Cham, 2019.

83. Vassanelli, Stefano, and Mufti Mahmud. "Trends and challenges in neuroengineering: Toward 'intelligent' neuroprostheses through brain-'brain inspired systems' communication." *Frontiers in Neuroscience* 10 (2016): 438.

84. Zhang, Yangan, Guichen Chen, Hang Du, Xueguang Yuan, Michel Kadoch, and Mohamed Cheriet. "Real-time remote health monitoring system driven by 5G MEC-IoT." *Electronics* 9, no. 11 (2020): 1753.

85. Haghi, Mostafa, Kerstin Thurow, and Regina Stoll. "Wearable devices in medical internet of things: Scientific research and commercially available devices." *Healthcare Informatics Research* 23, no. 1 (2017): 4.

86. Rovini, Erika, Carlo Maremmani, and Filippo Cavallo. "How wearable sensors can support Parkinson's disease diagnosis and treatment: A systematic review." *Frontiers in Neuroscience* 11 (2017): 555.

87. Olaronke, I., and Oluwaseun, O. "Big data in healthcare: Prospects, challenges and resolutions." In *2016 Future Technologies Conference (FTC)*, pp. 1152–1157, 2016.

88. Naveen, Soumyalatha, and Manjunath R. Kounte. "Key technologies and challenges in IoT edge computing." In *2019 Third International Conference on I-SMAC (IoT in Social, Mobile, Analytics and Cloud) (I-SMAC)*, pp. 61–65. IEEE, 2019.

3

Blockchain Architecture and Policy for Transforming Healthcare Industry

Medhavi Pandey and Nidhi Sharma
Delhi Technical Campus, Greater Noida, India

CONTENTS

DOI: 10.1201/9781003201960-3

3.1 Introduction

Blockchain is referred to as peer to peer connections over the internet, which enables decentralized databases and secure transactions in multiple locations without the obligation of any reliable arbitrator. The blockchain system is used for recording any kind of information related to a digital system where data is not stored as centralized data (unlike traditional databases where data is organized and kept in a centralized format). Blockchain saves the digitalized data in multiple places. Distributed ledger technology (DLT) is the term used for a cybernated system (digital system) where all such transaction affairs are recorded and communicated. A blockchain is primarily a digital ledger that is duplicated and disseminates across the different computer systems of a continuous network. It allows the recorded information to maintain its authenticity, so that no one can hack the system. The DLT contains an unchangeable cryptographic signature, which keeps all the recorded information safe and in multiple places.

The blockchain technology, also referred to as DLT, allows decentralized, unaltered data using cryptographic hashing, which can be transferred among the groups just like a google sheet. If you want some data from your team members, you can simply make a google sheet to make changes and access the sheet in a transparent manner, and hence add data to it. The blockchain concept is somewhat similar, though not as simple as we discussed in the example above. It adds chains to the blocks with a high level of security, which simultaneously permits access to the decentralized data in a secured and transparent manner, just like the bitcoin ethereum (Lichtigstein, 2018) which allows the adding up of blocks in a significant manner. Self-determining peer-to-peer networks manage the decentralized database. Also, timestamping servers are used to maintain and protect the essential records, necessitating that the data has not changed after a particular moment. Each block layout is done in a manner where the content of the next block is referenced with the previous one associated with the cryptographic hash.

Bitcoin came into the limelight in the year 2008. Nakamoto (2019) launched the concept of a genesis block, where each block carries the transactions and the information. All the interconnected chains carry the of different blocks, resulting in building a large number. The first generation of blockchain implementation is based on the concept of cryptocurrency, which was a bitcoin technology. In no time, this concept gained popularity with the public, who realized that without the intervention of any legal authority, the technology could be utilized for many other purposes. Then, the technology of blockchain 2.0 evolved in the year 2013–15, with the development of Ethereum. Vitilak Buterin introduced the concept of ethereum, with added functionalities of bitcoin, which became the second prominent digital token. Ethererum and bitcoin signalled both that digital money can be operated without government control and that they were introduced to complement the concept of the bitcoin. Ethereum used the concept of payment networks in a decentralized, open-ended software platform that can enter the computer code. Ether applications are not only bounded to store the codes but also facilitate the network's currency, programmatic contracts, and financial contracts. Whereas bitcoin was developed as a substitute for national concurrencies (which stimulates overall trading such as sales, exchange of goods, purchase), the concept of a medium of exchange came into the picture. Bitcoin stimulated overall trading practices and improved the efficiency of trading and the economy. Ethereum supports daily transactions and allows small contracts, which can perform numerous functions and decentralized applications, because of which there is a significant rise in cryptocurrency space. The Ethereum blockchain has established a proper ecosystem and has gathered an active community (Iredale, 2020).

The next, third-generation, technology manifests the applications of non-financial areas, which attempt to adapt the application beyond finance, which is furthermore benefited by blockchain (3.0) applications (Agbo et al., 2019). Third generation applications include use cases, decentralized applications that run over centralized servers, identity management, logistic monitoring, healthcare industry, sharing of medical records in a secured manner, cryptocurrency exchange (Androulaki et al., 2018; Burniske et al., 2016).

The evolution of blockchain has diversified its applications in numerous ways. Blockchain has gained popularity since 2008 and has captured the interest of different organizations and sectors, including the healthcare system and medical research. Blockchain suggested a process to solve critical healthcare challenges, such as medical records being secured properly, permitting secure access, and all sorts of privacy laws regarding patient data. It deals with the limitations and these critical issues of healthcare. In the present scenario, the blockchain system is considered as a remote monitoring technique for the healthcare system, with extended services and as an effort to restore patients/ public health through service providers. The Healthcare system includes its primary constituents, like the medical services core providers such as doctors, hospital administration, physicians, lab technicians, nurse, etc. (Vazirani et al., 2019). Then, there are hypercritical services like research based on medical science, with the medical insurance companies, doctors, and hospitals that come under this category.The category of beneficiary services includes public health and patient's health. This chapter addresses how these areas can use blockchain technology.

Blockchain is boosting technology thus, revolutionising technology in almost all the major sectors, including the public sector, entertainment, information services, healthcare, infrastructure, agriculture and mining, stock trading, crowdfunding, and more. As these companies use this technological concept in the digital ecosystem, it drives much greater transparency, efficiency, and veracity across all the fields. It reduces the risk of fraud and helps in raising scalability and functionality.

This chapter is categorized as follows: The overview of the blockchain concept, followed by an introduction to distributed ledger technology, detailing the DLT characteristics and properties. The second discusses blockchain architecture. The third section is about the architecture of healthcare, the concept of blockchain and the healthcare use case concept. The remaining section of the chapter summarizes the pros and cons of the blockchain concept within healthcare policy, its limitations, challenges, and future scope.

3.2 Overview of Blockchain

The substructure of blockchain technology related to healthcare industry is pen down here, as the detailed discussion about the blockchain is beyond the range of this chapter. Healthcare in blockchain is a leading light of this technology. It can address critical issues, for instance, but medical data can be too large to store, so sometimes it becomes unrealistic for small and medium scale healthcare industries in blockchain development. Also, there are issues related to privacy regulations of data, which is of major concern for sharing and ownership. Blockchain enables consolidated data records, which can be secured and updated on time. The data can be accessed and exchanged by consensus protocols. However, our discussion in this chapter needs to shed light on the basic purpose of solving healthcare problems using blockchain architecture.

3.2.1 A Walkthrough to Distributed Ledger Technology (DLT)

DLT legalizes the functioning of a predominantly accessible database, which allows distributed storage in a treacherous environment, with maximized efficiency and optimized transparency. Collaborations are generally among the organizations/industries and between individuals (Kannengießer et al., 2020). The key characteristics of DLT include:

- Append only – An append-only provides proper transactional data. The values and transactional data ledge does not overwrite any data and is used to provide full transactional history.
- Immutable – The transactional values or the data ledger ensures secured data, which is immutable and not tampered with, unlike other databases.
- Shared – The distributed ledger has a property of being shared in a network with multiple nodes, where all participants connect. In this, some nodes have a partial connection with the ledger while some nodes contain the complete state of a ledger. This characteristic of a DLT allows maximized transparency and well-ordered efficiency throughout the DLT network.
- Distributed – All the participants in the network are allowed to scale up nodes. This means the number of nodes can increase in DLT network. Every node has a duplicate of the ledger for transparency purposes. Also, the scalability factor reduces the bad actor attack impact on the consensus protocol (Frankenfield, 2021).

How is the information maintained in the ledger? How are record keeping arrangements done? How does DLT support all sort of transactions? How does the information in the ledger keep on updating? These are some technical design elements of DLT that answer all the above questions. Ledgers contain concise information of all transactions/balances of all the participants in DLT network. The account balance and other information related to transactions are maintained by ledgers. There are assets that are electronically maintained on the ledger, and there are assets that are native tokens or referred to as "native assets" which represent digital assets. The distributed ledger utilizes the facility of digital assets, digitally representing physical records, and records ownership by clearing or making settlements. However, blockchain that employs a chain of the transaction is one of a ledger. Transactions are recorded in blockchain implementations called blocks. These blocks are linked to the previous transactions, once these blocks are set as valid. DLT is responsible, which updates multiple nodes by the ledger.

Figure 3.1 describes connected nodes carrying their identical copy. As per arrangement's rules, within a certain time period, any changes in the ledger is reflected back in the copied nodes. A synchronized DLT system works with the consensus of nodes and a number of protocols that facilitates communication among them. The historical records and current state of nodes work with consensus among them. The term consensus here is referred to as a common state of the ledger, which all the participating nodes agree upon in a DLT network. Cryptographic tools like public key play a pivotal role in DLT, which identifies and

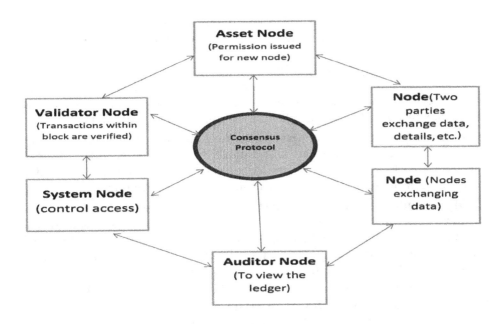

FIGURE 3.1
Ledger distributed across multiple nodes.

authenticates the participants. All the approved participants propose all the mandatory changes in the ledger, confirm the data records, and provide communication between protocols and all the nodes in the network. Each node uses cryptographic digital signatures and authenticates itself. These nodes now behave as validators and use cryptographic tools. The digital signature verifies and follows if the participant has genuine credentials or not. Cryptographic tools sometimes restrict the access to data to only approved parties, who can change and update information (Löber, 2017).

Figure 3.1 defines different nodes and how they are interconnect in the network. The system administrator controls the system access and imparts the services for standard-setting, dispute resolution, and regulatory reporting.

- Asset issuer node: this node allows or permits issuing new assets nodes.
- Proposer node: This node proposes the ledger for the new updates.
- Validator node: The validator node certifies the state modifications.
- Auditor node: It gives permission to view the ledger, but not to make any changes.

The nodes have the ability to check stored records and can see the transaction made (Löber, 2017).

3.2.2 Classification of DLT

The features of DLT represent technical characteristics as well as administrative characteristics. The technical features include the block interval, and administrative characteristics include verification of the node controller. These characteristics, when blended with the properties of DLT, influence the parameters of security and performance measures.

DLT systems are classified in three categories: permissionless, permissioned, and hybrid (Frankenfield, 2021). DLT has other characteristic features, shown here:

Permissionless distributed ledger: These features allow users to operate and maintain the data without the permission of any authority. Permissionless distributed ledger is a self-explanatory term that permits anyone to access DLT systems, and anyone can freely download it, as it is available for everyone (Frankenfield, 2021).

Permissioned distributed ledger systems: As the name suggest, this feature needs permission to access the DLT systems. Distributed ledger systems can issue and permit the validating blocks of users to access the ledger in a restricted manner. Authorized nodes maintain ledgers and restrict transactions in a secured manner (Frankenfield, 2021).

Hybrid distributed ledger systems: The hybrid distributed ledger system has both the features of permissionless distributed ledgers and permission distributed ledgers. Permission ledgers have the benefits of transparency, security, and allow restricted access to authorized users. The permissionless distributed ledger allows anyone to access the DLT network. Both characteristics give users flexibility to keep their data private or make it public, with optimized transparency features (Frankenfield, 2021).

The other characteristics of DLT systems are: The characteristics such as interoperability (allows communication between the distributed ledgers), maintainability (the degree of optimized efficiency, effectiveness among the ledgers), Smart Contracts (DLT design), Token Support (infers possible tokens, such as stability token, security, and utility token), Node Controller verification (defines the authenticity of a node's validating proceeding to join ledger), transaction content visibility (in DLT design, tcv can view all sort of transactions) and more. All these characteristics features are combined under the category of "flexibility" property. Auditability, compliance,and the extent of decentralization are all features that come under the "policy" property. Authenticity, confidentiality, and consistency are all features that come under the "security" property of DLT networks (Raj et al., 2019).

3.2.3 Properties of DLT

There are a few properties of the DLT system that define the following criteria in Figure 3.2 (Frankenfield, 2021):

Performance: This property allows a given task to be completed efficiently within a time span and with the use of resources from the distributed ledger.

Security: The data stored in a distributed ledger does not compromise security parameters. The consensus mechanisms permit responsiveness and robustness, which is an inherent trade-off of both of them. However, validating responsiveness allows for forks to reduce robustness in distributed ledger systems. To minimize this effect and to reinforce the security parameter, the targeted block at the very initial interim must be set to a certain value to confirm adequate transactions and cut down the hard block rate.

Flexibility: A distributed ledger gives freedom to customize and deploy applications.

Policy: It verifies, gives conditions, and the ability to operate to the distributed ledger.

Practicality: The degree of freedom to the users to achieve social targets with the technical constraint of distributed ledgers.

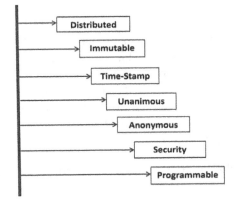

Properties of Distributed Ledger Technology (DLT)

- Distributed
- Immutable
- Time-Stamp
- Unanimous
- Anonymous
- Security
- Programmable

FIGURE 3.2
Properties of DLT.

Opaqueness: The extent to which operations and usage of the distributed ledger that cannot be tracked are defined by the opaque property.

3.3 Architecture of Block Chain

3.3.1 What is Block Chain?

Most people misunderstand blockchain architecture as something really complicated, but it is quite simple. A blockchain is nothing but a type of database. A database is a collection of data or information stored in a structured manner. For instance, it could be a table format to allow for simple searching and filtering for specific information. Blockchain is nothing but a chain of data or a chain of the transaction as blocks being chained together with each of them having a cryptographic signature, where each signature is called a hash, which is saved in multiple shared ledgers. It is supported by a connected process of nodes, which creates a network.

The functionality of the payment gateway permits secured transmission of the consumer's confidential data. It bridges a gap between a customer's bank processing tasks and the E-commerce website. Blockchain technology is defined under two categories:

- Public Blockchain: A permissionless blockchain allows anyone to participate and guarantees more secured features than a private blockchain. It allows the execution of consensus protocol. It also allows transaction censorship. The only drawback of this category is it requires immense computational power and has low privacy.

- Private Blockchain: A permission blockchain has peer to peer architecture, in which an invitation is required by the participants to access the network. Since the network keeps the restrictions for the participants, only validated invitations placed by the network are allowed to access. It requires low computational power and provides better privacy than public blockchain.

In a blockchain with a decentralized network, a node requests a transaction. In general, a transaction is initiated by its digital assets (bitcoin) when a seller submits a transaction. It is employed by private key cryptography (using a digital signature). These transactions are saved in a pool of transactions and are broadcasted to the blockchain network with every connected peer (node) where these are named as clients. At this step, on the basis of present criteria, peers need to select and validate the transactions. The way to validate the transactions makes use of a cryptographic algorithm.

Suppose a node wants to validate any transaction to know whether an instigator has enough balance between activating transactions. If the client (node) validates or verifies the transaction, then the node is appended in the block. Clients sometimes are called miners who use computational powers. They solve all computational puzzles and make enough effort to bring out the current block. If it is a successful attempt, then the miner gets an opportunity, and a new block is constructed. Every node communicates in the DLT network and among themselves to gain agreement. Since it is a decentralized technique, it does not require any centralized authority to validate transactions. This is done by consensus protocols. They communicate among the nodes. The concept of consensus protocols uses many advanced algorithms which have been specially developed for this purpose. In order to carry out the operations, the transaction request is sent by the users(node) to the blockchain (Angraal et al., 2017).

After the completion of transactions, a copy of each transaction record is added up to the ledgers. This property, known as an immutable ledger, never allows altering to remove anything. At this step, the transaction is established. After this, the other blocks link to the currently generated block, using a cryptographic hash pointer. The newly generated block is confirmed. In a similar manner, every time we need to append a new block in the chain, it will follow all the transaction steps by the time a newly generated block doesn't get confirmation (Monrat et al., 2019). The detailed architecture of blockchain is shown below in Figure 3.3.

3.3.2 Implementation of Blockchain in Health-Care

We are going to discuss some of the latest research on blockchain in health care, which includes some of the best studies and approaches. The detailed architecture is described below in Figure 3.4.

The two types of blockchain, private and consortium, segregate their structures' consent mechanism.

3.3.2.1 Key Initialization

Suppose there are some number of users -- let's say 'm' in this system. The set U defined as the users could be refer to as, $U = \{u_1, u_2, \ldots\ldots u_m\}$. In this healthcare system, we view doctor, pathologist, or software components like the cloud. Each user creates a public key pair cryptography algorithm, like (ElGama1). The public key pair of a user is denoted as k+ and k−, where k+ is said to be public key and k− is kept secret by the user Ui, and k+ is shared with all the users, using key distribution and contributors in the whole system.

3.3.2.2 Smart Contract

The smart contract is a set of directions that validates the information of more than one part, which are value-based on predefined measures related to the user's health statics.

BLOCKCHAIN ARCHITECTURE

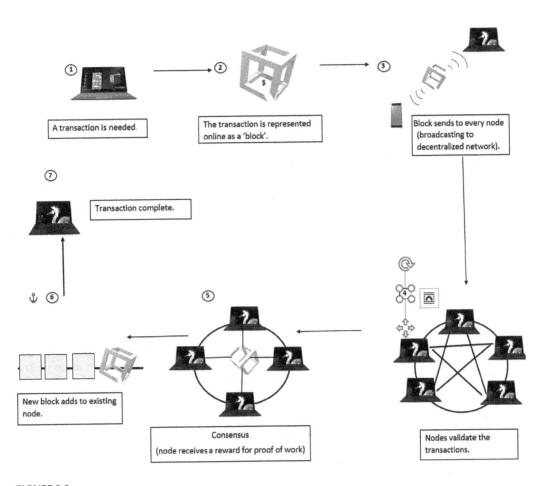

FIGURE 3.3
Blockchain architecture.

It is possible in the blockchain system to have single or multiple smart contracts. The agreement is generated by the system administrator only, who makes the decision of which part of the user's health records needs to be checked and verified. It's presumed that there is a complete user-health record. Among these records, a smart contract is generated and only 'R' parts need to be verified. A smart contract shall be constructed as 'SC', and referenced as smart contracts, which could be written as $SC = \{sc_1, sc_2, sc_3, sc_4 \ldots\ldots sc_w\}$ where the w is total quantity.

3.3.2.3 Transactions

In this architecture, a transaction is regulated such that it is linked to user health data and the sender's data. It is encrypted between the sender j and receiver k with the help of a secret key. The utilization of transactions is to transfer a user's health record. Now, there are three types of transactions in this system:

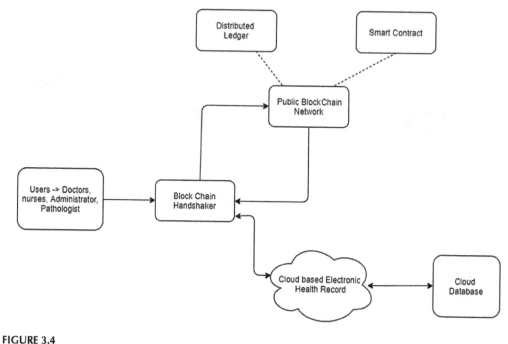

FIGURE 3.4
Blockchain in health-care.

1. Initially, the transaction is made by a doctor who carries a patient's health record to the blockchain handshaker for the next processing. The validation is done by the blockchain network. The IT or initial transaction could be a 'tuple'.

2. Blockchain transaction: It sends one's health record in the network, which is executed by blockchain handshakes.

3. Validated Transaction: It confirms the transaction in the network.

3.3.2.4 Transaction Template

It specifies this mechanism, in which it is created by an admin as stated by the format of the public blockchain network.

3.3.3 User Application

It provides two kinds of functionalities:

1. In this system, there are multiple types of users, such as nurses, doctors, admins, pathologists, and many more. Each one of them has discrete functionalities. The system creates application interfaces for the users and has distinct interfaces for distinct users, according to their defined roles.

2. An initial transaction is generated by a user based on some data, which can be the user's blood pressure or any other related symptom. Also, there will be some data generated by the system, like timestamps. The transaction is conveyed to the blockchain handshaker. It then verifies the user data and then creates a connection between the user and the blockchain handshaker.

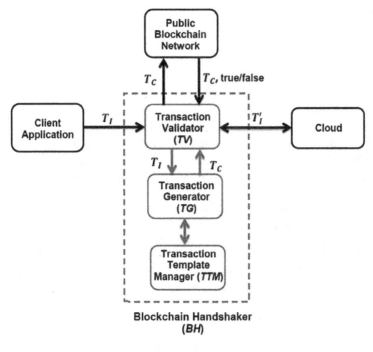

FIGURE 3.5
Blockchain Handshaker.

3.3.3.1 Blockchain Handshaker

In Figure 3.5, the Blockchain Handshaker is described. It is the core part of the architecture. This part behaves as a binding component, which further links user data, the cloud system, and the public blockchain network. The architecture described in Figure 3.5 has three subparts. They are mentioned below:-

1. Transaction generator: From an initial transaction phase, a blockchain is generated.
2. Transaction template manager: It holds a set of instant transactions templates for the network. The admin produces the transactions sets and it parts in corresponding smart contracts.
3. Transaction validator: It is the fundamental part of the blockchain handshaker. The transaction validator controls the whole interaction between blocks of the blockchain handshaker, cloud, and its network, and acquires the user application. The transaction validator receives a transaction from the user data and then sends it back to the transaction generator (Siyal et al., 2019).

3.3.4 Public Blockchain Network

Any public blockchain network could be used, such as Bitcoin or Ethereum. In this architecture, particularly, Ethereum is used. The public blockchain network comprises smart contracts, components of ledgers, and blockchain points. So, blockchain nodes obtain the transactions and validation formulated on smart contracts. If an acceptable transaction is established, the information is converted to the blocks. The acknowledgement is done in the form of a valid/invalid transaction.

3.3.4.1 Cloud

The cloud in this architecture grants us nearly similar features to what we see in the EHR management system. The initial assistance is just like hosting an EHR system. Another assistance is the storage facility. The cloud permits a huge database for storing users' health-related data. These systems receive T1 transactions from the blockchain handshaker, carry out all the pieces of the work involved in the transaction, and saves the transaction information in a cloud database.

The work which is proposed in this section is an approach taken from a well-established novel of tamper-resistance electronic medical record management by using open-source blockchain technology. In front of the existing approaches, this method gives a better mechanism that employs an abstraction layer that is called the "Blockchain Handshaker." The current approaches attempt to give solutions depending upon blockchain from scratch, which is a really inferior and expensive approach, and such procedures require a lot of changes in the existing system. In this system, a less complex architecture is created which allows non-dependency between business logic and the blockchain technology. Figure 3.5 represents a view of a prototype that inhibits the concept of an EHR management system. So, the proposed structure permits pre-established organizations to make use of an open source blockchain technology, with reduced complexity.

3.3.5 Blockchain Use Cases in Healthcare

This section focuses on one of the most interesting studies, which are categorized by use cases like electronic medical records, health insurance claims, pharmaceutical supply chain, and medical records.

3.3.5.1 Electronic Medical Record

One of the most important attributes is the Electronic Health Record, which can inter-changeably be known as the Electronic Medical Record. This attribute has the potential to connect the healthcare system. The EMR is an attribute which not only contains medical records of the patients, but also contains detailed historys. EHR especially focuses on the broader perspective of patients' health care. It provides clinical data details, as well as the overall health of patients, which is mapped with the blockchain technology and held up by EHR management. The Ethereum platform enables patients to gain information about who can access healthcare information (Xia et al., 2017). It focuses on record management, but lacks sharing of data on the cloud, as that sharing involves risk of displaying any private data. EHR and EMR related technology put forward a decentralized approach, data sharing among healthcare stakeholders in a secured manner. On the other hand, EMR applications implemented with blockchain include MedBlock (Fan et al., 2018) and Block HIE (Jiang et al., 2018). This provides a record searching mechanism. It supports in maintaining the block's address, which contains the patients' health records. This record is referenced on the corresponding blockchain (Jmaiel et al., 2020).

3.3.5.2 Health Insurance Claims

Blockchain technology has some inbuilt features and properties that we came across in this chapter. These features include transparency, policy, immutability, auditability. These characteristics provide encrypted and immutable data storage to medical insurance organizations. There are some limitations with this prototype, but blockchain has immense potential in the field of processing.

3.3.5.3 Remote Patient Monitoring

Blockchain plays a pivotal role to remotely accumulate biomedical data, as it possesses the properties of sharing, storing, and retrieving data. The patient medical data, which is to be fetched remotely, is done mainly by body area sensors, using IoT devices or mobile devices, allowing transmission of data on a Hyperledger Fabric application based on blockchain. Smart Contracts delivers automated interventions in a space safe environment. It assists in a real-time environment to monitor patients. IoT and artificial intelligence is heavily exploited in the E-health industry domain. When these technologies are combined with blockchain, it can access, store, share, and manage E-healthcare data (Jmaiel et al., 2020).

3.3.5.4 Pharmaceutical Supply Chain

The pharmaceutical industry is yet another identified use case. If the medications are not delivered or they are in short supply for the patients, havoc is created in anyone's life and can have serious consequences (Bryatov and Borodinov, 2019). This is one of the major problems to be addressed, and blockchain surely has the capability to work in this parameter. There is much research to be done to prevent spurious medications or drug supplys, though there are difficulties in identifying such counterfeits. However, there are blockchain technology-based solutions to these serious concerns (Haq and Esuka, 2018). Blockchain proposes its immutable, secure, and traceable features to verify any compliance to measure quality control over the pharmaceutical supply chain (Jmaiel et al., 2020).

3.4 Blockchain Opportunities for Health Data

The implementation of Blockchain technology in health care has made a significant alteration in health data management. Blockchain technology helps in generating medical records, and provides faster shifting of medical data in a safer mode. This diminishes the additional administrative costs and also allows the use of appropriate health data. In addition, the use of technology can reduce the need to depend upon the various mediators to oversee the exchange of important health related data.

As mentioned earlier, the medical data of a single patient can be divided into multiple areas, caregivers, custodians, and insurance providers, which implies that the complete medical history of patients are frequently blurred, mishandled, or the information is insufficient. Blockchain generated medical evidence can help teams in the healthcare sector to collect the scattered pieces of information and to store sensitive data. Therefore, the details of each patient, the instructions they received, the complete treatment, the facilities used, and other information, is kept in a secured manner that is updated in a timely fashion.

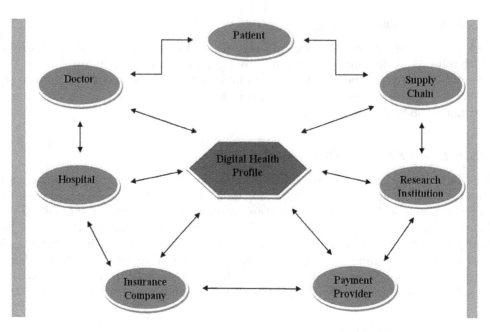

FIGURE 3.6
Opportunities offered by blockchain for health data.

It is ensured that confidential data is encrypted with a cryptographic scheme and is secured properly (Tandon et al., 2020).

This helps to untangle the primary function of health care providers to impart an effective, accurate, on time, and appropriate treatment to the patients. Pertinent data management of medical records is one of the key benefits of blockchain use in health care. Many of the issues affecting the healthcare industry, such as collaboration, data termination, fraud, and data loss during a disaster, can be eliminated.

The scope window of the use of blockchain technology in the healthcare profession is described below in Table 3.1.

3.5 Challenges of Blockchain Technology in Healthcare

With hundreds of reasons to indulge in this emerging technology, there are certainly some challenges also in the package. Significant reluctance is being shown by healthcare professionals, as well as by the general public. A few are mentioned below:

Data infringement: There can be a possibility of a data breach, as the data maintained in the blockchain records are easily accessible by any authorized source, which might lead to compromising the security of data. As healthcare-related data is very sensitive and is governed by strict laws relating to confidentiality, this could lead to a serious regulatory risk, which could outweigh the loss of easy access in an emergency.

Disadvantageous: Treatment centers show reluctance in accepting this technology, as it is in an emerging phase, and requires integration and implementation of a new system of operations that would override the existing system.

TABLE 3.1

Issues and Scope of Blockchain

Fields	Current Issues	Blockchain Healthcare Window of Opportunities
Health Data Correctness	Lack of universal medical records for health data. The resource providers generally maintain possess own database for patient's records which hampers the quality of treatment received by the patient	Universal Blockchain medical records can be maintained by the integration of Blockchain. The quality and correctness of treatment given to the patient improves significantly as all the facility providers will be using the universal records generated by the combination of blockchain and healthcare.
Health Data Standardization	Less than moderate standardization in storing, retrieving and sharing in terms of healthcare data. Information is negligently handled while transferring patient information to a custodian, one facility to another, one insurance provider to another.	Any health care facility can use the universally maintained Blockchain medical records regardless of said facility criteria.
Health Data Dependability	Scattered data records of the patient are easily alterable or distortable with negative intentions.	Blockchain data records are maintained in such a way that the records are unchangeable after their input is complete. Any changes in the input data require a long procedure and formalities with certain permissions and rights, which leads to the diminishing of theft and mishandling.
Health Data Steering Costs	An ample quantity of funds and time is required to handle unsystematic hospital records.	All the facility providers will be using the universal records generated with the combination of blockchain and healthcare
Prescription (Drug) Traceability	Plentiful fake prescriptions exist, without mentioning hazardous drugs which can be injurious to patients' health.	Data in blockchain records are unchangeable. Once the input related drugs prescription and other test profile is done, it becomes unalterable. Significant results in terms of eradication of feigned prescriptions and drug circulation.

Expensive: Blockchain technology requires a whopping amount of expense in the initial phase of installation, which might not be affordable for small and medium establishments.

3.6 Predictions about the Future of Medical Blockchain

The future of blockchain technology can be seen as blossoming and promising since in this technology, the rule of work is the decentralization of data in contrast to the existing centralized way of working and maintaining health data. Blockchain says that the patient is the one who should be and is the carrier of his/medical data records, instead of depending upon a single central source. Of Course, when some new technology is launched, it comes with a defined set of technical and non-technical challenges. Focusing on the opportunities that can be obtained using blockchain medical records, the procedure to collect, save, and fetch the data might involve huge costs and large numbers of steps, but the result is more significant and promising. New technologies, like artificial intelligence and machine learning, can be used to train the system for the future, ultimately reducing the complexity of the procedures involved.

3.7 Blockchain in Healthcare: A Revolution

Firstly, universal blockchain medical records can be maintained by the integration of blockchain and healthcare, also enabling the sharing of private and personal information without allowing any document or data to be misused. Because of decentralization systems and foolproof security, the hardware can be switched on these systems, which would eliminate data loss in any natural or man-made disasters. A time stamping mechanism is used to give the data a higher level of security.` Blockchain also provides a secure and streamlined payment management system so as to reduce dependence on clumsy and less secure procedures during the treatment of patients. Also, blockchain works and contributes in the field of research as it enables sharing data globally among healthcare researchers, permitting them to research, experiment, and study the patterns which can help treat critical and complex diseases.

In a cost-effective manner, the blockchain technology can eliminate a third party or mediator that generally tries to fetch or transfer data. Using Smart Contracts and compatible rules, it can verify, enabling access to the patient's data. Recently, developments in healthcare include mobile applications, allowing a patient to directly connect with a doctor by using apps.

This technology has immense potential to build integrated business models in accordance with healthcare operations, such as providing Pharma companies with a platform where they can get real-time data. This permits them to provide special assistance to their customers, like medical treatments, medicines, products, etc.

Lastly, blockchain also broadens the scope of all the facility providers globally to work together in a convenient way on universal database records, helping them to collaborate and reduce worldwide health care disparities while combating diseases.

References

Agbo, C. C., Mahmoud, Q. H., Eklund, J. M. (2019). Blockchain Technology in Healthcare: A Systematic Review. *Healthcare (Basel)*. April 4; 7(2): 56. doi:10.3390/healthcare7020056. PMID: 30987333; PMCID: PMC6627742.

Androulaki, E., Barger, A., Bortnikov, V., et al. (2018). Fabric, Hyperledger. A Distributed Operating System for Permissioned Blockchains. In *Proceedings of the Thirteenth EuroSys Conference; EuroSys '18*. New York, NY: Association for Computing Machinery, pp. 1–30: 15.

Angraal, S., Krumholz, H. M., Schulz, W. L. (2017). Blockchain Technology Applications in Health Care. *Circulation: Cardiovascular Quality and Outcomes* 10(9). doi:10.1161/CIRCOUTCOMES.117.003800.

Lichtigstein, A. (2018). *Who Is Vitalik Buterin*. Ethereum Founder. https://101blockchains.com/who-is-vitalik-buterin-ethereum/ (accessed May 5, 2021).

Bryatov, S., Borodinov, A. (2019). Blockchain Technology in the Pharmaceutical Supply Chain: Researching a Business Model Based on Hyperledger Fabric. In *International Conference on Information Technology and Nanotechnology (ITNT)*, Samara, Russia.

Burniske, C., Vaughn, E., Cahana, A., et al. (2016). *How Blockchain Technology Can Enhance Electronic Health Record Operability*. New York, NY: Ark Invest.

Fan, K., Wang, S., Ren, Y., et al. (2018). MedBlock: Efficient and Secure Medical Data Sharing Via Blockchain. *J Med Syst* 42: 136. doi:10.1007/s10916-018-0993-7.

Iredale, G. (2020). *History of Blockchain Technology: A Detailed Guide*. https://101blockchains.com/history-of-blockchain-timeline/ (accessed May 5, 2021).

Haq, I., Esuka, O. M. (2018). Blockchain Technology in Pharmaceutical Industry to Prevent Counterfeit Drugs. *Int. J. Comput. Appl.* 975: 8887.

Frankenfield, J. (2021). *Distributed Ledger Technology (DLT)*. https://www.investopedia.com/terms/d/distributed-ledger-technology-dlt.asp (accessed May 3, 2021).

Jiang, S., Cao, J., Wu, H., et al. (2018). BlocHIE: A Blockchain-based Platform for Healthcare Information Exchange. In *IEEE International Conference on Smart Computing (SMARTCOMP)*, pp. 49–56. IEEE.

Jmaiel, M., Mokhtari, M., Abdulrazak, B., et al. (2020). Application of Blockchain Technology in Healthcare: A Comprehensive Study. In *The Impact of Digital Technologies on Public Health in Developed and Developing Countries. ICOST*, vol. 12157. Springer, Cham. doi:10.1007/978-3-030-51517-1_23.

KannengießeR, N., Lins, S., Tobias, D., et al. (2020). Trade-offs between Distributed Ledger Technology Characteristics. *ACM Comput. Surv.* 53(2), article ID 42, May 2020. doi:10.1145/3379463.

Löber, K. (2017). *Distributed Ledger Technology in Payment, Clearing and Settlement: An Analytical Framework*. Bank for International Settlements. ISBN: 978-92-9259-031-4.

Monrat, A. A., Schelén, O., et al. (2019). A Survey of Blockchain from the Perspectives of Applications, Challenges, and Opportunities. *IEEE Access* 7: 117134–117151.

Nakamoto, S. (2019). *Bitcoin: A Peer-to-Peer Electronic Cash System*. Manubot. https://bitcoin.org/bitcoin.pdf (accessed May 5, 2021).

Raj, R., Rai, N., Agarwal, S. (2019). Anticounterfeiting in Pharmaceutical Supply Chain by Establishing Proof of Ownership. In *TENCON 2019–2019 IEEE Region 10 Conference (TENCON)*, pp. 1572–1577. IEEE.

Siyal, A. A., Junejo, A. Z., Zawish, M., et al (2019). Applications of Blockchain Technology in Medicine and Healthcare: Challenges and Future Perspectives. *Cryptography* 3(1): 3. doi:10.3390/cryptography3010003.

Tandon, A., Dhir, A., Najmul Islam, A. K. M., et al. (2020). Blockchain in Healthcare: A Systematic Literature Review, Synthesizing Framework and Future Research Agenda. *Computers in Industry* 122: 103290. ISSN: 0166-3615. doi:10.1016/j.compind.2020.103290.

Vazirani, A., O'Donoghue, O., Brindley, D., et al. (2019). Implementing Blockchains for Efficient Health Care: Systematic Review. *J Med Internet Res* 21(2): e12439. https://www.jmir.org/2019/2/e12439. doi:10.2196/12439.

Xia, Q., Sifah, E. B., Asamoah, K. O., et al. (2017). MeDShare: Trust-Less Medical Data Sharing among Cloud Service Providers via Blockchain. *IEEE Access* 5: 14757–14767.

4

Managing the Healthcare Industry using Big Data and Blockchain

Gautam Srivastava

GL Bajaj Institute of Management and Research, Greater Noida, Uttar Pradesh, India

CONTENTS

DOI: 10.1201/9781003201960-4

4.1 Introduction

The use of advanced technologies in healthcare is rapidly increasing. To increase efficiency and effectiveness, the modern healthcare system relies on technology (McGhin et al., 2019). Blockchain and big data are two critical and creative methods for improving an organization's standard and operating quality. These technologies lay the foundation for a wide range of healthcare domain applications (Tandon et al., 2020). Due to the high population density in both developed and developing countries, providing healthcare through traditional healthcare services becomes challenging. So, the adoption of information technology in healthcare is the need of the hour (Gordon and Catalini, 2018). The penetration of digitalized tools and techniques has forever altered healthcare. Blockchain and big data help to speed up operating processes, which has a direct positive effect on healthcare systems (Abu-Elezz et al., 2020). Blockchain paves the way for decentralised data and cryptocurrencies, making healthcare more effective. Blockchain is a distributed ledger. It also facilitates the exchange of data between two parties, making it easier for all healthcare stakeholders to operate efficiently (Zhang et al., 2018). The data distributed through blockchain is dispersed and immutable, so no one changes it. It improves communication and operational efficiency within hospitals. The use of blockchain to share information would assist in the protection of patients' privacy (Khan et al., 2020). The pharmaceutical industry is now benefiting from blockchain technology. It improves the digital marketplace for selling pharmaceutical products online. Pharmaceutical firms may use blockchain to market their drugs directly to consumers (Wu and Lin, 2019). Blockchain provides bid opportunities to the pharmaceuticals industry. The pharmaceutical industry is being modernized by blockchain technology. It introduces three important factors of the pharmaceutical industry: visibility, anonymity, and traceability. It enables approved centers to secure access to clinical trials (Fernando, 2019). The information could be shared securely and transparently due to the decentralized nature of blockchain. The use of blockchain facilitates the patient-centric approach (Farouk et al., 2020). Big data in healthcare refers to the massive volume of data produced every day in the healthcare industry. Big data is smart because it generates new sources of information that can be used for deeper research and analysis. It improves systematic processing capability and leads to determining data pattern recognition. In healthcare, big data assists the development and innovation of artificial intelligence. The healthcare sector is being transformed by big data (Dash et al., 2019). Big data can also be used to improve healthcare instruments. The use of big data allows for the prediction of potential healthcare needs (Senthilkumar et al., 2018). Blockchain and big data have many opportunities and challenges in healthcare. Healthcare performance is enhanced by integrating blockchain and big data. Both of these innovations have made inroads into the healthcare sector (Shi et al., 2020). Disease diagnosis using AI techniques can enhance the quickness of decision-making, and it can reduce the rate of false positives (Singh et al., 2021a).

4.2 Blockchain in Healthcare

Blockchain, a technology that was first introduced in 2009, is an electronic database record that is circulated in a decentralized way via a protected mechanism in computing devices (Nofer et al., 2017). The database is maintained in a decentralized manner using blockchain technologies. To provide a consensus system, blockchain has secure storage capability (Zheng et al., 2018). Blockchain's advanced features include various services such as integrity, traceability, and stability. A blockchain database is a unique category of database (Yaga et al., 2019). In comparison to previous tools, blockchain technology is more stable. Blockchain technologies are used in a variety of industries, including real estate, insurance, retail, and healthcare (Abadi and Brunnermeier, 2018). The integration of blockchain with IoT and AI are playing important roles in agriculture and healthcare fields to manage food supply chains, drug supply chains, traceability of products, smart contracts, monitoring the products, connecting, and intelligent prediction (Singh and Singh, 2020).

The healthcare industry requires data protection, usability, and affordability. Cost management is critical for the healthcare sector in a country like India. In the healthcare industry, blockchain technology ensures anonymity (Banerjee et al., 2018). Blockchain technology, also known as a distributed ledger, is a form of technology that lowers costs and improves transparency. The total cost of the healthcare sector is reduced as a result of using this technology. (Frizzo-Barker et al., 2020). Blockchain technology is now being used to address real-time problems in the healthcare industry. It also assists in the tracking of public records, the decentralization of data gathering, and the fulfilment of prescriptions (Bhattacharya et al., 2019).

The healthcare industry is being transformed by blockchain technology. Electronic medical records are the backbone of healthcare. It has become difficult to maintain healthcare records using conventional approaches due to the large amount of documentation and medical records (Bhuvana et al., 2020). Healthcare practitioners are dealing with issues like decentralized, unreliable, and corrupt records, which makes smooth functioning difficult. There are some companies, like Patientory, Medibloc, and Medicalchain, that are integrating the records of healthcare with the help of blockchain technology. They provide an individual patient with their whole medical history (Le Nguyen, 2018). The healthcare supply chain is also strengthened by blockchain. Blockchain improves the security of the healthcare supply chain and also improves monitoring of costs, time, and labour (Clauson et al., 2018).

Blockchain is made up of simple concepts and intriguing properties that are aligned with the complexities of the healthcare system. Blockchain functions as a distributed ledger, allowing it to keep track of all transactions in chronological order, with similar mutual copies maintained by all partners. This technology keeps track of various partners (De Aguiar et al., 2020). The benefit of blockchain technologies is that no one authority can assert ownership of the records. The decentralized data management scheme is known as the blockchain. This scheme protects data not just from tampering but also from disruption from the outside world (Attaran, 2020). All stakeholders of blockchain technologies have managed and selective access to data components, which are stored in a variety of validated blockchains in different locations. Each blockchain chain contains detailed information about the previous record in the chain (Maleh et al., 2020). The data in the blockchain is protected by encryption. One of the most valuable features of this system is that it removes the need for trust brokers to gain access to the records (Onik et al., 2019).

4.2.1 Challenges of Healthcare Data Management

1. *Information Sharing:* The healthcare sector needed decentralized data collection facilities in order to be sustainable. This data collection center assists administration in keeping and tracking individual patient records. This information can also be used for further study and advancement in the healthcare sector. For the decision-making

process, all stored data is important (Kannampallil et al., 2011). Most healthcare organizations often exchange this information with their customers, allowing each patient to take responsibility for their own wellbeing. Involvement of patients has become a pillar in the medical procedures in healthcare. Healthcare organizations are adopting more professional standards and regularly delivering health-related updates to their patients. The caretaker wanted to have access to their patient's records as well (Al-Janabi et al., 2017).

2. *Privacy Concern:* Since a patient's information is so personal, the protection of the data is also important. The healthcare information is confidential, and it is only shared with the individual concerned, with proper authorization. The healthcare industry is on the lookout for modern and creative technologies to protect patient data (Bansal and Gefen, 2010).

3. *Cost Reduction:* One of the most difficult problems is keeping the healthcare system's costs under control. The cost of healthcare, especially in the private sector, is extremely high. Private healthcare treatment is very expensive for the Indian middle class to afford, and the lower class could not afford it at all. Medical care consumes a large portion of the wealth of the Indian middle class. People in India are increasingly buying Mediclaim policies to assist them in urgent situations (Roggenkamp et al., 2019).

4. *Affordability:* The healthcare sector will benefit from blockchain technology because it is cost-effective. Blockchain technology can store and monitor vast amounts of healthcare data, while also safeguarding privacy. The protocol of blockchain connects all stakeholders without needing a costly layer of data. Data sharing that is more efficient often reduces waste. The Indian healthcare system needs modernization (McLellan et al., 2014).

4.3 Applications of Blockchain in Healthcare

4.3.1 Secure Healthcare Setup

Currently, the healthcare sector is run by a centralized information management system. This database management system is managed by a single person within the company (Rejeb and Bell, 2019). Hackers are finding it easier to gain access to this system. It is really easy to steal important information from a single data center. The blockchain infrastructure facilitates healthcare administration in preventing unauthorized access to the entire database (Hölbl et al., 2018). On a blockchain ledger, there is a large number of many individual players of varying degrees of access. If the blockchain network is properly incorporated in the healthcare system or organization, it will keep the data safe from a ransomware attack (Agbo and Mahmoud, 2019).

4.3.2 Payment System through Cryptocurrencies

One of the most significant advantages of the blockchain is being the ability to handle payments using Cryptocurrencies. It improves the financial model of the healthcare system's transparency (Kumar et al., 2018). Blockchain technology supports the reduction of healthcare fraud. The bill processing automation system would remove the involvement of third parties in the process, lowering total operating costs (Popovic, 2017). This tool is currently used by only a limited number of organizations. Any penny in the blockchain system can be mapped and registered, ensuring that no theft occurs during the billing process (Farouk et al., 2020).

4.3.3 Drug Traceability

The drug can be traced and secured thanks to blockchain technologies. Each new transaction in the block is unchangeable. This makes tracing and tracking data inside the block much simpler and ensures that the pharmacy supply chain is traceable and valid. Pharmacies that are registered under this system must be dependable (Zolfaghari et al., 2020). As a result, blockchain is being included in the central authority's control chain, which makes sense in these situations. Companies in the healthcare sector have granted themselves the freedom to pick the players in the supply chain. Also, registered users are granted access to this device (Hathaliya and Tanwar, 2020).

4.3.4 Clinical Trial and Data Security

Clinical studies are usually carried out to assess and verify the efficacy of medications used to treat particular diseases. The effectiveness of a drug's trial determines the drug's hypothesis testing (Tan et al., 2020). It may be applied on a bigger scope. A massive amount of data sets is needed to conduct a clinical trial. The analyst concentrates on data sets and, in some cases, conducts continuous testing (Mišić et al., 2019). The reports are examined using this information. Medical data is more reliable when stored using blockchain technologies (Angeles, 2019).

4.3.5 Single Patient Identification

Blockchain technology supports the preservation of individual medical records. Duplication of hospital reports and mismatches are not uncommon in healthcare records (Sharma et al., 2019a). Since there is only one database management system in conventional technologies, keeping error-free medical records becomes impossible. The blockchain system uses a hashed ledger to store all of the records (Dai and Tayur, 2020).

4.3.6 Digital Identity of Patients

It is important to provide a digital identity for each patient to provide them with reliable healthcare services. The data-based management system stores all of the patients' records (Algarni, 2019). Blockchain technology improves the database's stability and privacy. Mismatches and duplications of medical records are avoided, thus improving the quality of data records while lowering database management costs and reducing the number of errors in healthcare electronic records (Biswas et al., 2020).

4.4 Big Data in Healthcare

Big data is described as a vast amount of complex information that can be organized or unstructured. Data has been a must in our day-to-day lives, as it is required in almost all situations (Gu et al., 2017). Big data allows the healthcare system to create a machine learning model that can be used to design new healthcare equipment. The healthcare system that is based on data is more reliable and accurate. Healthcare and emergency facilities have benefited from the big data-driven healthcare infrastructure (Abouelmehdi et al., 2017). Big technology improves the healthcare system's decision-making capabilities. Big data has the potential to transform healthcare facilities. In today's healthcare sector, data is extremely important. Efforts should be made to include evidence of affordability and connectivity for the healthcare sector's improvement (Manogaran et al., 2018). Big data and information and communication technologies play a critical role in enhancing the delivery of public health services and prevention. Both developed and emerging countries have embraced the e-health platform, and they have had promising results (Batarseh et al., 2016). The pharmaceutical industry's business operations have been changed by big data. It is used to produce novel drugs and vaccines in a modern innovative research and development cell (Pesqueira et al., 2020). In the healthcare sector, big data has transformed the way people analyse, leverage, and manage information. Big data has predictive capabilities that can lower care costs while also improving quality of life. The average lifespan of a person is growing across the world as a result of modern healthcare, posing a new threat (Wang and Hajli, 2017). Big data allows health providers to conduct research and development and develop the right practices for the healthcare sector. There are many benefits of big data in healthcare that could save many lives. The treatment model has improved as a result of big data, becoming more reliable and successful (Palanisamy and Thirunavukarasu, 2019). Doctors and health providers now have even more knowledge about their patients thanks to big data, which allows them to cure patients more effectively. It contains detailed images of patients and tries to prevent them from being inconvenienced. We all agree that treatment is preferable to cure, and big data enables healthcare systems to prove this point (Yang et al., 2019).

4.5 Applications of Big Data in Healthcare

4.5.1 Prediction for the Staff

We can forecast the needs of nurses and physicians in a hospital using big data. Daily, the number of employees is determined by the number of admitted patients. This issue can be solved with the support of big data (Akoka et al., 2017). Also, data scientists could predict the workforce for future years. It aids in deciphering the pattern of patients admitted to hospitals in previous years. The information may be used to build a machine learning model (Galetsi et al., 2020). To do reliable forecasting, various statistical methods, such as time series, correlation, and regression, can be used. The predictive analyses' contribution helps in the cost optimization of healthcare. It improves management's ability to minimize additional labour costs by maximizing the number of employees (Mehta et al., 2019).

4.5.2 Electronic Records of Healthcare

One of the most popular uses of big data is database management, including anything a patient has recorded, such as lab test results, personal history, demographic statistics, and so on (Pramanik et al., 2017). The database stores all of the information in a stable format.

As a result, there is a reliable and stable unified data set. This information is used in the data collection procedure. The database's contents are shared with the public and private healthcare systems in a safe framework (Pashazadeh and Navimipour, 2018). One of the most significant benefits of big data is the elimination of paper records. This device will even give the patient an automatic alert for their weekly check-up. It allows healthcare administration to maintain detailed notes, which can be accessed by any approved individual in a matter of minutes (Pramanik et al., 2020).

4.5.3 Improve Patients' Engagement

A large number of patients are interested in smart medical devices that enable them to monitor their blood pressure, heart rate, and sugar level, among other things. Only trackable data allows for this kind of equipment. These sensors alert patients to potential dangers promptly (Saggi and Jain, 2018). These types of devices enable patients to keep track of their well-being. Big data allows researchers and scientists to create more advanced and effective medical instruments and products, which improves the ability to treat and avoid various health problems. These machines eliminate the need for patients to visit a doctor's office. For instance, a smartwatch may be very helpful for ordinary people to track their health. These devices could be designed by creating a machine learning model, which is only possible with big data (Chen et al., 2020).

4.5.4 Strategic Planning

Big data in healthcare improves the ability to prepare strategically and effectively, thus, developing a more sustainable business strategy (Syed et al., 2019). Big data enables healthcare to get a better understanding of the issue and find a solution through strategic planning. Big data technology allows administrators to interpret data more efficiently to identify the reasons that prevent patients from seeking proper care and health screenings (Khennou et al., 2018). A data scientist may create a system that represents an effective healthcare policy. The selection of data is also critical for successful strategic planning. It is impossible for healthcare to effectively leverage big data in the absence of appropriate strategic planning (Khennou et al., 2018) (Figure 4.1).

4.5.4.1 Repository

A consolidated and secure repository structure allows healthcare organizations to store all of their patient information in one place. It's a difficult job to plan and execute a repository structure. To sort the complicated big data, a lot of groundwork is needed. For research, all of the big data isn't required. As a result, data sorting and cleaning are necessary. Cleaning the data store in the archive is the first step in successful strategic planning.

4.5.4.2 Integration

Integration and collection of various datasets is a critical and difficult task. In the development of a full and accurate healthcare dataset, it is critical to link various data sources, enabling easy data access for successful strategic planning. Data integration has a huge effect on healthcare information system processing. These also remove the dataset's duplication.

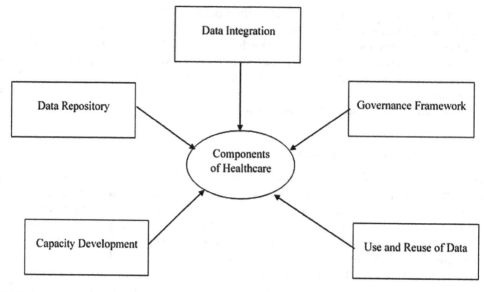

FIGURE 4.1
Components of data science in health care.

Source: Health Data for Informed Strategic Planning – Big Data Analysis (ibigdata.in)

4.5.4.3 Security

Healthcare data security is a big concern. If the data is large, privacy and data security are critical. Managing big data protection is a difficult challenge. To maintain all healthcare information in one consolidated location, an adequate system is required. It's not easy to keep these files secure. To keep the documents secure, high-security software is used. Maintaining the dignity of particular patients is difficult but necessary. To ensure the safety and protection of big data, organizations must have proper governance.

4.5.4.4 Support

A team of skills is required by a healthcare institution to clean the data, analyse it statistically, and interpret it using visualization software. Big data allows data scientists to create artificial intelligence capable of performing essential functions via automated processes. These artificial intelligence and deep learning models also improve the decision-making process' capabilities. It also creates an automated control structure that integrates all healthcare stakeholders. The support system assists in the handling of data questions used for research and decision-making.

4.5.4.5 Feedback

A well-structured database management system, backed up by advanced analytics, is essential for a successful and productive data strategy. Predictive analysis is extremely useful and valuable in the healthcare field, but it requires high-quality, reliable big data to be analysed. To scrutinise the data and reuse it for various healthcare purposes, strategic planning is needed. Artificial intelligence systems for smart hospitals are being developed as a result of ground-breaking analytical work. Super-speciality hospitals are becoming smart hospitals in both developed and emerging countries.

4.5.5 Predictive Analysis

Predictive analysis is one of the most powerful forecasting methods in all industries. Forecasting is also needed in the healthcare industry. The results of statistical forecasting assist hospitals in staffing for future years (Galetsi et al., 2019). They can predict the number of potential patients in the future. It's a never-ending process to improve health care. Big data enables researchers to keep track of all patient journeys, enhancing their ability to predict healthcare demand in the coming years (Baig et al., 2019). Predictive analytics allows healthcare administrators to monitor and maintain medical data in rural and remote areas. At a macro level, it increases healthcare delivery while lowering overall costs. Modern tools, such as ERP, can be used to create business-savvy healthcare solutions. The primary goal of predictive analysis is to make potential predictions. The researcher and analytics will use predictive analysis to examine the data's trend and pattern detection (Bates et al., 2018; Singh et al., 2021b). ML algorithms such as decision tree (DT), k-nearest neighbor (KNN), support vector machine (SVM), naïve Bayes, k-mean, q-learning, etc., help to do prognostic analysis.

4.5.6 Fraud Reduction

Many healthcare institutions are dealing with a serious data breach crisis. Data confidentiality should be a top priority for all healthcare organizations. Patients' confidential information is held by healthcare organizations and is very lucrative for black marketers. Any data leak has significant ramifications for healthcare (Lv et al., 2020). Analytics is being used by the majority of healthcare organizations to avoid threats and increase protection. Big data magnifies and exacerbates vulnerability issues, making the device more open. Advanced machine learning algorithms and a smart artificial intelligence model make healthcare more secure and stable. It may be able to detect illegal activities on its own (Anisetti et al., 2018). Big technology enables hospitals to develop new fraud monitoring and avoidance approaches. It improves the ability to detect outliers. Data-driven, stable systems save money and time, all of which are extremely valuable in healthcare (Anisetti et al., 2018).

4.5.7 Telemedicine

Telemedicine is the method of using information and communication technologies to treat a patient. It contributes to the provision of healthcare in rural and remote areas. A doctor seated in one location can be able to provide treatment to patients in another location (Sanchez-Pinto et al., 2018). Telemedicine programs are entirely reliant on information technology. Telemedicine allows people to speak with physicians over the internet, rather than personally attending the facility. Online surveillance, store and forward, and real-time interactive applications are only a few of the telemedicine services available. Long-term hospital delivery and patient retention are also made possible by telemedicine (Habl et al., 2016). Telemedicine is advantageous for people who live in areas where treatment is scarce. Patients and physicians can collaborate further due to digital technology. Telemedicine is a cost-effective, accessible, and patient-focused platform (Sood and Bhatia, 2005).

4.6 Healthcare 4.0

In the digital innovation path, healthcare is rapidly approaching healthcare 4.0. Its goals are to empower healthcare professionals to assist patients who are located far away. Healthcare is being transformed and revolutionized by technologies such as augmented reality and virtual reality applications (Kumari et al., 2018). A healthcare infrastructure that is equipped with cutting-edge technology will provide a more affordable, cost-effective, and comprehensive variety of services. It further assists in the training and education of the paramedical staff of rural areas (Kumar et al., 2020). Healthcare 4.0 is more patient-centric and anticipates potential healthcare sector needs, enhancing facilities. It hastens the development and acceptance of automated healthcare solutions. Healthcare 4.0 is focused on the collection of vast amounts of data and the use of the data to improve healthcare quality. It further improves the healthcare system's applications (Tanwar, 2020). The healthcare infrastructure of today's world is more digital than in past eras, enabling patients to receive more reliable and accessible healthcare facilities. Healthcare 4.0 can significantly increase healthcare quality and patient satisfaction. In healthcare 4.0, resolving privacy and security problems is crucial (Baitharu and Pani, 2016). Healthcare 4.0 improves the capacity to predict and prevent disease. Healthcare 4.0 is associated with industry 4.0. Healthcare 4.0 is focusing on an automation network that converts conventional hospitals into smart hospitals. Healthcare 4.0 relies heavily on automated computers and robotics. Artificial intelligence technologies that drive hyper-personalization of treatment are at the heart of healthcare 4.0. It is reshaping the healthcare ecosystem, which has a strong impact on patients. It has a significant impact on the ability to sustain and build a healthy society (Hathaliya et al., 2019). The patients benefit from the sharing of information among all healthcare stakeholders. Image and information retrieval capabilities are improved due to cutting-edge artificial intelligence technologies. Data extraction is essential for accurate predictive analysis, which assists in the development of future medical devices (Sharma et al., 2019b) (Figure 4.2).

4.7 Blockchain in Healthcare 4.0

Blockchain technology is playing a crucial role in healthcare version 4.0. The healthcare sector is making great strides in the direction of digitalization (Tanwar et al., 2020). Blockchain provides security to sensitive information and distributes the data to all the stakeholders in a transparent manner. It provides reliable data flow in the vast network and has security in data protection and transparency (Agbo et al., 2019). Blockchain is an emerging technology in the healthcare sector that not only provides security and privacy but also enable patients to have all the medical records. The patients are the owners of the data, and they have the authority to share their data (Clim et al., 2019). Blockchain is an emerging electronic ledger that has to have a significant impact on the emergence of healthcare 4.0. Blockchain technology has tremendous potential in healthcare 4.0. A blockchain is a revolutionary tool that provides data integrity and privacy (Sookhak et al., 2020). Blockchain can resolve many healthcare challenges and has various applications in healthcare 4.0, like data analytics, database management, telemedicine, electronic billing, etc. Blockchain technology is modernizing the healthcare infrastructure (Modgil and Sonwaney, 2019). Blockchain enhances

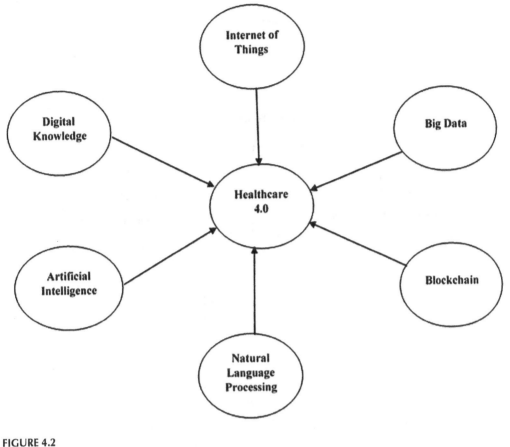

FIGURE 4.2
Digital foundation of Healthcare 4.0.

Source: Javaraman et al. (2020)

the security of data, which generates trust among the stakeholders. The stakeholders could view the data which is authorized by the owner, i.e., patients. A decentralization system through blockchain offers safe storage and distributed digital information. Blockchain effectively and efficiently resolves the problem of traceability and trust (Khatoon et al., 2020) (Figure 4.3).

4.8 Big Data in Healthcare 4.0

Big data has a vital role in industry 4.0. In the present digitalized world, sensors are playing a critical role in all sectors. Healthcare 4.0 is also untouched by it (Rallapalli et al., 2016). The healthcare sector is becoming more dependent on clinical data, which enhances the size of the medical records. Big data accelerates the modernization of healthcare. Big data enhances the decision-making process in the healthcare system (Cirillo et al., 2019). Big data is used in developing the machine learning model and artificial intelligence, which

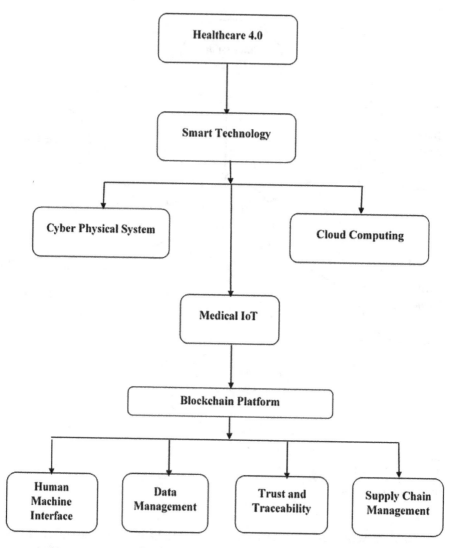

FIGURE 4.3
Blockchain and Healthcare 4.0.

Source: Mukherjee et al. (2020)

smooth the functioning of healthcare. It provides the various high-tech solutions to the healthcare industry. Big data is used to develop various architect solutions for the healthcare system. Various kinds of medical equipment could be developed, based on big data. Big data is an important pillar for healthcare 4.0. Big data in healthcare is classified into major four types, data of various kinds of medicine, patient's data, clinical data, and the data of medical experiments (Dayal and Singh, 2016). The applications of big data are vast in healthcare 4.0. Big data is also used to keep the medical records available to the world and also be able to integrate that data to help future researchers. Big data is used in data management and data warehouses, which are used for effective and efficient decision-making processes, online analysis, digital transactions, etc. Big data is used in data mining and developing a machine learning model for healthcare 4.0 (Reinhardt et al., 2020).

4.9 Conclusion

This chapter focuses on the importance of blockchain and big data. Combining blockchain and big data is an invigorating combination for healthcare 4.0. Both tools help accelerate the process and functioning of the healthcare system. Healthcare is rapidly moving toward healthcare 4.0. Blockchain and big data both are enhancing the automation system in healthcare through artificial intelligence. In healthcare 4.0, traditional hospitals are transforming into smart hospitals, which is the need of the hour. Developed countries have already implemented healthcare 4.0, and rapidly-developing nations are moving swiftly toward it. These tools help to enhance the operational efficiency of the healthcare industry. The medical instruments developed based on big data are more reliable and efficient. It also increases the efficiency of healthcare professionals to cure patients. Patients have full records of their medical history and they are authorized to share this information. Digitalization in the healthcare system is very essential to increase efficiency and effectiveness. Blockchain and big data smooth the various applications and processes of healthcare.

References

Abadi, J., and Brunnermeier, M. 2018. *Blockchain Economics*, No. W25407. National Bureau of Economic Research. doi:10.3386/w25407.

Abouelmehdi, K., Beni-Hssane, A., Khaloufi, H., and Saadi, M. 2017. Big data security and privacy in healthcare: A review. *Procedia Computer Science*, 113, 73–80. doi:10.1016/j.procs.2017.08.292.

Abu-Elezz, I., Hassan, A., Nazeemudeen, A., Househ, M., and Abd-Alrazaq, A. 2020. The benefits and threats of blockchain technology in healthcare: A scoping review. *International Journal of Medical Informatics*, 142(10): 104246. doi:10.1016/j.ijmedinf.2020.104246.

Agbo, C. C., Mahmoud, Q. H., and Eklund, J. M. 2019, June. Blockchain technology in healthcare: A systematic review. *Healthcare* 7, no. 2, 56. Multidisciplinary Digital Publishing Institute. doi:10.3390/healthcare7020056.

Akoka, J., Comyn-Wattiau, I., and Laoufi, N. 2017. Research on Big Data – A systematic mapping study. *Computer Standards and Interfaces*, 54, 105–115. doi:10.1016/j.csi.2017.01.004.

Algarni, A. 2019. A survey and classification of security and privacy research in smart healthcare systems. *IEEE Access*, 7, 101879–101894. doi:10.1109/ACCESS.2019.2930962.

Al-Janabi, S., Al-Shourbaji, I., Shojafar, M., and Shamshirband, S. 2017. Survey of main challenges security and privacy in wireless body area networks for healthcare applications. *Egyptian Informatics Journal*, 182, 113–122. doi:10.1016/j.eij.2016.11.001.

Angeles, R. 2019. Blockchain-based healthcare: Three successful proof-of-concept pilots worth considering. *Journal of International Technology and Information Management*, 273, 47–83.

Anisetti, M., Ardagna, C., Bellandi, V., Cremonini, M., Frati, F., and Damiani, E. 2018. Privacy-aware big data analytics as a service for public health policies in smart cities. *Sustainable Cities and Society*, 39, 68–77.

Attaran, M. 2020. Blockchain technology in healthcare: Challenges and opportunities. *International Journal of Healthcare Management*, 1–14. doi:10.1080/20479700.2020.1843887.

Baitharu, T. R., and Pani, S. K. 2016. Analysis of data mining techniques for healthcare decision support system using liver disorder dataset. *Procedia Computer Science*, 85, 862–870. doi:10.1016/j.procs.2016.05.276.

Banerjee, M., Lee, J., and Choo, K. K. R. 2018. A blockchain future for internet of things security: A position paper. *Digital Communications and Networks*, 43, 149–160. doi:10.1016/j.dcan.2017.10.006.

Bansal, G., and Gefen, D. 2010. The impact of personal dispositions on information sensitivity, privacy concern and trust in disclosing health information online. *Decision Support Systems*, 492, 138–150. doi:10.1016/j.dss.2010.01.010.

Batarseh, F. A., and Latif, E. A. 2016. Assessing the quality of service using big data analytics: With application to healthcare. *Big Data Research*, 4, 13–24. doi:10.1016/j.bdr.2015.10.001.

Bates, D. W., Heitmueller, A., Kakad, M., and Saria, S. 2018. Why policymakers should care about "big data" in healthcare. *Health Policy and Technology*, 72, 211–216. doi:10.1016/j.hlpt.2018.04.006.

Bhattacharya, P., Tanwar, S., Bodke, U., Tyagi, S., and Kumar, N. 2019. Bindaas: Blockchain-based deep-learning as-a-service in healthcare 4.0 applications. In *IEEE Transactions on Network Science and Engineering*. IEEE: 1242–1255. doi:10.1109/TNSE.2019.2961932.

Bhuvana, R., Madhushree, L. M., and Aithal, P. S. 2020. Blockchain as a disruptive technology in healthcare and financial services – A review based analysis on current implementations. *International Journal of Applied Engineering and Management Letters (IJAEML)*, 41, 142–155. doi:10.5281/zenodo.3822463.

Biswas, S., Sharif, K., Li, F., and Mohanty, S. 2020. Blockchain for E-health-care systems: Easier said than done. *Computer*, 537, 57–67. doi:10.1109/MC.2020.2989781.

Chen, P. T., Lin, C. L., and Wu, W. N. 2020. Big data management in healthcare: Adoption challenges and implications. *International Journal of Information Management*, 53, 102078. doi:10.1016/j.ijinfomgt.2020.102078.

Cirillo, D., and Valencia, A. 2019. Big data analytics for personalized medicine. *Current Opinion in Biotechnology*, 58, 161–167. doi:10.1016/j.copbio.2019.03.004.

Clauson, K. A., Breeden, E. A., Davidson, C., and Mackey, T. K. 2018. Leveraging blockchain technology to enhance supply chain management in healthcare: An exploration of challenges and opportunities in the health supply chain. *Blockchain in Healthcare Today*, 13, 1–12.

Clim, A., Zota, R. D., and Constantinescu, R. 2019. Data exchanges based on blockchain in m-health applications. *Procedia Computer Science*, 160, 281–288. doi:10.1016/j.procs.2019.11.088.

Dai, T., and Tayur, S. 2020. OM forum—Healthcare operations management: A snapshot of emerging research. *Manufacturing and Service Operations Management*, 225, 869–887. doi:10.1287/msom.2019.0778.

Dash, S., Shakyawar, S. K., Sharma, M., and Kaushik, S. 2019. Big data in healthcare: Management, analysis and future prospects. *Journal of Big Data*, 61, 1–25. doi:10.1186/s40537-019-0217-0.

Dayal, M., and Singh, N. 2016. Indian health care analysis using big data programming tool. *Procedia Computer Science*, 89, 521–527. doi:10.1016/j.procs.2016.06.101.

De Aguiar, E. J., Faiçal, B. S., Krishnamachari, B., and Ueyama, J. 2020. A survey of blockchain-based strategies for healthcare. *ACM Computing Surveys CSUR*, 532, 1–27. doi:10.1145/3376915.

Farouk, A., Alahmadi, A., Ghose, S., and Mashatan, A. 2020. Blockchain platform for industrial healthcare: Vision and future opportunities. *Computer Communications*, 154, 223–235. doi:10.1016/j.comcom.2020.02.058.

Fernando, E. 2019, September. Success factor of implementation blockchain technology in pharmaceutical industry: A literature review. In *2019 6th International Conference on Information Technology, Computer and Electrical Engineering (ICITACEE)*, pp. 1–5. IEEE. doi:10.1109/ICITACEE.2019.8904335.

Frizzo-Barker, J., Chow-White, P. A., Adams, P. R., Mentanko, J., Ha, D., and Green, S. 2020. Blockchain as a disruptive technology for business: A systematic review. *International Journal of Information Management*, 51, 102029. doi:10.1016/j.ijinfomgt.2019.10.014.

Galetsi, P., Katsaliaki, K., and Kumar, S. 2019. Values, challenges and future directions of big data analytics in healthcare: A systematic review. *Social Science and Medicine*, 241, 112533. doi:10.1016/j.socscimed.2019.112533.

Baig, M. I., Shuib, L., and Yadegaridehkordi, E. 2019. Big data adoption: State of the art and research challenges. *Information Processing and Management*, 566, 102095. doi:10.1016/j.ipm.2019.102095.

Galetsi, P., Katsaliaki, K., and Kumar, S. 2020. Big data analytics in health sector: Theoretical frame-work, techniques and prospects. *International Journal of Information Management, 50*, 206–216. doi:10.1016/j.ijinfomgt.2019.05.003.

Gordon, W. J., and Catalini, C. 2018. Blockchain technology for healthcare: Facilitating the transition to patient-driven interoperability. *Computational and Structural Biotechnology Journal, 16*, 224–230. doi:10.1016/j.csbj.2018.06.003.

Gu, D., Li, J., Li, X., and Liang, C. 2017. Visualizing the knowledge structure and evolution of big data research in healthcare informatics. *International Journal of Medical Informatics, 98*, 22–32. doi:10.1016/j.ijmedinf.2016.11.006.

Habl, C., Renner, A. T., Bobek, J., and Laschkolnig, A. 2016. *Study on Big Data in Public Health, Telemedicine and Healthcare*. Final Report. Publisher: European Commission

Hathaliya, J. J., and Tanwar, S. 2020. An exhaustive survey on security and privacy issues in Healthcare 4.0. *Computer Communications, 153*, 311–335. doi:10.1016/j.comcom.2020.02.018.

Hathaliya, J. J., Tanwar, S., Tyagi, S., and Kumar, N. 2019. Securing electronics healthcare records in healthcare 4.0: A biometric-based approach. *Computers and Electrical Engineering, 76*, 398–410. doi:10.1016/j.compeleceng.2019.04.017.

Hölbl, M., Kompara, M., Kamišalić, A., and Nemec Zlatolas, L. 2018. A systematic review of the use of blockchain in healthcare. *Symmetry, 1010*, 470.

iBigdata. n.d. ibigdata.in/works/using-health-data-for-informed-strategic-planning/ (accessed April 15, 2021).

Jayaraman, P. P., Forkan, A. R. M., Morshed, A., Haghighi, P. D., and Kang, Y. B. 2020. Healthcare 4.0: A review of frontiers in digital health. *Wiley Interdisciplinary Reviews Data Mining and Knowledge Discovery, 102*, e1350. doi:10.1002/widm.1350.

Kannampallil, T. G., Schauer, G. F., Cohen, T., and Patel, V. L. 2011. Considering complexity in healthcare systems. *Journal of Biomedical Informatics, 446*, 943–947. doi:10.1016/j.jbi.2011.06.006.

Khan, F. A., Asif, M., Ahmad, A., Alharbi, M., and Aljuaid, H. 2020. Blockchain technology, improvement suggestions, security challenges on smart grid and its application in healthcare for sustainable development. *Sustainable Cities and Society, 55*, 102018. doi:10.1016/j.scs.2020.102018.

Khatoon, A. 2020. A blockchain-based smart contract system for healthcare management. *Electronics, 91*, 94. doi:10.3390/electronics9010094.

Khennou, F., Khamlichi, Y. I., and Chaoui, N. E. H. 2018. Improving the use of big data analytics within electronic health records: A case study based OpenEHR. *Procedia Computer Science, 127*, 60–68. doi:10.1016/j.future.2019.06.004.

Kumar, M. S., Raut, R. D., Narwane, V. S., and Narkhede, B. E. 2020. Applications of industry 4.0 to overcome the COVID-19 operational challenges. *Diabetes & Metabolic Syndrome: Clinical Research & Reviews, 145*, 1283–1289. doi:10.1016/j.dsx.2020.07.010.

Kumar, T., Ramani, V., Ahmad, I., Braeken, A., Harjula, E., and Ylianttila, M. 2018, September. Blockchain utilization in healthcare: Key requirements and challenges. In *2018 IEEE 20th International Conference on e-Health Networking, Applications and Services Healthcom*, pp. 1–7. IEEE. doi:10.1109/HealthCom.2018.8531136.

Kumari, A., Tanwar, S., Tyagi, S., and Kumar, N. 2018. Fog computing for Healthcare 4.0 environment: Opportunities and challenges. *Computers & Electrical Engineering, 72*, 1–13. doi:10.1016/j.compeleceng.2018.08.015.

Le Nguyen, T. 2018, August. Blockchain in healthcare: A new technology benefit for both patients and doctors. In *2018 Portland International Conference on Management of Engineering and Technology PICMET*, pp. 1–6. IEEE. doi:10.23919/PICMET.2018.8481969.

Lv, Z., and Qiao, L. 2020. Analysis of healthcare big data. *Future Generation Computer Systems, 109*, 103–110. doi:10.1016/j.future.2020.03.039.

Maleh, Y., Shojafar, M., Alazab, M., and Romdhani, I., eds. 2020. *Blockchain for Cybersecurity and Privacy: Architectures, Challenges, and Applications*. CRC Press.

Manogaran, G., Varatharajan, R., Lopez, D., Kumar, P. M., Sundarasekar, R., and Thota, C. 2018. A new architecture of Internet of Things and big data ecosystem for secured smart healthcare monitoring and alerting system. *Future Generation Computer Systems, 82*, 375–387. doi:10.1016/j. future.2017.10.045.

McGhin, T., Choo, K. K. R., Liu, C. Z., and He, D. 2019. Blockchain in healthcare applications: Research challenges and opportunities. *Journal of Network and Computer Applications, 135*, 62–75. doi:10.1016/j.jnca.2019.02.027.

McLellan, A. T., and Woodworth, A. M. 2014. The affordable care act and treatment for "substance use disorders": Implications of ending segregated behavioral healthcare. *Journal of Substance Abuse Treatment, 465*, 541–545. doi:10.1016/j.jsat.2014.02.001.

Mehta, N., Pandit, A., and Shukla, S. 2019. Transforming healthcare with big data analytics and artificial intelligence: A systematic mapping study. *Journal of Biomedical Informatics, 100*, 103311. doi:10.1016/j.jbi.2019.103311.

Mišić, V. B., Mišić, J., and Chang, X. 2019, August. Towards a blockchain-based healthcare information system. In *2019 IEEE/CIC International Conference on Communications in China ICCC*, pp. 13–18. IEEE. doi:10.1109/ICCChina.2019.8855911.

Modgil, S., and Sonwaney, V. 2019. Planning the application of blockchain technology in identification of counterfeit products: Sectorial prioritization. *IFAC-PapersOnLine, 5213*, 1–5. doi:10.1016/j.ifacol.2019.11.080.

Mukherjee, P., and Singh, D. 2020. The opportunities of blockchain in health 4.0. In *Blockchain Technology for Industry 4.0*, pp. 149–164. Springer, Singapore. doi:10.1109/BigDataCongress.2017.85.

Nofer, M., Gomber, P., Hinz, O., and Schiereck, D. 2017. Blockchain. *Business & Information Systems Engineering, 593*, 183–187. doi:10.1007/s12599-017-0467-3.

Onik, M. M. H., Aich, S., Yang, J., Kim, C. S., and Kim, H. C. 2019. Blockchain in healthcare: Challenges and solutions. In *Big Data Analytics for Intelligent Healthcare Management*, pp. 197–226. Academic Press. doi:10.1016/B978-0-12-818146-1.00008-8.

Palanisamy, V., and Thirunavukarasu, R. 2019. Implications of big data analytics in developing healthcare frameworks – A review. *Journal of King Saud University-Computer and Information Sciences, 314*, 415–425. doi:10.1016/j.jksuci.2017.12.007.

Pashazadeh, A., and Navimipour, N. J. 2018. Big data handling mechanisms in the healthcare applications: A comprehensive and systematic literature review. *Journal of Biomedical Informatics, 82*, 47–62. doi:10.1016/j.jbi.2018.03.014.

Pesqueira, A., Sousa, M. J., and Rocha, Á. 2020. Big data skills sustainable development in healthcare and pharmaceuticals. *Journal of Medical Systems, 4411*, 1–15. doi:10.1007/s10916-020-01665-9.

Popovic, J. R. 2017. Distributed data networks: A blueprint for big data sharing and healthcare analytics. *Annals of the New York Academy of Sciences, 13871*, 105–111.

Pramanik, M. I., Lau, R. Y., Azad, M. A. K., Hossain, M. S., Chowdhury, M. K. H., and Karmaker, B. K. 2020. Healthcare informatics and analytics in big data. *Expert Systems with Applications, 152*, 113388. doi:10.1016/j.eswa.2020.113388.

Pramanik, M. I., Lau, R. Y., Demirkan, H., and Azad, M. A. K. 2017. Smart health: Big data enabled health paradigm within smart cities. *Expert Systems with Applications, 87*, 370–383. doi:10.1016/j.eswa.2017.06.027.

Rallapalli, S., Gondkar, R., and Ketavarapu, U. P. K. 2016. Impact of processing and analyzing healthcare big data on cloud computing environment by implementing hadoop cluster. *Procedia Computer Science, 85*, 16–22. doi:10.1016/j.procs.2016.05.171.

Reinhardt, I. C., Oliveira, J. C., and Ring, D. T. 2020. Current perspectives on the development of Industry 4.0 in the pharmaceutical sector. *Journal of Industrial Information Integration, 18*, 100131. doi:10.1016/j.jii.2020.100131.

Rejeb, A., and Bell, L. 2019. Potentials of blockchain for healthcare: Case of Tunisia. *World Scientific News, 136*, 173–193.

Roggenkamp, H., Abbass, A., Town, J. M., Kisely, S., and Johansson, R. 2019. Healthcare cost reduction and psychiatric symptom improvement in posttraumatic stress disorder patients treated with intensive short-term dynamic psychotherapy. *European Journal of Trauma & Dissociation*, 3(3): 100122. doi:10.1016/j.ejtd.2019.100122.

Saggi, M. K., and Jain, S. 2018. A survey towards an integration of big data analytics to big insights for value-creation. *Information Processing & Management*, 545, 758–790. doi:10.1016/j.ipm.2018.01.010.

Sanchez-Pinto, L. N., Luo, Y., and Churpek, M. M. 2018. Big data and data science in critical care. *Chest*, 1545, 1239–1248. doi:10.1016/j.chest.2018.04.037.

Senthilkumar, S. A., Rai, B. K., Meshram, A. A., Gunasekaran, A., and Chandrakumarmangalam, S. 2018. Big data in healthcare management: A review of literature. *American Journal of Theoretical and Applied Business*, 42, 57–69. doi:10.11648/j.ajtab.20180402.14.

Sharma, D., Singh Aujla, G., and Bajaj, R. 2019a. Evolution from ancient medication to human-centered Healthcare 4.0: A review on health care recommender systems. *International Journal of Communication Systems*, e4058. doi:10.1002/dac.4058.

Sharma, R., Zhang, C., Wingreen, S. C., Kshetri, N., and Zahid, A. 2019b. Design of Blockchain-based Precision Health-Care using soft systems methodology. *Industrial Management & Data Systems*. 120, no. 3, 608–632. doi:10.1108/IMDS-07-2019-0401.

Shi, S., He, D., Li, L., Kumar, N., Khan, M. K., and Choo, K. K. R. 2020. Applications of blockchain in ensuring the security and privacy of electronic health record systems: A survey. *Computers & Security*, 101966. doi:10.1016/j.cose.2020.101966.

Singh, P., and Singh, N. 2020. Blockchain with IoT and AI: A review of agriculture and healthcare. *International Journal of Applied Evolutionary Computation (IJAEC)*, 11(4), 13–27. doi:10.4018/IJAEC.2020100102.

Singh, P., Singh, N., and Deka, G. C. 2021a. Prospects of machine learning with blockchain in healthcare and agriculture. In *Multidisciplinary Functions of Blockchain Technology in AI and IoT Applications*, IGI Global: pp. 178–208. doi:10.4018/978-1-7998-5876-8.ch009.

Singh, P., Singh, N., Singh, K. K., and Singh, A. 2021b. Diagnosing of disease using machine learning. In *Machine Learning and the Internet of Medical Things in Healthcare*, Elsevier: pp. 89–111. doi:10.1016/B978-0-12-821229-5.00003-3.

Sood, S. P., and Bhatia, J. S. 2005. Development of telemedicine technology in India: "Sanjeevani" – An integrated telemedicine application. *Journal of Postgraduate Medicine*, 514, 308.

Sookhak, M., Jabbarpour, M. R., Safa, N. S., and Yu, F. R. 2020. Blockchain and smart contract for access control in healthcare: A survey, issues and challenges, and open issues. *Journal of Network and Computer Applications*, 178, 102950. doi:10.1016/j.jnca.2020.102950.

Syed, L., Jabeen, S., Manimala, S., and Alsaeedi, A. 2019. Smart healthcare framework for ambient assisted living using IoMT and big data analytics techniques. *Future Generation Computer Systems*, 101, 136–151. doi:10.1016/j.future.2019.06.004.

Tan, L., Tivey, D., Kopunic, H., Babidge, W., Langley, S., and Maddern, G. 2020. Part 2: Blockchain technology in health care. *ANZ Journal of Surgery*, 9012, 2415–2419. doi:10.1111/ans.16455.

Tandon, A., Dhir, A., Islam, N., and Mäntymäki, M. 2020. Blockchain in healthcare: A systematic literature review, synthesizing framework and future research agenda. *Computers in Industry*, 122, 103290. doi:10.1016/j.compind.2020.103290.

Tanwar, S. 2020. *Fog Computing for Healthcare 4.0 Environments*. Springer Nature, Switzerland AG. doi:10.1007/978-3-030-46197-3.

Tanwar, S., Parekh, K., and Evans, R. 2020. Blockchain-based electronic healthcare record system for healthcare 4.0 applications. *Journal of Information Security and Applications*, 50, 102407. doi:10.1109/TNSE.2019.2961932.

Wang, Y., and Hajli, N. 2017. Exploring the path to big data analytics success in healthcare. *Journal of Business Research*, 70, 287–299. doi:10.1016/j.jbusres.2016.08.002.

Wu, X., and Lin, Y. 2019. Blockchain recall management in pharmaceutical industry. *Procedia CIRP*, 83, 590–595. doi:10.1016/j.procir.2019.04.094.

Yaga, D., Mell, P., Roby, N., and Scarfone, K. 2019. Blockchain technology overview. *arXiv preprint arXiv:1906.11078*. doi:10.6028/NIST.IR.8202.

Yang, Y., Zheng, X., Guo, W., Liu, X., and Chang, V. 2019. Privacy-preserving smart IoT-based health-care big data storage and self-adaptive access control system. *Information Sciences, 479,* 567–592. doi:10.1016/j.ins.2018.02.005.

Zhang, P., Schmidt, D. C., White, J., and Lenz, G. 2018. Blockchain technology use cases in healthcare. In *Advances in Computers,* vol. 111, pp. 1–41. Elsevier. doi:10.1016/bs.adcom.2018.03.006.

Zheng, Z., Xie, S., Dai, H. N., Chen, X., and Wang, H. 2018. Blockchain challenges and opportunities: A survey. *International Journal of Web and Grid Services, 144,* 352–375. doi:10.1504/IJWGS.2018.095647.

Zolfaghari, A. H., Daly, H., Nasiri, M., and Sharifian, R. 2020. Blockchain applications in healthcare: A model for research. *arXiv preprint arXiv:2008.05683.*

5

Integration Aspects of AI, IoT, Big Data, and Blockchain in Healthcare Industry

Ashwani Kumar
UCER, Greater Noida, India

Deena Nath Gupta and Rajendra Kumar
JMI, New Delhi, India

CONTENTS

DOI: 10.1201/9781003201960-5

5.1 Introduction

Artificial Intelligence (AI), Internet of Things (IoT), Big Data, and Blockchain technologies have been revolutionizing the field of the Healthcare Industry. AI assists in the improvement of diagnoses, the forecasting of outcomes, and the exploration of tailored healthcare. The Machine Learning (ML) part of AI is an effective technique for diagnosing and predicting disease (Singh et al., 2021). Imagine being in excruciating pain around your heart and walking into your doctor's office (or teleconferencing software) to visit him. The doctor enters your symptoms into their computer, which pulls up the most up-to-date information base they canincorporate to diagnose and cure, which they may have conveyed as a BANET (Body Area Network) sensor device. During your MRI scan, a sophisticated healthcare device aids in finding the abnormalities that are too small for the laboratory personnel's vision to detect. Doctors may even recommend using a smartphone app in conjunction with the device already owned to track the parameters and the variety of problems. A continuous blood glucose monitor, unlike your watch, delivers continuous reading. It's possible that your ring is taking your temperature. Finally, a computer system analyses your medical records and the medical history of your family to recommend therapy paths that are specifically suited to you.

Thousands of people collect data in order to come closer to the quantified self. Scales and activity monitors are examples of Internet-connected devices that communicate measurements and record user behaviour in milliseconds. A fetal heartbeat wearable is also available (Roham et al., 2011). Many integrated devices now measure perspiration and other factors, in addition to pulse and movement. To solve new issues, high-tech devices need high-tech solutions. Atrial fibrillation is defined as a heart rate of more than 300 beats per minute (rather than 60–80 beats per minute). Patients suffering from the disease are 33 percent more likely to getting dementia, and 70% of them will die froma stroke (Hénon et al., 2006). Anticoagulants and blood thinners are two treatments that are 80% successful.

Hospital professionals are increasingly developing gadgets to make use of the huge volumes of data provided by patients and to respond when the results are concerning. A program developed by the University of California sets an example in this domain. Heart patients weigh themselves at regular intervals witha wireless scale. The device identifies dangerous weight increases and notifies clinicians, who schedule a meeting with the patient before emergency admission is required. Despite their potential, these devices have a high desertion rate of more than 30% after a time of active use. The software program has evolved into an engagement channel, allowing them to combine behaviour changing psychology withlong-term behaviour modification and usage.

Follow-up contact with a healthcare provider is required, along with the intelligent monitoring systems. The technique could be significantly improved by connecting with other devices, facilities, and programs, thereby reducing the in-hospital treatment. Medical shops that transmit data through ad-hoc networking isone of the most current smart device ideas. If a patient has not taken their medicine, they will be called via phone to discuss and help them comply with their medication schedule. Apps that can detect skin cancer and analyze urine are available. IoT has opened up a slew of possibilities for improving patient care while simultaneously lowering healthcare costs.

Blockchain is a piece of software that was created by combining many pre-existing technologies to give it its distinct characteristics. A bank cardis atrusted intermediaryand a financial transaction central authority. The land register is a secure sanctuary for property ownership information. These centralized databases are vulnerable to being hacked and altered. Blockchain aims to address privacy and security issues in data management, while also facilitating data interchange between physicians, hospitals, healthcare systems, and insurance companies by using a decentralized, immutable database. Blockchain with IoT and AI is creating a revolution in the healthcare industry (Singh and Singh, 2020)

The rest of the chapter discusses the following topics. Artificial intelligence is described in Section 5.2. The applicability of IoT in Healthcare is discussed in Section5.3. Data isdiscussed in Section5.4 in all its details. Healthcare data is discussed in Section5.5. The uses of Blockchain in Healthcare arediscussed in Section5.6. Section 5.7projects the future of healthcare. The conclusion is presentedin Section 5.8.

5.2 Artificial Intelligence

Artificial intelligence (AI) is the process of mimicking human intellect in machines that have been programmed to think and act in the same way humans do. Artificially intelligent machines are capable of remembering human behaviour patterns and adapting to meet their needs. There are several virtual assistants out there that can accurately predict our music preferences;cars can now drive themselves;and a personcould pay theirbills just by speaking to anassistant. The first research into AI was sparked by Alan Turing's book,"Computing Machinery and Intelligence." He questioned machines' ability to think. In his book, he posed the question, "Can Machines Think?" which sparked a flurry of AI research and, as a result, a slew of thesis proposals.

In 1956, Dartmouth college professor John McCarthy coined the term AI. According to him, "every aspect of learning and intelligence could be duplicated by machines if it is well described." When it comes down to it, AI is nothing more than code. It is based on algorithms that are designed to mimic human behaviour, as demonstrated in Figure 5.1. AI is a computer science abstraction. According to IBM, 90 percent of global data was created in the previous two years (Blasiak, 2014).

In the next decade, it is anticipated that there will be 150 billion networked measuring sensors, which is 20 times the global population (Helbing, 2018). Everything is becoming smarter as a result of the exponential data being generated. Because there are so many

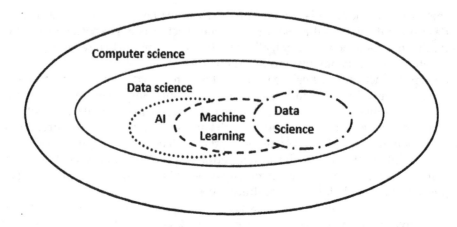

FIGURE 5.1
Role of AI and ML in computer science.

potentials with so much data, the focus has shifted to the learning process and the development of intelligent systems. The more data a system receives, the more it can learn and, thus, generate more precise outcomes. AI and ML are only recently being used and applied in enterprises and healthcare. As a result, ML applications in hospital networks are innovative, intriguing, and fascinating. The future of health is interwoven with data from every possible source, including patients, the environment, and clinicians themselves, with more devices than people on the planet (Ivanov et al., 2013). AI and ML have the potential to revolutionize health care.

5.2.1 Investigating AI

AI is intelligence presented by computers (Nwana, 1996). The development of features that boost the ability to manipulate and move is one of AI's key principles. The following are examples of AI:

1. Getting a system to think rationally and provide better output.
   - Automated Reasoning, proof planning, and whatnot.
2. Learn-ability, discover-ability, and predict-ability of a program.
   - ML, DM, and SKD.
3. Human interaction of a program.
   - Natural Language Processing (NLP)
4. Enabling machines to navigate intelligently.
   - Robotics

Fewerdatasets and the inability to analyze large volumes of data have hampered the intelligence components of AI in the past. Data is now available in real-time, thanks to the rapid expansion of mobile phone usage, digital gadgets, and the IoT (Gupta and Kumar, 2019). Weak AI and Strong AI are the two forms of AI that are classified based on how well they perform when doing a task. Weak or narrow AI is AI that performs just the most basic and straightforward tasks. These systems are not humanoid, but they can appear intelligent if

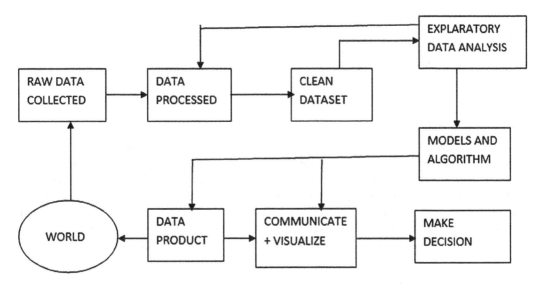

FIGURE 5.2
Decision making procedure in Data Science.

properly trained. Consider a chess game in which the system computes all moves and rules and determines every potential scenario. Weak AI is more powerful than strong AI. They have the ability to think in human terms. The two primary enablers are ML and data science.

Arthur Samuel of IBM created the term ML in 1959, when he proposed teaching computers what they need to know about the world. ML was born out of the observation of patterns. To conclude, ML is the study of computer algorithms that learn from their experiences and data to improve themselves automatically. It's regarded as a form of artificial intelligence, the interdisciplinary field of science that uses science methods, procedures, algorithms, and systems to develop new knowledge and gain insight from data and apply it across a range of disciplines.

Data is used in all AI processes. AI project teams work with data, which might be small or large in size. Real-time data needs real-time analytics when it comes to large data. Scientists or engineers who specialize in data discovery, interpretation, and management, develop mathematical models using data; also, communicating insights and findings derived from data to technical audiences are among their technical duties. Finally, big data is impossible to achieve without data science. The data science team usually has two primary responsibilities. First, the team starts with an issue/question and uses data to answer it. Second, insight and intelligence are extracted through data analytics. Figure 5.2 depicts the procedure.

5.2.2 Real-Time Big Data Learning

Because of the lack of data, AI progressed initially progressed slowly compared to now. Datasets were limited in size before the emergence of smartphones and lower-cost computation systems. Consequently, this lackhad a significant impact on the development of artificial intelligence. Today's era has changed the field; ML is maturing, and the transition to an evidence-based, data-driven strategy is becoming easier. Technology has evolved to the point where it can now access these massive databases and rapidly build ML applications.

Almost every action in the twenty-first century leaves a transactional imprint. When raw data is acquired and converted into meaningful information/knowledge that affects practices, it becomes valuable. The project and circumstances define its value. The resultcould be more personalized interactions or increased data and insight exchange inside a hospital or institution.

5.2.2.1 Drug Discovery

ML has the potential to be utilized in fundamental drug development for a wide range of applications, from early drug compound screening to predicting success rates based on biological characteristics. R&D discovery technology includes things like sequencing of next-generation. A pharmacological existence is not needed now for the drug to be successful. Digital drugs and patient data are revealing answers to diseases that were previously progressive and thought to be chronic. For example, the Low Carb Program is used by over three lakh people with type-II diabetes (Summers and Curtis, 2020).

5.2.2.2 Follow-Up Care

In the healthcare business, readmission to the hospital is a major cause of concern. Doctors and governing bodies are striving for the health of the patients after they return home after being admitted to the hospital. Digital health coaches assist with aftercare. Patients can question assistants about their medicines, be reminded to take them, and assistantsinterview patientsabout their symptoms and communicate crucial information to doctors (Summers and Curtis, 2020). For disabled patients in some countries, such as India, butlers help people communicate with their healthcare providers by providing online call facilities, i.e., removing many barriers to communication.

5.2.3 Harnessing the Power of AI in Healthcare

Several important difficulties must be tackled before AI and ML can be effectively applied and incorporated into hospital systems.

5.2.3.1 Understanding Gap

A considerable gap exists between stakeholder awareness and AI and ML applications. For the use ofAI and ML toprogressin hospitals, the capacity to convey concepts, methodologies, and testing is crucial. For healthcare to move closer to precision medicine, data sharing and convergence are crucial. A successful healthcare strategy necessitates the formation of data science teams focused on data analysis. Data investment is the approach that must be taken. Experts in data science are necessary to improve value for both patients and providers.

5.2.3.2 Fragment the Data

Reliability and integration are two hurdles that a Data is exercising currently. Patients use iPads, Fitbits, and watches to collect data, and doctors collect biomarkers and demographic information daily. During the patient's experience, this data is never mixed. Furthermore, there are no infrastructures in place to process and analyses this greater collection of data in a practical and trustworthy manner. Additionally, EHRs must be digitized in a fashion that allow patients and caregivers to access them at any time. COVID-19 accelerates data source linkage. Functional data is still developing in its early phases. A data fabric is a unified ecosystem that incorporates architecture, technology, and resources to help with enterprise decision-making management and improvement.

5.2.3.3 Appropriate Security

Simultaneously, enterprises have security and regulatory concerns, particularly when it comes to managing patient data and ensuring that it is always accessible. Furthermore, many healthcare institutions are still employing outdated software that is more vulnerable to cyber-attacks. WannaCry malware devastated the NHS's digital infrastructure (National Health Service). The ransomware, which has its origins in the United States, encrypts data on computers and demands $300–600 in bitcoin in exchange for access (Department of Health and Social Care, 2018). The ransomware attack hit over 16 healthcare organizations in England and Scotland, including hospitals and GP (General Practice) surgeries. People were instructed that they could only seek medical care in an emergency in particular places. The NHS is only one of many worldwide organizations that have been devastated by ransomware, which claims to have attacked healthcare devices in 150 nations.

5.2.4 Conversational AI

AI systems that can communicate are referred to as conversational AI. Individuals interact with conversational AI systems using voice rather than a text or code-based user interface. A growing number of products, businesses, and services are using chatbots for customer service. Alexa, Amazon's voice-activated AI assistant, is capable of performing all these tasks by combining natural language with algorithms, including recipe creation, ordering items, calculating calories in meals, or summoning a cab.

Conversational AI is becoming increasingly popular. A smart speaker is owned by one in every five Americans, and Facebook Messenger has over 100,000 chatbots (Zumstein and Hundertmark, 2018). AI chatbots' capabilities improve with time. Healthcare assistants have the potential to be smart personal assistants. It has direct applicability for the less abled because it simply involves the use of the voice to carry out activities or instructions. Conversational AI in healthcare can answer simple questions that do not require a doctor's attention. New parents, for example, might ask a conversational AI as many questions as they desired without being embarrassed or wasting the time of a healthcare professional.

The AI voice will answer questions about what temperature to bathe babies at, how long to letthem sleep, and whether they are meeting developmental milestones. Answers to many questions can be found using search engines. Most patients who seek information about their symptoms, on the other hand, have limited knowledge of how to assess qualitystudiesand may come across contradictory data, as well as misleading facts (or fake news), that can be confusing.

Patients can use a medical AI chatbot to get immediate care. Continuing with the preceding example, it would be inconvenient for a child's new parents to go to the doctor for answers to each inquiry or concern about a symptom (such as a chesty cough). However, medical proof is required. Conversational AI is becoming increasingly important in healthcare, when it allows digital access to healthcare teams and the world, which currently cannot be detected just by algorithms.

5.2.4.1 Diagnosing Disease

Medical scans can evaluate diabetes symptoms or detect them (Agrawal et al., 2019; Chauhan et al., 2021) and breast cancer signs can also be detected using AI. Many disease detection algorithms are now in use in medicine, indicating that they have considerable potential. Many AI resources aren't subjected to peer review or academic rigor. The software, supervision and validation datasets for the algorithm, comparison data, evaluation of output, and findings of neural networks are all important details that must be verified.

5.3 Internet of Things

The adoption of big data and AI in healthcare has been accelerated by recent digital upheavals. AI technologies are trained using data of all types, forms, and sizes. Academic institutions and entrepreneurs alike are developing rapid prototype solutions with more appealing health and engagement claims. IoHT devices, which are enabling a slew of new innovations that are improving people's lives, have expedited the merging of technology and medicine (Wallace et al., 2014). Health monitoring by people is now possible because healthcare is now mobile and not confined to waiting rooms only.

The challenge of storing, indexing, and analyzing vast volumes of data has hampered AI's intelligence element in the past. Data is now available in real-time, thanks to the exponential development of smartphone usage, digital gadgets, increasingly digitized systems, wearables, and the IoT. IoT refers to the ever-increasing number of smart, interconnected gadgets and sensors, as well as the enormous volumes of data they generate. Devices, services, and, eventually, humans all exchange data (Gupta and Kumar, 2020). You could also hear terms like IIoT and IoHT, which refer to other IoT verticals.

A follow-up consultation might benefit greatly from interaction with other devices, services, and systems, potentially replacing clinical intervention with a nurse's phone call instead. Medicine dispensers that take data from Bluetooth and detect if medication has been taken are among the latest smart gadget innovations. It will be discussed and encouraged that the user takes their medication on a regular basis if they have not been following that recommendation. Skin cancer detection apps and urine analyses can both be found on the app store.

The IoT has opened up a slew of new possibilities for improving patient care while simultaneously lowering healthcare expenses. Big data refers to both structured and unstructured data sources, both traditional and unique. As data becomes more diverse, so does the scope of what codes and ML technology in hospitals can accomplish? Diversity in big data can take the following forms:

- Data types include, but are not limited to, text, numbers, music, video, and photographs.
- User requirements and use cases are the focus of this section.
- Data value: Is the data suitable? This would suggest a focus on data quality in terms of its use. Data of higher quality does not automatically mean more data.

There are numerous data sources to choose from, just as there are numerous data applications. Access points and users are examples of these. The amount of data available is growing at an alarming rate. As more IoHT devices are developed, it will become increasingly important to distinguish important data from noise.

5.4 Data

Data can be available all over the place. Datafication is being pushed forward by global disruption and multinational initiatives. We live in a time when almost everything is being digitalized (or datafied). With this data production technique, new and potentially useful forms of data can be created. A push is underway to improve intelligence in municipalities as a whole. Cities and towns will begin to collect a range of information in real-time to ensure the quality of life of entire communities in the not too distant future,as the human-computer connection becomes increasingly ingrained in smart therapy.

Data can be found everywhere around us. There isa plethora of options available. The global demand for data collection, analysis, and visualization has risen as a result of big data from linked devices, embedded sensors, and the IoT. In the COVID-19 case, countries and practitioners were able to share data, especially regarding risk factors and chronic conditions associated with the new Coronavirus. Traffic lights should capture data such as air quality, visibility, and traffic speed in addition to directing traffic. One might wonder if a speeding ticket could be reversed based on a smart watch's temperature or a smart ring's average heart rate. Data can take the form of characters, text, words, numbers, images, music, and video. Data is divided into two categories: structured and unstructured. Before it can be used as information, it must be interpreted. Data that has been arranged or categorized and has some relevance (or values) for the recipient is known as information.

Data is transforming the healthcare industry, as new incentives and payment systems are introduced due to two major shifts: the need to control rising costs and the emergence of digital health, which is democratizing the healthcare system by relieving individuals of their physical constraints through the use of new devices. Changing medical trends are reshaping the medical system. Nowadays, social media and the Internet provide quick access to online health information and make patients more knowledgeable about their health. Patient-generated data is regularly generated, and patients want access to their own data. A personalized approach to treatment is a key component of evidence-based medicine.

Patients and healthcare practitioners have voiced a strong desire for full clinical data to be made available so that more reasonable treatment decisions can be made based on existing evidence. According to a survey published by diabetes.co.uk in 2019, one out of every three patients wish to engage in data sharing, but fewer people are allowed to do so. Because subtleties in subpopulations are uncommon and difficult to detect in small samples, combining separate datasets into larger populations provides more reliable proof.

5.4.1 Data Governance

Data governance is a philosophy that is linked to data security. The general population is expected to be unwilling to provide their data due to privacy concerns. Following numerous sets of laws needs disaster recovery and protection, and network infrastructure is critical to meeting these requirements. In order to provide the best care to patients, healthcare businesses must upgrade their network infrastructure. Patients were able to connect with healthcare practices during COVID-19. The influence of this small objective is global. When healthcare professionals see data, they feel compelled to act. As a result, when people emailed their healthcare providers, the fact that they received responses altered how therapy was given (Liu et al., 2020). Should a system that can detect illness risk warn a patient that it is monitoring the impending outcome?

These once-futuristic ideas are becoming a reality because of the rise of digitally connected gadgets and ML applications, and debate on these subjects is crucial to advancement. What if the pancreatic cancer test prevents me from obtaining life insurance? With the usage of the data of a patient, there are substantial privacy concerns, both in terms of what data should be kept private and what data is beneficial. Many people feel that AI's impartiality raises it beyond moral difficulties; however, this is not the case. Environmental learnings are just as rational and unbiased as AI algorithms. Data can reveal social relationships, political affiliations, religious beliefs, and sexual orientation, and it is raising new ethical questions about the use of health data.

5.4.2 Types of Data

Structured data is frequently saved in a database and organized according to a model or schema. Almost every company is aware of this type of information and may even be making good use of it. Structured data is set up in a way that makes it easy to find and retrieve information. For this purpose, structured data is usually stored in a relational database. Anything that isn't structured is referred to as unstructured data. There is no model or format for unstructured data. Unstructured data is difficult to access and obtain because it lacks evident arrangement. Due to its raw and unorganized character, structured data takes less effort to evaluate than unstructured data. However, natural language processing (NLP) and other data science and ML tools are providing assistance for sentiment classification in unstructured, informal datasets. It is possible that unstructured data will not always be able to be converted into a structured model. For example, uniform fields in the transmission of information via email or notice include the time sent, the subject, and the sender. The post's contents, on the other hand, will be tough to categorizeand examine.

Structured and unstructured data have overlapping features, whereas semistructured data is in the middle. In relational databases and data tables, hierarchical data schemas are the norm. Semistructured data does not necessarily follow this rule. In contrast, semistructured data is characterized by tags and markers that group records and fields and separate semantic properties.

5.4.3 Big Data

Big data is a collection of vast amounts of both traditional and digital data that may be analyzed and discovered. The term "big data" refers to databases that are too massive to fit within a standard relational database structure for storage and processing. A key component of big data is its scale; however, scale alone does not explain the entirety of its significance. We can use big data analytics to discover hidden patterns, links, trends, and preferences, among other things, so stakeholders can make smarter, better decisions. For this function, ML develops a toolkit of methodologies that may be enforced to datasets. Figure 5.3 depicts Laney's three Vs of big data (Chauhan and Sood, 2021; Ivanov et al., 2013).

Volume – Volume is the generated and processed quantity of data. The sheer amount of data complicates the storage capacity, indexing capability, and retrieval process. **Variety**– Big data has a wide range of data types and existence, necessitating effective storage,

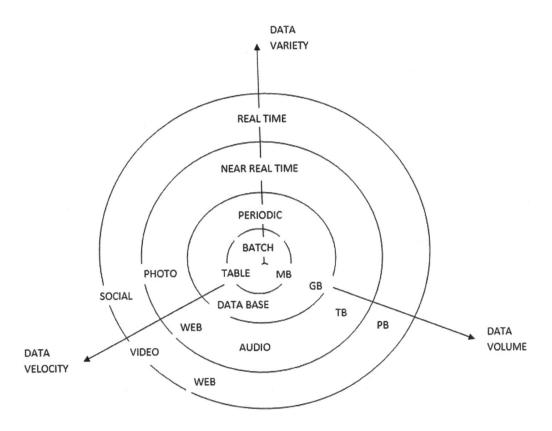

FIGURE 5.3
The three vs of Big Data.

analysis, and processing technologies. **Velocity** –Big data is accumulating at a fast pace, creating both demands and obstacles. These three have long been a source of contention among data scientists. In addition to the three Vs of big data, there are two further types of data to consider: data veracity and data significance. To better understand big data's incredibly dynamic existence, Mark van Rijmenam proposed four more Vs: variability, veracity, visualization, and value.

5.4.3.1 Volume

Laney highlighted the first V, or the thesis that there is a lot of it, as a crucial feature of big data in 2001. The demand for storage and its accompanying costs have traditionally limited big data adoption. This problem has been overcome by moving data centers from on-premises to the cloud. Even better, it comes with features like security and scalability. As a result, there have been significant storage cost savings. Cloud computing is a type of distributed computing that is delivered over the internet. Whether it's offered by public health systems, states, pharmaceutical companies, or corporations, big data isn't new in healthcare. Different characteristics of Volume is illustrated in Figure 5.4.

Patient's data is collected on a continual basis, both digitally and non-digitally.For analysis and enforcement needs, data is consumed, controlled, and produced. Until 2020, a patient's electronic health record (EHR) will not be accessible. Many companies are

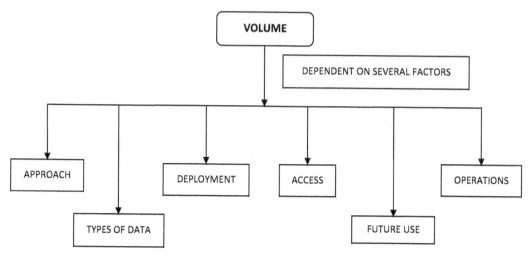

FIGURE 5.4
Different characteristics of volume.

working to put this data on the blockchain, a decentralized network framework that is transforming access to health data. Data is copious, simple to use, and has been demonstrated to be reliable. Most healthcare providers, on the other hand, do not use it for the following reasons.

- The collection of patient data takes place outside of the healthcare system.
- Data provided by patients must be incorporated and explored as part of a larger medical record or health timeline.
- Patient data includes behavioral and environmental health indicators in addition to medical markers.

Healthcare organizations continue to pique attention due to the possibility of cost reductions. The incidence of type 1 diabetes in children in the United Kingdom was recently spatially mapped on social media using the hashtags #facesofdiabetes and #letstalk. Users' sentiments were also assessed, and ML methods were used to help users identify post categories. The holy grail of personalized treatment is people-powered data and its near-real-time use. In the banking, oil, and retail industries, datafication is well underway. Anyone and any organization may get into this increasing data stream thanks to the rise of health wearables and mobile healthcare.

5.4.3.1.1 Coping with Data Volume

To use a large amount of data relevant to your organization, storage must be reliable and low cost. The ideal storage option is influenced by a number of factors, including:

- Strategy: The cost of storing data rises in tandem with the amount of data stored. As a result, the project and regulatory criteria will determine whether detailed data should be collected. Catchall techniques against high volume storage are now possible, thanks to low-cost cloud storage technologies.

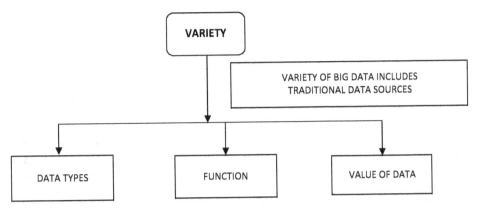

FIGURE 5.5
Different characteristics of variety.

- Data types: Consider if you'll be storing organized or unstructured data. Video, music, and image storage would be more energy-intensive than text storage.
- Deployment: Choose whether to deploy the solution locally, remotely, or in the cloud.
- Accessibility: Determine the platform for the solution viz. an app, a web interface, an intranet, or another method. Operational tasks include structuring of data, the architecture of process, archiving of data, and recovery of information, case recording, and other legal specifications.
- Future usage: Consider new data sources and system extensions. Because of the spread structure of datasets, inertia in big data implementation has long been linked to the decentralized character of such systems.

5.4.3.2 Variety

Big data encompasses both traditional and novel data sources, both organized and unstructured. Variation in data can take the following forms, as it can with a variety of sources: Text, numbers, audio, video, photographs, and other data formats are examples. This feature includes use cases and user specifications. Figure 5.5 is depicting different characteristics of Variety.

5.4.3.3 Velocity

The computer hardware infrastructures that facilitate data velocity have special challenges. Cloud computing offers the ability to instantly store and handle enormous amounts of data. Because of its storage and cost flexibility, cloud computing is the favoured method for large data projects. The cloud can store petabytes of data, and hundreds of servers can be scaled up and down in real-time to suit demand. Even more advantageous is the fact that computer power is both inexpensive and readily available.

Following the earthquake in Haiti in 2010, Twitter data proved to be a more effective technique. In a separate study, social media sites surpassed government disease surveillance approaches in terms of speed and accuracy in detecting cholera progression. Because CPS devices, embedded sensors, and other gadgets are so common, data can be transferred without a MAC address or Internet connection almost soon after it is created. Data is generated at a breakneck speed. Data acquired in the previous two years is commonly considered to outnumber data generated from the beginning of time untilthen.

5.4.3.4 Variability

There is surprisingly little predictability in big data. This term describes the significance of data that varies over time. Analysis of sentiment requires a high degree of variability. Several tweets could have a completely different meaning if just one phrase is changed. Variabilityis often used interchangeably with "variety." There may be five kinds of roses offered by a florist, for example. There is nothing more important than variety. A white rose will be different in form and smell, depending on the day of the week you visit the florist. There is always variation in the world. For sentiment analysis to be reliable, algorithms should be able to comprehend the context and gain insight into the true meaning of words in that context. Despite advancements in artificial intelligence, this still remains a challenging task.

5.4.3.5 Veracity

Data that is useless, no matter how abundant, will remain useless. Veracity in the context of data utilization relates to the truthfulness of data and if the quality of data is optimal and applicablein terms of biases, noise, and abnormalities. Different characteristics of veracity is depicted in Figure 5.6.

A number of factors can influence data validity, including the following:

- Data entry: Was all of the information correct? Is there a data entry audit trail?
- Data management: How reliable is the data as it moves through the system?

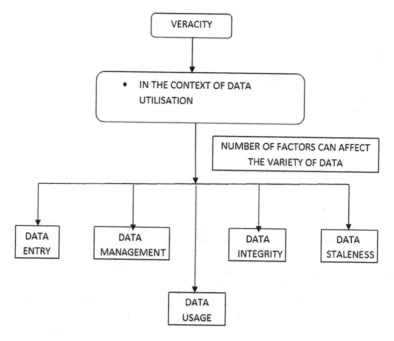

FIGURE 5.6
Different characteristics of veracity.

- The integrity of the data: Is the data properly referenced and reported?
- Data staleness: Is the data suitable for use? Is it up to date and pertinent?
- Actionability: Can the information be useful in achieving objectives? Is it moral to use this information?

The six Cs of reliable data will assist you in determining the authenticity of the data you use in your initiatives. Clean, comprehensive, current, consistent, compliant, and collaborative datasets are crucial.

- Clean data: Data quality techniques include reduplication, standardization, verification, matching, and processing. Because clean data is free of contamination, it may be used to make strong quality decisions. Clean data is the hardest barrier to overcome when it comes to user confidence.
- Complete data: Solid decision-making is enabled by consolidated data infrastructures, methodologies, and procedures.
- Current data: Data that is current is often thought to be more dependable than data that is out of date. When does data cease to be current, then? Does separating the signal from the noise become more difficult as the amount of real-time, current data grows?
- Consistent data: Consistent data must be used in order to enable the readability of a machine. It provides cross-compatibility to the devices, as well as metadata.
- Compliant data: Stakeholders, customers, legal law, or a new policy can all influence compliance rules. Despite the existence of numerous data infrastructures and standards, data science as a subject continues to face new challenges that demand regulation and legislation. Compliance may be defined differently by various stakeholders. Internally, criteria will be in place to guarantee that data satisfies different standards. Both parties must agree on data accessibility and shared in compliance with internal and external regulations. A data and knowledge governance board is commonly seen in businesses.
- Collaborative data: The 6th C is data coordination, which ensures that both the data management and business management priorities are aligned. The sixth C is more concerned with how you manage data than with the data itself. However, all of the Cs must be present in order for data to be trusted. The characteristics of Six Cs are depicted in Figure 5.7.

Metadata includes details as well as notes and comments. It's vital to invest capital in strategic information management to guarantee that assets are accurately identified and preserved in a taxonomy. This enables faster linkage of the dataset and supports a uniform asset management strategy, ensuring that finding, retrieving, and sharing the file will be easy. On the other hand, big data brings with it a plethora of metadata, allowing businesses to generate information and capitalize on it (Malde et al., 2012). In essence, this gives customers more human-friendly results, increasing click-through and conversion rates.

5.4.3.6 Visualization

Visualization refers to the appropriate analysis and visualizations required to make large data visible, understandable, and actionable. Although visualization may appear to be simple, complex presentation of datasets is crucial for the knowledge and progress of

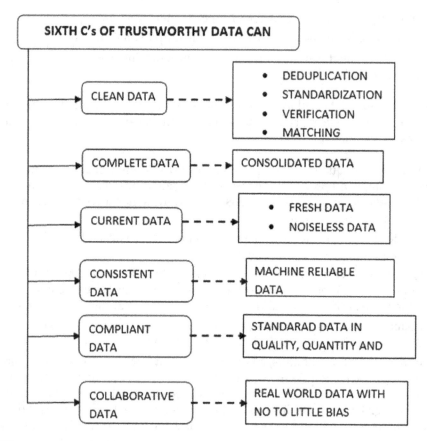

FIGURE 5.7
Characteristics of six Cs.

its users. When it comes to communicating insights gained from datasets to users, data visualization is often the most significant component. To fully benefit from data science approaches, users must understand the outcomes of data analysis and investigation. A lack of data strategy is linked to poor data visualization: if clear objectives and use cases aren't identified, displaying data outputs may be challenging due to a lack of clarity.

5.4.3.7 Value

Is the information appropriate for the purpose for which it was gathered? In terms of application, this would suggest a concentration on data quality. There are numerous sources of data, values, classes, and use cases to choose from, just as there are numerous data applications. Access points (such as the Internet, the telephone, SaaS [software as a service]) and consumers are among them. The amount of data available is growing at an alarming rate. The ability to distinguish valuable data bits from noise will become increasingly important as additional healthcare IoT devices become available. An example of wearable biomedical sensors is presented in Figure 5.8.

Data can be exchanged immediately after it is generated, without the requirement for a MAC address or Internet connectivity, because cyber-physical devices, embedded sensors, and other gadgets are so widespread. Data is generated at an incredible rate. It is

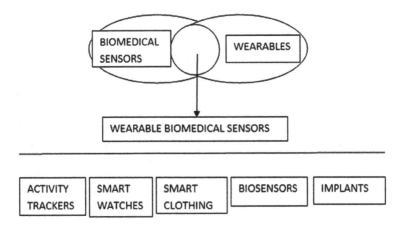

FIGURE 5.8
Wearable biomedical sensors.

often assumed that data generated in the past two years outnumber data generated from the beginning of time until that moment. Dealing with a high degree of data generation is a daunting issue for businesses. Wearable gadgets and sensors, as well as their use in clinical healthcare, will continue to gain popularity. The key to enhancing clinical value is to use a variety of different and heterogeneous data sources. The term "value" refers to how useful data is. It's vital to establish faith in data by guaranteeing its quality and usability. This will be assessed qualitatively and quantitatively in the healthcare industry. Medical influence on a person's outcomes or behaviour change, participation, impact on systems, and commercialization are all examples of limiting value (cost saving, cost benefits, etc.).

5.4.4 Information Discovery

The ability to convert raw data into useful information to drive behaviours and procedures demonstrates its usefulness. Unstructured analysis of data is a branch of data science that aims to extract information from it. Researchers can now sequence the DNA of humans in seconds, forecast a terrorists attack, figure out responsible genes for different diseases, and determine how likely you are to respond to Facebook advertisements. Data analysis may help businesses realize the strength of their data and uncover the most important data to their company goals, outcomes, and decisions. Stakeholders are usually interested in the knowledge gained from data analysis.

5.4.5 Security of Information

Patient data security and privacy are both in jeopardy. When dealing with sensitive health information, security and privacy concerns are appropriately raised. Data analysis, storage, administration, and application technologies originate from different sources, placing data at risk. Cybersecurity is a major problem. There have been major data breaches in the healthcare industry. When it was discovered that the sensitive data of thousands of patients was stored on hard drives that were auctioned on eBay, the ICO in the United Kingdom sanctioned the Brighton & Sussex University Hospitals NHS Trust (Lambert, 2016).

Anthem, a health insurance company, based in the United States, has undergone the greatest healthcare data breach to date. As a result of the issue, about 70 million current and former users' personal details were exposed.

Medical equipment poses a particular security problem due to its technological diversity. From smartphone health apps to injections, medical devices form a close network, presenting new chances for intruders (Leavitt, 2010). This form of action is considered dangerous, although it is understood that it can be helpful for individuals who are more technically savvy. In the past, fans "hacked" insulin pumps and continuous glucose monitoring to operate as an artificial pancreas. The main concern is that a similar device weakness, if exploited, might result in data breaches and, potentially, mortality among those who rely on medical devices. Finding a balance between disturbance and advancement is a trial and error process these days. Today's disruptors were yesterday's innovators.

5.5 Healthcare Data

Small and large use cases,patients, professionals, and transactions create vast volumes of data, as healthcare stakeholders are well aware. Here are a few instances of cutting-edge hospital data applications.

5.5.1 Predicting Waiting Times

Data from different hospitals are taken to predict the number of patients likely to attend each institution on a day-by-day and hour-by-hour basis (Renaud et al., 2009). Admission rates at different times were predicted using time series analysis techniques. This information was made available to all surgeries and clinics, demonstrating the usability of data in enhancing efficiency. Most clinics are demonstrating how data is still being used in healthcare.

5.5.2 Reducing Readmissions

Hospital costs can be controlled in the same way as waiting times are controlled. Critical patient clusters can be identified using data analytics, based on different parameters. Using these findings, necessary care is provided to the needy patients in order to lower readmission frequencies. By successfully identifying at-risk patients, EHR analytics for a hospital in the US reduced the frequency of readmission of patients to almost half.

5.5.3 Predictive Analytics

The preceding examples may be correct in calculating waiting durations and readmission frequencies, utilizing less data. The same data-analytics concept can be applied to disease prediction and care democratization on a large scale. Optum Labs has acquired electronic health records (EHRs) for more than 30 million patients in the United States to improve hospital operations. The goal is for physicians to make data-driven, educated decisions in real time, resulting in better patient care. The algorithms were trained and evaluated on 30 million health records to identify individuals. Patients' age and socioeconomic status can be considered by providers when assessing care on both an individual and group basis, not just when estimating risk but also when offering treatments for the best out-come for patients.

5.5.4 Electronic Health Records

EHRs have yet to achieve their full potential. Patient authorization is required for records to be exchanged via protected computer systems, and they are accessible to both public and private sector healthcare professionals. Each record is made up of a single editable file, allowing physicians to make changes over time without worrying about data duplication or inconsistencies. Despite the fact that EHRs make perfect sense, universal deployment is proving tough. According to HITECH research, EHRs are used by up to 94 percent of quali-fying hospitals in the US. Europe has sunk further into the abyss. The European Commission has set a deadline of 2020 for the creation of a consolidated European health record system.

Kaiser Permanente in the US has built a software system that allows them to share data across all of their locations, while also making EHRs easier to use. According to a McKinsey estimate, the data-sharing system saved $1 billion by lowering the frequency of office visits and lab testing (Wolf, 2009). Patients with cardiovascular disease had better outcomes because of a data-sharing policy. The electronic health record is turning into blockchain, a distributed ledger to democratize and decentralize data access.

5.6 Using the Blockchain in Healthcare

The transition from paper-based patient health records to electronic health records (EHR) is often acknowledged as a significant step forward in healthcare. By digitizing patient data, some of the traditional limitations of centralized data repositories can be overcome. In this model, however, the provider retains control of the medical records. Blockchain technology, which has the potential to change data access, security, and trust, was popularized by the bitcoin cryptocurrency. In conventional healthcare, blockchain has yet to be implemented.

5.6.1 Tamper-Proof Security

One can trace the hash forward and backwards all the way to the first block of the block-chain. To update a block in the present, all blocks corresponding to a transaction must be updated simultaneously, in all records across all nodes holding copies of the ledger. Validity is determined by the longest chain of occurrences. Blockchain technology is based on crypto-economic and game theory principles. In order to be recognized, any competitor chain should have a faster time to completion than the existing one. This would require significant investments in computers, energy, and resources. Miners compete for the hon-our of verifying blocks. Miners are paid in bitcoin for validating blocks since excellent behavior costs money in terms of electricity and computing power.

The creation of a shared data will make it possible for hospitals to access healthcare data with enhanced security and privacy.

- Backup is created by decentralizing and encrypting the data.
- The blockchain has become more democratic. A version of the truth can be contrib-uted or stored by anyone.

- The general truth is held through securing unanimity about occurrences.
- Time-stamping provides a transparent and auditable ledger of events.
- Game theory, cryptoeconomics, and assurance of censorship-free events.

5.6.2 Supply Chain Verification

The technology can be used for the verification of the supply chain. It may be used to validate components of every supply chain link because it is designed in an historical and auditable manner. It was possible to verify that the cold delivery chain for carrying insulin from the producer to the pharmacy had not been tampered with and was kept at the proper temperature. This is currently being utilized to combat counterfeit medicine in developing countries. It's also being created to improve the security of genetic data, addressing the privacy concerns that vast amounts of genomic data raise.

5.6.3 Patient Record Access

Patients are requesting to see their medical records. When it comes to determining the appropriate way to communicate sensitive medical data with unnamed third parties, this is a huge concern. Third parties face a challenge in safeguarding patient privacy, while assuring data integrity. Without the need for human interaction, presenting patient records on a properly verified blockchain will provide a cryptographic guarantee on data quality. Transactions would be generated by providers or consumers who provide health data. To access data, users must give a signature, timestamp, and private key. A full patient health record can be generated with the help of a digital signature in all records stored on the blockchain. A blockchain can be used to register each EHR addition, which generates an auditable, immutable trail of transactions and provides assurance that the most recent version of the record is being used. Patient verification would be required for any access to or processing of data. Blockchain is decentralized, so any party approved by the ecosystem can join it without apprehension.

5.7 What Is the Future of Healthcare?

Over the years, sensors will get smaller and faster so that patient health profiles will eventually contain sleep analytics, continuous blood glucose data, heart rate, blood pressure, and projected calorie burn. An electronic wristwatch will track different health indicators of the patient. Embedded biodegradable sensors will perform important health care functions, such as monitoring patients' vital signs. The importance of behavioural economics in our daily lives will grow.

5.7.1 Straps for Stress

Wearables are important for tracking stress and relaxing the mind. With wearable devices that track breathing and heart rate, it can help people identify signs of stress and keep a better eye on their health. There are fitness trackers with mindfulness features, and headphones send waveforms to the brain (Office of the Chief Economist, 2019).

5.7.2 UV Detector

Researchers at Northwestern University have developed UV sensors that can precisely measure a person's exposure to UV light. Short exposure to UV can reduce the risk of melanoma and heatstroke since UV is known to be a potent carcinogen (Haghi et al., 2017).

5.7.3 Ingenious Tattoos

Researchers at MIT and Harvard have developed smart tattoos that embed sensors in the skin (Heo and Takeuchi, 2013). The biological composition of the interstitial fluid reacts with smart tattoo ink to show the state. Tattoos will be able to fade over time, lasting as long as they are needed and only visible under specific lighting conditions. A blood glucose smart tattoo, for example, may turn red when blood glucose is high but blue when blood glucose is low.

5.7.4 Appropriate Medicines

There are many ways to make medicines smart. Patients and their healthcare team can receive timely reminders if they've forgotten to take their medicine, if smart medication tracks when and how much they've taken. The lids on bottle caps and the pill packets of pill packets are Bluetooth enabled to remind patients to take their medications. Insulin pens generate a steady stream of data, which is automatically uploaded to the cloud, accessible through a digital smartphone interface. Inhalers with smart sensors can easily detect an impending attack before the user even recognizes it (Payne et al., 2020).

5.7.5 Insulin That Is Smart

Smart insulin is a type of smart medicine that adjusts to changing blood glucose levels automatically. Insulin is released in proportion to blood sugar levels, whether they are low or high. A smart insulin patch developed by researchers at the University of North Carolina is used to give insulin by using a microneedle. There is no risk of the beta cells being rejected by the immune systems of persons with type 1 diabetes because they are kept in a patch on the outside of the body (Panchal et al., 2011). Patients are in the ideal position to understand what is going on inside their bodies, and they are more prepared than ever to visit the doctor. Patients are more aware, educated, and health-conscious than ever before. However, in varying degrees, this might result in mental distress and hypochondria.

Patients should keep in mind that trained healthcare experts can conduct a far more thorough examination. One of the reasons why the medical industry hasn't always adopted a patient-centered approach could be because of this. A 2019 poll found that using the platform enhanced 87 percent of patients' interactions with their healthcare professionals, with 75 percent expressing a better understanding of their condition. In a 2015 survey, the same amount of patients claimed they had a better understanding of their ailment, but just 20% said their relationships with their healthcare providers had improved. In particular, when it comes to illness management and geriatric care, connected medicine has a lot of promise for overcoming new health concerns.

5.7.6 Patient-Centered by Design

The usage of user data and third-party services can help to improve the precision of therapies. Through digital treatments and self-management smartphone apps, patients can gain the knowledge, skills, and tools they need to take charge of and maximize their health. Stopping smoking, exercising more, and losing weight are all examples of lifestyle changes that can be treated with behavioural therapy, while also tackling significant chronic conditions. One's behavior has an impact on chronic diseases and how they are managed (Saslow et al., 2018).

5.8 Conclusion

A smart hospital provides a differentiated patient experience in addition to providing clinical excellence and a lean supply chain. Advanced analytics and electronic health records are among the elements that make up a continuous learning environment in smart hospitals. People will be able to make better treatment decisions due to the growing use of technology and AI. Patients will be treated by the most qualified physician during nonemergency consultations over the Internet, as AI prioritization allows for fast treatment. Adherence and responsibility will be measured and maintained through a combination of offline physical and online digital care.

The integration of AI, IoT, Big Data, and Blockchain in healthcare brings a completely automated environment for patients. When a patient arrives at the hospital, an automated and streamlined admittance process cuts down on the time they have to wait. A clinical-grade wearable will track the vital signs of patients during their stay in the hospital. The medical team can view the measurements wirelessly through a dashboard. The top priority is given to discovering and resolving anomalies. In the future, hospitals will transform into data centers, which will take advantage of data to increase efficiency, reduce errors, and improve treatments and equipment decisions. Patients will be rewarded with cryptocurrencies if they continue to make reasonable and healthy lifestyle choices, and healthcare will be provided as a service.

References

Agrawal, V., Singh, P., and Sneha, S.. 2019 "Hyperglycemia Prediction Using Machine Learning: A Probabilistic Approach." In *International Conference on Advances in Computing and Data Sciences*, pp. 304–312. Springer, Singapore.

Blasiak, K. 2014. "Big Data: A Management Revolution." *Helsinki Metropolia University of Applied Sciences Bachelor of Business Administration International Business & Logistics Thesis*, 50.

Chauhan, P., and Sood, M. 2021. "Big Data: Present and Future." *Computer* 54 (4): 59–65. doi:10.1109/MC.2021.3057442.

Chauhan, T., Rawat, S.,Malik, S., and Singh, P. 2021. "Supervised and Unsupervised Machine Learning based Review on Diabetes Care." In *2021 7th International Conference on Advanced Computing and Communication Systems (ICACCS)*, vol. 1, pp. 581–585. IEEE.

Department of Health and Social Care. 2018. "Lessons Learned Review of the WannaCry Ransomware Cyber Attack." *Department of Health & Social Care*, February, pp. 1–42. www.nationalarchives.gov.uk/doc/open-government-licence/%0Ahttps://www.england.nhs.uk/wp-content/uploads/2018/02/lessons-learned-review-wannacry-ransomware-cyber-attack-cio-review.pdf.

Gupta, D.N., and Kumar, R. 2019. "Lightweight Cryptography: An IoT Perspective." *International Journal of Innovative Technology and Exploring Engineering (IJITEE)*8 (8): 700–706. https://www.ijitee.org/download/volume-8–issue-8/.

Gupta, D.N., and Kumar, R. 2020. "Generating Random Binary Bit Sequences for Secure Communications between Constraint Devices under the IoT Environment." In *INCET*, pp. 1–6.

Gupta, D.N., Kumar, R., and Kumar, A. 2020. "Efficient Encryption Techniques for Data Transmission Through the Internet of Things Devices." In *IoT and Cloud Computing Advancements in Vehicular Ad-Hoc Networks*, edited by V. Jain, O. Kaiwartya, N. Singh, and R.S. Rao, 1st ed., pp. 203–228. Pennsylvania, PA: IGI Global. doi:10.4018/978-1-7998-2570-8.ch011.

Haghi, M., Thurow, K., and Stoll, R. 2017. "Wearable Devices in Medical Internet of Things: Scientific Research and Commercially Available Devices." *Healthcare Informatics Research*23 (1): 4–15. doi:10.4258/hir.2017.23.1.4.

Helbing, D. 2018. "Towards Digital Enlightenment: Essays on the Dark and Light Sides of the Digital Revolution." In *Towards Digital Enlightenment: Essays on the Dark and Light Sides of the Digital Revolution*, May, pp. 1–222. doi:10.1007/978-3-319-90869-4.

Hénon, H., Pasquier, F., and Leys, D. 2006. "Poststroke Dementia." *Cerebrovascular Diseases*22 (1): 61–70. doi:10.1159/000092923.

Heo, Y.J., and Takeuchi, S. 2013. "Towards Smart Tattoos: Implantable Biosensors for Continuous Glucose Monitoring." *Advanced Healthcare Materials*2 (1): 43–56. doi:10.1002/adhm.201200167.

Ivanov, T., Korfiatis, N., and Zicari, R.V. 2013. "On the Inequality of the 3V's of Big Data Architectural Paradigms: A Case for Heterogeneity." November. http://arxiv.org/abs/1311.0805.

Lambert, P. 2016. "The Data Protection Officer: Profession, Rules and Role." CRC Press, 37 (5). doi:10.31228/osf.io/759cj.

Leavitt, N. 2010. "Researchers Fight to Keep Implanted Medical Devices Safe from Hackers." *Computer*43 (8): 11–14. doi:10.1109/MC.2010.237.

Liu, Q., Luo, D., Haase, J. E., Guo, Q., Wang, X.Q., Liu, S., Xia, L., Liu, Z., Yang, J., and Yang, B.X. 2020. "The Experiences of Healthcare Providers during the COVID-19 Crisis in China: A Qualitative Study." *The Lancet Global Health*8 (6): E790–798. doi:10.1016/S2214-109X(20)30204-7.

Malde, M., Kothari, M., and Shah, M. 2012. "Open Graph Interface for Uniform Access to E-Learning Resources." *International Journal of Computer Applications*58 (18): 37–39. doi:10.5120/9385-3881.

Nwana, H.S. 1996. "Software Agents-Nwana.Pdf." pp. 1–49. http://www.upv.es/sma/teoria/agentes/softwareagents-nwana.pdf.

Office of the Chief Economist. 2019. "Progress and Potential: A Profile of Women Inventors on U.S. Patents." *IP Data Highlights*, no. 2: 84–86.

Panchal, A., Shah, V., and Upadhyay, U.M. 2011. "Insulin Drug Delivery Systems: A Review." *International Journal of Research in Pharmaceutical Sciences*2 (4): 484–492.

Payne, N., Gangwani, R., Barton, K., Sample, A., Cain, C., Burke, D., Newman-Casey, P.A., and Shorter, K. 2020. "Medication Adherence and Liquid Level Tracking System for Healthcare Provider Feedback." *Sensors (Switzerland)*20 (8): 1–18. doi:10.3390/s20082435.

Renaud, B., Labarère, J., Coma, C., Santin, A., Hayon, J., Gurgui, M., Camus, N., et al.2009. "Risk Stratification of Early Admission to the Intensive Care Unit of Patients with No Major Criteria of Severe Community-Acquired Pneumonia: Development of an International Prediction Rule." *Critical Care*13 (2). doi:10.1186/cc7781.

Roham, M., Saldivar, E., Raghavan, S., Zurcher, M., Mack, J., and Mehregany, M. 2011. "A Mobile Wearable Wireless Fetal Heart Monitoring System." In *2011 5th International Symposium on Medical Information and Communication Technology, ISMICT 2011*, pp. 135–138. doi:10.1109/ISMICT.2011.5759813.

Saslow, L.R., Summers, C., Aikens, J.E., and Unwin, D.J. 2018. "Outcomes of a Digitally Delivered Low-Carbohydrate Type 2 Diabetes Self-Management Program: 1–Year Results of a Single-Arm Longitudinal Study." *JMIR Diabetes*20 (8). doi:10.2196/diabetes.9333.

Singh, P., Singh, N., Singh, K.K., and Singh, A. 2021. "Diagnosing of Disease Using Machine Learning." In *Machine Learning and the Internet of Medical Things in Healthcare*, pp. 89–111. Academic Press.

Singh, P., and Singh, N. 2020. "Blockchain with IoT and AI: A Review of Agriculture and Healthcare." *International Journal of Applied Evolutionary Computation (IJAEC)*11 (4): 13–27.

Summers, C., and Curtis, K. 2020. "Novel Digital Architecture of a 'Low Carb Program' for Initiating and Maintaining Long-Term Sustainable Health-Promoting Behavior Change in Patients with Type 2 Diabetes." *JMIR Diabetes*5 (1): 22–25. doi:10.2196/15030.

Wallace, P.J., Shah, N.D., Dennen, T., Bleicher, P.A., and Crown, W.H. 2014. "Optum Labs: Building a Novel Node in the Learning Health Care System." *Health Affairs*33 (7): 1187–1194. doi:10.1377/hlthaff.2014.0038.

Wolf, H. 2009. "What Health Systems Can Learn from Kaiser Permanente." *Health International*, pp. 19–25. http://www.mckinsey.com/insights/health_systems_and_services/what_health_systems_can_learn_from_kaiser_permanente_an_interview_with_hal_wolf.

Zumstein, D., and Hundertmark, S. 2018. "Chatbots: An Interactive Technology for Personalized Communication and Transaction." *IADIS International Journal on Www/Internet* 15 (1): 96–109.

6

Security and Privacy Aspects of AI, IoT, Big Data and Blockchain in Healthcare Industry

Apoorva Joshi
Career College, Bhopal, India

Ambrish Kumar Sharma
NRI College, Bhopal, India

Sanjeev Gour
Career College, Bhopal, India

Pratima Guatam
RNTU University, Bhopal, India

CONTENTS

DOI: 10.1201/9781003201960-6

6.1 Introduction

6.1.1 Privacy Preservation in Big Data, AI/ML

AI/ML forces the requirement of privacy preservation to a completely different level of discussion than has been common since big data or machine learning came into existence. Despite that fact, before we talk about the privacy issue in the context of machine learning, let's look at the techniques that have been built and used to mine large datasets over time.

The privacy implications of AI have also gotten a lot of coverage. Smart voice robots, probe boxes, and other AI technologies can annoy users or steal personal information from those in the normal public. A recommended framework can quickly unearth the browsing and purchase histories of users. Without a huge amount of original data, it is not possible to create accurate AI models. On the other hand, the AI system in use makes data collection easy. Real data, such as our consumption patterns, medical records, online purchases, interactions, and personal data like sports and diet, will expose our privacy. As AI technology advances, a growing number of AI applications are being used to mine private data, including both legitimate and illegitimate operations. People are becoming more aware of the value of privacy rights. One of the most critical research topics in AI privacy security is how to strike a balance between AI data use and privacy.

6.1.2 Privacy-Preservation in Blockchain for IoT

The number of medical patients in many countries is skyrocketing, making it increasingly impossible for the person who is linked to healthcare data to find primary physicians or caregivers. As IoT technology rises, wearable device use has increased in patient care, allowing for remote monitoring of patients. This technology will also enable doctors to handle a larger number of patients. Patients are monitored and cared for outside of the traditional clinical setting, using remote patient monitoring (RPM). For starters, that provides patients with an inherent simplicity of process. Patients could communicate with health care service providers as needed. Such a process also lowers the cost of medical devices and raises the standard of treatment. This is a primary reason why healthcare professionals are looking for ways to make RPM available to the general public. A specifically built tracking device that helps to track and send healthcare data, with smart contracts, a smartphone with internet, and an RPM framework, may be the critical components of an RPM system, as shown in Figure 6.1.

Wearable devices and the Internet of Things (IoT) play a critical role in both RPM and the ongoing movement that would a build Smart Cities structure. Easy-to-use, wearable device sensors would gather patient health data and send it to a required location, like a hospital, pathology lab, or medical institution, to identify a problem or particular disease, making care easier. As a result of patient data being stored, analyzed, and transferred, we see a Big Data scenario emerge. In healthcare, wearable devices are small and intelligent electronic devices that work with microcontrollers and can be incorporated in clothes or used as accessories. They are unnoticeable, easy to use, and equipped with advanced

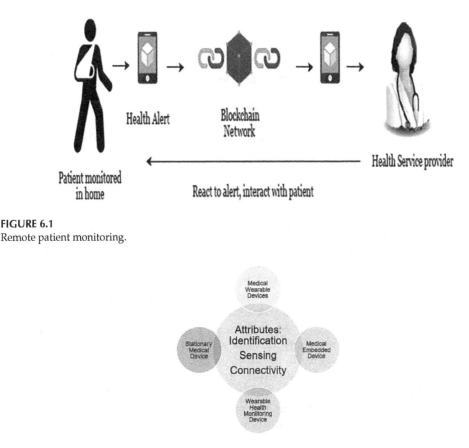

FIGURE 6.1
Remote patient monitoring.

FIGURE 6.2
Healthcare IoT topology.

technological features like data transfer, that are wireless, input data in real-time, and are alerting mechanisms for errors. These devices will give healthcare providers vital information, including blood pressure, breathing patterns, and blood sugar levels. There are four types of healthcare devices (Figure 6.2):

Stationary Healthcare Equipment: equipment that can only be used in a particular area.

Healthcare Embedded Equipment: equipment that can be implanted within the body (e.g., pacemakers)

Wearable Healthcare Equipment: Wearable equipment that is a medically prescribed device (e.g., Nebulizer).

Market Products: Wearable healthcare monitoring equipment (e.g., Smart-watch, Fuel band, etc.)

The pill with a sensor was approved by the Food and Drug Administration (FDA) on November 13, 2017. This pill is able to detect whether a patient has taken it or not. The pill's sensor communicates with a wearable device pad, which then sends the message to a smartphone app. This technology has the potential to revolutionize chronic disease treatment and mental health disorders. The basic network of this wearable equipment embedded

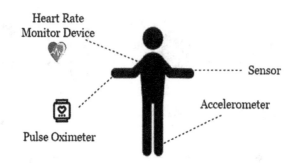

FIGURE 6.3
Wearable devices for the patients.

with special application-software, sensors, actuators, and networking that enables the wearable device to communicate and share data is one of the major projects of the Internet of Things (IoT) (Figure 6.3). We will not only be able to see this wearable equipment transmitting healthcare data in a future smart-city, but we also will be able to see them transmitting financial data. As wearable devices become more interconnected, they will share a wide range of information. As a result, the concepts raised here about wearable healthcare devices and blockchain technology have a far broader scope than we can demonstrate or imagine here. Such technology necessitates reliable data exchange in order to manage such patient data between institutions. Health information is extremely confidential and revealing it could put the patient at risk of being exposed. Furthermore, the existing data-sharing structure is based on a centralized architecture that necessitates centralized trust.

Databases containing personal information usually have columns/attributes that fall into one of the following categories in terms of privacy:

(a) PII (Personally Identifiable Information) – these are data in .cvv file or an excel sheet that can be used to identify individuals or connect with them (e.g., email address, social security number, etc.).

(b) QI (Quasi-Identifiers) – these are columns that are not actually useful on their own, including other QIs, query results, and some external data to identify a person's data (e.g., age, gender, pin code, etc.).

(c) Sensitive Data/Columns – these are not basically PII or QI attributes, but include data about the individual person that needs to be hidden for various reasons (e.g., STD diseases, income, live location (Geo location), and more.

(d) Non-sensitive Data/Columns – these are the attributes that do not match with any above points (e.g., hobby, country).

6.2 Security and Privacy Aspects of Emerging Technology in Healthcare Sector

Privacy is a notoriously difficult term to describe, especially in the healthcare sector. One common viewpoint currently holds that privacy is linked to context. The role players involved, the mechanisms like Big-data, IoT, AI blockchain, and many more emerging technologies by which information is accessed, the pace of access, and the intent of access all influence how information will flow. When these contextual laws are broken, we call it a privacy violation. Such violations may occur as a result of the wrong actor gaining access to the information, the mechanism through which information can be accessed being violated, or the object of access being inappropriate, among other things. When we consider moral explanations for why such breaches are problematic, we may divide them into two groups (with some simplification): consequentialist and deontological concerns. There are two caveats: first, certain privacy breaches fall into both categories. Second, some of the questions we raised apply to "small data" collection as well. However, in big data environments, the number of people affect the magnitude of the consequences, and the challenge for aggrieved people to take preventive or self-help steps all appear to rise.

6.2.1 Consequentialist Concerns

Consequentialist issues arise as a result of negative implications for the individual whose privacy has been invaded. There may be tangible negative effects, such as an increase in one's long-term-care insurance premium due to additional details now available as a result of a violation of privacy, job discrimination, or the discovery of one's HIV status by those in one's circle or a social circle, etc. Consider the possibility of increased anxiety if one believed one was now vulnerable to identity fraud, long before any misuses of one's identity had occurred.

6.2.2 Deontological Concerns

The existence of deontological considerations is not contingent on the occurrence of negative consequences. The fear of a privacy breach manifests in this category even though no one uses a person's information against them or if the person is unaware that a breach has occurred. Even if no damage has been done, a privacy violation will cause harm. Assume that as part of a broader data dragnet, an entity unwittingly or unintentionally gains access to data you store on your smartphone. The company discovers the data is worthless to them after analyzing it, including images you took of a humiliating personal ailment, and removes the record. We will never know what happened. Many sources that might be analyzing your data are from other countries and will never meet us or someone who knows us. It's difficult to say we have been harmed in a consequentialist context, but many people believe that the lack of control over one's records, the invasion, is ethically questionable in and of itself, even though one haven't been harmed. This is a matter of deontology.

6.3 Technologies used in Privacy for Healthcare Data

To facilitate the delivery of effective and proper treatment, healthcare organizations store, manage, and distribute massive quantities of data. Nonetheless, protecting these records has been a difficult task for decades. Adding to the confusion, the healthcare sector remains one of the most unsafe to commonly reported data error. In reality, attackers generally use data mining methods and techniques to open sensitive data or information and make it openly accessible, which results in a data breach occurring. As a result, it is a tough task that businesses attempt to adopt medical-data protection strategies that hide critical assets while still meeting regulatory requirements. Numerous technologies are available for the protection and privacy of healthcare data. The following are the most commonly used technologies.

6.3.1 Authentication

Establishing or verifying that statements made by or about the subject are valid is called authentication. Authenticaton plays a precious role in every area, from securing access to business networks to safeguarding user personal identities, and ensures that the user is the correct person and is eligible to have the access that is claimed. For example, TLS (Transport Layer Security) and its ancestor, SSL (Secure Sockets Layer), use encryption protocols that provide secure communications over networks like the Internet. TLS and SSL provide cryptographic network connections from start to end at the Transport Layer (Zhang et al., 2010). In an applications such as web searching, E-mail, faxing, messaging, and VoIP (Voice-over-Internet-Protocol), these types of implementation protocols are widely used. Also, they manually use a trusted certification authority; SSL/TLS are used to authenticate the main server. In addition, the BullsEye algorithm is used to track all hidden data from every angle (Shafer et al., 2010). This algorithm ensures data protection and manages the relationships between the original and replicated data. Only approved people are able to read or write critical data. The one-time pad algorithm is mainly used in research (Yang et al., 2013) and suggests a novel and simple authentication model. It prevents passwords from being communicated between servers. Both the healthcare records provided by providers and the identity of patients should be checked at each point of access in a healthcare system.

6.3.2 Encryption

Data encryption is a very useful technique for avoiding unknown or unauthorized access to confidential data or information. These technologies maintain safety and retain the data ownership from the different data-centers to every point (including mobile devices used by pharmacies, doctors, chemists, and data administrators), and those are stored in the cloud. Medical data is provided by healthcare organizations to both patients and medical professionals, making it easier to include new health records or a entry. Despite this, various encryption algorithms have been developed and implemented (AES, RSA, Rijndael, RC6, 3DES, DES, RC4, Blowfish, and many more); however, it is mainly dependent on the proper selection of encryption algorithms (Somu et al., 2014). To implement safe cloud-storage remains a tough task.

6.3.3 Data Masking

Data Masking basically replaces sensitive data with an unidentifiable value, but it does not use cryptography because the original value cannot be recovered if it is masked. This reason generates a technique of de-identification or masking of PI-personal identifiers, such as pin code, zip code, name, and other methods like suppressing, bucketization, and generalizing quasi-anonymization. Sweeney (2002) and Can et al. (2018) introduced k-anonymity; this method protects against identity disclosure, but it fails when we talk about protect against attribute disclosure. Truta et al. (2006) proposed p-sensitive anonymity, a means of preventing both identity and attribute disclosure. The main difficulty in anonymizing high-dimensional data sets is a common problem for many approaches (Chawala et al., 2005). When we talk about minimizing cost for securing a big data implementation, this technique has a major advantage. When protected data is migrated onto the platform from a secure source, masking eliminates the need for additional security measures to be applied to the data while it is available on platform.

6.3.4 Access Control

Users can connect with a KDD system once they have been given their username and password and authenticated, but they have a permit only for limited access through a limited access control policy, which basically depends on what type of privilege and rights are given by the practitioner to a patient or a third party. This is a one of the efficient and adaptable methods for granting permissions to patients and third parties. The model generally used for this setup is Electronic health record (EHR) access control model, which is Role-Based Access Control (RBAC) [12] and Attribute-Based Access Control (Hagner, 2007; Mohan et al., 2010). When it is used in the medical system, RBAC and ABAC have some limitations. When we talk about cloud-oriented storage, a dynamic access control scheme based on the CP-ABE and symmetric encryption algorithm is also proposed in the research (Zhou et al., 2014). To obtain the high level of security we need (the fine-grained access control while maintaining protection and privacy), we recommend hybrid technologies with other security mechanisms, such as encryption and access control methods.

6.3.5 Confidentiality

Advanced persistent threats, or APTs, have emerged in recent years as targeted attacks against information systems, with the primary goal of smuggling recoverable data to the attacker. As a result, invading patient privacy is becoming an increasing concern in the world of big data analytics, posing a challenge for organizations to solve these various complementary and important issues. In reality, data protection controls data access over the data lifecycle, while data privacy determines who may able to view personal data, like hospital, pathology, or where the sensitive information may reside. Data privacy is based on the privacy policies of hospitals and laws. A recent incident published by Forbes magazine raises issues about patient privacy. These incidents force big data researchers to think about maintaining privacy during the analytics of data. Medical data privacy is therefore a vital issue that must be taken into consideration.

6.4 Legal Measures Taken for Healthcare Data

6.4.1 Data Protection Laws

To counter the growing thicket of relevant data privacy regulations, it is more important than ever that healthcare organizations can handle and maintain the safety of person's sensitive information, as well as focus on risks and legal obligations in processing personal data. For this, different countries have their different data protection policies and regulations. Table 6.1 lists the data security legislations and laws in some of the countries, as well as key features.

TABLE 6.1

Privacy Related Acts in some Countries

Country	Law	Salient Features
USA	HIPAA Act and HITECH Act	For maintaining national standards, transactions are developed. Individuals aged 12–18 are granted the right to privacy. The affected must sign a consent document. The Patient Safety Work Product must remain confidential. Individuals who violate the confidentiality clauses face personal penalties. Protect the confidentiality and protection of EHR(Electronic Health Records).
EU	DPD – Data Protection Directive	Protecting personal data which contain sensitive information is fundamental rights of people which affect there freedoms, especially their right to privacy while personal data is processed
Canada	PIPEDA – Personal Information Protection and Electronic Documents Act	People are granted the right of information and they must know whether their personal information is being used or stored, and organizations are expected to protect this information in a safe and secure manner (Meiko Jensen, 2013).
UK	DPA – Data Protection Act	Individuals have the right to control their data and knowledge about themselves. Personal data should not travel to a country or territory outside the Europe. It guarantees an acceptable degree of data subject rights and freedoms.
Morocco	Act 2009	By establishing the CNDP unit, they authorized and restrictedthe use of personal information and sensitive data by data controllers in any data analyzer (Chafiol-Chaumont, 2013).
Russia	RFLPD (Russian Federal Law on Personal Data)	They depend on controllers to take all appropriate technological steps to maintain the personal data secure from unauthorized access.
India	IT Act and IT Act	For sensitive personal data or documents, use fair security practices. Provides compensation to those who have suffered an unjust loss or income. Services under the terms of a lawful contract face imprisonment and/or a fine.
Brazil	Constitution	People's private lives, respect, and reputation are maintained, with rights to compensation for personal loss or social harm caused by their abuse.
Angola	Data Protection Law	Collection and processing of sensitive data is only permitted in a legal way that permits such processing and authorization from the APD.

6.5 Methods of Privacy Preservation used in Big Data/ML/AI

A conventional approach for protecting data or information in big data is briefly listed here. While particular procedures have worked in the past to protect a patient's privacy, their shortcomings have contributed to the development of newer approaches.

6.5.1 De-identification

Methods of preventing the use of sensitive data of a person by hiding any data that may able to identify the patient information, either by removal of unique patient identifiers, or by the statistical method, require the patient to check or verify that information and that enough identifiers have been distorted. However, outsiders could be able to obtain external data by the de-identification technique in big data. A consequence is that de-identification is insufficient to secure the privacy of big data. Building powerful privacy-preserving methods to avoid the possibility of re-identification makes the technique more feasible. To improve this conventional methodology, we use the following methods:

(a) k-anonymity

(b) l-diversity

(c) t-closeness

6.5.1.1 k-Anonymity

This technique depends on K value. As k value increases, the lower the chance of re-identification. Due to k-anonymization, the technique can cause data distortions, and thus greater information loss. Furthermore, if the quasi-identifiers information is together with another publicly accessible information platform available to separate individuals' data also in k-anonymization, then the sensitive attribute which contains an identifier such as "(like Disease)" or one of the any other identifiers will be revealed. So many measures for quantifying information loss due to anonymization have been suggested, but they do not represent the actual utility of data.

k-Anonymity Many data owners, including government departments and hospitals, claim that data, such as medical records, can be kept anonymous if sensitive details such as the name of the patient, pin code, and contact number are withheld and the rest are released. However, by connecting the data with other publicly available data, the individual may be re-identified. When noise is introduced to a dataset, such as false values or special symbols, it can provide anonymity, and it can also lead to incorrect analytical results in records. When we talk about data mining, different analytical techniques are involved (Sweeney, 2002) that use generalization, bucketization, or suppression methods to enable data disclosure. If at least' k' times the quasi-identifiers reappear per tuple value of the quasi-identifiers, the tuple is distinguishable from each other, and the table is said to k-anonymized.

The k-Anonymity principle The table is said to be k-anonymous if each and every value is different and indistinguishable, by the minimum value of (k-1) records, from the same table in a given dataset. The higher the value of k, the better the privacy security. Some methods used in K-Anonymity are:

- **Generalization** To assemble tuple recognition less discrete, generalization is a method for representing the values of the attributes in a table. The attribute is specified as a ground-domain, and as a domain value increases, it affects the result of the generalization. This is referred to as the domain hierarchy of generalization. If the table has already surpassed k-anonymity (Meyerson et al., 2004) within the table, K-minimum generalization is used for private tables with unique values. The main disadvantage of this technique is it requires a high degree of generalized value if it contains some smaller outliers, i.e., tuples, attributes that happen less than k-times.

- **Suppression** Endorse k-anonymity, suppression is combined with a generalization. Suppression is a tactic used to change or mask certain values in quasi-identifiers. The suppressed-value is indicated by an asterisk (*), which can be applied to be in hierarchies for domain-value and generalization. In the generalization section's example, the mapped value can be suppressed as Z1 (0212*, 0212*), then further suppressed to Z2 (021**), and finally to maximum suppression (*****).

- **Pros of k-Anonymity** Protects against personal identity disclosure by preventing connections to a cloud stored data with the values less than k. This makes it impossible for the adversary to connect sensitive data to external data. The cost of developing this device is significantly lower than that of other anonymity approaches, such as cryptographic solutions (Iyenger et al., 2002). In particular, k-anonymity algorithms like Datafly, Incognito, and Mondrian are widely used in PPDP.

- **Cons of k-Anonymity** Drawbacks of this technique include unsorted matching, complementary release, minimizing the temporal attacks. This method has many drawbacks, including a significant lack of usefulness when used for high-dimensional data, and the need for extra caution if the data has already been anonymized.

- **Homogeneity attack:** The sensitive attributes are not diverse enough; this can result in groups that reveal personal information. Assume P and Q are rivals, and P knows Q lives in a particular pin-code and is a fixed age, and P wants to know Q's medical condition. As a result of P's information of Q, P will see that the information is the same as a variety of medical tuples. All have the same medical condition (sensitive information), i.e., HIV. As a result, the k-anonymous data should be sanitized further by breaking the sensitive values inside the record with identical quasi-identifier values.

- **Background knowledge attack:** Background knowledge attack is the perpetrator that provides the knowledge of the individual's sensitive information with additional reasoning, the essential characteristics of the individual that can reveal more information. Consider P and R to be colleagues, and P would like to know if R's personal information was discovered in the same patient list as Q's. R is a 45-year-old Asian woman who lives in a specific zip code, according to P. Regardless, R's medical history indicates that he or she may be suffering from one of the three health issues: like HIV, kidney failure, or viral-infection. P infers heart disease from R, based on the context knowledge from P that R avoids high calories and has low blood pressure. As a result, history awareness attacks on k-anonymity are possible.

6.5.1.2 L-Diversity

L-diversity is a form of grouping based anonymization which reduces the granularity of data presentation to protect privacy in large data sets. This model is DER which stands for Distinct, Entropy, Recursive (Ton A., 2015), and is an expanded version of k-anonymity, The l-diversity shows the issues of the k-anonymity model, such as the need to preserve identities. The primary issue with that method is if we want to make data protected by l-diverse, but a sensitive column doesn't have many different values, one can insert fictitious data. This fictitious data may increase protection. As a result, the L-diversity has some cons on skewness and similarity attack. Therefore, it cannot protect against attribute disclosure.

The use of l-diversity was proposed as a way to address the disadvantages of k-anonymity. They also introduced a novel extension to k-anonymity that can ensure data privacy, even without exposing the adversary's context information to prevent attribute disclosure. This strategy is based on the assumption that each sensitive attribute is "well-represented" in each category. By implementing the k-anonymity concept (Machanavajjhala, 2006; Samarati, 1998), this strategy is a modification of k-anonymity.

The l-Diversity Principle: A k-anonymous table is said to be l-diverse if the equivalence class in the table has at minimum values for each sensitive column (Akbar et al., 2018). Following are some guidelines for elucidating the term "well-represented":

l-Diversity: a value appears more often than other values within the equivalence group.

Entropy l-Diversity: The entire data must have at least log(l) entropy for each equivalence group. In the case of a table with low overall entropy, this strategy may be prohibitive if only a few of the values are identical.

Recursive (c, l)-Diversity: a table is said to conform to this rule if the sensitive values in each parallel group do not occur too frequently or too rarely (Simi et al., 2017).

Pros of l-Diversity: Provides greater distribution of sensitive attributes within the population, thus enhancing data security. Protects against knowledge failure and is an extension of the k-anonymity technique, but because of faster working and execution by the l-diversity algorithm, l-diversity is better than k-anonymity.

Cons of l-Diversity: Provides greater distribution of sensitive attributes within the population, thus enhancing data security. Protects against knowledge leakage, and it is extended version of k-anonymity technique.

6.5.1.3 T-Closeness

T-Closeness is a refinement of anonymization focused on the l-diversity community. T-closeness model (Li et al., 2007) is a form of extended l-diversity method that uses its column values separately and allows for the separation of data records for that particular column. The main pros of this method are to hide attribute disclosure, but as the size of information is grown, it can result in the risk of re-identification.

Increasing the granularity of the information perceived improves the t-closeness approach called l-diversity. The researcher's knowledge extends beyond the overall table, including the datasets. But it is limited to the level of detail on specific data. As a result, there is a smaller gap between the identifier and hyper properties. The EMD (Earth Mover's Distance) is used to calculate the distance.

Advantage of T-Closeness: T-Closeness protects against homogeneity and knowledge attacks in k-anonymity by preventing the disclosure of attributes that protect data privacy. This specifies the attribute's proximity, which is l-diversity restriction.

Disadvantage of T-Closeness: The relationship between t-value and information acquired is difficult to define when using the EMD (Earth Mover's Distance) as a privacy measure of t-closeness. The equivalence group's sensitive column tuples must be identical to those in the overall data.

6.5.2 HybrEx

In cloud computing; HybrEx (the hybrid execution model) (Priyank et al., 2016) is a model for maintaining privacy and confidentiality of the data. It only uses public clouds for non sensitive records and computations that are listed as public. For example, when the healthcare site uses organizational data or is conducting computations, its use of public clouds poses no privacy or confidentiality danger. The model executes a private cloud for a healthcare organization's datasets that contain sensitive private data. Before a job is executed, it considers data sensitivity and integrates with protection. The issue with HybrEx is that it ignores the key created at public and private clouds and only considers cloud as an antagonist.

More precisely, the HybrEx model is used to control privacy or confidentiality danger. The HybrEx model is used for the healthcare organization's critical, private data and computation, and it makes use of their own cloud. Additionally, applications require access to

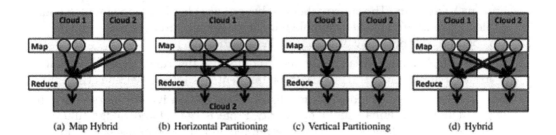

FIGURE 6.4
Execution categories for HybrEx MapReduce.

both private and public data, it is partitioned and runs on both private and public clouds. The model is shown in Figure 6.4, which includes an HybrEx execution structure for partitioning and running programs.

The key advantage of the HybrEx model is that it has its own privacy incorporation, which allows you to add more computing and cloud storage resources from public clouds to a private cloud without worrying about confidentiality and privacy. The HybrEx model avoids the issue of public cloud trustworthiness by partitioning data and computation. Which solution offers the same degree of privacy protection and confidentiality for local computing? Organizations are now considering integrating private and public clouds for capability and efficiency reasons,. The HybrEx model will provide these companies with the added advantage of confidentiality and privacy. To more thoroughly investigate this broad path, we first concentrate on how to implement the HybrEx model in execution, using Hadoop Map-reduce and HBase.

It can be challenging to provide equitable output over a vast area due to Map-reduce's all-to-all communication style and master-slave design. Finally, a Map-reduce job gives a unique chance to realize the HybrEx paradigm, since it is subdivided into jobs that run successfully.

This category is referred to as Map hybrid, as shown in Figure 6.2a. We use CloudBurst (Samarati, 2001), a bioinformatics MapReduce program, to demonstrate this. Simply put, it applies a genome sequence comparison algorithm that can be used to support other biological studies. In the Map step, CloudBurst uses the method to process on both the citations and fixed genomes. As a result, during the Map process, HybrEx MapReduce can safely use the public cloud for reference genomes, while storing target genomes in the private cloud. The Reduce process in CloudBurst, on the other hand, generates (possibly) private outputs, such as the result of a patient's genome comparison. In practice (Sirota, 2010). HybrEx MapReduce can automate these use-cases by using different types of clouds for different levels, since it seamlessly blends private and public clouds. This is referred as horizontal partitioning, as seen in Figure 6.2b.

Partitioning vertically The *New York Times* used MapReduce, running on Amazon EC2, to convert scanned images of public domain papers to .pdf file. Each original article was made up of several small TIFF images, which were "glued" together by a MapReduce job to generate one PDF file per article. HybeEx MapReduce naturally supports this. Vertical partitioning is the term we use to describe this group. This category is depicted in Figure 6.4c. These companies mostly use their private cloud for processing public data, but they may need to scale out to a public cloud on occasion. As shown in Figure 6.4, HybrEx Map-reduce can accomplish this by simply using both private and public clouds in Map-reduce (d). This is referred to as "hybrid."

Research Directions and Challenges To adopt the HybrEx model and achieve integration with protection, we must address three key challenges: data partitioning, device partitioning, and integrity. The following challenges affect our work:

- **Data Partitioning** As the HybrEx model recommends partitioning for confidentiality and privacy, the issue of how to partition data arises immediately. We use two labels to answer this question, a private label and a public label. Basically, these labels are recognized by HybrEx Bigtable and HybrEx MapReduce, which evaluate data and computation placement accordingly. Information flow management methods used in high level programming languages like .jif and Asbestos are influenced by the use of labels. These methods use labels to manage and monitor how data travel between system elements, so we just need labels to decide where information and computation are placed. Labelling can be done when data is imported into HybrEx Bigtable through a MapReduce job.

- **System Partitioning** As the HybrEx model uses both private and public types of cloud, in every implementing the HybrEx model must divide its elements and components by putting some in the public and others in the private cloud. There are three sub questions to ask:

  How to prevent public elements from accessing the whole data.

  How to keep private elements safe from accessing data

  How to reduce the communication costs, as all are necessary for us.

- **Integrity** To solve the issue of integrity, the HybrEx model maintains the hash table of data of a public cloud in the private cloud. But HybrEx Bigtable checks the accuracy of public data when it is requested, or proactively through the sampling method. HybrEx uses MapReduce tests, the integrity of the results from the public cloud in two modes, that basically provides different standards of fidelity for computation integrity. Primary mode is complete integrity testing, in which the private cloud performs a re-execution of any MapReduce task performed by the public cloud. This is primarily provided by HybrEx MapReduce to allow auditing when an entity needs to check the accuracy of previous public cloud computations.

6.5.3 Identity based Anonymization

This method is a form of data sanitization, with the aim of preserving privacy. It is the method of encryption or extraction of PII (personally identifiable information) from datasets in order to keep the individuals described in the data anonymous. The key challenge with this method is balancing anonymization, privacy protection, and security, and to evaluate user data while preserving identities, big data techniques are used. Intel uses an internal web portal that is made more convenient by accessing weblog pages in big data resources. Personal identifying information (PII) had to be removed from the repository. However, this has little bearing on the use of big data/ML techniques for analysis or the ability to re-identify in order to investigate suspicious activity. Intel developed an open framework for anonymization (Sedayao et al., 2014) to fulfil the major benefits of Cloud storage, allowing a range of tools that are used in de-identifying and re-identifying weblog data. Healthcare data has some properties that are defined in the standard definition of anonymization literature during the implementing architecture phase. Intel determined that the anonymized data was subject to correlation, despite covering identifiable Personal Information such as usernames and IP addresses. Basically it is a case study of an enterprise's anonymization implementation, explaining the specifications and implementations that occurred when using anonymization to protect privacy in the business sector--but it affects every sector. K-anonymity based metrics were used in this investigation of anonymization efficiency. Intel mainly uses Hadoop technique to evaluate anonymized data and knowledge. It is necessary to properly evaluate anonymized datasets in order to determine a vulnerability attack.

These techniques ran into problems when they were used to evaluate usage data while protecting users' identities using anonymization, privacy techniques, and big data techniques. Intel developed an open framework for anonymization to fulfil the major benefits of Cloud storage (Yong Yu et al., 2016). This made it possible to use a number of resources to de-identify and re-identify web log data. Medical organizations data has some properties that vary from the typical examples in anonymization. Obviously PII means Personal identification information, including user-name and IP addresses. Intel discovered that an anonymized record was vulnerable to attacks. Basically, it was discovered that User Agent knowledge closely corresponds to individual users, after examining the trade-offs of fixing these vulnerabilities.

6.5.4 Blockchain Privacy Architecture

In this architecture, there are three components. The first is the patient, who must first register his personal information, as is the case in most block chain-based healthcare applications (Nakamoto et al., 2008). The information about the patient will then be stored in a database server, which will be split into three servers. He can access his account at any time and perform a check-up by entering his symptoms value, As an output, a patient can learn whether the patient is normal, pre-diabetic, or diabetic. The second component is the doctor, who must go through the same registration process as the patient, and can access information about the patient's check-up history and current state of disease using his login id and password. The doctor can obtain patient information directly from the servers where the information is stored. The doctor may only display the patient's data; the patient does not have permission to make any changes to the data. The doctor will send the prescription to the patient via e-mail, based on the patient's background and checkup results. The third element is the administrator, who has full access to all elements and can read and write data. Administrators must also register for the device data in order to gain access to perform any read or write operations. This ensures that the administrator is a respected member of the company. An organization has granted the administrator the authority to manage the entire system. He can get data directly from these decentralized servers, but he can't change it. Only the administrator has access to the data. If a third party, such as a hacker, tries to change something on one of the servers, the rest of the servers are disabled, and the data that the hacker has access to is double encrypted hash value making it extremely difficult to crack. For maintaining these systems, we use AES Encryption Algorithm.

6.5.4.1 AES (Advanced Encryption Standard) in Healthcare

Basically, AES is a cryptographic algorithm that is used to encrypt data. Concerning medical data, the amount of medical image transmission has expanded significantly. E-health requires the transmission of digital visual data on a regular basis. Medical transmission security is also becoming a bigger issue. In the medical field, for example, the need for quick and secure diagnosis is critical. The security of healthcare data has become increasingly critical in recent years. Encryption or data concealing algorithms can be used to protect this multimedia data. Data compression is required to reduce the transmission time. So far, some resolutions that integrate image encryption and compression have been presented (Hylock et al., 2019). Evaluate the performance of traditional cryptography like data encryption standard, international data encryption algorithm, and advanced encryption standard, as well as compression methods like Joint Photographic Experts Group and others. As the new encryption standard, AES uses a block cipher to jumble computations on a predetermined block size of 128 bits, using the key and round integers. The core function is repeated for a number of cycles, the number of which is determined by the key length. The resistance of the AES algorithm against cryptographic algorithms assaults improves as the number of cycles used increases.

For the deployment of Rijndael-based algorithms (AES) in medical data. To begin, we show a selection element associated with the input state, key length, and number of iterations utilized in our method to adapt to a variety of platforms (Oh-Ju-Young et al., 2010). Secondly, the basic picture or simple-text can be flattened using the Huffman method to minimize the input file sizes, while also halving the AES-encryption time. Finally, by using loop unrolling and merging methods into our algorithm, we may reduce the amount of effort spent programming to execute AES.

6.5.4.2 AES Encryption Algorithm

For a 128-bit stack, follow the AES (Azougaghe et al., 2015; Zhang et al., 2018) encryption steps:

> From the cipher key, create a series of round keys.
>
> Load the block data into the state array (plaintext).
>
> To the starting state list, append the initial round key.
>
> Manipulate the state for nine rounds.
>
> Complete the tenth and final state manipulation round.
>
> Make a copy of the final state array as encrypted data (ciphertext).

- The AES algorithm is used to obtain the hash value, and pailliers is added to the AES hash value for re-encryption. The user would receive an email stating that someone attempted to modify the data on that computer using the MAC address and IP address. The key goal is to protect the patient's data from any malfunctioning. On this proposed scheme, the following attacks are possible:
- Denial of Service (DoS)
- Sybil attack
- Eclipse and Routing Attacks.

6.6 Result and Discussion

We looked into the security and privacy issues of Bigdata/AI/ML by exploring current methods and strategies for achieving a secured system and privacy for individual sensitive information, which are extremely beneficial to healthcare societies. We concentrated on highlighting privacy and security approaches and methodologies, emphasizing their focus and utility. To answer unique privacy difficulties, in particular specialized big data/AI/ML analytics, which established an effective and privacy-preserving cosine similarity computing algorithm, would necessitate extensive research. Many studies have looked into the benefits and drawbacks of using anonymization, privacy security, and Big Data methodologies to assess usage data while maintaining users' identities. However, it continues to use the K-anonymity strategy, which is susceptible to a connection attack. Aside from these articles, many researchers suggested a two-phase top-down specialization that could be a scaled TDS method for anonymizing broad data sets on the cloud using the Map Reduce system. However, it employs an anonymization strategy that is susceptible to a correlation attack. The suggested variety of privacy concerns related to big-data/ML/AI applications is also restricted, since classification of patients and profiling can easily discriminate based on gender, age, physical condition, and social issues, etc. Proposed is an anonymization technique to boost-up the anonymization of big-data/ML streaming, which requires some more research in this field to design and implement. Many methodologies and algorithms are proposed that provide data security and privacy that limits the confidence level in the cryptographic server.

In this chapter, we focus on the private blockchain framework, where data is decentralized, but access rights are granted by centralized authorities, leading to issues such as data protection, data alteration, and so on, since it does not use proof of work, which are extremely difficult mathematical problems to solve in order to obtain permission rights to modify data. To solve this issue, a centralized authority grants access to a private blockchain, but users' read, write, and update rights are limited. The data attribute, which is the diabetic symptoms, is split into three servers. The user who has access to the data can obtain it directly from the decentralized servers, but he cannot change it. Only the administrator has access to the data. If a third party, such as a hacker, attempts to modify a computer, the rest of the servers will be disabled, and the data that the hacker attempts to access will be in double encrypted form, making it extremely difficult to crack. The AES algorithm is used to produce the hash value, and pailliers is added to that AES hash value for re-encryption and key generation. When anyone wants to alter the data on that computer using the MAC address and IP address, the user will receive an email. The key goal is to protect the patient's data from any malfunctioning.

6.7 Conclusion and Future Work

Big data/AL/ML has limitless applications in health-science, KDD, medical-care, and personal healthcare. But it has a so many hurdles and barriers in this path, such as technological difficulties, privacy and security concerns, and a lack of professional talent, are preventing it from reaching its full potential in the healthcare sector. Researchers in this area consider Big data/AI/ML protection and privacy to be a major roadblock. We've looked at several examples of good similar work from around the world in this article. In the context of bigdata/ML in the healthcare sector, privacy problems are involved in the whole life cycle, which was discussed in the chapter, as well as the benefits and drawbacks of existing privacy and security technologies. There are more approaches, such as "Hiding a needle in a haystack," "Attribute based encryption method," "Access control method," "Homomorphic-encryption," and "Storage path encryption." These lists contain many more techniques commonly used for maintaining patient privacy in healthcare. On the other hand, the focus of the insights will be on how to solve the scalability challenge of big data/AI/ML privacy and protection in the healthcare era. We'll go one step further in the future and use the Map-Reduce system to simulate alternative approaches to solving the problem of balancing protection and privacy models.

When we focuses on the private blockchain's security issues by making it safer for data privacy and granting access control only to authenticated users who have permission for rights, such as read, write, and update, as defined by their position. This AES method keeps the evaluation factors of availability, honesty, and confidentiality intact. Because of quantum computers, the use of blockchain could be phased out. The application of this strategy can be expanded in the future by focusing on the prevention of attacks such as DOS Sybil and others.

References

Zhang, R., and Liu, L. Security models and requirements for healthcare application clouds. In *IEEE 3rd International Conference on Cloud Computing*, 2010.

Shafer, J., Rixner, S., and Cox, A.L. The hadoop distributed filesystem: Balancing portability and performance. In *Proceedings of 2010 IEEE International Symposium on Performance Analysis of Systems & Software (ISPASS)*, March 2010, WhitePlain, NY. pp. 122–133.

Yang, C., Lin, W., and Liu, M. A novel triple encryption scheme for hadoop-based cloud data security. In *Emerging Intelligent Data and Web Technologies (EIDWT), 2013 Fourth International Conference On*, pp. 437–442, 2013.

Somu, N., Gangaa, A., and Sriram, V.S. Authentication service in hadoop using one time pad. *Indian J Sci Technol* 7 (2014): 56–62.

Akbar, F., Mawengkang, H., and Efendi, S. Comparative analysis of RC4+ algorithm, RC4 NGG algorithm and RC4 GGHN algorithm on image file security. In *IOP Conference Series: Materials Science and Engineering*, vol. 420, no. 1, p. 012131. IOP Publishing, 2018.

Simi, M.S., Sankara Nayaki, K., and Sudheep Elayidom, M. An extensive study on data anonymization algorithms based on k-anonymity. In *IOP Conference Series: Materials Science and Engineering*, vol. 225, no. 1, p. 012279. IOP Publishing, 2017.

Can, O. Personalized anonymity for microdata release. *IET Information Security* 12, no. 4 (2018): 341–347.

Truta, T.M., and Vinay, B. Privacy protection: P-sensitive k-anonymity property. In *Proceedings of 22nd International Conference on Data Engineering Workshops*, p. 94, 2006.

Chawala, S., Dwork, C., Sheny, F.M., Smith, A., and Wee, H. Towards privacy in public databases. In *Proceedings on Second Theory of Cryptography Conference*, 2005.

Mohan, A., and Blough, D.M. An attribute-based authorization policy framework with dynamic conflict resolution. In *Proceedings of the 9th Symposium on Identity and Trust on the Internet*, 2010.

Hagner, M. Security infrastructure and national patent summary. In *Tromso Telemedicine and eHealth Conference*, 2007.

Zhou, H., and Wen, Q. Data security accessing for HDFS based on attribute-group in cloud computing. In *International Conference on Logistics Engineering, Management and Computer Science (LEMCS)*, 2014.

Li, N., et al. T-Closeness: Privacy beyond k-anonymity and L-diversity. In *Data Engineering (ICDE) IEEE 23rd International Conference*, 2007.

Ton, A., and Saravanan, M. *Ericsson Research.* http://www.ericsson.com/research-blog/data-knowledge/big-data-privacy-preservation, 2015.

Samarati, P. Protecting respondent's privacy in microdata release. *IEEE Trans Knowlege Data Eng* 13, no. 6 (2001): 1010–1027.

Machanavajjhala, A., Gehrke, J., Kifer, D., and Venkitasubramaniam, M. L-diversity: Privacy beyond k-anonymity. In *Proc. 22nd International Conference Data Engineering (ICDE)*, p. 24, 2006.

Samarati, P., and Sweeney, L. Protecting privacy when disclosing information: K-anonymity and its enforcement through generalization and suppression. Technical Report SRI-CSL-98–04. SRI Computer Science Laboratory, 1998.

Sweeney, L. K-anonymity: A model for protecting privacy. *Int J Uncertain Fuzziness* 10(5) (2002): 557–570.

Meyerson, A., and Williams, R. On the complexity of optimal k-anonymity. In *Proc. of the ACM Symp. on Principles of Database Systems*, 2004.

Iyenger, V. Transforming data to satisfy privacy constraints. In *Proceedings of the ACM SIGKDD*. 2002, pp. 279–288. 54.

LeFevre, K., Ramakrishnan, R., and DeWitt, D.J. Mondrian multidimensional k-anonymity. In *Proceedings of the ICDE*, 2006, p. 25.

Priyank, J., Manasi, G., and Nilay, K. Big data privacy: A technological perspective and review. *J Big Data* 3 (2016): 25.

Sedayao, J., and Bhardwaj, R. Making big data, privacy, and anonymization work together in the enterprise: Experiences and issues. In *Big Data Congress*, 2014.

Yong, Y., et al. Cloud data integrity checking with an identity-based auditing mechanism from RSA. *Future Gen Comput Syst* 62 (2016): 85–91.

Nakamoto, S. *Bitcoin: A Peer-to-Peer Electronic Cash System*. La Vergne, TN: BN Publishing, 2008.

Jensen, M. Challenges of privacy protection in big data analytics. In *2013 IEEE International Congress on Big Data*, 2013.

Chafiol-Chaumont, F., and Falkman, A-L. *Data Protection Overview (Morocco)*, 2013.

Sirota, P. *Keynote: Making Hadoop Enterprise Ready with Amazon Elastic MapReduce. Hadoop Summit*, 2010.

Zhang, Y., Yang, M., Zheng, D., Lang, P., Wu, A., and Chen, C. E_cient and secure big data storage system with leakage resilience in cloud computing. *Soft Comput* 22 (2018): 7763–7772.

Azougaghe, A., Kartit, Z., Hedabou, M., Belkasmi, M., and El Marraki, M. An e_cient algorithm for data security in cloud storage. In *Proceedings of the 2015 15th International Conference on Intelligent Systems Design and Applications (ISDA)*, Marrakech, Morocco, December 14–16, 2015.

Oh, J-Y., Yang, D-I., and Chon, K-H. "A selective encryption algorithm based on AES for medical information." *Healthcare Informatics Research* 16, no. 1 (2010): 22.

Hylock, R.H., and Zeng, X. "A blockchain framework for patient-centered health records and exchange (HealthChain): Evaluation and proof-of-concept study." *Journal of Medical Internet Research* 21, no. 8 (2019): E13592.

7

Impact of AI, IoT and Big Data Analytics in Diseases Diagnosis and Prediction

Ambrish Kumar Sharma
NRI College, Bhopal, India

Apoorva Joshi
Career College, Bhopal, India

CONTENTS

7.1 Introduction

Artificial intelligence (AI) refers to a computer that simulates the human intelligence process (Tsai et al., 2014). The Internet of Things is integrated with an AI system that monitors people's health based on sensor outputs. The IoT is largely comprised of embedded sensors, so the older embedded devices continue to send data streams to internet associates in order to store the analyzed data. This value is occupied in order to give the user's time a boost. The Internet of Things (IoT) is the foundational infrastructure that connects the physical and digital worlds (Pham et al., 2015). IoT technology entails machine-to-machine communication, which allows machines to exchange information over the internet without the need for human interaction. The health-related information sensing technology is

DOI: 10.1201/9781003201960-7

a daily movement based on medical check-ups outside of a hospital and in the patient's home. Patients must be monitored under the care of a doctor after the disease has been identified. The benefits of real-time monitoring through connected devices may also lie in the ability to maintain healthy lifestyles in the face of medical occurrences such as asthma, lung cancer, blood-sugar issues, pulmonary problems, chronic bronchitis, and so on (Pieczenik et al., 2007).

The IoT device gathers and transmits health data, such as stress and sugar levels, electroencephalograms (EEG), or electrocardiograms (ECG). This type of information should be collected and sent to the appropriate doctor, medical officer, researcher, official agency, etc., who is an expert who needs to look at the relevant data (regardless of their location, time, or computer) for research or to care for a patient. IoT enables and can effectively deliver capability sharing, data movement, and exchange of information system-to-system. Bluetooth, Wi-Fi, Ż-wave, and other unique trendy protocols are examples of property protocols (Madhumathi et al., 2018). Thus, if the resource army wishes to change the trend, it must first address the health and illness of patients, as well as initiate innovative approaches for individual care. Big data is better for evaluating historical databases, due to factors such as the number, variety, and speed of the data to be analyzed (Teece, 1998)..

In a nutshell, as illustrated in Figure 7.1, Big data is defined by its main three attributes, V3, i.e., V1-volume, V2-velocity, and V3-variety. Big data is a term that describes a large collection of data that continues to grow over time. The volume of big data is equivalent to that of conventional data, but on a considerably bigger scale. The variability of the statistics that wish to be studied is not old, and it consists of both structured and unstructured information. The velocity is produced in a typical manner. This technology could also become more popular as new technology emerges, such as the internet of things, where devices and sensors continuously generate data. AI combines large amounts of data with fast and consistent techniques, allowing machine formatted code to automatically go beyond the data's patterns and choices.

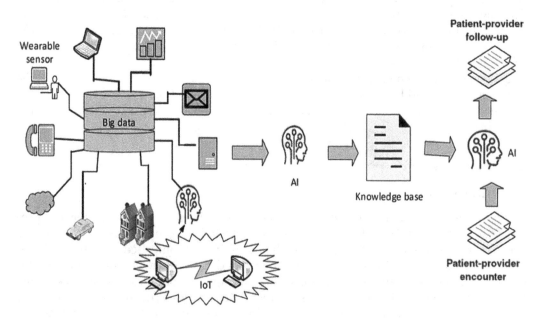

FIGURE 7.1
Pictorial representation of extraction of information by using IoT devices based on AI.

It poses a number of fundamental issues:

- What are our options for using efficient disease prevention to minimize the growing number of patients?
- What are our options for providing high-quality services, while lowering healthcare costs?
- What are our options for making the most of IT's position in detecting and mitigating risk at an early stage?

Using intelligent data mining tools to glean knowledge from the vast amount of health information is an obvious answer to these questions. Researchers working on data analytics are on the verge of making significant advances in patient care. In the healthcare industry, data analytics technologies have a lot of promise. Early disease detection and treatment are now possible thanks to data processing, machine learning, and data mining. Many countries use early disease detection and monitoring systems.

7.2 Background

In the medical literature, the benefits of AI have been extensively explored (Dilsizian et al., 2014). It might also be able to learn and self-correct based on feedback to improve accuracy. AI might employ powerful algorithms to "learn" features from a large amount of healthcare data, and then apply the findings to improve clinical practice. AI systems that give up-to-date medical knowledge from journals, textbooks, and clinical procedures may support physicians in providing proper patient care. Furthermore, an AI device gathers useful data from a large number of patients to aid in creating real-time inferences for health risk alerts and predictions. In addition, an AI device could help to reduce diagnostic and treatment errors in human healthcare practice (Patel, 2009).

7.2.1 Healthcare Data

In order for AI systems to be utilized in healthcare, they must first be "trained" utilizing data from clinical operations, such as screening, diagnosis, and therapy assignments, so that we may learn about comparable groups of subjects, correlations between subject attributes, and desired results. During the diagnosis stage, a large amount of the AI literature analyzes data from diagnosis imaging, genetic testing, and electro-diagnostics. For example, when processing diagnostic images with vast volumes of data, radiologists should use AI technologies (Gillies et al., 2016). The use of irregular genetic expression in long non-coding RNAs to diagnose gastric cancer was investigated by Li et al. (2016) and for determining the location of neuro damage, an electro-diagnosis support device was developed by Shin et al. (2010).

These data sources differ from picture, genetic, and electro-physiological records because they contain vast amounts of narratives, with no specific structure, such as medical-matters, that cannot be specifically analyzed. As a result, the AI applications that go with the data focus on converting unstructured material into machine-readable electronic medical records ('EMR). To increase the accuracy of congenital abnormality identification, Karakülah et al. (2014) employed AI to infer phenotypic traits from case reports.

7.2.2 Disease Focus

Despite the fact that AI research in healthcare is developing, much of it is still focused on a disease that is not avoidable. We will go over a few examples below:

1. Carcinoma: In a double-blinded validation analysis, İBM Watson for oncology, as proved by Şomashekhar et al., would be a reliable AI tool for helping cancer diagnosis. Clinical images were analyzed by Esteva et al. (2017) to classify skin cancer subtypes.
2. Neurology: Bouton et al. (2016) developed an AI system to help quadriplegic patients regain control of their movements. Farina et al. (2017) looked at the efficiency of an offline man/machine interface that uses the discharge timings of spinal motor neurons to control upper-limb prosthesis.
3. Cardiology: Dilsizian and Şiegel et al. (2014) spoke about how the AI system could be used to diagnose heart disease using cardiac images.

Early detection is critical because early treatment for all three illnesses is necessary to prevent patients' health from deteriorating, and all are primary causes of death. Furthermore, by enhancing research methods, genetics, etc., which is the AI system's ability, early diagnosis may be possible. AI has been used in the past to treat a variety of other ailments. Two recent examples are Long et al. (2017), who used ocular image evidence to diagnose congenital cataract disease, and Gulshan et al. (2016), who employed retinal fundus images to identify referable diabetic retinopathy.

7.3 Challenges, Diseases, Diagnosis, and Prediction

Analysis of large and complex quantities of data by hand is both costly and impractical. Big data analytics has a lot of advantages for disease detection and treatment, but it also has a lot of drawbacks and difficulties when it comes to adapting big data analytics techniques. Access to data and limitations contribute to the difficulty. Because there are so many patients, it is difficult to take into account all of these factors when developing a cost-effective and reliable preventive scheme.

The researcher can develop an effective preventive method as a result of the proliferation of medical information systems and improved linkage between physicians, patients, and health records. Healthcare software generates a large amount of complex data. Traditional methods lag behind in transforming such facts to become information that can be used to make decisions, and medical personnel have barely begun to use advanced information technology. Massive advancements in H/W, S/W, and communication technology have provided outlay and cost-effective solutions by improving the quality of care, appropriately evaluating risk, and minimizing duplication of effort, opening up new options for inventive prevention. Massive amounts of data are all obstacles to the development of such a system. Disease prevention relies heavily on data exchange between various healthcare systems, so interoperability is critical to the success of the prevention system, even as the healthcare sector is still evolving. The guidelines for illness prevention and intervention included in ISO standards are an important component, but they are not yet fully developed in the healthcare industry. There are numerous stakeholders (HL, ISO, and IHTSDO) who are working to solve semantic interoperability, with the aim of having a shared data representation. Healthcare data comes in a variety of formats. Furthermore, the widespread adoption of sensors that can be worn for body care has resulted in a massive increase in the volume of heterogeneous data. Data integration is needed for successful prevention methods. For years, clinical data documentation has taught clinicians to archive data despite how much data would be gathered and evaluated, in one of the most efficient ways conceivable. Clinicians are hesitant to implement electronic health record systems for reporting because they attempt to standardize data collection. The correctness and completeness of the database have a direct impact on the accuracy of data analysis.

Finding problems in data is difficult, and correcting the data is even more difficult, particularly when data is incomplete. Using incomplete data will almost always result in incorrect results. Ignoring incomplete data, on the other hand, introduces bias into the study, leading to false conclusions. We need advanced data analysis and association techniques to derive valuable information from vast volumes. Other considerations include data protection and liability, capital costs, and technological issues. Another big stumbling block in the implementation of a preventive scheme is data protection. HIPAA certification is held by the majority of healthcare organizations; however, it does not guarantee data protection or security because HIPAA focuses on security (Patil et al., 2014). With the a lot of use of smart-wearable devices, mobile phones, and online access to data, that data is becoming increasingly vulnerable. Furthermore, since these devices may not be equally accessible due to economic barriers, it may exacerbate racial and ethnic disparities.

7.4 Theory Related to Prediction of Diseases

Huge data from IoT devices has a major impact on health informatics and telematics. Computing is the primary driver in IoT, and it is evolving as a solution to information overcrowding and inefficiencies in critical systems. As the co-word investigation reveals, stability, safety, and information transport are major technological concerns within the smog computing domain. It predicted the emergence of novel medical informatics and telemetics to address this shortcoming. Only a few examples include periodic and distant healthcare observation systems, ubiquitous sensing by reasoning systems, life support systems, IoT based primarily systems for illness intervention, and health emergency and alerting systems. From an interconnection of embedded computing devices to an interconnection of smart sensor devices, the Internet of Things has evolved. However, when used in the context of a smart city, It poses worries about processing and storage power limitations. Signals in real time obtained by smart sensors and IoT devices, such as electroencephalogram (EEG), are typically complex and involve advanced computing.

To resolve this dilemma, Amin et al. (2019) developed a deep learning model that outperforms high-tech systems in terms of accuracy. For identification and classification, the cognitive healthcare paradigm incorporates IoT cloud technologies. Two CNN models were utilized, both of which had been pre-trained on a typical EEG-dataset. Raw time domain EEG signals were fed into a CNN model for classification, suggesting that EEG data may be used for end-to-end learning. The cognitive module then makes a decision based on the patients' needs for resources and medical assistance. The healthcare sector is confronted with numerous issues in storing and processing data in order to derive information from it. The increasing amount of healthcare data generated by health tests and screenings necessitates the development of new approaches for its management. To overcome this issue, Liyakathunisa et al. (2019) proposed a new technique for observing an individual's healthcare situation, which relies heavily on electronic sensor and IoT devices. During remote monitoring, the health safety advantage to both the unhealthy and stable population is achieved by the use of intelligent algorithms, facilities, and methods that allow for quicker diagnosis and expert intervention, for more effective treatment options.

Array-based comparative genomic hybridization is routinely used to detect changes in genomic DNA. Machine learning techniques are used to assess data acquired by IoT devices linked to the human body. As a result, rather than simply discovering patterns within the data, algorithms that can distinguish increases and decreases within supported numerical deliberations are required. To overcome this difficulty, Gunasekaran Manogaran et al. (2018) propose a replacement methodology that employs an efficient and scalable methodology to detect DNA range variations across the ordination. To represent DNA range amendment around the ordination, this work combines a Bayesian hidden markov model and a gaussian mixture clustering technique. Measuring performance criteria such as accurately predicted, miss predicted, precision, and error are used to evaluate the expected modification detection algorithmic program's performance. Big data and high-performance computing innovation are being used to solve a number of issues, including health care, education, transportation, and more. Diabetic retinopathy and age-related macular degeneration are two chronic disorders that can cause visual loss if not detected early. To solve this issue, Arun das et al. (2019) introduced AMD-Res, a 152-layer web convolutional neural network that analyzes photos to categorise and verify the severity of AMD disorders. Key contributions are the following:

- Using IoT in a big data network, collect real-time medical knowledge about a patient.
- A genome-wide association analysis using regularization to predict disease.
- All other precautionary measures, such as doctor's advice.
- Incorporate a sensor into the human body.

7.5 Classical Approach and Philosophy

The emphasis of preventive care is on measures to reduce potential health risks by detecting and preventing disease at an early stage. A successful disease prevention approach lowers disease risks, slows disease progression, and alleviates symptoms. It is the most effective and cost-effective method of disease prevention. Main, secondary, and tertiary preventive measures techniques are divided into three stages. Disease prevention can be used at any stage, in conjunction with a patient's medical history, with the intention of halting the disease's progression. It aims to minimize the number of new cases by implementing strategies such as exercise, or vaccinaton against.communicable disease (Patil et al., 2014).

As a result, it is most useful when a patient's condition is suspected. Risk factor mitigation, general health promotion, and other preventive measures are examples of key prevention strategies. This can be accomplished by health education and promotion programs that promote healthy lifestyles and environmental health approaches.

Secondary treatment is most effective for those in the asymptomatic stages since it aims to cure the disease, delay its development, or reduce its effects. It aims to minimize the

TABLE 7.1

Prevention Level

Prevention Stages	Outcomes
First	Security and promotion of health in particular
Second	Diagnosis and treatment prior to the onset of symptoms
Third	Early symptomatic illness has a disability cap

number of cases by detecting diseases early and slowing or stopping their development, Detecting cardiovascular patients after their first cardiac event, blood testing for toxicity, eye exams for myopia, and nutritional adjustments are just a few examples. Procedures to diagnose by disease screening, like radiography for the detection of early-stage prostate cancer, are a popular approach to secondary prevention. The primary goal of tertiary disease prevention is to improve the patient's quality of life. Once a disease has been diagnosed and managed in its acute therapeutic process, treatment and rehabilitation are used to lessen the effect of the disease on the patient. To predict the likelihood of a patient contracting disease, there is a requirement for substantial medical performance and patient skills (Table 7.1).

7.6 AI Disease Prediction Model

A wearable sensor can be found on the knee, shoulders, hand, hips, forearm, and other body parts. Sensors are used in the identification and prediction of diseases in humans. Patient data is gathered, including demographics, cancer diagnosis characteristics, heart conditions, diabetes, blood pressure, and so on. They are said to respond to biological vital signs, body movements, and organic compounds after that. Data handling can be broken down into several steps, such as data pre-processing and evaluation. The authentic waveform from the annoying signal is recovered in the pre-processing unit. The signal's frequency and time domain are examined. Using the optimality criterion, function extraction is performed. The data on diseases could be categorized to produce a well-defined diseases database for a better decision-making study, as shown in Figure 7.2.

To ever be utilised as a procedure, although the internet of things is significant in the IT industry, disease prediction without human involvement is far more essential. In this study, we employ AI and an IoT computer to construct a disease prediction strategy in a large data scenario. Many predictive analytic algorithms have been developed using IoT devices, although AI in conjunction with IoT devices is unusual. Deep learning is built using data mining algorithms. Data acquired from patients is displayed in Figure 7.3.

7.6.1 GARIC Architecture

Generally speaking, a neuro-fuzzy scheme is implemented using GARIC architecture, i.e., Generalize-Approximate-Reasoning-Intelligence-Control. Specifically, the critical step involved in developing colorectal cancer predictive models is data-mining big data and report review. Data accuracy is ensured by pre-processing information obtained from various sources to eliminate duplicates and oddities. GARIC architecture was used to process and classify the data collected about the patient (Muthu et al., 2020).

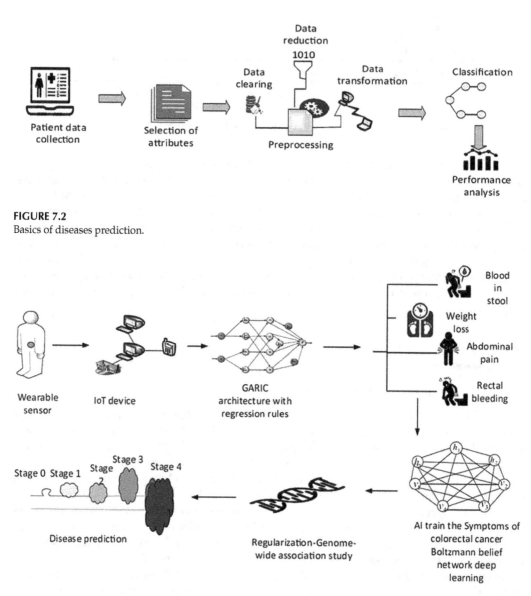

FIGURE 7.2
Basics of diseases prediction.

FIGURE 7.3
Diagram of the Internet of Things (IoT) with AI-based disease prediction.

The human body's wearable sensing element is used to predict diseases. Nowadays, some individuals are afflicted with a variety of diseases, so disease severity can be anticipated ahead of time.

7.7 IoT Device

IoT software is a e-health monitoring and actual current time tracking device that is used to treat patients. Health professionals can now operate remotely and have instant access to patient data, thanks to the internet of things and artificial intelligence (AI). Furthermore,

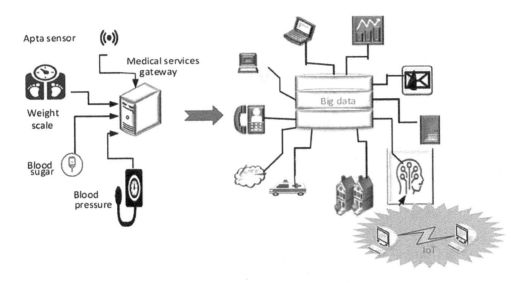

Apta sensor

Medical services gateway

Weight scale

Blood sugar

Blood pressure

Big data

IoT

FIGURE 7.4
Big data and the Internet of Things (IoT) for health care solutions.

the AI and IoT combine data from various instruments, resulting in accurate diagnoses. Massive data is used to collect information for the purposes of knowledge storage and analysis. It enables businesses to investigate the effect of behavior on disease by using colorectal cancer monitoring devices and applications.

E-medical records, gene sequencing, medication research, portable sensors, etc., are among the sources of health data. These instruments provide more reliable data than self-reported data. The doctor can use an internet program to access medical records. When a critical condition arises, a warning will be a message sent to the physician's attention. Then he'll be able to use the machine, which will help him predict diseases. When necessary, the doctor will consult a patient's previous medical history, as shown in Figure 7.4.

7.8 Big Data Analytics

The term "big data" came about as a result of the requirement to analyze massive amounts of unstructured data collected every second from diverse data sources. Traditional analytics tools are often not suited to process such unstructured data and extract insights. The challenge with big data is figuring out how to do research as quickly as possible while yet keeping a fair level of accuracy. Machine learning models are being used in new data analysis approaches as a result of big data. Big data in healthcare refers to vast amounts of health-related information gathered from a variety of sources, including medical imaging, pharmaceutical data, electronic health records, and so on. Pham et al. (2020) defined big data as "physician notes, X-Ray records, case history, list of doctors and nurses, and details regarding outbreak areas" in the context of COVID-19. In the context of contact tracing, big data refers to contact information obtained from a variety of sources, such as hotels, airports, and restaurants, that can be used to track down everyone who has had close contact with a confirmed case of COVID-19. While there is no official definition for contact tracing big data analytics, we define it as the collection and analysis of social history contact information from a range of sources that is always expanding and developing.

The following are some of the features:

- Volume refers to the amount/size of data that must be processed.
- The consistency of findings from a processing device is referred to as veracity in this study.
- Value refers to what the consumer can gain or receive as a result of the analysis;
- Variety refers to the various types of data produced, such as structured and massive data.
- Velocity refers to how rapidly data is generated.

7.8.1 Big Data Analysis Interaction Monitoring

Interaction monitoring using large data is a critical area for communicable diseases by combining different data sources, including social media messages with meta-data and tags, passenger lists, metro digital wallets, car logs, and the use of credit cards. Though maybe not exact, it could also be possible to define key aspects from the spot on social media narrative to verify that an user is in a specific area at a particular time by providing a monitoring model that can monitor people even if they have no tracking equipment and cell devices. Keeling et al. (2020) formulated a contact tracking model to estimate infection transmission rates. This pattern detected potential individuals infected before extreme diagnosis is made, but if not done "rapidly too much" it will have social ramifications. One of the most important aspects of human social interaction was the enormous wide variation who meet this definition of "interaction." In social meetings, the use of ethnic diversity to evaluate a dynamical system throughput depends on reliable, often scant, data. Big data will help make sure that communication is clear, in order to determine the transmission rate on a huge scale. The architecture of data is nevertheless important to ensure data fusion, sharing, and examination in a big data world. The database schema can improve the monitoring of various components. When large data is gathered from virtual communities, a disease outbreak can be reconstructed early. Quasi datasets and bitstreams typically inform how an efficient outbreak determination in the early stages of an outbreak should be adapted in the core technologies (Bragazzi et al., 2020).

7.8.2 Cognitive Computing Scenario Identification

In finding any alleged new or recorded incidents, Qin et al. (2020) used media platforms search indices (SMSIs). To prevent the emergence of COVID-19, SMSI compiles a list of symptomatology, including cough, tuberculosis, fever, and chest pain, which appear on websites with social networking keywords. The movement of people has been considered the key mode for spread of pathogens. Social media posts could in this respect help to identify any details of the purported risk of complications. Responses may nevertheless not be reliable or confident, This is among the most significant challenges in big data analysis in social media. It means allowing health officials to outline adequate answers in order to create the relevant detection system, using key phrases as strategy. The COVID-19 pandemic

TABLE 7.2

An Overview of Machine Learning

Parameters	Platform Applications
Storm	For serology data streams with a focus on message processing.
S4 and Kafka	Modular construction is supported for decentralized data integration, inspired by the MapReduce concept.
Flink	For heterogeneous systems, which can deal with a massive amount of data in memory in a short period of time.
Apache Spark	Collection can be done in batches.

is unfortunately spreading worldwide. Big data offers an appropriate means of mapping and integration. IoT devices can be furnished with sophisticated tools for modelling complex COVID-19 simulation models [14] that can help develop an understanding and care of the viral disease. Consequently, schemes for sentiment analysis are vital. Notwithstanding, the sheer data volume and speed at which it needs to be processed requires a machine learning intrusion. Table 7.2 provides a list of structures and their key technologies for Predictive Analytics.

Despite the economic scope of COVID-19 scenarios, cloud computing services can allow efficient security and confidentiality through disparate datasets (Mohamed et al., 2019). Stream statistical analysis entails real-time insights, and given the geographical scope of COVID-19 instances, large datasets can ensure efficient secure exchange through distinct data-sets. Real-time, decreased spark streaming platforms include Storm, Splunk, and Apache. The advantage is that cloud computing provides a robust security enviroment by delegating the parallel processing technique to its analytics system via "boss" and "task node." S4 is a pluggable hard copy or electronic for rapid creation of massive data communication in a shared local culture. Kafka is a log collection system that is free and open-source. Flink is a stream processing dispersed processing platform that performs data processing as a "cyclic data flow of multiple iterations" It cuts the time it takes to compute data by using a series of iterations. For clustering and classification, Apache Spark employs machine learning algorithms. By transferring information to the Spark runtime system, data can be mapped, reduced, and filtered.

7.9 Big Data Analytics Tools in Healthcare

Traditional prevention programs are mostly concerned with promoting healthcare benefits, when the marginal expense of an intervention is high. The USA spent more than 80% of its budget on disease treatment and complications, compared to just 2–3% on prevention, despite the fact that many of these diseases can be avoided at an early stage (Bosworth, 2010). Health-care spending does not guarantee improved health-care system quality. Investing in prevention will help to save money, while also improving the quality and reliability of health care. Many countries are under severe financial and resource constraints. Early disease detection and prevention play a critical role in lowering mortality rates and healthcare costs.

TABLE 7.3

Methodologies for Large Datasets

Parameter	Definition
Presto	Massive amount of data is obtained, and a distributed SQL query engine is used to analyze it.
HDFS	HDFS provides the Hadoop cluster with underlying storage and distributes them through several servers/nodes.
MapReduce	Breaks down a mission into subtasks and collects the results, making it effective for large amounts of data.
Jaql	Jaql is a functional language with a weakly typed syntax and slow evaluation. It is part of IBM's Hadoop-based Big Data platform.
PİG	Both types of data, i.e., structured/unstructured, can be assimilated.
Avro	By defining data types, context, and scheme, it makes data encoding and serialization easier, which enhances data structure.

7.10 Outcomes and Forecast Evaluation

A number of considerations stroke prognosis and illness mortality. In terms of enhancing forecast accuracy, AI technologies outperform traditional methods. Zhang et al. (2013) proposed a model for predicting three-month overall survival by looking at biological functions 48 hours after a stroke and using decision tree to aid diagnostic and treatment. Asadi et al. (2014) compiled clinical information from 107 patients who had intra-arterial treatment for acute anterior or backward circulation stroke. The experts analyzed the data with a machine learning algorithm and SVM, and achieved an accuracy rate of over 70.0%. They also employed knn classifier to identify characteristics that influence the outcome of arterial occlusion for brain arteriovenous malformations (Asadi et al., 2016). Their methods had a 97.5 percent accuracy rate, despite the fact that standard regression analysis models only had a 43 percent accuracy rate. Birkner et al. (2007) employed an optimum algorithm to predict 30-day morbidity, and their findings were more accurate than earlier methods. King et al. [38] also employed SVM to calculate stroke mortality at discharge. They also advocated for the use of synthetic plurality frame interpolation to eliminate the bias in stroke outcome prediction caused by imbalance in several data sets. Brain imaging has been used to predict the outcome of stroke treatment. Chen et al. (2016) employed machine learning to assess cerebral edema contralateral infarction using CT scan data. They developed a random forest that is more effective and dependable than standard methods for detecting nerve cells and analyzing changes in CT imaging. Using cognitive performance generated from MRI and functional MRI data, Siegel et al. (2016) employed ridge regression and multiplex learning to predict cognitive impairment following stroke, using ridge reduction and busy learning.

7.11 Conclusion and Discussion

Accurate diagnosis/assessment in the health sector is dependent on data collection and analysis. Data collecting has gotten considerably better. Preventive treatment is one area of medicine where data analytics has a big impact, helping practitioners to thwart disease before it takes hold. In order to address what we call "risk reduction services," organizations would have access to data insights gurus, healthcare professionals, data, and predictive analytics procedures, and assets. We've identified the challenges as well as given the right that must be examined prior to adopting any method. Each platform's algorithms are detailed in depth, along with execution instructions. We talked about why AI is being utilized in healthcare, showed how AI has examined different types of medical information, and surveyed the most prevalent disease types for which AI has been utilized. Machine learning and language generation processing, the two primary types of AI products, were then thoroughly examined. For machine learning, we concentrated on arguably one of the best previous approaches, SVM and artificial neural, as well as the newer image recognition methodology. The three primary types of application areas in adjuvant treatment were then discussed. Both a neural networks (ML) piece for handling with metadata (images, EP data, genetic analysis) and a natural language processing (NLP) component for mining irregular texts are required in a successful AI architecture. The advanced algorithms must be trained using medical information well before the system can aid clinicians with medical imaging and therapy advice.

References

Amin, S.U., et al. Cognitive smart healthcare for pathology detection and monitoring. *IEEE Access* 2019; 7: 10745–10753.

Asadi, H., Dowling, R., Yan, B., et al. Machine learning for outcome prediction of acute ischemic stroke post intra-arterial therapy. *PLoS One* 2014; 9: e88225.

Asadi, H., Kok, H.K., Looby, S., et al. Outcomes and complications after endovascular treatment of brain arteriovenous malformations: A prognostication attempt using artificial Intelligence. *World Neurosurg* 2016; 96: 562–569.

Birkner, M.D., Kalantri, S., Solao, V., et al. Creating diagnostic scores using data-adaptive regression: An application to prediction of 30–day mortality among stroke victims in a rural hospital in India. *The Clin Risk Manag* 2007; 3: 475–484.

Bosworth, H. *Improving Patient Treatment Adherence: A Clinician's Guide*. Springer, Berlin, 2010.

Bouton, C.E., Shaikhouni, A., Annetta, N.V., et al. Restoring cortical control of functional movement in a human with quadriplegia. *Nature* 2016; 533: 247–250.

Bragazzi, N.L., Dai, H., Damiani, G., Behzadifar, M., Martini, M., and Wu, J. How big data and artificial intelligence can help better manage the COVID-19 pandemic. *Int. J. Environ. Res. Public Health* 2020; 17: 3176.

Chen, Y., Dhar, R., Heitsch, L., et al. Automated quantification of cerebral edema following hemispheric infarction: Application of a machine learning algorithm to evaluate CSF shifts on serial head CTs. *Neuroimage Clin* 2016; 12: 673–680.

Das, A., et al. Distributed machine learning cloud teleophthalmology IoT for predicting AMD disease progression. *Futur Gener Comput Syst* 2019; 93: 486–498.

Dilsizian, S.E., and Siegel, E.L. Artificial intelligence in medicine and cardiac imaging: Harnessing big data and advanced computing to provide personalized medical diagnosis and treatment. *Curr Cardiol Rep* 2014; 16: 441.

Esteva A., Kuprel, B., Novoa, R.A., et al. Dermatologist-level classification of skin Cancer with deep neural networks. *Nature* 2017; 542: 115–118.

Farina, D, Vujaklija, I, Sartori, M, et al. Man/machine interface based on the discharge timings of spinal motor neurons after targeted muscle reinnervation. *Nat Biomed Eng* 2017; 1: 0025.

Gillies, R.J., Kinahan, P.E., and Hricak, H. Radiomics: Images are more than pictures, they are data. *Radiology* 2016; 278: 563–577.

Gulshan, V., Peng, L., Coram, M., et al. Development and validation of a deep learning algorithm for detection of diabetic retinopathy in retinal fundus photographs. *JAMA* 2016; 316: 2402–2410.

Karakülah, G., Dicle, O., Koşaner, O., et al. Computer based extraction of phenoptypic features of human congenital anomalies from the digital literature with natural language processing techniques. *Stud Health Technol Inform* 2014; 205: 570–574.

Keeling, M.J., Hollingsworth, T.D., and Read, J.M. E_cacy of contact tracing for the containment of the 2019 novel coronavirus (COVID-19). *MedRxiv* 2020: 1–10.

Li, C.Y., Liang, G.Y., Yao, W.Z., et al. Integrated analysis of long noncoding RNA competing interactions reveals the potential role in progression of human gastric Cancer. *Int J Oncol* 2016; 48: 1965–1976.

Long, E., Lin, H., Liu, Z., et al. An artificial intelligence platform for the multihospital collaborative management of congenital cataracts. *Nature Biomedical Engineering* 2017; 1. doi:10.1038/s41551-016-0024.

Madhumathi, R., et al. A comprehensive survey of IoT edge/fog computing protocols. In *Handbook of Research on Cloud and Fog Computing Infrastructures for Data Science*, pp. 85–107. IGI Global, 2018.

Manogaran, G., et al. Machine learning based big data processing framework for cancer diagnosis using hidden Markov model and GM clustering. *Wirel Pers Commun* 2018; 102(3): 2099–2116.

Mohamed, A., Najafabadi, M.K., Wah, Y.B., Zaman, E.A.K., and Maskat, R. The state of the art and taxonomy of big data analytics: View from new big data framework. *Artif. Intell. Rev* 2019; 53: 989–1037.

Muthu, B., Sivaparthipan, C.B., Manogaran, G., Sundarasekar, R., Kadry, S., Shanthini, A., and Dasel, A. IoT based wearable sensor for diseases prediction and symptom analysis in healthcare sector. *Peer-to-Peer Networking and Applications* 2020 Nov; 13(6): 2123–2134.

Patel, V.L., Shortliffe, E.H., Stefanelli, M., et al. The coming of age of artificial intelligence in medicine. *Artif Intell Med* 2009; 46: 5–17.

Patil, H.K., and Seshadri, R. Big data security and privacy issues in healthcare. In *2014 IEEE International Congress on Big Data*, pp. 762–765, 2014.

Pham, Q-V., Nguyen, D.C., Huynh-The, T., Hwang, W-J., and Pathirana, P.N. Artificial intelligence (AI) and big data for coronavirus (COVID-19) pandemic: A survey on the state-of-the-arts. *IEEE Access* 2020; 8.doi:10.20944/preprints/202004.0383.v1.

Pham, T.N., et al. A cloud-based smart-parking system based on internet-of-things technologies. *IEEE Access* 2015; 3: 1581–1591.

Pieczenik, S.R., and Neustadt, J. Mitochondrial dysfunction and molecular pathways of disease. *Exp Mol Pathol* 2007; 83(1): 84–92.

Qin, L., Sun, Q., Wang, Y., Wu, K-F., Chen, M., Shia, B-C., and Wu, S-Y. Prediction of number of cases of 2019 novel coronavirus (COVID-19) using social media search index. *Int. J. Environ. Res. Public Health* 2020; 17: 2365.

Shin, H., Kim, K.H., Song, C., et al. Electrodiagnosis support system for localizing neural injury in an upper limb. *J Am Med Inform Assoc* 2010; 17: 345–347.

Siegel J.S., Ramsey L.E., and Snyder A.Z., et al. Disruptions of network connectivity predict impairment in multiple behavioral domains after stroke. *Proc Natl Acad Sci USA* 2016; 113: e4367–4376.

Teece, D.J. Capturing value from knowledge assets: The new economy, markets for know-how, and intangible assets. *Calif Manag Rev* 1998; 40(3): 55–79.

Tsai, C-W., et al. Data mining for internet of things: A survey. *IEEE Commun Surv Tutor* 2014; 16(1): 77–97.

Zhang, Q., Xie, Y., Ye, P., et al. Acute ischaemic stroke prediction from physiological time series patterns. *Australas Med J* 2013; 6: 280–286.

8

Blockchain Technology Based Healthcare Supply Chain Management

Murari Kumar Singh

Sharda University, School of Engineering and Technology, Greater Noida, India

Narendra Singh

GL Bajaj Institute of Management and Research, Greater Noida, India

Rajnesh Singh

GL Bajaj Institute of Technology and Management, Greater Noida, India

Pushpa Singh

KIET Group of Institutions, Delhi-NCR, Ghaziabad, India

CONTENTS

8.1 Introduction

Blockchain technology is a major emerging technology that has a major impact on real-world applications. Blockchain is a chain of cryptographically linked blocks in a distributed environment that maintains trust between individuals without reliably knowing

DOI: 10.1201/9781003201960-8

each other (Wu et al., 2019). Figure 8.1 shows the timeline evolution of blockchain. Due to the emerging trend in healthcare and medicine toward user-centered care, traditional healthcare technology is losing billions of dollars each year due to insufficient data integration. Increasing data integration means that traditional information technology for health is losing billions of dollars annually. Implementation of blockchain with emerging technology, such as the Internet of Things (IoT) and Artificial Technology (AI), is in its early phases. There may be several research challenges related to privacy, smart contract security, interoperability, and transparency, particularly in healthcare and agriculture (Singh and Singh, 2020).

Healthcare records are the backbone of every modern healthcare system, and traditional supply chain management (SCM) in medicine or healthcare products can be untrusted, tempered, or cost-effective. The goal of this chapter is to show ways to integrate blockchain technology in the healthcare and healthcare SCM sectors. Blockchain will help keep medical records safe and secure by putting health records on the blockchain. Smart contracts can run on a blockchain, enhancing quality in healthcare by giving interoperable access to health data, the pharmacy, physicians, labs, insurers, and data storage, creating efficiency in the medical supply chain, and heightening security, etc. (Ante, 2020).

The use of blockchain SCM for medicine or health care products can be securely and easily handled, then used to verify the authenticity of healthcare products. This chapter also provides a brief description of potential future directions in the field of the healthcare industry.

8.2 Supply Chain Management in Healthcare

The supply chain usually states the resources required to provide goods or services to different entities participating in the supply chain. Healthcare SCM is an emerging field within SCM, and motives to improve principles and practices are related to concepts in humanitarian SCM (Tabaklar et al., 2015). The healthcare industry encounters many technical challenges, such as customer dissatisfaction, increasing cost of health services, patient to doctor chain management, bill payment, slower network services, reimbursement for services, and recent technological services. Some of the challenges for the healthcare SCM are listed below:

8.2.1 Lack of Data Integrity

These supply chains must be linked together. Centralization of purchasing channels is needed. Services must share agreements in order to qualify for higher tier rates. The supply chain will not be cost-effective until these changes are made, thus the systems that it encompasses will remain inefficient.

8.2.2 Inadequate Workflow Design

Many procedures are duplicated unnecessarily in the healthcare supply chain. The explanation for this is that the supply chain's networks and organizations are not related. Several of the activities could be programmed and combined in such a way that all participants could openly exchange information.

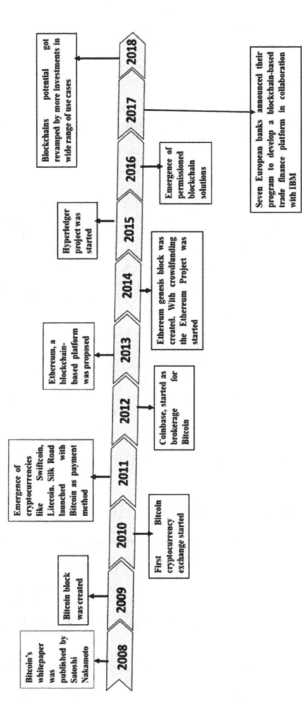

FIGURE 8.1

Timeline evolution of blockchain.

8.2.3 Shortages of Healthcare Products

The healthcare supply chain may be disorganized as a result of this shortage. Providers are required to either buy more costly alternatives or keep a large backup inventory of goods that are at risk of running out of stock, which adds to the expense of inventory management and product expiration.

8.2.4 Shortage of Quality Data

The lack of advanced analytics is a common problem among providers. Since they don't have access to sophisticated modeling tools or real-time reports, health professionals know that their decisions aren't well-informed.

8.2.5 Unexpected Hidden Costs

The hidden costs of any commodity are a challenge for healthcare providers. Historically, most providers have only considered the cost of the product and the cost of shipping. However, there are added costs, such as inventory storage. Complete landed supply costs must be factored into providers' budgets.

These reasons reenforce the health industries' need to implement a new intelligent structure that can meet these requirements and sustain them in the competitive environment. Healthcare SCM is not an easy process. Healthcare SCM comprises obtaining resources, managing supplies, and supplying goods and services among doctors, patients, and hospitals, as shown in Figure 8.2. Healthcare SCM enhances the efficiency of hospitals, physicians' practices, and patient care.

There are three main players of hospital SCM, i.e., doctor, patient and hospitals. The healthcare supply chain is conclusively going to be adopted quicker than other businesses because of stated challenges that are difficult to address with emerging technologies and could be better covered by blockchain technology. The raw materials and data about medical products and services typically drive through numerous independent players, such as manufacturers, providers, distributors, insurance firms, hospitals, and numerous governing agencies. Healthcare SCM encompasses the flow of various medical product types and

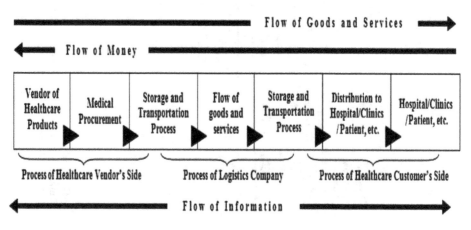

FIGURE 8.2
Supply chain management process in healthcare.

the involvement of many participants. The primary objective of healthcare supply chain is to offer medical products in a quicker, more transparent manner. The participants in the healthcare supply chain can be categorized into three groups, such as producers, purchasers, and providers (Mathew et al., 2013).

The healthcare supply chain starts with the medical product producer, where medical devices and equipment are produced and sent to a distribution center. A hospital can either purchase directly from the manufacturer/distributor, or the transaction can be directed through a group purchasing organization on behalf of the hospital. From the hospitals, products and services are directly supplied to the patient and doctor. Following are the trends in healthcare SCM.

1. Executives of the healthcare supply chain will be required to improve and enlarge their skill set in the future. The "ideal" supply chain leader will have four skills: interaction, bargaining, research, and delivery. They may have worked in SCM, human resource management, project management, health care, or technology in the past. They will have a master's degree, a credential in Lean/Six Sigma, and leadership experience.

2. Healthcare SCM will be reshaped due to the push for people in health supervision, for keeping people healthy, and keeping people with chronic medical problems as healthy as possible–ideas that will reshape the healthcare supply chain.

3. Risk-based contracting between providers and suppliers would change the way supply chains are built. Under value-based payment arrangements with payers, health care providers are taking on more clinical and financial risk, and they need to share that risk with suppliers.

4. By 2021, software and technology will drive the healthcare SCM market to $2.2 billion. In four years, the healthcare SCM industry would be worth $2.22 billion. An agreement with the Food and Drug Administration's Unique Identification Initiative, increasing pressure on hospitals and health systems to increase effective performance and profitability, and rising implementation of cloud-based SCM are all factors driving market expansion.

5. The practice of big data analytics used to improve SCM would become more popular. The improved use of progressive analytics to enhance SCM efficiency will be driven by predicting supply chain outcomes accurately.

There has been a significant change in the hospital sector, with market drivers for healthcare SCM, including increased competition, extremely high expenditures, increasing fragmentation of the healthcare sector, shorter product lifecycles, and the removal of trade barriers.

8.3 Overview and Architecture of Blockchain

Most database systems today employ a centralized client-server architecture. A client (user) in this system can change the information stored on the centralized server. The centralized authority has control over the entire server database and can control and make decisions regarding the several access control procedures defined on the data stored in the database. They even have the authority to validate a user's credentials before allowing them to access the database. Blockchain may be an effective alternative for resolving challenges

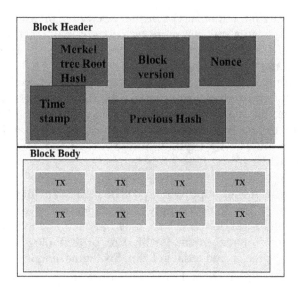

FIGURE 8.3
Block structure.

in traditional centralized systems. A blockchain is a collection of cryptographically inter-connected blocks that are used to store and transfer data in a distributed, transparent, and tamper-proof manner. Every block is made up of a list of transactions that are connected together by cryptographic pointers. Such connections safeguard the blockchain's integrity and resistance to tampering (Javed et al., 2020).

A block header consists of various fields, like nonce, previous hash, Merkle-root, and timestamp. A link to the trailing edge is made when fresh data is uploaded to the block-chain, extending the blockchain by one block or unit. As more data is contributed to the blockchain, the chain becomes longer and larger. All transaction history in a block can be easily recorded, traced, and validated by the blockchain network users (Zhang et al., 2019). When one block in the chain is changed or modified, the encryption links will be broken, disrupting the blockchain as a whole. It enables the user to check the data's precision doubling. By using decentralized systems, the risk of a centralized control system can be reduced. The database authority has centralized security controls for all users of the data-base. By storing and creating structural data storage, the blockchain secures the network. This makes it easier to track records or transactions with heterogeneous data in databases with blockchain technology. Figures 8.3 and 8.4 show block structure and an example of blockchain, consisting of blocks (Shi et al., 2020).

The consensus mechanism is one of the most significant features that create a secure, trusted, and transparent blockchain. A majority of system members must agree on each transaction before it can be confirmed. Table 8.1 shows some important blockchain charac-teristics that make it ideal for future industrial and health applications.

8.3.1 Architecture of Blockchain

Figures 8.5 and 8.6 display the elementary architecture of the blockchain (Wu et al., 2019), a transaction in blockchain (Figure 8.5) has various steps and needs to be verified. The trans-action is recorded in the block structure, where numerous bits of information are required, like timestamp, nonce, transaction list, previous hash, Merkle root, and current block hash.

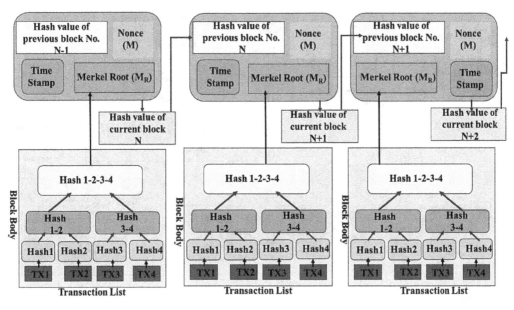

FIGURE 8.4
Example of blockchain consisting of a sequence of blocks.

TABLE 8.1

Characteristics of Blockchain

Open Source	It provides all blockchain network users with open source access.
Decentralized	All of the system's historical data and transactions can be kept, updated, accessed, and monitored across many systems.
Transparent	All the systems on the network have the same and an updated copy of the public ledger. With network consensus, the transaction is recorded and stored on the blockchain network, and it is visible and traceable throughout its lifetime.
Immutable	Once the digital asset is stored in the blockchain network, no one can modify or delete it. Blockchain provides and controls immutability using a timestamp and hashing the transactions.
Irreversible	In each blockchain, a specific and verifiable record is kept for every transaction ever made.
Anonymity	Each node on the blockchain can safely access, transfer, store, and update data without the need for a third party.
Ownership	Each blockchain-exchanged document stores its own records with a single Hash code.
Smart Contracting	A smart contract is a self-executing contractual application that runs and executes on the blockchain platform and is typically designed to include rules and conditions. It is also known as a crypto contract and was first proposed by Nick Szabo in 1994. Smart contracting supports quick-response operations in supply chains.

The transaction is also recorded by the user when requested. This newly generated block is broadcast among all the peer nodes in blockchain network. A blockchain network generates hashes using the SHA-256 (Secure Hash Algorithm-256) method, and each block is cryptographically linked to the hash of the previous block on the chain. This cryptographically linked property makes the chain unbreakable, and if anyone tries to add a new block, it must be authenticated by all network nodes or smart contracts, as well as a consensus mechanism. The consensus process ensures that the nodes participating in the validation

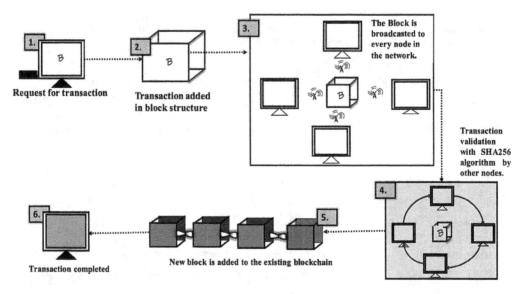

FIGURE 8.5
The basic architecture of blockchain.

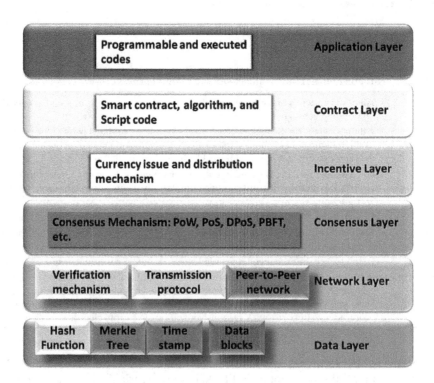

FIGURE 8.6
The layered architecture of blockchain.

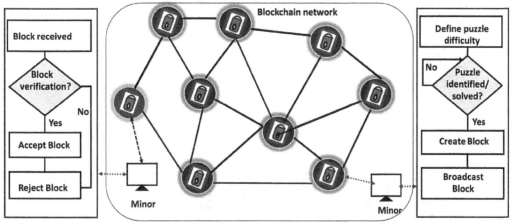

FIGURE 8.7
Working of consensus mechanism on blockchain network.

receive a good result by following the order in which the transactions should occur. Once a transaction has been validated and inserted into the chain, it cannot be changed; it can only be appended to the new transaction list in a block. Figure 8.7 shows the general working principle of consensus mechanism on the blockchain network. This immutable property of a ledger results in a secure and reliable transaction in the network.

A blockchain system is currently divided into four types: i) public, ii) private, iii) consortium, and iv) hybrid blockchain (Lin and Liao, 2017).

All records are open to the public, and anyone can contribute to the consensus mechanism in a public blockchain. Only a restricted number of pre-selected nodes will be allowed to participate in the consensus method in a consortium blockchain, which banks and government organizations commonly employ. Only nodes from a single business are permitted to participate in the consensus process in a private blockchain, which is utilized in SCM, asset monitoring, and other applications. Since it is entirely managed by one entity, a private blockchain is considered a centralized network. The consortium blockchain, which numerous organizations developed, is still partially operational. Since only a limited number of nodes will be chosen to decide the consensus, it would be decentralized. The advantages of private and public blockchains are combined in hybrid blockchains. Table 8.2 shows the comparison of public, private, and consortium blockchain technology.

8.4 Blockchain for Supply Chain Management

Blockchain technology can be implemented to increase inventory transparency and traceability in the supply chain. It would be especially useful in circumstances where there is no central trust entity, and neither party wants to share information directly.

The integration of content, knowledge, and financial flows in a network of companies or organizations is known as SCM. To manufacture and deliver goods and services to consumers, multiple supply chain partners must collaborate. The SCM principle radically alters the nature of a company because regulation is no longer based on direct control of

TABLE 8.2

Comparison of Blockchain Technologies

Benefits	Risk
Predictive planning, better assets utilization	Poor AI execution
Optimizing operating cost	High cost implementation
Improve decision making	Data security
Reduced lead time	Centralized system
Scalable	Trust with unknown nodes

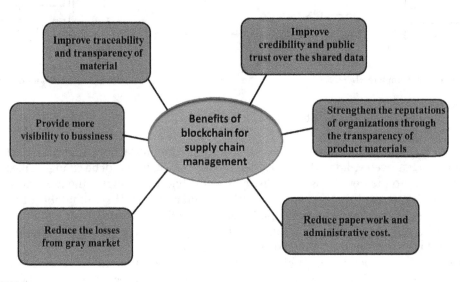

FIGURE 8.8
Benefits of blockchain in SCM.

internal business processes but rather on integration through supply chain member organizations (Lai et al., 2004).

Figure 8.8 represents the benefits of blockchain in SCM. The fundamental advantage of blockchain for SCM is that it allows participants to record information such as location, price, quality, date, certification, and other relevant data. The availability of this information within the blockchain enhances material traceability and transparency in the supply chain, as well as company visibility and gray market losses. Some other benefits of the blockchain in the supply chain are the improvement of credibility and public trust over the shared data, strengthening an organizations' reputation through the transparency of product materials, and reducing paperwork and administrative cost.

8.5 Blockchain and Healthcare Supply Chain Management

Because of the growing impact of digital technology on our health system, as well as globalization, rising adoption of information systems, open market drug and medicine sales, and global sharing of electronic health records, a complicated system of confidentiality, transparency, and authenticity of the above information has emerged.

On January 30, 2020, the WHO (World Health Organization) declared a public health emergency owing to the appearance of a new coronavirus known as SARS-CoV2, which is linked to the disease COVID-19, and the epidemic became a pandemic on January 11, 2020 (World Health Organization, 2020). The epidemic has sped up the global supply chain, but giving transparency, mentoring medications and medical equipment, and creating end-to-end visibility has been tough. The penetration of the collective category of substandard and falsified (SF) medicines, often known as counterfeit drugs, is a serious and familiar threat to the pharmaceutical supply chain, as depicted in Figure 8.8. Apart from product and drug counterfeiting, a healthcare facility's SCM may be disrupted by a lack of product registry and packaging problems (Moosivand et al., 2019).

In Africa, over 100,000 people are dying each year because of improper dosages of counterfeit drugs purchased from unknown or unfundable suppliers, according to a WHO (World Health Organization) survey (WHO, 2017).

Blockchain is critical for securely transferring data among groups of people, regardless of their trustworthiness or cross-checking. Blockchain is often run on a distributed ledger and can be integrated into a new workflow or modified protocols to meet unique needs. Because all transactions are recorded on the ledger, and every node in the blockchain preserves a record of the transaction, it is uncomplicated to rapidly check the drug's origin, vendor, and distributor. Moreover, the blockchain's distributed ledger allows healthcare administrators and physicians to verify and confirm supplier credentials (Narayanaswami et al., 2019). Figure 8.9 shows the blockchain-enabled flow from raw information to retailers, physicians, hospitals, and third parties for medical equipment and pharmaceuticals. Transaction records are stored in a new block in each step and validated prior to the next step in the chain of healthcare. When raw information or material is collected to be sent to the plant, a block is created that includes information and data sources. This information is recorded in the digital public ledger as a type of transaction. Once the collection of raw information is completed, this information, along with raw material, is sent to the

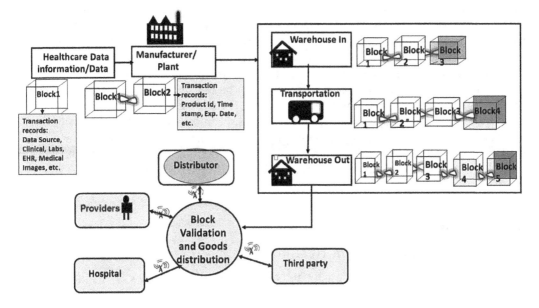

FIGURE 8.9
Blockchain-enabled SCM in healthcare.

TABLE 8.3

Benefits and Threats of a Blockchain in Health Care SCM

Benefits		Threats	
Patient related	Health Information Exchange	Technical threats	Slow processing speed
	Clinical trials		Scalability issues
	Managing medical insurance		Authorization and security issues.
	Pharmaceutical supply chain	Social threats	Social Acceptance
Organization related	Tracking patient's health data		Regulation Issues
	Personalized Healthcare	Organizational threats	Lack of technical skills
	Monitor patient's health status		Transaction and installation cost
	Security authorization		Interoperability issues

manufacturing plant. Every item manufactured by the plant has a unique identity (like product-id) which is integrated with other transactions having a time stamp, expiration date, etc., in a new block. This new block is cryptographically linked with the previous one, making it a blockchain. Following the mass production of products in a manufacturing plant, pharmaceutical products are gathered in a warehouse for further distribution, where transactions such as expiration date, lot number, and in-time can be recorded in a new block. During distribution from "warehouse-in" transportation details, which are also included in the blockchain, the transaction may include mode of transportation, factors affecting parameters such as temperature, humidity, and transport out time. "Warehouse-out" is directly connected to third parties, hospitals, distributors, or doctors. Warehouse-out details are also included in a block, the same as the warehouse-in. The receivers (like doctors) and third parties can validate and verify information about the received product.

In the case of pandemic events like the current one, blockchain can provide innovative and effective solutions to improve a variety of disease prevention and disease management operations, therefore boosting clinical risk management. The rapid and uncontrolled occurrence of coronavirus and its rapid spread worldwide has revealed that existing health care surveillance systems are not only unable to respond quickly to a public health emergency but also the evident absence of advanced prediction systems that are based on large-scale clinical data sharing, which can prevent or minimize such emergencies.

Pharmacies and healthcare professionals may better understand the supply chain through an appropriate and timely authentication process, ensuring that valid medicines continue to reach the people who need them most. In this aspect, blockchain technology has a lot of potential for building a reliable provider network that allows healthcare administrators to protect patients from shady vendors. Some benefits and threats of a blockchain technology in healthcare SCM can be summarised as shown in Table 8.3.

8.6 Benefits of Blockchain in Healthcare

The idea of blockchain can be characterized as a decentralized framework inside of which chronicled or value-based records are kept up, put away, and recorded across a shared organization of personal computers known as hubs. It depends intensely on set up cryptographic strategies. So you are excused if you think blockchain is predominantly about

Cryptocurrency. While talking about blockchain, individuals regularly interface it to cryptos and Bitcoin. Be that as it may, blockchain is considerably more than cryptographic money with regard to the strength of an application. However, without this innovation, the presence of digital forms of money, for example, Ethereum or Bitcoin would not have been conceivable. Every specific unit of the said advanced record is known as a block. Crypto Technology ties these blocks together, making them, in a real sense, changeless. Regardless of how you take a gander at it, medical care joined with blockchain is a match made in paradise. This innovation can associate the divided frameworks that can deliver bits of knowledge to all the more likely inspect the worth of customized care.

The rapid advancement of blockchain innovation has pulled in wide consideration from governments and monetary establishments. However, blockchain innovation has step by step been brought into the clinical field, including clinical information applications, clinical record sharing, individual security assurance, clinical installments, and medication that hasn't been forged, etc, Right now, clinical information is not vulnerable to worries about abuse or wasteful utilization of a blockchain. Here are different ways a blockchain can contribute to healthcare:

Master Patient Lists: Often, when managing medical services information, records get confused or copied. Additionally, extraordinary EHRs have an alternate construction for each field, recognizing that there are various methods of entering and controlling the most straightforward informational indexes. With blockchain, the whole informational index is hashed to a record and not simply the essential key. The client would search for the location; there can be different addresses and numerous keys, yet they will all respect a solitary patient distinguishing proof.

Claim Adjudication: Since blockchain chips away at an approval based trade, the cases can be consequently checked when the organization concurs about the manner in which an agreement is executed. Additionally, since there is no focal position, there would be fewer blunders or cheating.

Supply Chain Management: Blockchain-based agreements can help medical care associations observe an inventory request through its whole life cycle. How is the exchange occurring, whether the agreement is effective, or if there are any postponements.

Interoperability: Interoperability, the actual guarantee of blockchain, can be acknowledged by the utilization of modern APIs to make EHR interoperability and information stockpiling a dependable interaction. If blockchain networks are imparted to approved suppliers safely and uniformly, that would kill the expense and weight-related information compromise.

Accessibility: Data created from various sources, including wearable gadgets, can be simply directed into a clinical chain that can be utilized by patients to effectively audit their clinical record history, regardless of whether they are housed in circulated capacity areas. However, the information is put away in a decentralized organization, and there is no single place of attack (Hussein et al., 2018), which diminishes the danger of inaccessibility to patient record keeping. The patients can, at that point, specifically and safely, share access of their own, with any trusted outsider they wish. Moreover, well-being-related administrations and clinical products have the advantages of patient information available from numerous storehouses (Chitchyan and Murkin, 2018; Yang et al., 2019), giving upgraded openness. However, constant admittance to information would improve clinical consideration coordination and improve clinical consideration in clinical crisis circumstances.

Improved Transparency: The provenance highlight of the blockchain suggests that any augmentations to the blockchain are noticeable to the entirety of the patient's organization individuals. Given that information is unchanging, any unapproved alterations can be analyzed as inconsequential. With regard to fake prescriptions, for instance, a blockchain application will actually want to track crude drug materials to the completed item in a changeless and shared circulated record.

Help discover fake medications in the medication store network, considering that blockchain members confirm the information in the chain, conceivably with the mix of IoT against fake gadgets; Fill in is an open norms innovation that will eventually improve the nature of data sharing process from irrelevant data sets with numerous members in the medication inventory network. This kind of blockchain application can possibly change the medication store network into a common, straightforward, and dependable open information design that could incorporate different members and locales. Despite the current arrangements are vulnerable to being altered by a "blockchain-empowered" enemy with altering abilities during assembling, the inventory and administration framework could make drug duplicating a non-issue (Hussein et al., 2018). Clinical laborer preparing is progressing, subsequently blockchain has the potential to be utilized to regulate by recording and checking the range of abilities when preparing and schooling clinical staff. The provenance includes permits following instructive substances to their sources. Another basic advantage of blockchain is the capacity of wellbeing claims, as it includes delicate information that necessitates assurance and checking. Blockchain can likewise improve the proficiency of the protection guarantee measure as it can give close to continuous case preparing, check on advantage qualification and give preauthorization to suppliers.

Improved Security: Medical data is touchy information that should be kept hidden and secure. With information breaks on the ascent, it is basic to guarantee the security and protection of all clinical records, including yet not restricted to test imaging and protection information. In 2015, the Health and Human Services (HHS) office detailed that secured protected information breaches influenced more than 113 million people. Generally, 99% were hacking casualties, while just 1% suffered different types of information penetrate. HHS additionally revealed that network workers (107 million) and EHRs (3 million) are the main sources of data breaches. On account of the decentralization included in blockchain, no single information point can be hacked to take patient records. However, decentralization of the information records gives a changeless history of events, in the event that the information is private/public, and the set of experiences can be made straightforward. One account of private information can be jumbled by ascertaining and putting away the hash number. Blockchain information is encoded and requires the patient's private key to be decoded. A programmer won't peruse the patient information, even upon access. A lucky symptom of the greater security is a higher patient trust in assent recording frameworks: Patients can add assent proclamations any time in their consideration venture – sure that the blockchain will hold them safely (Zhang and Poslad, 2018).

Improved Performance: The term decentralization of a blockchain improves execution bottlenecks that come from regular organization correspondence. Incorporating IoT with blockchain, as proposed in (Griggs et al., 2018) can also decrease the requirement for physical checkups. However, blockchain innovation would give a functioning criticism circle in such a situation, to give ongoing far off tolerant observing and clinical intercessions that would permit conveyance of notices to all elaborate gatherings consequently.

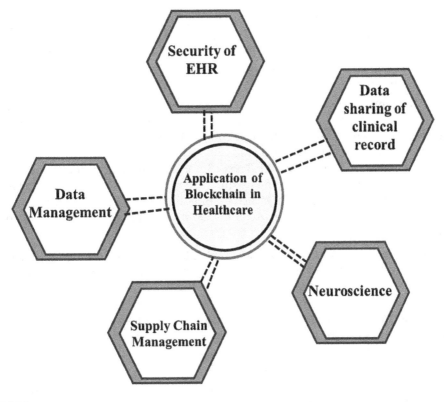

FIGURE 8.10
Application of blockchain in healthcare.

8.6.1 Application of Blockchain in Healthcare

Blockchain can utilize its innovation and inalienable highlights in an assortment of uses across numerous applications shown in Figure 8.10. Applications vary from features as they are not intrinsic to the system; however, they are measures that, in the blockchain, innovation can be applied to give another prerequisite. Applications discussed are information chain sharing, security, information administrations, inventory network, and executives (Khezr et al., 2019).

Data sharing of clinical record: Sharing of the clinical record is one primary and fundamental aspect to increase the nature of medical services suppliers and create a good framework of the medical service. Sharing clinical or medical records could be possible between people.

Security: Blockchain innovation has arrived at an extraordinary boom in the medical area because of its significance in conquering the EHR's security difficulties in healthcare. EHRs can possibly improve the conveyance of medical services. It is made when a patient is conceded to a clinic and when a doctor analyzes a patient, or when an asymptomatic outcome, for example, a MRI sacn is put away in the EHR system (Bahga and Madisetti, 2013). Therefore, security of such advanced data is given most extreme priority, and at present, would be utilizing blockchain for free from any danger medical services information. Keeping the worth of information and diminishing stockpiling costs for information, the board in medical services blockchain innovation assumes a huge part. Because of its remarkable capacity, blockchain technology is the lone response for getting advanced data, and it keeps on assuming an urgent part later on for big business information by the board.

Data Management: Healthcare organizations are also information-driven, and the volume of information is created just like other organizations. Medical IoT devices are creating massive volumes of the data collected and shared to laboratories and organizations for examinations (Shen et al., 2019). Presently, a primarily focus is given to the data collection from the medical record, and to further move for disease diagnosis and prediction by using machine learning techniques (Singh et al., 2021). However, data security and management is also required. Introduction of blockchain in healthcare records sharing enables secure, transparent data management without any third party authentication.

Electronic health records data management: Electronic health records (EHR) is electronic health related information used to store and access the patient information. There may arise new challenges for the security of patients' information. Storing records in blockchain provides patients' benefits to access and share their healthcare information (Dimitrov, 2019). Blockchain enables a secure methodology to interchange the health information of medical data in the healthcare business over a decentralized peer-to-peer network.

Supply Chain Management: SCM is a problematic possibility in healthcare services; with dissipated demand surrounding medical supplies, medicines, and essential medical equipment assets, trading off the store network measure may directly affect the health of patients. WHO (2017) specified that more than 100,000 persons die in Africa due to inadequate dosing from fake medications requested from unknown or untrustworthy sellers. Moreover, the medication duplicating, lack of an item in inventory, and bundling blunders in a medical services office may interrupt the complete SCM. Blockchain is a particularly significant innovation to check all SCM processes from drug manufacturer to supplier to distributor to venor to end-user or hospital inventory. Each block in the blockchain keeps a record of the conversation, and confirms the beginning of the medication, the vendors, and the wholesaler right away. Moreover, the carried record of the blockchain permits healthcare specialists and doctors to check and authorize the providers' agreements (Narayanaswami et al., 2019).

8.6.2 Predictions of Fate of Blockchain in the Healthcare

The extent of blockchain in medical services turns upward and promising as it tackles a portion of the major problems besetting the industry. Although, blockchain is decentralized and not normal for most of the medical services records that are incorporated, we imagine a reformist future. Moreover the future is where blockchain acts as a component of a system in which the patients will become stewards of their own clinical information, instead of depending on a central source. The interaction and number of steps to record, discover, and get the information can be difficult and various, yet with the assistance of emerging advances like Machine Learning and AI, these issues will get settled ultimately.

8.7 Challenges of Blockchain Technology in Healthcare

While blockchain in the healthcare industry is getting perhaps the most convincing patterns in medical services application improvement, there are still a few difficulties that should be survived if this arising technology is to be used to its maximum capacity. In addition, the potential snags to this innovation could be specialized difficulties; however, what is all the more conceivably obtrusive is social hindrances, guidelines, and enactment arrangements. For example, you may have somebody who can't manage the cost of a health tracker, and accordingly can't utilize one for following their clinical information when they visit a hospital or staff. Possibly there is a guideline set up that confines the utilization of blockchain technology in certain offices as a result of an apparent absence of financing (Bell et al., 2018). Strategy change with regards to new innovation can move rapidly at times, or it may come about more gradually. It's hard to anticipate, yet it will be entrancing to perceive what the following 10–15 years get this region. The numerous utilizations for blockchain appear to be plainly obvious. Anybody related with the medical services industry ought to perceive the potential dependence on what has effectively been developed and retrofitted with this kind of technology.

Healthcare Data Interchange: Data should pass between medical services suppliers to essential outsiders, safety net providers, and patients, while meeting information security guidelines in the medical services area.

Cross Country Interoperability: Having a solitary norm for patient information trade takes into consideration simplicity of passing information between medical services suppliers, which inheritance frameworks regularly don't give.

Medical Device Tracking: Medical gadgets following from inventory network to decommissioning considers a quick recovery of gadgets, counteraction of superfluous repurchasing, and extortion investigations.

Drug Tracking: As with clinical gadgets, blockchain offers the capacity to follow the chain of care from production network to patients, taking into consideration frictionless reviews and anticipation of fake medications.

8.8 Role of Blockchain on Covid-19

Covid-19 is a global health emergency, and the healthcare industry has an opportunity to integrate emerging technologies to monitor, control, and manage covid-19. There is a requirement for secure data that may deliver accurate information regarding covid-19 from various sources. These sources are government and private hospitals and experimental laboratories that can deliver data of covid-19 patients. This data may not be authentic since it is not examined and suitably stored and probably not collected according to set procedures (Sharma et al., 2020).

Blockchain technology has the potential to solve this problem by offering a distributed ledger or digital database that comprises data that can be concurrently used and shared inside a widespread decentralized and publicly accessible network. A blockchain is a distributed ledger used to collect scrambled blocks of data and create a chain. Blockchain

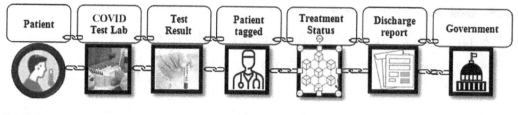

FIGURE 8.11
Blockchain in tracking Covid-19.

technology has primarily consisted of blocks, miners, and nodes. Blockchain is a chain of many blocks. A block is similar to a page of a ledger or record book. The miners can generate a novel block of chains by using the method of mining. Nodes are electronic devices that retain a replica of the blockchain and keep its network functioning (Bashir, 2018; Kaur et al., 2021). The blockchain contributing nodes are utilized for patients, testing labs, different hospital departments, and government sites. The data on the ledger are patient demographic records, sample test results, tags for the patient according to their health status, treatment plans, discharge summary, and government, as shown in Figure 8.11. Blockchain technology can be applied in collecting and monitoring covid-19 data in the following set of connected blocks of the blockchain.

- The first Block 1 is created as a *patient* block, consisting of all basic information of patients who are coming for the covid-19 test.
- Second Block 2 is for the covid *testing lab*, consisting of all related testing information, staff information, sample collections, and billing information.
- The third block is related to the test result block, which can transparently represent the positive and negative status of a patient. That information can also be visible to the patient block, testing lab block, and next connected block.
- Next connected Block 4 tagged the patient as either hospitalized or home quarantined, as suggested by the Doctor.
- Treatment is Block 5, which contains all the patient's treatment-related information. The number of the patients admitted to ICU, the number of patients relying on oxygen, who occupied a bed, etc., are also recorded in a secure database.
- The discharge report is Block 6, which contains information on the number of patients recovered and the number of deaths due to covid-19, in a transparent manner.
- The government is called Block 7, which can trace and record all covid-19 information from block 1 to block 7. The government and health organizations enable tracing and monitoring of covid-19 patients at each block, with consistency and precision (Papadopoulos et al., 2020).

All data from block 1 to block 7 comprises a distributed ledger that includes evidence that can be used concurrently and jointly inside a widely distributed and publicly available network. All covid-19 information is unchangeable, transparent, and secure through the use of cryptographic hashing. Blockchain technology enables numerous possible potentials for the covid-19 pandemic, like outbreak tracking, patient tracing, medical equipment tracking, and healthcare SCM. This information can be collected from each block and processed

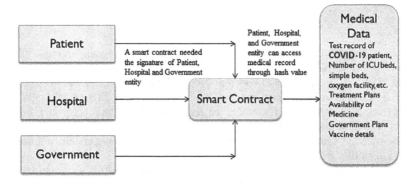

FIGURE 8.12
Smart contract in healthcare.

data into the scale of big data. These data can be part of AI-based learning techniques, such as supervised and unsupervised learning, and can predict the positivity rate, recovery rate, treatment plan, effective medicine, and medical equipment SCM, with the stakeholders. Blockchain can support the effective planning of government policy and resource deployments for the different healthcare sectors (Marbouh et al., 2020).

Smart contracts provide secure transactions and agreements to be carried out among patient, hospital and government entities as shown in Figure 8.12. Through the hash value, these entities can access medical records/data from the distributed environment. Distributed Ledger Technology (DLT) enables the secure storage of medical data. IoT based best-connected channel model is designed to provide the fastest communication among the participating entities in a heterogeneous environment (Singh and Agrawal, 2018).

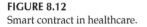

8.9 Conclusion

Blockchain is transparent, distributed, immutable, secure, and easily traceable and trackable from one place to another. In this chapter, we have discussed blockchain architecture for healthcare that manages the SCM of the hospital. Blockchain enables digital data transactions for distribution on a peer-to-peer network as a distributed ledger that can be privately or publicly distributed to all users on the network. Blockchain replaces traditional SCM. Blockchain quickly created and connected a block for drug manufacturers, vendors, and the distributor. Blockchain technology plays a vital role in treating or collecting data for active patients, recovered patients, and medication plans, during the covid-19 pandemic. One significant advantage of blockchain in the healthcare supply chain is to provide access to all end users (doctors, hospitals, third parties) and authenticate the transactions of the public ledger.

A chain from the patient to the government can offer transparent information to each connected block. The different blocks can be patients, a testing lab, hospital departments, and government sites that used a smart contract to share the medical documents on the digital ledger.

References

Ante, L. "Smart contracts on the blockchain – A bibliometric analysis and review." *Telematics and Informatics*, no. 57 (2020): 101519.

Bahga, A., and Madisetti, V.K. "A cloud-based approach for interoperable electronic health records (EHRs)." *IEEE Journal of Biomedical and Health Informatics* 17, no. 5 (2013): 894–906.

Bashir, I. *Mastering Blockchain: Distributed Ledger Technology, Decentralization, and Smart Contracts Explained*. Packt Publishing Ltd, 2018.

Bell, L., Buchanan, W.J., Cameron, J., and Lo, O. "Applications of blockchain within healthcare." *Blockchain in Healthcare Today* 1, no. 8 (2018).

Chitchyan, R., and Murkin, J. "Review of blockchain technology and its expectations: Case of the energy sector." *arXiv preprint arXiv:1803.03567* (2018).

Dimitrov, D.V. "Blockchain applications for healthcare data management." *Healthcare Informatics Research* 25, no. 1 (2019): 51.

Griggs, K.N., Ossipova, O., Kohlios, C.P., Baccarini, A.N., Howson, E.A., and Hayajneh, T. "Healthcare blockchain system using smart contracts for secure automated remote patient monitoring." *Journal of Medical Systems* 42, no. 7 (2018): 1–7.

Hussein, A.F., ArunKumar, N., Ramirez-Gonzalez, G., Abdulhay, E., Tavares, J.M.R.S., and de Albuquerque, V.H.C. "A medical records managing and securing blockchain based system supported by a genetic algorithm and discrete wavelet transform." *Cognitive Systems Research* 52 (2018): 1–11.

Javed, M.U., Rehman, M., Javaid, N., Aldegheishem, A., Alrajeh, N., and Tahir, M. "Blockchain-based secure data storage for distributed vehicular networks." *Applied Sciences* 10, no. 6 (2020): 2011.

Jayaraman, R., AlHammadi, F., and Simsekler, M.C.E. "Managing product recalls in healthcare supply chain." In *2018 IEEE International Conference on Industrial Engineering and Engineering Management (IEEM)*, pp. 293–297. IEEE, 2018.

Kaur, S., Chaturvedi, S., Sharma, A., and Kar, J. "A research survey on applications of consensus protocols in blockchain." *Security and Communication Networks*, 2021, 22, 2021. doi:10.1155/2021/6693731

Khezr, S., Moniruzzaman, M., Yassine, A., and Benlamri, R. "Blockchain technology in healthcare: A comprehensive review and directions for future research." *Applied Sciences* 9, no. 9 (2019): 1736.

Lai, K.-H., Ngai, E. W. T., and Cheng, T. C. E. "An empirical study of supply chain performance in transport logistics." *International Journal of Production Economics* 87, no. 3 (2004): 321–331.

Lin, I.-C., and Liao, T-C. "A survey of blockchain security issues and challenges." *IJ Network Security* 19, no. 5 (2017): 653–659.

Marbouh, D., Abbasi, T., Maasmi, F., Omar, I.A., Debe, M.S., Salah, K., Jayaraman, R., and Ellahham, S. "Blockchain for COVID-19: Review, opportunities, and a trusted tracking system." *Arabian Journal for Science and Engineering* vol. **45**, **no.** 9895–9911 (2020): 1–17. doi:10.1007/s13369-020-04950-4

Moosivand, A., Ghatari, A.R., and Rasekh, H.R. "Supply chain challenges in pharmaceutical manufacturing companies: Using qualitative system dynamics methodology." *Iranian Journal of Pharmaceutical Research (IJPR)* 18, no. 2 (2019): 1103.

Mathew, J., John, J., and Kumar, S. "New trends in healthcare supply chain." In *Annals of POMS Conference Proceedings*, Denver, CO, pp. 1–10. 2013.

Narayanaswami, C., Nooyi, R., Govindaswamy, S.R., and Viswanathan, R. "Blockchain anchored supply chain automation." *IBM Journal of Research and Development* 63, no. 2/3 (2019): 1–7.

Papadopoulos, T., Baltas, K.N., and Balta, M.E. "The use of digital technologies by small and medium enterprises during COVID-19: Implications for theory and practice." *International Journal of Information Management* 55 (2020): 102192.

Reda, M., Kanga, D.B., Fatima, T., and Azouazi, M. "Blockchain in health supply chain management: State of art challenges and opportunities." *Procedia Computer Science* 175 (2020): 706–709.

Sharma, A., Bahl, S., Bagha, A.K., Javaid, M., Shukla, D.K., and Haleem, A. "Blockchain technology and its applications to combat COVID-19 pandemic." *Research on Biomedical Engineering* (2020): 1–8. doi:10.1007/s42600-020-00106-3

Shen, B., Guo, J., and Yang, Y. "MedChain: Efficient healthcare data sharing via blockchain." *Applied Sciences* 9, no. 6 (2019): 1207.

Shi, S., He, D., Li, L., Kumar, N., Khan, M.K., and Choo, K.-K.R. "Applications of blockchain in ensuring the security and privacy of electronic health record systems: A survey." *Computers & Security* 97, (2020): 101966. doi:10.1016/j.cose.2020.101966

Singh, P., and Singh, N. "Blockchain with IoT and AI: A review of agriculture and healthcare." *International Journal of Applied Evolutionary Computation (IJAEC)* 11, no. 4 (2020): 13–27.

Singh, P., and Agrawal, R. "A customer centric best connected channel model for heterogeneous and IoT networks." *Journal of Organizational and End User Computing (JOEUC)* 30, no. 4 (2018): 32–50.

Singh, P., Singh, N., Singh, K.K., and Singh, A. "Diagnosing of disease using machine learning." In *Machine Learning and the Internet of Medical Things in Healthcare*, pp. 89–111. Academic Press, 2021.

Tabaklar, T., Halldórsson, A., and Kovács, G. "Borrowing theories in humanitarian supply chain management." *Journal of Humanitarian Logistics and Supply Chain Management* 5, no. 3 (2015): 281–299.

World Health Organization. *A Study on the Public Health and Socioeconomic Impact of Substandard and Falsified Medical Products: Executive Summary.* No. WHO/EMP/RHT/SAV/2017.02. World Health Organization, 2017.

Wu, M., Wang, K., Cai, X., Guo, S., Guo, M., and Rong, C. "A comprehensive survey of blockchain: From theory to IoT applications and beyond." *IEEE Internet of Things Journal* 6, no. 5 (2019): 8114–8154.

World Health Organization. "Naming the coronavirus disease (COVID-19) and the virus that causes it." (2020). https://www.who.int/emergencies/diseases/novel-coronavirus-2019/technical-guidance/naming-the-coronavirus-disease-(covid-2019)-and-the-virus-that-causes-it (accessed May 26, 2021).

Yang, J., Onik, M.M.H., Lee, N.-Y., Ahmed, M., and Kim, C-S. "Proof-of-familiarity: A privacy-preserved blockchain scheme for collaborative medical decision-making." *Applied Sciences* 9, no. 7 (2019): 1370.

Zhang, R., Xue, R., and Liu, L. "Security and privacy on blockchain." *ACM Computing Surveys (CSUR)* 52, no. 3 (2019): 1–34.

Zhang, X., and Poslad, S.. "Blockchain support for flexible queries with granular access control to electronic medical records (EMR)." In *2018 IEEE International Conference on Communications (ICC)*, pp. 1–6. IEEE, 2018.

9

Challenges and Future Prospects of IoT in Healthcare

Saru Dhir, Shradha Sapra, and Madhurima Hooda

Amity University, Greater Noida, India

CONTENTS

9.1 Introduction

Globally, various research projects have been exploring different scientific solutions to increase health care provisions in order to support the already developed services by enhancing the utilization of IoT. There has been an increased effort to create healthcare applications and services driven by IoT. Moreover, this research is also concerned with how IoT addresses elderly care, the personal health of an individual, healthcare management in

DOI: 10.1201/9781003201960-9

chronic disease, and much more. This paper also shows how the advances using various technologies in sensors, web applications, and other devices have motivated the development of affordable healthcare devices, leading to the growth of IoT in the field of medication (Riazul Isla et al., 2015). The IoT is becoming a huge trend in this era of technology and has the potential to affect the whole traditional business range. IoT can revert for an extensive variety of apps, for example, management of waste, smart urban communities, traffic blockage, structural wellbeing, mechanical control, medicinal services, etc.

In the object oriented worldview, everything on the planet is considered an object, yet in the IoT world view, everything on the planet is considered a smart object, which enables them to interact with each other through web technologies practically or physically. Continuously, new innovations are being discovered in order to fulfill the needs of individuals. Earlier Internet availability started to multiply in big businesses and the customer market, yet was still constrained in its utilization as a result of the low execution of the system interconnections.

Section 9.1 discusses medicinal services which are based on the IoT technology, increment personal satisfaction, and raise the client's experience as well. Section 9.2 talks about IoT layers. IoT has a multi-layered architecture, which is categorized into four different stages: sensing, network, service, and interface layers. Section 9.3 highlights IoT Healthcare Technology. There exist many IoT based health care tools that may have the capability to transform the IoT-based health care services, like Cloud computing, Big Data, Grid computing, etc. Section 9.4 emphisizes services and applications on IoT healthcare. Various IoT based healthcare services are notification services, web services, cross-network conventions, etc. Section 9.5 evaluates IoT Popularity Index by using the data from Google Scholar and publications on IoT. Section 9.6 discusses challenges in IoT Healthcare. Numerous researchers have been working on the design and implementation of different IoT based health care services. Yet, there are few difficulties and issues that should be addressed deliberately. At last, Section 9.7 provides conclusions and future prospects of the research.

This information could provide support to analysts, researchers and IoT professionals who are working in the field of IoT healthcare technologies.

9.2 Literature Review

It was discovered in one of the research projects that the Internet of Things, which rejects PDAs, PCs, and tablets, would be able to develop an estimated 26 billion units in 2020, which is approximately an increment of 30 fold from 0.9 billion in 2009 (Sobhan Babu et al., 2014).

One of the most vital trends of IoT is the simplicity of financially effective collaborations through the consistent and secure network crosswise over individual patients, facilities, and medicinal service associations (Goyal et al., 2021). Health issues, like chronic syndrome and other medical crises, rely upon these medicinal service systems driven by updated remote technologies (Kazmi et al., 2017). Medicinal servers and related medical databases help a great deal in the expansion of health based records. IoT has been undertaken with significant interest by scientists to utilize the skills of the IoT healthcare network system. As of now, there exist various iterations and models in this arena that are supporting healthcare centers to provide better services to the patients (Pang, 2013). Moreover, some protocols are also being introduced for sending the IoT advancements to the healthcare industry in various nations around the world (Sapra et al., 2018).

It was observed that in COVID-19, there are number of studies done on healthcare that are based on the use of IoT for healthcare. A number of different applications of IoT was identified for healthcare (Javaid and Haleem Khan, 2021).

An IoT based architecture was presented that represents the scalability requirement, reliability, and security in terms of distant, health observing devices for COVID-19 patients (Paganelli et al., 2021).

A health care architecture was proposed for using IoT on a large scale for communication between different devices (Haghi et al., 2020). There are a number of studies that focused on different architectures based on security and privacy in healthcare applications (Krishnamoorthy et al., 2021; Said and Tolba, 2021).

9.3 IoT for Healthcare

IoT provides supports to various healthcare applications, such as wireless health checking, chronic syndrome, etc. Consistency of treatment and pharmaceuticals at home is another vital potential application. A long these lines, different medicinal gadgets, sensors, and symptomatic gadgets could be seen as smart gadgets. Medicinal services that are based on the IoT technology raise personal satisfaction and the customer's experience, as well.

9.4 IoT Layers and Services

IoT has a multi-layered architecture which is categorized into four different stages as follows:

A. Sensing Layer: This is the primary layer that integrates with all the various kinds of hardware connected to the physical world and gathers all the required i formation.

B. Networking Layer: This is the second layer of IoT. It provides support to the network and transfers the data within the different networks.

C. Service Layer: This layer accomplishes all the different kinds of services that are going to satisfy user needs.

D. Interface Layer: This is the top-most layer that gives coordinated effort techniques to clients and different applications to examine all the data, conveying every one of the ideal yields.

There are various kinds of IoT services available:

A. Smart Wearable Devices: These devices may be utilized by those patients who need to gather information concerning their well-being, for example, blood pressure level, pulse rate, and glucose level sent over different sensors on the wearable technologies, which are further directed to smartphones.

B. Smart Homes: Whereas sensors may distinguish the adjustments in temperature and the ventilating systems may be checked. Home surveillance cameras can catch any interlopers and send the notices to the property holders through mobile applications.

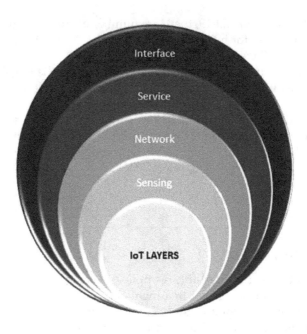

FIGURE 9.1
IoT layers.

TABLE 9.1

IoT Services at Each Layer

	Wearable's	Smart Homes	Smart Cities
Interface	Google Glass, Smartphones, FitBit, Samsung Gear, Smartwatches	Smart Thermostat, Smart door lock, Smart Energy management, Smart Lights	Smart Parking, Smart Traffic and Transportation System, Smart Environment, Connected Cars.
Service	Monitors the health status of patient like BP, Glucose Level	Monitoring the working of smart devices in home	Monitors the traffic, Environment in the city
Networking	Bluetooth	Wifi	VANET
Sensing	Cardiac Health, Withings BP, Fuelband	Daily Activities	Drone Ambulances

C. Smart Cities: The traffic and transport systems may be checked through IoT technologies to achieve smart cities (Baruah et al., 2019). Information may be gathered and examined to recognize the updates in traffic networks and transportation systems.

9.5 IoT Healthcare Technology

There exist many IoT based health care tools that may have the capability to transform the IoT-based health care services:

A. CLOUD COMPUTING: The assimilation of this technology toward IoT-based health care services ought to grant facilities overall admittance to mutual assets and offer various services on demand over the system, to address different issues.

B. GRID COMPUTING: Grid computing, which is also known as "Cluster Computing" is the base of cloud computing, which has the ability to address medicinal sensor nodes.

C. BIG DATA: It can incorporate gigantic measures of necessary health information produced from different medicinal sensors, and it also allows devices to enhance the proficiency of significant health analysis.

D. NETWORKS: Diverse network systems are a component of the physical framework of the IoT centered health care network system, ranging from network systems for short-range (for example: WBANs, WPANs, 6LoWPANs, WSNs, and WLANs (Bhardwaj et al., 2019)) to networks for long range communications.

E. AMBIENT INTELLIGENCE: As end customers in health care networks are all human beings, the utilization of ambient intelligence is vital. It helps to learn human behavior continuously and execute the activity required that is activated by any event.

F. AUGMENTED REALITY: A fundamental component of IoT, augmented reality is of great importance in the medical field. It is helpful in monitoring surgery and other health components.

G. WEARABLES: The health and well-being of patients can be encouraged by using wearable devices that are used to gather related health information about the patient and monitor the health status continuously, using IoT technologies.

9.6 IoT Health Care Services and Applications

IoT centered health care networks play a fundamental part in many areas, which include monitoring aging patients with chronic ailments and other serious health issues, and also managing the health and wellbeing of the individuals. IoT based applications are additionally categorized as different applications, such as: single-condition and clustered-condition.

A single condition application can be an accomplice to a particular disease or confusion, however a clustered application contracts with various contaminations or conditions all together.

9.6.1 Services

IoT services give a specific solution. These consist of notification services, web services, cross-network conventions, etc. Various IoT based healthcare services are as follows:

9.6.1.1 Ambient Assisted Living (AAL)

The Ambient Assisted Living (AAL) service is an IoT stage motorized by man-made brainpower which is utilized to address the prosperity of old and disabled individuals. The principle objective behind AAL is to lengthen the life of matured persons in an accommodating and safe manner. The results given by ambient assisted living services have the ability to make elderly people feel self-confident by guaranteeing more obvious self-sufficiency.

9.6.1.2 The Internet of m-Health Things (m-IoT)

M-wellbeing, otherwise called versatile processing, utilized as therapeutic sensors, m-IoT illuminates a medical care structure which connects the 6LoWPAN with existing 4G organizational frameworks for online m-wellbeing administrations in the future. There are some particular characteristics intrinsic to the mobility of sharing entries in m-IoT which further prompts to conceptualization of m-IoT services.

9.6.1.3 Adverse Drug Reaction (ADR)

An Adverse Drug Reaction (ADR) is the damage caused by addicting medication. It determines the medication by using NFC empowered devices. The information collected is then organized to detect whether the medication provided is suitable with its hypersensitive profile and e-health records.

9.6.1.4 Community Healthcare (CH)

Observing community healthcare (CH) accompanies the idea of building up a system that covers a range of information about a neighbourhood community. The setup could be an IoT-based healthcare system, a civil hospital, neighbourhood, or a rural community. In each manner, a specific administration called Community Healthcare (CH) is unavoidable for meeting combined specialized needs as a bundle. A supportive IoT stage for checking rural health care has been scheduled and found to be energy efficient.

9.6.1.5 Children's Health Information (CHI)

Uncovering issues that deal primarily with kids' prosperity while fostering the well-being of the general populace, and specifically on provisions for children with social, emotional, or mental health problems and help for their family members is essential. This issue has convinced researchers to develop a specific IoT administration, known as "Children's Health Information (CHI)," to present this necessity in an acceptable way.

9.6.1.6 Wearable Device Access (WDA)

Distinctive non-interferring sensors have been delivered for different extents of therapeutic claims created explicitly for WSN-grounded medical services organizations. These sensors are effective in passing data to comparable organizations that are utilizing IoT. On the other hand, a wearable gadget could aid in gathering attributes suitable for the IoT plan. Therefore, the need for transmitting sensors inserted in wearable items is apparent. In this particular circumstance, creating a functional method for wearable information access (WDA) is essential. The consolidation of wearable administrations in applications is a duscussion point for when to use IoT for WSNs. This strategy presents a model system that can be recycled as a piece of a wide collection of medical care applications by various flexible figuring contraptions, for instance, smart watches and cell phones.

9.6.2 IoT Healthcare Applications

It may be seen that administrations have been used to make applications; however applications are clearly used by customers and patients. Subsequently, administrations are designer driven; however, applications are customer driven (Lin et al., 2017; Mishra et al., 2018). Diverse IoT-based medical care applications, with both single-condition and bunched condition applications, are as follows:

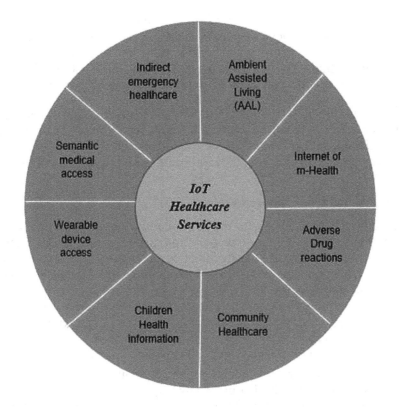

FIGURE 9.2
IoT healthcare services.

Source: Sapra et al. (2018).

9.6.2.1 Single-Condition Applications

i. GLUCOSE LEVEL SENSING: Diabetes is a collection of metabolic diseases in which the sugar levels in blood are high for a significant time period. Blood glucose checking reveals explicit examples of changes in blood glucose and offers help in planning meals, work outs, and restorative conditions. In m-IoT, techniques for glucose checking and sensors from the patients are connected through an IPv6 network, and are shown to be enormously helpful to organizations and suppliers.

ii. ELECTROCARDIOGRAM MONITORING (ECG): The use of ECG consolidates the assessment of the essential pulse. The use of IoT to ECG to check the pulse can give the most improbable information and should be used to its fullest degree. An exploration presents an IoT-based ECG observing framework made from a distant, conventional recuperation transmitter and a distance tolerating processor.

iii. BLOOD PRESSURE MONITORING: Blood Pressure could be continuously monitored with a wireless communication interface between a health center and a health post. The Withings BP gadget is dependent on a relationship with an Apple cell phone (Nguyen et al., 2017)

iv. Body Temperature Monitoring: The temperature of our body is a fundamental sign when monitoring homeostasis. The possibility of m-IoT as a sensor to detect internal body heat and to note any internal heat level changes is a productive use of the m-IoT system (Kodali et al., 2015).

v. OXYGEN SATURATION MONITORING: Heartbeat oximetry is a logical choice for the external checking of levels of saturation of oxygen in the blood. The coordination of IoT with heartbeat oximetry is helpful for development based restorative clinical benefits applications. The wearable heartbeat oximeter Wrist OX2 by Nonin works with a network reliant upon a bluetooth prosperity gadget profile.

In this overview, we have designated a portion of the forward thinking research that altogether could contribute to the future improvement of Healthcare 4.0 frameworks. We have distinguished the critical exploration holes and introduced the advanced best in class of medical care frameworks, presenting the Healthcare IoT Application and Service Stacks.

9.6.2.2 Clustered-Condition Applications

i. REHABILITATION SYSTEM: As medication and recuperation can restore the functioning of individuals with incapacity or imperfections, they offer a vital part of the remedy. The IoT can overhaul rehabilitation processes and facilities to ease issues associated with a growing populace and the shortage of wellbeing experts. IoT-based progress can shape a structure to facilitate long distance consultations for guidance toward complete recuperation. There are various IoT-based recuperation systems, for instance, an organized request structure for jails, the reclamation practice of hemiplegic patients and a shrewd city clinical recuperation system.

ii. MEDICATION MANAGEMENT: The resistance issue in medication addresses a certifiable danger to general wellbeing and brings about vast financial waste over the world. To conquer this issue, IoT offers few empowering game plans. A shrewd technique for restorative boxes for an IoT-based remedy the executives planned includes a model procedure of the I2Pack and the iMedBox and checks the system by field preliminaries. This procedure accompanies measured fixing based on delamination materials constrained by distant correspondences (Pace et al., 2017).

iii. WHEELCHAIR MANAGEMENT: Many experts have endeavored to make amazing wheelchairs with complete automation for handicapped people. Conceivably, the effort could be possible through the use of IoT. A structure for wheelchair customers based on IoT innovation is proposed where the design goes with WBANs joined along various sensors whose limits are custom fitted to IoT necessities. Intel's IoT division proposed another IoT based associated wheelchair which can check the individual sitting on the seat and assemble data around the customer's general climate, considering the rating of a space's accessibility.

iv. IMMINENT HEALTHCARE SOLUTIONS: Many therapeutic contraptions are available; however, there exists no precise show of incorporating those devices into IoT frameworks. Different medical care discussions with connections to IoT that seem quickly drawing to a conclusion are hemoglobin openness, sporadic cell improvement, cancer therapy, correcting eye debilitation, skin disease, and remote medical procedures (Gupta et al., 2017; Sarkar and Saha, 2017).

v. SMARTPHONES: The development of gadgets with a smart phone controlled sensors which use the IoT technology as the key feature has increased in recent years.

Diagnostic applications are utilized to get access to analytic and treatment data. Medication reference applications normally give names of medications, their symptoms, measurements, costs, and distinguishing characteristics. Literature scan applications encourage searches for medical literature databases to search for proper medicinal data.

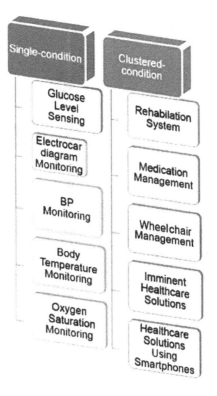

FIGURE 9.3
IoT healthcare applications.

9.7 IoT Popularity Index

9.7.1 Publication Data (2011–2017)

The quantity of distributions for IoT and IoT for medical services is growing. Utilizing the information from *Google Scholar*, Figure 9.4 exhibits the number of distributions for IoT and IoT for medical services since 2011. There has been an increase in the quantity of distributions for the term IoT consistently from 6,610 in 2011 to 36,300 in 2016. Also, for the class of IoT for healthcare, the level of distributions has likewise been expanded ceaselessly from 324 in 2011 to 6,030 in 2016. Yet, in 2017, there has been a slight decrease in the IoT usage for medical services distributions down to 35,200 in IoT publications and 5,020 mentions of IoT for Healthcare distributions. The investigation shows that in spite of a large number of IoT distributions, there is still room to utilize IoT for Healthcare.

9.7.2 Publication Record (2015–2020)

In Figure 9.4: Popularity Index of IoT and IoT for healthcare is represented through different research publications from 2011 to 2017.

Below Table 9.2 represent the publication data for IoT in healthcare of conferences, journals, magazines, articles and books through different publishers, such as *IEEE, ACM*, and *Science Direct* from 2015 to2020.

IoT and IoT for Healthcare

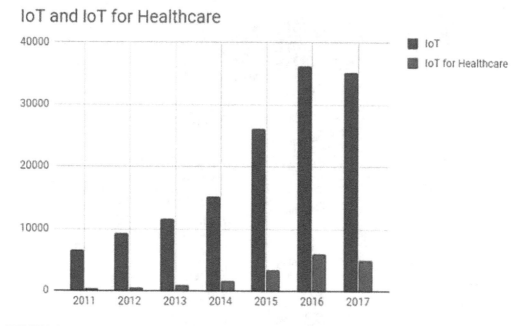

FIGURE 9.4
IoT popularity index.

TABLE 9.2

Research Publication Data for IoT in Healthcare (*IEEE, ACM* and *Science Direct*)

Publishers	Conference	Journals	Magazines	Articles	Books
IEEE	1,488	386	63	61	30
ACM	15,201	2,093	527	500	102
Science Direct	2,322	2,082	126	156	452

Based on the above data, Figure 9.5 represents the graphical representation that shows *ACM* has highest publication data from the last six years. Figure 9.5 also represents the research publication data in journals, magazines, articles and books.

Table 9.2 and Figure 9.5 specify the complete research publication data from 2015 to 2020, where Table 9.3 elaborates each year's publication data, i.e., from 2015 to 2020. Here it specifies the publication data from different publishers in different years. Here it is also observed that researchers regularly worked on IoT in respect to health care. As there is a pandemic situation due to COVID-19, it was also an increase observed in the number of publications about health care centers.

Figure 9.6 represents the graphical representation for last six years of publication in *IEEE, ACM,* and *Science Direct.* It is observed from the graph also, that in every year there is a continuous increase in research publication on the topic "IoT in Healthcare." Researchers continue to work on IoT, healthcare and how we can improve healthcare using IoT.

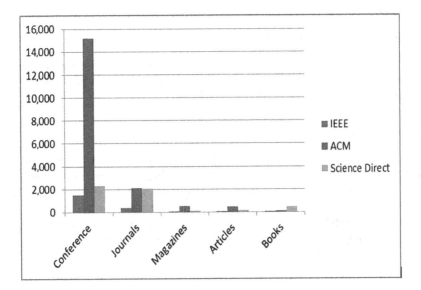

FIGURE 9.5
Graphical representation of different publications.

TABLE 9.3

Research Publication Data for IoT in Healthcare in Last Six Years

Publishers	2015	2016	2017	2018	2019	2020
IEEE	99	136	268	367	443	525
ACM	1,438	2,035	2,875	3,401	4,110	4,205
Science Direct	111	223	363	605	893	1,449

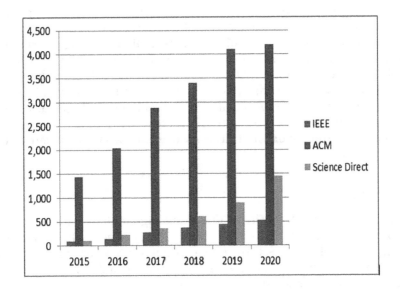

FIGURE 9.6
Graphical representation of research publications in last six years.

9.8 Challenges in Health Care

Numerous researchers have been working on the design and implementation of different IoT based health care services. Yet, there are a few difficulties and issues that should be deliberately addressed. Some of them are as follows:

9.8.1 Data Management

- Data storage and management: One of the significant research worries for the following couple of years may be the means by which to store information created by objects instead of the human population (Routray and Anand, 2017). With a specific end goal, we have to utilize systems and structures to assemble, store, and manage information formed in IoT procedures. Also, we require investigation apparatuses which could help in examining the created information for better results and upgrading the execution and generation of various applications.

- Data integrity: Data Integrity is one of the most noteworthy challenges in a data-centric environment. Detecting gadgets must assemble and offer information which is necessary to play out a required operation and guarantee that information isn't kept or shared endlessly. The processes of sharing and gathering information must utilize integrity as a major scale along with some standard protocols.

- Data confidentiality and privacy: As IoT deals with tracking, detecting, and associating daily existence objects utilized by people, this includes more concerns in regard to data protection and data leakage. This additionally delivers a lot of individual client data and thus increases the requirement for providing security and confidentiality (Usak et al., 2019). This generates a need for creating secured procedures for the collection of information and accessing it.

- Data interoperability: Patients would conceivably be gathering unmistakable data while utilizing these different restorative gadgets. For instance, a patient experiencing diabetes may consistently assemble the glucose reading and return it to their primary care physician, while also potentially gathering information related to their asthma issue on an alternate contraption, which may go to their asthma specialist. Numerous times, that the information the patient gathers stays in the limit lines of every one of the systems and IoT merchants and isn't perceptible to different structures. Henceforth, with the shortfall of more broad acknowledgment of adequate interoperability, data from different IoT gadgets may remain held in each individual framework and drop its worth to whatever is left of a patient's consideration bunch.

9.8.2 Device Management

- Device mobility and heterogeneity: One of the highlighting features in the enhancement of IoT is the versatility of smart devices. However, dealing with this gigantic measure of portable devices turns into a crucial test too. IoT utilizes the utilization of these gadgets with a greater rate of heterogeneity and versatility, so it must use frameworks that help these device properties.

- Device security and backup: Portable devices of IoT must be protected against assaults as these nodes might be the most prime targets of the assault and could

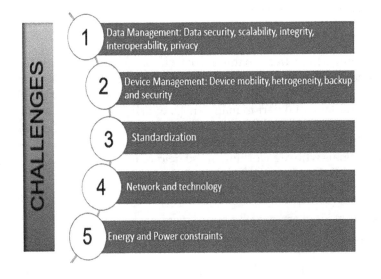

FIGURE 9.7
Challenges in IoT for healthcare.

easily give a portal to the attacker to get into the framework for harmful actions. This gives an assaulter an advantage to disturb the entire IoT operation significantly (Anjali and Kalbande, 2021).

1. Standardization: Modern IoT applications still do not have the worldwide principles that IoT empowered devices needs to take after. These models are extremely critical and have a major part for adaptability (scalability) and interoperability of IoT on a worldwide scale (Vashishtha et al., 2018).

2. The major associations that are working for setting principles for IoT are ANSI, IEEE, the European Committee for Electro-Technical Standardization, and the China Electronics Standardization Institute. In addition, these principles will likewise make it simple to persuade industrialists to utilize IoT empowered advancements.

3. These IoT empowered devices might utilize standard conventions and encryption systems possession, keeping in mind the end goal to make interoperability conceivable.

4. Network and technology: Considering the design, an IoT medicinal services system could be one of three kinds: data-centric, service-centric, and patient-centric designs. In the data-centric plan, health construction could be categorized into objects on the basis of collected health information of the patient. The healthcare structure is allotted by association of attributes that they should give in service-centric plan. In the patient driven plan, health care structures are separated by the contribution of patients and their relatives they deliberate for treatment. In such manner, the solution to the topic of which IoT network is the best suitable for health care resolves.

5. Power constraints: For constant running of IoT operations, gadgets will require a continuous power supply. These gadgets are not sufficiently rich, as far as memory and processing speed is concerned. So, these energy bound gadgets must be conveyed with lightweight components device communication and detection.

9.9 Conclusion

The IoT is becoming a huge trend in this era of technology and has the potential to affect the whole traditional business range. An increased number of determinations have been made in healthcare service and applications driven by IoT. IoT grounded health care network systems play a fundamental part in many areas, which include monitoring aging patients with chronic ailments and other serious health issues, and managing the health and well-being of the individuals. In sum, this paper could provide support to analysts, researchers, and IoT professionals who are working in the field of IoT healthcare technologies.

9.10 Future Prospect

The IoT healthcare system is still expanding. The IoT healthcare system has introduced many healthcare applications which have enhanced the structural working of the healthcare industry, yet there are some challenges faced by these technologies. Several issues, such as data management issues that include data privacy, storage, scalability and interoperability, device management challenges like device mobility, backup and security, standardization, network issues, and energy and power constraints are expected to facilitate a better healthcare network system.

References

A. Kazmi, M. Serrano, A. Lenis, et al. "A QoS-aware integrated management of IoT deployments in smart cities." In *IEEE 10th Conference on Service-Oriented Computing and Applications (SOCA)* (2017).

A.L. Paganelli, P.E. Velmovitsky, et al. "A conceptual IoT-based early-warning architecture for remote monitoring of COVID-19 patients in wards and at home." *Journal of Internet of Things* (2021).

A. Vashishtha, S. Dhir, and M. Hooda. "Smart cities in India: Revamping the street lighting system using IoT." In *Advanced Informatics for Computing Research (ICAICR)* (2018). Vol. 956. Springer, Singapore.

Y. Anjali, and D.R. Kalbande. "Ensuring security and privacy in IoT for healthcare applications." In *Cognitive Engineering for Next Generation Computing: A Practical Analytical Approach* (2021).

B. Sobhan Babu, K. Srikanth, T. Ramanjaneyulu, et al. *IoT for Healthcare* (2014).

B.Y. Lin, H.W. Hung, S.-M.T. Seng, et al. "Highly reliable and low-cost symbiotic IoT devices and systems." In *IEEE International Test Conference (ITC)* (2017).

S. Goyal, N. Sharma, B. Bhushan, et al. "IoT enabled technology in secured healthcare: Applications, challenges and future directions." In A. E. Hassanien, A. Khamparia, D. Gupta, et al. *Cognitive Internet of Medical Things for Smart Healthcare. Studies in Systems, Decision and Control*, vol. 311 (2021). Springer, Cham. doi:10.1007/978-3-030-55833-8_2.

H.H. Nguyen, F. Mirza, M. Asif Naeem, et al. "A review on IoT healthcare monitoring applications and a vision for transforming sensor data into real-time clinical feedback." In *IEEE 21st International Conference on Computer Supported Cooperative Work in Design (CSCWD)* (2017).

S. Krishnamoorthy, A. Dua, and S. Gupta. "Role of emerging technologies in future IoT-driven Healthcare 4.0 technologies: A survey, current challenges and future directions." *Journal Ambient Intell Human Compute* (2021). doi:10.1007/s12652-021-03302-w.

M. Haghi, S. Neubert, A. Geissler, H. Fleischer, N. Stoll, R. Stoll, and K. Thurow. "A flexible and pervasive IoT-based healthcare platform for physiological and environmental parameters monitoring." *IEEE Internet Things J.* 7 (2020): 5628–5647. doi:10.1109/JIOT.2020. 2980432.

M. Usak, M. Kubiatko, M. Shabbir, et al. "Health care service delivery based on the internet of things: A systematic and comprehensive study." *Int. Journal of Communication System* 33 (2019).

Md. Javaid, and Ibrahim Haleem Khan. "Internet of Things (IoT) enabled healthcare helps to take the challenges of COVID-19 Pandemic." *Journal of Oral Biology and Craniofacial Research* 11–12 (2021): 209–214.

N. Gupta, H. Saeed, S. Jha, et al. "Implementation of an IoT framework for smart healthcare." In *International Conference of Electronics Communication and Aerospace Technology (ICECA)* (2017).

P.D. Baruah, S. Dhir, and M Hooda. "Impact of IoT in current era." In *International Conference on Machine Learning, Big Data, Cloud and Parallel Computing (COMITCon)* (2019), pp. 334–339. ISBN: 978-1-7281-0211-5. IEEE.

P. Pace, R. Gravina, G. Aloi, et al. "IoT platforms interoperability for active and assisted living healthcare services support." In *Global Internet of Things Summit (GIoTS)* (2017).

R.K. Kodali, G. Swamy, and B. Lakshmi. "An implementation of IoT for healthcare." In *IEEE Recent Advances in Intelligent Computational Systems (RAICS)* (2015).

S. Bhardwaj, S. Dhir, and M. Hooda. "Automatic plant watering system using IoT." In *Second International Conference on Green Computing and Internet of Things (ICGCIoT)* (2019), pp. 659–663.

S.K. Routray, and S. Anand. "Narrowband IoT for healthcare." In *International Conference on Information Communication and Embedded Systems (ICICES)* (2017).

S.M. Riazul Isla, D. Kwak, M. D. Humaun Kabir, et al. *The Internet of Things for Health Care: A Comprehensive Survey* (2015).

S. Mishra, M. Hooda, S. Dhir, and A. Sharma. "iCop: A system for mitigation of felonious encroachment using GCM push notification." In *Advances in Intelligent Systems and Computing*, vol. 731 (June 13, 2018). Springer. ISBN: 978-981-10-8848-3.

S. Sapra, M. Hooda, A. Chhabra, and S. Dhir. "Smart med-minder." *Indian Journal of Public Health Research & Development* 9, no. 11 (2018): 661.

S. Sarkar, and R. Saha. "A futuristic IoT based approach for providing healthcare support through E-diagnostic system in India." In *Second International Conference on Electrical, Computer and Communication Technologies (ICECCT)* (2017).

O. Said, and A. Tolba "Design and evaluation of large-scale IoT-enabled healthcare architecture." *Applied Science* 11 (2021): 3623. doi:10.3390/app11083623.

Z. Pang. "Technologies and architectures of the Internet-of-Things (IoT) for health and well-being." In *Comput. Syst., KTH-Roy. Inst. Technology*, Stockholm, Sweden, 2013.

10

The Future of AI, IoT, Big Data and Block Chain Technology in Healthcare Industry: Challenges and Open Issues

Upasna Joshi

Delhi Technical Campus, Greater Noida, Uttar Pradesh, India

CONTENTS

DOI: 10.1201/9781003201960-10

10.1 Background and Motivation

AI consists of two words, "Artificial Intelligence" (Holzinger et al., 2019). Intelligence can be defined an ability of an individual to have more win-win conditions as compared to other fellows in a game. Machines are trained artificially like a human to solve the complex problems in an efficient way. Artificial intelligence is all about what teaches the machines/ devices to be more intelligent, so that they can efficiently think like a human being (Vrontis et al., 2021).

Artificial intelligence (AI) and related innovations are becoming more common in business and culture, and they're starting to emerge in the health care system. Many areas of healthcare services, as well as service provision within suppliers, funders, and medical companies, may be transformed by these innovations (Bullock et al., 2020). Nowadays, with the revolution in technology, the world is constantly changing. We have more devices around us than people, and devices are getting linked with us somehow in many ways. Smartphones and virtual assistants have become a part of our day to day life. From buying groceries to locating a partner, even daily chores and exercise have become simpler with the ease of technology (Mintz et al., 2019). Big data, artificial intelligence (AI), and optimization are at the core of the development of many of the world's most successful products, from Google to Uber, Alexa to Netflix. Smart devices and artificial intelligence, which are fostering a range of creativity that continues to change lives, further accelerated the fusion of technology and knowledge. Users can now track their wellness without the help of a physician (HCP) thanks to the arrival of health information technology.

Those changes were before COVID-19, a viral infection that changed the digital age. The World Health Organization (WHO) declared the coronavirus disease 2019 (COVID-19) outbreak a public health emergency on January 30, 2020, and it was classified as a pandemic months later (Allam et al., 2019; Briganti et al., 2020; Kaul et al., 2020). In the field of medicine, digital health has always played a significant role. Even so, the need to keep people connected and safe in their homes has been a challenge. Coronavirus accelerated the speed of adoption of digital technology in every sense. One of the most important weapons in the fight against the pandemic and maintaining healthcare service through the crisis was digital health. Similarly, algorithms can improve back-office procedures, improving patient hospital experiences while also saving money by decreasing waste and inefficiency--money that may then be invested in better patient care. Machine learning will benefit everyone in the long run, whether it's family physicians or assistants at the bedside. Data science will provide constructive feedback to boost productivity, consistency, and accuracy.

Speedy digital transformation is fostered by data insight and real-world proof, in which regulations are striving to stay up-to-date. A series of researches have shown us that AI might outperform as compared to the people assigned at vital health emergencies like disease diagnosis. Machine learning algorithms are already rivalling radiologists in detecting dangerous diseases like cancer and advising scholars to create new ways for such testing phases. The simulation of the artificial agents placed in adverse environments to get the information about current scenarios is the part of AI as well as. The tasks performed by the agents having certain types of characteristics, which will be like identification, understating, knowledge, real-time problem solving, learning, and execution of plans already planned. Artificial intelligence includes the different algorithms and techniques.

Training consists of reasoning based techniques; learning includes pattern prediction, character recognition, natural language processing, image recognition, and predication based upon the existing data, robotic applications, and nature-inspired learning.

10.1.1 History about Artificial Intelligence

Artificial intelligence is not a new branch of science. Ai emerged with the emergence of the modern computer system around the 1940s and 1950s. In the 1950s, computer scientists proposed a Turing test to see if either the machine could learn on its own or not. For this test, two people play roles of an interrogator and another, who checks the performance with the machine. The aim is to fool the interrogator to believe that it is human. If the machine successfully does so, then the conclusion is that the machine can think.

Due to recent advancements in artificial intelligence, its applications have been increased and used in many fields of study.

10.1.2 Architecture of Artificial Intelligence

Artificial intelligence revolves around us in every area of the field. It is the future of the next era, where we can feel its presence in every place at our home, at the office, in a building, inside the car, etc. Researchers are currently working in the field of study where they are trying to create devices that can beat human intelligence in any problem-solving tasks (Johnson et al., 2018; Nichols et al., 2019; Xu et al., 2019). The AI branches are mainly categorized into six branches, which are illustrated in the following figure.

In spite of its numerous applications, AI is planning its prominent role in field of Healthcare. The various AI tools present in the market are regularly updated and extensively used by physicians and practitioners. By using AI techniques, practitioners can perform the task efficiently, with less time and cost. It is expected that the artificial intelligence market size will grow exponentially from the present market size by 45% until 2026. The major reason behind this substantial growth is that the complexity and volume of healthcare data is increasing day by day necessitating the need to reduce the cost of computation by using various AI tools (Kreminski et al., 2020). The other major reason includes the multidisciplinary productions of products used for healthcare sectors. These tools aim to provide a common platform for all the users and end-users of the healthcare industry to provide and allocate resources that will benefit the time-saving process. The last and main motive to adopt such technology is that major giant biotechnologies and pharmaceutical companies need an advantage in increasing the productions of drugs and vaccines.

Initially, to train the data, data from various healthcare industries are collected to understand the relations and associations in the groups, clinical data, and in the different clinical diagnosis systems. The outcomes of the process generate features and significant characteristics, which are generally helpful in further processes. The clinical data may be the result of images, graphics, physical recordings, and electronic recordings from devices or

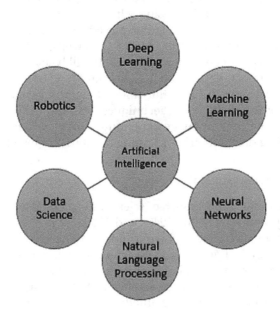

FIGURE 10.1
Categorization of AI specific areas.

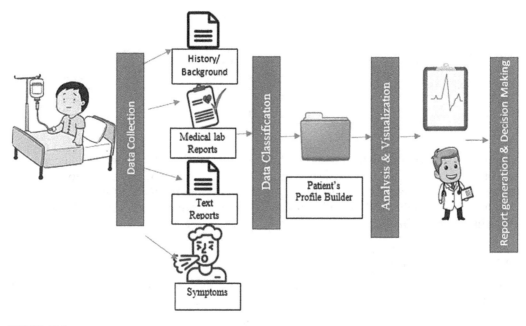

FIGURE 10.2
Architecture of AI based applications in healthcare.

in other formats. Until now, AI researchers and analysts have studied and worked on the various formats of this prospect. A major study of work is done on medical diagnosis images and on the genetic diagnosis, data collected using the electronic diagnosis images. Based upon the numerous amounts of data collection, AI techniques can be divided into two major categories. The first is the machine learning (ML) solution, and the second is natural language processing. Using the ML tools and techniques, one can conclude the disease diagnosis mechanism with the outcome as a result of the basis of characteristics and traits. In later used techniques, un-structured form data is aggregated and fed to some specific electronic devices and the outcome is regenerated through ML techniques by structural data.

10.1.3 Comparison to Traditional Machine Learning Mechanisms

The conventional approach includes all the useful ML algorithms that are able to train and manipulate the clinical data in an untestable format based upon the patient characteristics or may be depending upon the interests of medical practitioners. The medical data feed for training to the machine may be a patient's information (like height, weight, age, sex, pulse rate, oxygen level, etc.) or may be disease-oriented information like diagnosis results imaging, Electro physical test results, clinical test record, or data of physical examination. This data may also be composed of indicators related to diseases like cancer, where the indicator of tumours have size, shape, and spots (Keltch et al., 2014). To understand the concepts better, let patient have nth attributes as m^{th} patient as Xmn and resultant is Ymn. Usually based upon the desired results, ML algorithms are subdivided into supervised and unsupervised learning. The foremost reason for using the later one is forecasting through the association between the attributes of the patient and a desired results. Unsupervised

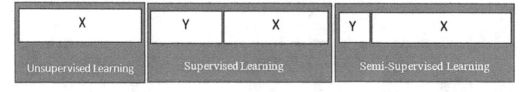

FIGURE 10.3
Categorization of ML approaches.

learning usually performs feature extraction. Other than these two, there is the combination of both the approaches, called semi-supervised learning, which is useful for the problem where information about outcome is not present (Hussain et al., 2020).

Some of the mainly used algorithms of AI in the Medicare industry are briefly discussed in the literature of this study.

10.1.3.1 Support Vector Machine

The first algorithm which is widely used in research work is support Vector machine (SVM). With the purpose of classification and regression, SVM uses the hyper plane, which can be used to categorize the data point manageably into such areas so that margins between the two different data points must be relevant. With the upcoming problem of missing clinical data, this can be used for diagnosis of the diseases like cancer and types of tumor, etc.

10.1.3.2 Neural Networks

These networks are represented in forms as different layers of neuron composed of input layer, hidden layer, and outcome layer. There may be multiple hidden layers respective to the objective function for generating the outcome. The structure is inspired from the behavior of the human brain, which consists of neurons that receive the signals, processes the data, and sends it to the output layer. In healthcare mainly, Neural Networks are used as Conventional Neural Network (CNN) and Recurrent Neural networks (RNN). The basic difference between the two is that the first one can take only fixed input blocks and generate fixed size outputs, whereas lthe second one will be helpful for more complicated problems that have variable data size of input and output. Neural Network has been used

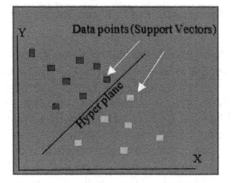

FIGURE 10.4
Support vector machines.

for the analysis of medical images, feature detection, and also predicting the future importance of drugs by identifying them through chemical structures. Google Deep Mind and IBM Watson have successfully developed the data learning model to use this approach, which is helpful for scanning the images through MRI for cardiac arrest.

With the diagnosis of any disease, affirmation is a very important aspect of making some medical decisions. For such purposes, the best is logistic regression, used for configuration of disease risk management analysis and used by the physicians for prediction and time analysis. It works on dependent variables only, whereas linear regression (Ahmadi et al., 2018) works on dependent and independent variables through the association between the variables to help detect the risk factors, as well predict the actual disease causing problems.

10.1.3.3 K-Nearest Neighbor Classification

Such classification techniques are used for the process for classification of data on the basis of nearest neighbor located. It is used widely for prediction and classification purposes.

Although AI is expanding exponentially in Medicare, still there are some major issues to be encountered. With the increase in research in the same area, various techniques are developed with time changes. But out of all projects, few of the approaches are successfully implemented in clinical trials. Still, there are some gaps in the study of the art and clinical practice. Some of them are listed in this section.

10.1.4 Key Challenges

Modeling through Machine Learning/AI tools: The number of AI tools is increasing, and researchers are expanding their scope, which is very satisfying. AI had a huge impact on the lives of humans. There are so many start-up companies, too, that are investing money in AI healthcare. The algorithms for disease diagnosis and prediction may use tons and tons of data to train the model, which requires huge computability that is not effectively used in normal computers. Although with enhancement in cloud and parallel, researchers can solve such a problem effectively, there are still some issues that medical staff and distributors need to face while running such models, as they consume much time, too.

10.1.4.1 Limited Knowledge of AI Tools

Nowadays, AI tools are being connected to every device in our home. They are a better way out than using the classical methods of solving real-time problems. Still, there are some regions worldwide where AI approach is distant; in that region, people are not connected through the internet; they have no providers like Google Cloud or Amazon Services. Underprivileged areas are most affected by the inability to use such techniques. Another limitation behind machine modeling is that it requires a lot of human effort to work effectively, for example, a machine learning algorithm that can categorize the image as a tumour or not requires the complete set of the algorithm to work with a good amount of accuracy, whereas a medical expert can easily categorize the study of a tumor in a minute. So, it's really a struggle to attain the level of accuracy and to reach a human level thinking process.

10.1.4.2 Implementation Issues

AI tools work only on data, but if the patient does not provide accurate data or refused to provide the data how can he be the diagnosis? Also, to make AI systems more efficient than today is a tedious task, as we know that AI has evolved through the various stages of development. Researchers want AI to create a human brain like a machine, and so imply that understanding how the machines derive the results are AI black-box problems which need to be solved with utmost priority.

10.1.4.3 Acceptance in Issues

AI solutions are not easy generated. If we are successful in doing so, using them for applications is also tedious work. There is gap between the industry that is using the tools and developers who are developing the tools. Hence, the patients and medical staff must be educated to the use of AI-based systems. Patient trust is a major issue in this area of study since we need data from the patient end, and patients also must trust AI based treatment. For example, AI based surgery through robotics includes the data from patients and other staff because we can't risk the patient's life, as AI systems always have ambiguous output. Also, patients should be mentally prepared to understand that being operated on by AI robotics can save time and resources of the overall system. In this case, the healthcare industry and developers need to build trust among patients and educate themselves and medical staff. Hospitals and the Medicare industry can build their own Ai based use-case, which involves the right strategy for implementation and deployment. Thus, this is not a single issue problem, AI problems are designed for every stakeholder.

10.1.4.4 Regular Monitoring

AI equipment can only solve the problems related to healthcare and data, which can be helpful in disease diagnosis, but if the patient is in adverse condition, expertise from the medical staff can only be helpful because then there is a requirement of regular monitoring of patients. Also, tracking the patients' mobility while being present in the room can only be provided by the medical staff. Sensors and ML algorithms can only give notifications and advice to the staff, but can't treat the patients and ensure recovery in some cases.

10.1.5 Open Issues

Also, there are some open issues that need to be addressed and that need lots of research. Healthcare security is a prominent concern, which includes the volume of patient and industrial data that can be misused in any way. According to some insider reports, 75% of healthcare data is under threat. Data security and privacy are the needs of the day. Also, systems must provide a guarantee to the users about the security and efficient use of data at any cost. Other than that, there are some social, cultural, ethical, and legal issues, too. These issues are region-based country-based or people based. The implication of issues causes the delay in the development of AI techniques and tools.

Sharing of databases and health records in the public domain evokes security issues. There is a need for high-end security to make the process secure and efficient in every way. No standards have been followed or implemented on the AI technology. Hence, the need for policymakers and stakeholders to set those standards is urgent.

Besides that, any AI systems also face some technical challenges that include transportation, energy resources, hardware and maintenance cost, and telecommunication networks. Such issues can also degrade the performance of AI in the healthcare industry.

10.2 Role of IoT Industry in Healthcare with its Vision and Scope

In the healthcare industry, patients are dependent on hospital management and doctors for regular health updates. With the use of IoT, a new recommendation system is emerging that can advise based on the health status of patients bysimply sending information through sensors or other nodes. Remote monitoring and remote sensing of patients and regular updates on the status of patients is only possible through IoT (Ngu et al., 2016). The healthcare industry and management can get regular updates even when they are not with the patients and can check for the updates regularly. IoT has revolutionized the healthcare industry through smart devices, and it's easy to use. Long queues in hospitals and clinics can be avoided if a patient directly connects to the physician through an app, and physicians can judge the patient's status based on their information. It is mush easier to monitor the patients and get updates whenever required than to go through the traditional system of visits to clinics and hospitals (Huh et al., 2017). This interaction process also includes the involvement of the patient as the doctor learns about the current status every time. Everything revolves around the data. The algorithms are getting the inputs and are producing the output through the machine learning process, so IoT is based upon the data and converting the data into an action format. Regular updates from patients, with no need for an emergency visit, can be helpful in improving their health status. Devices of IoTs connect with hardware responsible for generating the reports of patients.

10.2.1 Importance of IoT in Healthcare

The importance of IoT is not limited to certain applications of Healthcare. It is an emerging technology and increases its scope day by day. With the increase in its applications, some significant advantages of this technology are listed below:

10.2.1.1 Regular Monitoring

Devices connected to the internet, and in other formats, are useful in achieving the goals/ aim of physicians; they can observe, devise, and deduce some decisions based upon the status of the patient's health. Smart devices connected to each other through the internet are responsible for transforming the data from a raw format to a structural format and, with the help of physicians, can make decisions easily (Lee et al., 2015). Data can be collected in a format and stored on the cloud under the access of authorized persons only, which provides security and safety to data.

10.2.1.2 Reliability and Functionality

The major objective of the IoT is to enhance the connectivity of the device in order to enable the data to move freely inside the assigned systems that regulate efficiency and effectiveness. Based on various well advanced IoT protocols, IoT devices can detect the location of illness within seconds, thus saving time by giving results instantly.

10.2.1.3 Data Analysis

The vast amount of data related to patients, their history, and backgrounds and also related to the diseases are stored in the cloud. The analysis of such data and deducing the information is a major task. To do so, various IoT devices with ML techniques help to solve complex problems in a short time.

10.2.1.4 Instant Notification and Tracking

The data collected from the patients is transmitted to the system administrators/doctors from time to time. In case of any emergency or in any critical situation, patients get updates from the physicians and follow the instructions accordingly. Thus the IoT serves as a connecting platform among the devices.

10.2.1.5 Research Analysis

Apart from various applications, healthcare data can be used to discover and make new drug discoveries. The vast amount of data stored in the cloud is operated through supercomputers for research purposes (Elhoseny et al., 2018; Victor et al., 2021).

10.2.1.6 Improvement in Diseases Diagnosis

The diseases can be diagnosed with the help of various classical techniques that take a lot of time. IoT has made this process simple and relevant for all the users to diagnose the disease before time.

10.2.1.7 Fault Reduction

The data gathered from the various platforms help to visualize the patterns and characteristics with the minimum cost and errors. Based upon these advantages of IoT, the healthcare industry is booming and acting as a warrior for every disease or new challenge ever come. The question is how the data is accessed from the patient's body and how it reaches the next level of information. The solution to this problem is sensor devices or IoT nodes (Wu et al., 2020) these nodes are actually responsible for transmitting the information from source to destination.

10.2.2 Wearable Sensors

The nodes are used in the devices for hearing aid problems. They are placed inside the device and transform the sounds/information from the real world to the actual sound. The device is helpful in filtering and equalizing the layered sounds.

10.2.3 Ingestible Sensors

These are tiny nodes placed inside a patients' body that get information and updates regarding patients' bodies. These sensors are really helpful in various diseases and helped to regulate and monitor on a daily basis.

10.2.4 Motion Sensors

The nodes give the live tracking location of the patients, especially in the case of elderly patients and in the case of child movement. These nodes are acquitted with the GPS-enabled devices responsible for tracking the patients and people in any scenario.

10.2.5 Parameters based Sensors

These devices track the daily activity of a patient for the physician to get updates on various parameters like heart rate, blood pressure, body temperature, etc. These devices are equipped with the various sensor nodes used to detect the body's vital signs at anytime.

10.2.6 IoT Architecture in the Healthcare Industry

The architecture of IoT depends upon the use and application of the healthcare industry and where it is applied. The basic components behind the architecture of IoT based medical applications are explained below:

10.2.6.1 Infrastructure

The infrastructure of IoT based medical applications involve the software and hardware, as well as devices included to form the complete structure/framework.

10.2.6.2 Sensors

The tiny devices have limited storage so batteries are used to collect the data and aggregate it in any manner, then transmit it to the mobile station (Kumar et al., 2017; Patel et al., 2016). Depending upon the application, sensors are used inside the applications.

10.2.6.3 Connectivity

Communication between two endpoints is only possible through high-end connectivity. The smart devices are connected through the internet or with other technology like Bluetooth to provide the communication media between the nodes.

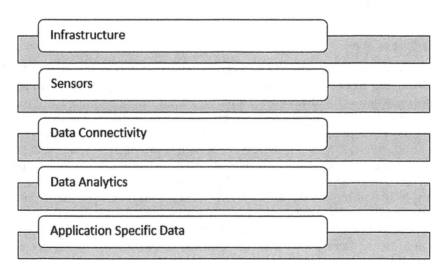

FIGURE 10.5
IoT framework in healthcare.

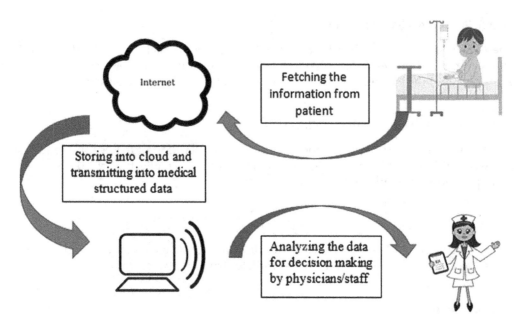

FIGURE 10.6
Framework of IoT healthcare applications.

10.2.6.4 Data Analysis

Data analysis is the concept of visualizing and analyzing the data to fetch results or decisions from them.

10.2.6.5 Application Specific

The smart IoT devices get input from smart monitors and displays showing the vital descriptions of health status and patient's reports.

10.2.7 Paradigms of IoT

In the last few decades, numerous research projects have been underway in the healthcare industry, and technology is playing a great role in managing the simulation part. Healthcare management is always a hot topic of interest for industrialists and researchers. With the demand in drug supply and a huge increase in health issues, there is a need to acquire the system capable of performing in every environment. Communication among patients, healthcare staff, and distributors is essential to provide information in the desired time period (Moosavi et al., 2015; Zgheib et al., 2017). IoT provides the one-stop platform for all the users who can have direct or indirect interest in the process. In India, medical facilities have also improved day by day. But because of its large population, it is a challenge. A new buzzword for IoT in the medical industry is 'IoMT'. IoMT is connected to sensor devices and health equipment used by the healthcare and medical field to monitor and track the patient's status. With the increase in the devices that generate medical reports, the IoMT system (with medical ecosystems, healthcare data, and other images) is capable of admirable output using data repositories like data servers and the cloud. Various companies are investing in the market based upon IoMT products like robotics, smart home, smart hospitals, smart speakers, and devices for the elderly. Consequently, the wearable industry is booming for the medical sector, and predictions are that, by 2025, this industry will be worth around $75 billion. The major devices have been introduced to the market. IoMT uses the vital signs and parameters through which these devices can interact with the patients and physicians. Hardware for IoT devices includes the built-in sensors, TCP-IP integration, and security information is that are incorporated in hardware devices like Arduino Yun, Raspberry Pi, etc. (Maktoubian et al., 2019).

10.2.8 Wireless Body Area Network with IoT Based Healthcare Industry

Generally, sensor nodes are placed in the body to detect and monitor the vital signs from the patient's body. These sensors are ingested by the patients or placed on the surface of the body. They are useful to diagnose diseases that are not easy to detect and where the reach of any device is not possible to capture the images. Thus, with the devices, the network is formed outside the body of a patient to aggregate and transmit the data. This information is used by the observer for furture recommendations. The network is called a Wireless Body Area Network (Bajaj et al., 2020; Onasanya et al., 2019). Smartphones and smart devices act as the bridge between WBAN and IoT and are helpful in the detection of diseases at early stages, sending notifications and emergency calls to the doctors. The key components in the development of WBAN are wearable sensors. The tiny nodes have certain issues, too, which may cause problems and affect the system's efficiency over time. These tiny devices have limited storage and battery capacity, so power restriction is a major concern in IoT enabled body area networks. Thus, with the aim of energy harvesting, such modules and techniques are developed so that the system becomes more flexible and relevant.

WBANs coordinate with a biochemical sensor network that really is intuitive and highly advanced, to control real-world medical problems. WBANs can be categorized into three hierarchical levels. The first level is composed of a Body Area Network, where Body Sensor Nodes (BSNs) are inserted in the human body to measure the medical parameters. These

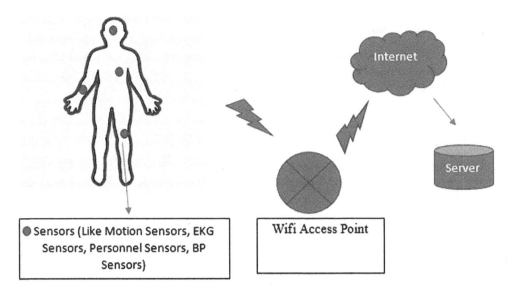

FIGURE 10.7
Configuration of body area network.

nodes send the data to the nodes controller of the body (NCs). The NCs aggregate and communicate further to the Base station placed outside the body. Data get stored in a cloud that can be easy to access by specific medical applications placed in hospitals, clinics, or homes, etc. In the case of Intra-WBANs, due to dynamic physical phenomena, energy consumption and the short span of batteries are the key design issues (Kumar et al., 2020; Pang 2013). In the case of any diabetic patients or any corona virus-infected patients, patient temperature, oxygen level, and pulse rate are essential after every interval of time. The data collected get stored at the hospital internal server, where the patient has access to data through a mobile or PC. This pandemic era has given researchers a new direction to research in the current field of study. WBANs coordinate with a biochemical sensor network that really is intuitive and highly advanced, to control the real-world medical problems.

Out of all the many protocols that have been designed; the Zig Bee protocol is most popular, in which transmission is made through an internet connection or Wi-Fi or Bluetooth. This is designed for short distances, i.e., around 300 meters, whereas Bluetooth has a lesser range of 10 meters for small scale data aggregation. Wi-Fi has a wider range, with high intensity of speed and bandwidth. It is used for long-range communication between the nodes and devices.

10.2.9 Relevance to COVID-19 Situation

The corona virus has become a major concern nowadays due to its drastic infectious spread over almost all the countries in the world. Not only the general populace, but frontline workers, including doctors, staff, and health workers, got this infection in huge numbers. Also, with the increase in cases all over the world, it is observed that the shortage of beds has become a serious problem (Kallel et al., 2021; de Morais et al., 2021). These two issues also boost the development of IoMT, where the patient can be cured without visiting hospitals. Thus, the spread of virus can be minimized also. Patient travel and direct contact with health workers (and vice versa) can be avoided by such techniques. This technology is also cost-effective and time-saving in all ways.

10.2.10 Challenges in IoMT

Divergence of the applications of IoT in all areas, like telemedicine, tele-consultancy, traffic control, and smart living has changed the world; but, with the increase in the impact of such technology, there are many challenges to face (Selvaraj et al., 2020). including these discussed below:

10.2.10.1 Reliability

The major concern that affects the overall efficiency and performance is Reliability. The system must perform in all vulnerable situations where even the chance of failure may occur. Also, at every point of time, the information must be accurate and consistent. Integrity must be ensured in the system.

10.2.10.2 Safety

As an IoMT system is composed of lots of devices and components, it must be designed to provide safety to every user operating the system. The devices must not harm any other being who is in contact with the device directly or directly.

10.2.10.3 Security

As the systems may collect the information or data from one user or among multiple users, security is a major concern. Security of data and information stored on large server farms, local servers, or the cloud is essential, so there is a need for implementation and policy guidelines that make the network connection more secure and safe to use.

10.2.10.4 Authorization and Authentication

Verification of the authorized user who wants to access the data and validation of that data is essential. Failing verification and validation, the system must ensure that the data must not be accessed.

10.2.10.5 Accuracy and Integrity

There is a huge gap between the research and implementation. The physical world problems are different than the virtual world mechanisms, so the system must be able to adapt to rapid changes accordingly to the environmental conditions. Also, it must support all the modelings of classical medical systems and their requirements. Output in the defined time period and the resultant output is also a major issue that must be faced by the innovators and designers.

10.2.10.6 Cost Effectiveness

The infrastructure includes a combination of hardware and software parts. The components required to manufacture the medical systems are not very effective. Due to such issues, many countries are lagging behind on such technologies, as there are so many places in the world that are not connected to the internet itself. Without basic internet infrastructure, the probability of adoption of such technology is negligible.

10.2.11 Future of IoT

A pandemic like COVID-19 may only be cured or prevented with the IoMT enabled technology, as this technology provides a way to adopt to new changes to the market. Clinics and hospitals are providing tele-consultancy and adopting new scenarios in this pandemic, where patients cannot interact directly with physicians. In such cases, wearable devices have given a new direction to the pandemic disease where patients can self-monitor and treat themselves when with limited resources (De Michele et al., 2019).

With increased development in the 5 G networks, the future of IoT is augmented with faster communication speed between the patient and care providers than the 4 G technology. With adherence to IoT devices, patients can use smart devices at home to monitor the sleep rate, pulse rate, oxygen level, and body temperature, etc. The sensors that regulate the complete systems are directly or indirectly connected with the devices and generate the notifications at every new level or for any reminders. Thus new pandemic roll has increased the progress and adoption of new technology, and also increases the challenges for its advancements. IBM is utilizing this technology in hospitals to check washing hands of patients.

Another example is, in case of any accidents while using IoT devices, track the patient's status and search for nearby hospitals to suggest them for an emergency call or ambulance.

This pandemic era has given researchers a new direction to research in the current field of study. The scope of the evolution in medical industry is not limited to home treatments or the development of smart devices and sensors. The scope of this innovative industry is vast.

10.3 Big Data in Healthcare Industry

The field of study allows collection of a large scale volume of data, visualization, analysis, and using it in any form according to a given set of problems by the data designer and analyzer. Big Data has opened new ways to analyze the data and use it in any form. The applications have been expanded in every field of our life. But for the healthcare industry, big data has proven to be a boon to mankind. The technology can minimize the treatment cost, prediction, and prevention of deadly diseases and is useful in discovering drugs. With the expansion in population worldwide and continuous reduction of resources, humans are facing new challenges regularly (Baro et al., 2015). The collection data and analyses of data based on the techniques and approaches have given a new medical industry direction. The health professionals are finding a new solution for medical issues with the help of such technological evolutions (Senthilkumar et al., 2018).

Traditional systems failed to organize and analyze the qualitative and quantitative data of huge volume. Although there are many definitions of Big Data, it is well known for its 3 Vs. (Volume, Velocity, and Variety). This statement implies that data in the world is changing and increasing day by day in its volume already known for its size. Velocity refers to the speed of processing, storing, and analyzing the data, whereas the last keyword, variety, indicates the managed and unmanaged data used in an optimized way in different applications. In spite of this, Big Data has changed the way of organizing structured and unstructured

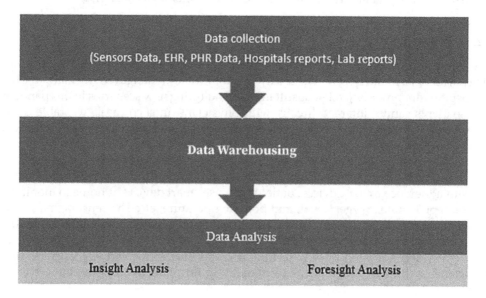

FIGURE 10.8
Process in data analysis.

data in any form, collecting from various resources like hospitals, clinics, a patient's record, and history data to solve complex problems in a lesser amount of time. It means that the aggregation is done by digitizing everything in any way and analyzing to make some decisions in the large volume of data, which is organized in such a structured format that it can be easy to use through the software and combination of hardware devices and other system processes.

Healthcare is a major sector of investment nowadays. Despite its numerous applications and aim of wellness, diagnosis and health treatment consist of major components of healthcare professionals and facilities. The data storage and ease of accessing the data are important; to make the process easy, Electronic Health Records (EHR) helps to store the majority of data, storing the information related to the patient's history, disease diagnosis, and treatment process information (like results, medical lab reports). The treatment and diagnosis of diseases in a given time constraint is essential. Other than the EHR, the other digital systems like (Electronic Medical Record) EMR, Personal Health Record (PHR), and all the record-based systems have vast potential to enhance the healthcare service, efficiency, productivity, and healthcare facility costs. Using such real-time systems of medical care facilities have increased the speed of generating the results and predicting diseases, diagnosis of diseases, and sending the notifications regularly and on time. The digital medical system helps to monitor periodically and is dedicated to improving productivity in estimated costs. Sources of data are not limited but are diversified in every sector, either public sector or private. The following figure shows the diversification of Big Data sources from various fields.

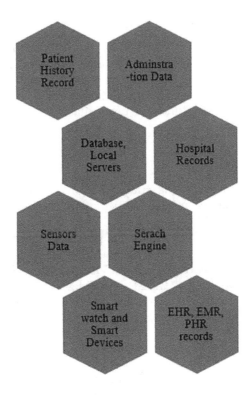

FIGURE 10.9
Application of big data.

10.3.1 Applications of Big Data

The big data application are expanding its fields and sector in every way.

10.3.1.1 Wellness of Mankind

The various smart devices, like smart watches, smartphones, and other gadgets, have become a part of everybody's life. These devices track and control oxygen levels, blood pressure levels, and physical activities. Finally, the data that get stored in cloud servers can be used for further analysis and research.

10.3.1.2 Diseases Diagnosis and Prediction

Diseases are diagnosed through the latest technology. Big Data uses AI and ML techniques to quantify the data and classify the data. Then, in the end, apply the best strategy for the resultant output it generates. Predication of pandemic and epic diseases and their cause and prevention techniques of illness may be diagnosed through Data mining and analysis.

10.3.1.3 Reduction in Errors

A decision support system like Medware helps reduce prescription errors and save millions of patients' lives. According to the study, prescription errors affect millions of people and put their lives at risk.

10.3.1.4 Reduction in Overall Cost

The data managed by the cloud and analyzed by big data analytics gives clinical insights not otherwise possible. Also, such expert systems advise physicians regarding treatment and medicines, thus avoiding guesswork. Also, it deeply analyzes the patient data and predicts the patient's health status sooner to ignore the risk by giving the prevention. It also predicts the system processes, finds the best suitable protocols available and predicts the outcome.

10.3.1.5 Research and Study

The major part of Big Data helps find the study of new medicines and their discovery trends in diseases and overcome the system's techniques and implementation. The research using Big Data in healthcare is useful to simplify complex problems that humans cannot solve, and is even beneficial to analyze and predict the pandemic disease and find methods like vaccination and drugs to overcome such diseases. For example, many researchers have published their works on the pandemic Corona Virus (COVID-19). The research indicates the trends and future spread of virus and also provides techniques to maintain social distancing, observe masks at public places, and prevent infection rate predication based upon the symptoms.

10.3.1.6 Social Cause Prediction

A large volume of data from various countries and different peoples are gathered to analyze the data in its trends. In its strategies, the data source collection is based on geographic, cultural, or demographic factors.

10.3.2 Challenges in Big Data

Despite its emerging application, many challenges are also faced, as discussed below:

10.3.2.1 Data Storage

The storage of a large volume of data is one of the primary issues that can arise, but many applications can be multiple local storage servers. The usage of server storage provides access of data at all times. Another option of external storage of data is expensive but provides reliability. The organization must comply with selecting the best storage strategy that fulfils the demands of the user's requirements while also being available any time.

10.3.2.2 Data Cleaning

The process of excluding unwanted information from relevant data is a cumbersome task. It requires the AI/ML approach(s) to establish the complete setup for this task. Although it can be done manually, it is really difficult to execute the filtration process without any error in the case of large scale data. The process must be adopted to remove the unintended information without harming any data flow and actual data.

10.3.2.3 Data Security

Many security attacks, phishing, hacking, and ransom attacks are common dangers. Organizations are also working on security protocols and implementing them to avoid any malicious attacks on their data. Some major security reasons that are in focus are encryption, data hiding approaches, firewalls, and authentication processes.

10.3.3 Scope in Healthcare

The scope of healthcare has provided new ways for researchers, academicians, industry, and entrepreneurs to work and invest in the future of the Medicare industry. The future work needs to be comprised of many capacities that are detailed here:

1. The medical organization prerequisite is to establish a big data research center through which it can manage the entire information of data and where reliability is a major concern.
2. An organization is required to decide and select the best out of all strategies, depending upon the data of an organization.
3. The big data developers should focus on the milestones, aims, and objectives of adjusting the data analytics to the organizations.
4. The regular interval of trends, security, internal and external systems, applications, and software developments give the long-term solutions to the organizations.

10.4 BlockChain in Healthcare

In healthcare, the government is investing on a regular basis; also, a major part of GDP is investing in this area, but still hospital prices are rising. Blockchain can improve performance and attain the efficiency to manage diseases. Blockchain is the set of chunks of data linked together in the form of a block. Each block is linked to other blocks through the set of cryptographic keys. These keys are to be kept in some record format like hash keys to provide the connectivity to the combination of nodes. The advantages of the high scale technology mainly include the network's security, verification, and authentication approaches to the authorization process (Sylim et al., 2018). The applications are applied to many healthcare fields, where security is the main aim of technology. The public data records are easy to access for such problems. Private, secure blockchains are providing the solution to the problems. The application includes the authorization and verification of the users. It also provides the security and policies for data connectivity to an organization. With the increase in electronic health records, medical reports and lab data, the blockchain has the solution to improve the quality and security of data. It can aggregate the data from various resources, generate the digital record based on the data parameters, and send it to the physician to treat the patients.

The blockchain has expanded its arms, including major applications. The work of research is under the following consequent areas. Blockchain provides a one-in-all platform to facilitate the digital data where different physicians, hospitals and medical reports get uploaded on the cloud to analyze it and to generate a one record file used for predication, treatment, diagnosis, etc. Additionally, to maintain the secure transaction and safe supply chain integration among the suppliers and consumers, dealers will be required. The new drug discovery and research are benefited through this approach. The process forms the rule-based criteria through the data it executes. For example, what if, in an emergency, the patients get the updates and alerts through the profile and provide the gateway for payment to the providers.

10.4.1 Challenges and Open Issues of Blockchain Technology

The challenges of the blockchain industry include the difficulty in marinating the data storage and sending the data for further applications (Haq et al., 2018). There is the requirement to overcome the following challenges before adopting the technology in the healthcare field.

10.4.1.1 Cultural Revolution

The adoption of technology among patients and physicians is the major concern of the day. There are still cases where doctors physically examine the patients and prescribe the medicines on paper. In these scenarios, technology needs a lot of time to transform the records from paper to digital records. Another issue can arise when the technology does not accept the records that are left blank. In such cases, the obstacles are bigger. People behaviour is another factor caused by cultural, socio, and economic factors; thus, technology acceptance is the question mark.

10.4.1.2 Distributed Data

The healthcare data is not centralized and also impossible to place entirely at one place. Due to its distributed nature and undefined format, it is problematic to tackle the data. This data is composed of various other components to make it useful in an application and consolidation in one platform is challenging.

10.4.1.3 Business Aspects of the Data

Data can't be shared with other agencies in any form. For example, by transferring the patient's data to hospitals, the data can be misused or used by other business companies for their use.

10.4.1.4 Viable Technology

Still there is no hard core proof that any emerging technology can the save the patient's life. The technology needs lots of changes and improvements to find the best solution to any emergency or dynamic problem.

10.5 Conclusion

The day is not far when robots can perform the surgeries, and smart devices operate and advise the patients, using the technologies like AI, Big Data, BlockChain, and IoT. With the advancement in recent trends of technology (AI, Big Data, BlockChain and IoT), it will be taking the world in its hand. The day is not far when the patient's death date is predictive also. The development is increasing day by day and is unstoppable. Although these applications are very beneficial in reducing the patients time and money, it is still hard to understand and depend on the technology to put a patient's life on stack. Devices are trained to suggest diets, sleep patterns, medicines, health status, etc. Healthcare has the potential to unlock all the locks of traditional clinical systems through technological innovations. In fact, there is a need to remove the obstacles to attain efficiency and better performance of the healthcare industry.

References

Allam, Z., and Dhunny, Z.A. "On big data, artificial intelligence and smart cities." *Cities* 89 (2019): 80–91.

Ahmadi, H., Bouallegue, R., Viani, F., and Massa, A. "An improved prediction based strategy for target tracking in wireless sensor networks." *International Journal of Internet Technology and Secured Transactions* 8, no. 3 (2018): 453–468.

Bullock, J., Luccioni, A., Pham, K.H., Lam, C.S.N., and Luengo-Oroz, M. "Mapping the landscape of artificial intelligence applications against COVID-19." *Journal of Artificial Intelligence Research* 69 (2020): 807–845.

Briganti, G., and Moine, O.L. "Artificial intelligence in medicine: Today and tomorrow." *Frontiers in Medicine* 7 (2020): 27.

Baro, E., Degoul, S., Beuscart, R., and Chazard, E. "Toward a literature-driven definition of big data in healthcare." *BioMed Research International* (2015).

Bajaj, K., Sharma, B., and Singh, R. "Integration of W.S.N. with IoT applications: A vision, architecture, and future challenges." (2020): 79–102.

De Michele, R., and Furini, M. "IoT healthcare: Benefits, issues and challenges." In *Proceedings of the 5th E.A.I. International Conference on Smart Objects and Technologies for Social Good*, pp. 160–164, 2019.

de Morais Barroca Filho, I., Aquino, G., Malaquias, R.S., Girão, G., and Menêzes Melo, S.R. "An IoT-based healthcare platform for patients in I.C.U. beds during the COVID-19 outbreak." *IEEE Access* 9 (2021): 27262–27277.

Elhoseny, M., Ramírez-González, G., Abu-Elnasr, O.M., Shawkat, S.A., Arunkumar, N., and Farouk, A. "Secure medical data transmission model for IoT-based healthcare systems." *IEEE Access* 6 (2018): 20596–20608.

Huh, S., Cho, S., and Kim, S. "Managing IoT devices using blockchain platform." In *2017 19th International Conference on Advanced Communication Technology (ICACT)*, pp. 464–467. IEEE, 2017.

Haq, I., and Esuka, O.M. "Blockchain technology in pharmaceutical industry to prevent counterfeit drugs." *International Journal of Computer Applications* 180, no. 25 (2018): 8–12.

Holzinger, A., Langs, G., Denk, H., Zatloukal, K., and Müller, H. "Causability and explainability of artificial intelligence in medicine." *Wiley Interdisciplinary Reviews: Data Mining and Knowledge Discovery* 9, no. 4 (2019): e1312.

Hussain, A.A., Bouachir, O., Al-Turjman, F., and Aloqaily, M. "AI techniques for COVID-19." *IEEE Access* 8 (2020): 128776–128795.

Johnson, K.W., Soto, J.T., Glicksberg, B.S., Shameer, K., Miotto, R., Ali, M., Ashley, E., and Dudley, J.T. "Artificial intelligence in cardiology." *Journal of the American College of Cardiology* 71, no. 23 (2018): 2668–2679.

Keltch, B., Lin, Y., and Bayrak, C. "Comparison of A.I. techniques for prediction of liver fibrosis in hepatitis patients." *Journal of Medical Systems* 38, no. 8 (2014): 1–8.

Kumar, N. "IoT architecture and system design for healthcare systems." In *2017 International Conference on Smart Technologies for Smart Nation (SmartTechCon)*, pp. 1118–1123. IEEE, 2017.

Kreminski, M., Dickinson, M., Mateas, M., and Wardrip-Fruin, N. "Why are we like this?: The A.I. architecture of a co-creative storytelling game." In *International Conference on the Foundations of Digital Games (FDG 2020)*, pp. 1–4. IEEE, 2020.

Kumar, K., Kumar, N., and Shah, R. "Role of IoT to avoid spreading of COVID-19." *International Journal of Intelligent Networks* 1 (2020): 32–35.

Kallel, A., Rekik, M., and Khemakhem, M. "IoT-fog-cloud based architecture for smart systems: Prototypes of autism and COVID-19 monitoring systems." *Software: Practice and Experience* 51, no. 1 (2021): 91–116.

Kaul, V., Enslin, S., and Gross, S.A. "History of artificial intelligence in medicine." *Gastrointestinal Endoscopy* 92, no. 4 (2020): 807–812.

Lee, I., and Lee, K. "The Internet of Things (IoT): Applications, investments, and challenges for enterprises." *Business Horizons* 58, no. 4 (2015): 431–440.

Moosavi, S.R., Gia, T.N., Rahmani, A.-M., Nigussie, E., Virtanen, S., Isoaho, J., and Tenhunen, H. "S.E.A.: A secure and efficient authentication and authorization architecture for IoT-based healthcare using smart gateways." *Procedia Computer Science* 52 (2015): 452–459.

Maktoubian, J., and Ansari, K. "An IoT architecture for preventive maintenance of medical devices in healthcare organizations." *Health and Technology* 9, no. 3 (2019): 233–243.

Mintz, Y., and Brodie, R. "Introduction to artificial intelligence in medicine." *Minimally Invasive Therapy & Allied Technologies* 28, no. 2 (2019): 73–81.

Ngu, A.H., Gutierrez, M., Metsis, V., Nepal, S., and Sheng, Q.Z. "IoT middleware: A survey on issues and enabling technologies." *IEEE Internet of Things Journal* 4, no. 1 (2016): 1–20.

Nichols, J.A., Herbert Chan, H.W., and Baker, M.A.B. "Machine learning: Applications of artificial intelligence to imaging and diagnosis." *Biophysical Reviews* 11, no. 1 (2019): 111–118.

Onasanya, A., and Elshakankiri, M. "Smart integrated IoT healthcare system for cancer care." *Wireless Networks* (2019): 1–16.

Pang, Z. "Technologies and architectures of the Internet-of-Things (IoT) for health and well-being." PhD diss., KTH Royal Institute of Technology, 2013.

Patel, K.K., and Patel, S.M. "Internet of things-IoT: Definition, characteristics, architecture, enabling technologies, application & future challenges." *International Journal of Engineering Science and Computing* 6, no. 5 (2016).

Senthilkumar, S.A., Rai, B.K., Meshram, A.A., Gunasekaran, A., and Chandrakumarmangalam, S. "Big data in healthcare management: A review of literature." *American Journal of Theoretical and Applied Business* 4, no. 2 (2018): 57–69.

Sylim, P., Liu, F., Marcelo, A., and Fontelo, P. "Blockchain technology for detecting falsified and substandard drugs in distribution: Pharmaceutical supply chain intervention." *JMIR Research Protocols* 7, no. 9 (2018): e10163.

Selvaraj, S., and Sundaravaradhan, S. "Challenges and opportunities in IoT healthcare systems: A systematic review." *S.N. Applied Sciences* 2, no. 1 (2020): 1–8.

Victor Hugo, C., and Hareesha, K.S. *IoT in Healthcare and Ambient Assisted Living.* Edited by Gonçalo Marques and Akash Kumar Bhoi. Springer, 2021.

Vrontis, D., Christofi, M., Pereira, V., Tarba, S., Makrides, A., and Trichina, E. "Artificial intelligence, robotics, advanced technologies and human resource management: A systematic review." *The International Journal of Human Resource Management* (2021): 1–30.

Wu, T., Fan W., Qiu, C., Redouté, J.-M., and Yuce, M.R. "A rigid-flex wearable health monitoring sensor patch for IoT-connected healthcare applications." *IEEE Internet of Things Journal* 7, no. 8 (2020): 6932–6945.

Xu, J., Yang, P., Xue, S., Sharma, B., Sanchez-Martin, M., Wang, F., Beaty, K.A., Dehan, E., and Parikh, B. "Translating cancer genomics into precision medicine with artificial intelligence: Applications, challenges and future perspectives." *Human Genetics* 138, no. 2 (2019): 109–124.

Zgheib, R., Conchon, E., and Bastide, R. "Engineering IoT healthcare applications: Towards a semantic data driven sustainable architecture." In *eHealth*, vol. 360, pp. 407–418. Springer, Cham, 2017.

11

Modern Machine Learning and IoT Applications for Personalized Healthcare: Opportunities and Challenges

P. Sriramalakshmi, Shreyaa Parvath Rajkumar, and R. Nivedhithaa
Vellore Institute of Technology, Chennai, India

CONTENTS

DOI: 10.1201/9781003201960-11

11.1 Introduction

Personalized healthcare is a term used to describe the process of recording and analyzing data about the particular patient's clinical history and risk factors and providing personalized treatment and care. The term has gained popularity recently due to the increase in production of wearable sensor network devices in the market. These wearable devices are also known as IoMT devices.

Internet of Medical Things or IoMT is popularly known as a collection of medical devices and/or applications that can link to healthcare information technology systems using networking technologies (Al-Turjman et al., 2020). It minimizes the need for extraneous hospital visits and the burden of the healthcare systems by connecting patients to their doctors and aiding the relay of a large amount of data over a secure network. The way healthcare is approached worldwide has changed radically with the expansion of the Internet of Medical Things or IoMT as it is commonly referred, owing to the growth of smart sensors and devices in the healthcare sector.

The market includes smart appliances, namely, wearables and medical/vital monitors, strictly for healthcare purposes on the body, at the patient's house, or in a community, or in clinics and hospitals, and real-time location, telehealth, and other services. Some examples of IoMT devices are discussed in Section 11.3.

IoMT can be classified into various segments as listed below:

11.1.1 On-Body Segment

This segment can be customarily categorized based on their target users; these could be daily consumers who use consumer health wearables or hospitals which require medical and clinical-grade wearables.

- Consumer health wearables:
  This category comprises devices that are not under any regulation by healthcare and medical authorities and are mainly used for personal health and individual wellness.

  E.g.,: activity trackers, bands, wristbands, sports watches, etc.
- Clinical-grade wearables:
  On the other hand, these devices are under regulation and used in association with the supporting platforms that are certified by health authorities. Devices of this kind require the concurrence of specialist advice or a prescription from a doctor.

  E.g., The Smart belt, introduced by Active Protective, which combines its fall detection capabilities with a hip safe-guarding deployment for aged users, Halo

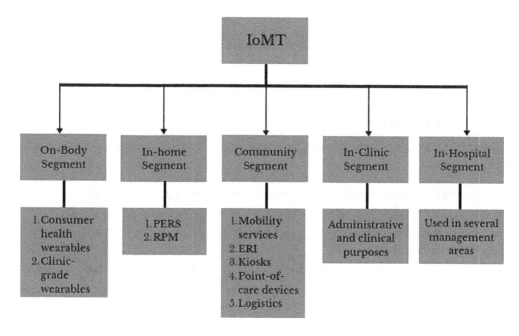

FIGURE 11.1
Segments of IoMT.

Neuroscience's Halo Sport headset, aimed to stimulate areas of the brain responsible for muscle memory, strength, and toleration during strenuous physical activity; and Neurometrix Quell, a wearable device with neuromodulation capabilities that can provide relief from chronic pain on the sensory nervous level.

11.1.2 In-Home Segment

This includes personal emergency response and remote patient monitoring systems:

- A Personal Emergency Response System (PERS) is a diffusion of wearable devices and a live call center service to increase self-reliance for the patients. It allows the patient to communicate and receive emergency medical care.
- Remote Patient Monitoring System (RPM) integrates home monitoring devices and sensors used for chronic disease management. The benefits of the system are mentioned in Section 11.2.2.

11.1.3 Community Segment

This segment includes five components:

- Mobility services
- Emergency Response Intelligence
- Kiosks
- Point-of-care devices
- Logistics

11.1.4 In-Clinic Segment

It includes IoMT devices employed for administrative and clinical purposes. An example of such a device is a cloud-based examination platform for doctors/physicians/specialists to assess patients at any point.

11.1.5 In-Hospital Segment

This segment consists of devices used in hospitals in several management areas, such as the following:

- Asset management monitors that track the assets throughout the facility.
- Personnel management helps to keep track of staff efficiency and productivity.
- Patient flow management enhances patient experience by monitoring the patient arrival times and so on.
- Inventory management helps reduce inventory costs and improve staff efficiency.
- Environment and energy monitoring help keep optimal conditions in the patient rooms and storage areas. It also oversees the usage of electricity.

Data procured from smart healthcare devices (wearables, ingestible sensors, etc.) can be effectively gathered and computed to analyse evaluative conditions by using Artificial Intelligence (AI) and Machine Learning (ML) based algorithms. Various machine learning algorithms such as SVM, Decision Tree, KNN, Random Forest, etc., are used for disease diagnosis and prediction (Singh et al., 2021a). The types of learning: supervised, unsupervised, semi-supervised, and reinforcement learning. Some commonly used ML algorithms, such as decision tree (DT), k-nearest neighbor (KNN), support vector machine (SVM), naïve Bayes, k-mean, q-learning, etc., techniques also help in disease diagnosis and prediction (Singh et al., 2021b). Cloud based architectures like Big Data analysis do not perform well and are not reliable when security and latency-critical IoT applications are taken into consideration. In the case of the user being a patient with time-sensitive healthcare requirements, the necessity for a device with greater reliability and accessibility is high. Disconnection from the network or bandwidth variations can have a fatalistic impact.

Recently, the use of architectures involving Fog and Edge Computing has seen significant growth.

- *Edge Computing* occurs on a gateway device (device that is physically close to the sensor) or a device that is connected to the sensor. Some examples of edge nodes are smartphones, smart watches, microcontrollers, etc.
- *Fog computing* nodes operate at LAN levels. They involve bigger devices like PCs and local servers that may be physically farther away from the sensors.

The above two paradigms are usually carried out together, and they have a reduction in latency and higher availability.

On one side, the mobile cloud computing model (MCC) boasts superior rates of data transmission, but suffers from limited coverage. Whereas the mobile edge computing model (MEC) provides a lower rate of latency. In the IoT-based field of healthcare, a progressive transition from MCC to MEC and reliable edge models has been noticed in recent years.

11.2 Modern Machine Learning and IoT Applications for Personalized Healthcare

11.2.1 Architecture

As mentioned above, the use of architectures involving Fog and Edge Computing has seen notable growth in recent years. In the personalised healthcare domain, the use of these architectures pertains to designing remote monitoring models that are part of the field and wearable sensor networks used for fulfilling preventive and predictive methods in systems of personalised healthcare. The contributions toward this in the scientific community mostly include fog nodes that exist in the form of local servers that perform collection, analysis, and processing of the data generated by IoMT devices.

In earlier times, most of the proposals for remote monitoring of the patients were, for the most part, PC based systems. For example, they used data generated by ECG and accelerometers to inform the doctor or clinician regarding episodes of irregular and elevated heart rates, which helped mitigate precarious situations. Subsequently, the use of microcontrollers to collect data from sensors saw huge growth (Greco et al., 2020).

In the last few years, the growth of IoT technology has led the way to various smarter solutions for several aspects of the healthcare industry. These solutions utilize both software platform domains and network architectures. The aspects that are addressed include the following:

- pediatrics, and geriatric care
- monitoring chronic diseases
- epidemic disease care
- cyber-physical systems in the medical domain
- private healthcare and fitness

The architecture for general solutions aimed at health monitoring problems is split into two categories, namely, static remote monitoring and dynamic remote monitoring.

Static remote monitoring is for patients who are supposed to be in a building, i.e., in their home or in the hospital, whereas dynamic remote monitoring is for patients that need to be monitored when they are on-the-go.

For general solutions, a multilevel architecture is employed, as depicted in Figure 11.2. It could involve various computation levels, such as edge, fog, and cloud computing.

- Edge Computing Level: In this level, portable devices such as smartphones, smartwatches, and other compact devices are pre-process and perform ancillary elaborations on the data collected from IoMT devices (such as wearables).
- Fog Computing Level: Here, PCs, gateways, and servers collect the data sourced from the in-field sensor networks in association with edge devices for local computing and processing.
- Cloud Computing Level: In the cloud computing level, cloud services perform high level processing, complex computations, and remote data storage.

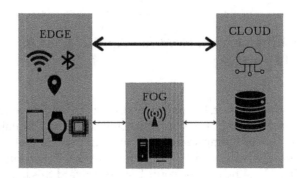

FIGURE 11.2
Multilevel architecture with various computation levels.

11.2.2 Opportunities and Benefits

The benefits of smart, personalized healthcare are listed below:

11.2.2.1 Simultaneous Reporting and Monitoring

Given the case of a medical and health-related emergency like a heart attack, automated monitoring enabled in real-time via the connected devices holds the potential to save millions of lives. With the help of an IoMT device (e.g.,: wearable) linked to an app on the patient's smartphone, the connected devices can obtain all necessary medical and fitness information and status.

The linked device is capable of collecting and furthermore transferring data such as blood pressure measures, blood glucose levels, weight, O2 saturation, ECG, EMG, etc.

This resultant data is stored virtually with the help of cloud services and is shared with the concerned doctors, physicians, and specialists as per the authorization from the authority in charge of access control (Shehabat & Al-Hussein, 2018). This helps the authorized persons in monitoring the medical information of the patient.

11.2.2.2 End-to-End Connectivity

Through healthcare mobility solutions, the Internet of Things helps in automating healthcare and the patient healthcare workflow. End-to-end connectivity helps in providing greater data security and governance. It eliminates the issues revolving around security, such as network vulnerability. The administrator will be able to determine which devices from which places can connect to the network at a particular time.

As IoMT continues to develop, it should be able to support digital mobility and digitalization. Hence, aiding clinical use cases and several devices is crucial.

Having a more coherent interface will become indispensable as new kinds of data streams and devices find their way into more clinical and managerial systems. To make high-speed decisions and troubleshoot issues effectively requires an inclusive view of your network's performance. A thorough network solution can offer a singular view of both your wired and wireless network from the edge to the private cloud. A good network management tool should have an excellent user interface, with insights that aid complex decision making. An end-to-end solution will help with the above using a single device.

11.2.2.3 Affordability

It enables transfer of data between the connected devices, interoperable compatibility, machine-to-machine interaction, data exchange and transmissible data that makes services immensely cost efficient. It brings down costs by limiting non-essential visits to the hospitals. It also employs resources of improved quality, in turn augmenting the allocation processes and planning of resources (Shehabat & Al-Hussein, 2018).

11.2.2.4 Data Miscellany and Analysis

The tasks of the administrator entails the tedious task of managing a huge amount of data. Data that is collected from the connected digital appliances could be subjected to analysis and assorted through mobility solutions provided by the capabilities of IoT. These capabilities can decrease the collection of raw data, providing the means and motivation to drive important solutions in healthcare with the help of data-driven inferential analytics and insights that can prevent human error while speeding up the process.

Good network analytic tools will give the administrator a view of all the applications running on the network, the patients using them and the reaction time for each application. This provides a microscopic view into the constituents of the system, including performance insights, users, locations, and appliances, which will help in making data-driven decisions and also help in troubleshooting issues rapidly.

11.2.2.5 Patient Tracking and Event Driven Alerts

Life-threatening situations can be avoided safely with the help of patient tracking and alerts, allowing one to safeguard patient health in critical situations with the help of continual notifications and event driven and real-time alerts for the careful and correct monitoring, analysis, and diagnosis.

IoT paves the way for healthcare related mobility solutions which helps in realizing real-time patient tracking, providing necessary alerts and monitoring; this, in turn results in better patient-side treatment, with the proper involvement and intervention of physicians and/or specialists, thus improving the delivery of complete patient healthcare.

Additionally, this helps to ensure that, in the case of patients who have recently undergone close-monitoring in a hospital environment and have been cleared to return to their independent lives, emergency help is always available (Simon et al., 2019).

11.2.2.6 Remote Medical Assistance

When a patient needs to contact persons for any medical and health-related assistance and is not able to reach them due to location and knowledge related inhibitions (Shehabat & Al-Hussein, 2018), IoT-powered mobility solutions could provide help for the patient with required medical assistance whenever required.

Prescriptions can also be accessible to the patient by means of IoT device enabled delivery chains used expressly for healthcare tasks. Hence, using devices connected to the patient's smartphone, their vitals can be monitored when they are outside medical facilities. It also allows for the continuous monitoring of the patient status, and the effectiveness of preventive check-ups and control measures.

11.2.3 Challenges

11.2.3.1 *Cyber Security and Privacy*

Though IoMT has a lot of benefits, they are not widely adopted at a larger scale due to the security and privacy issues involved. IoMT involves the usage of various sensors to monitor body temperature, blood pressure, heart rate, etc. The devices are connected to our phones, cars, and homes through the internet. Due to this, the obtained data stored in the devices become vulnerable and prone to attacks by cybercriminals. Hackers with malicious intentions can access the sensor data to steal or modify it.

People may not prefer sharing their health reports as it may have a substantial amount of sensitive data. Ransomware attacks, fraudulent health claims, and fake alerts are some of the possible issues.

A few factors that cause security concerns are lack of encryption, heterogeneity of devices, and access control (Anmulwar et al., 2020). Some are listed below.

11.2.3.2 *Architecture*

Usually, manufacturers prioritize cost savings over security. Therefore the IoT devices do not have enough space to perform upgrades as they use smaller hard disks to reduce cost. This design flaw resulted in a cascade of ramifications that led into the devastating 2016 Mirai botnet attack, which caused the temporary shut down of the websites of major commercial tech companies, including Twitter, Netflix, and Spotify (Surya, 2016). If something similar to this incident happens in the healthcare sector, it may result in fatal consequences.

11.2.3.3 *Lack of Encryption*

Sensors to gateway communication and gateway to cloud communication is not encrypted, making it easy for hackers to hack into the systems. IoT devices, in general, operate with low energy and lesser computing power to implement algorithms to ensure security.

11.2.3.4 *Heterogeneity of Devices*

IoT devices such as fitness watches, medical sensors, and pollution monitoring devices are all unique. Therefore, the same encryption will not work on every device. All these devices are incorporated with the user's cars, phones, other home appliances, etc., creating the difficult task of securing a system with several components.

11.2.3.5 *Accessibility Control*

Data accessibility is easier in comparison to security, which is considered only as an add-on during device development. Only authorized persons/administrators should have access to the patient's data.

11.2.3.5.1 *Data Handling*

At any given time, there are about 3.7 million devices that are employed for monitoring the different parts of the human body. This figure is expected to have exponential growth as time moves on (Sahoo et al., 2019). This is mainly due to the endless variation of the state that occurs in the human body, which results in the continual generation of data.

Data is collected from the sensors, which are worn or implanted inside the human body, then specific application-based algorithms are used for processing and ultimately, an inference is made. Here, the collected data are of various formats. Due to heterogeneity, there are no standardized data collection formats in health care. As the data collected are enormous and unstructured, the time required for processing increases. High-performance computing (HPC) systems are required to process large volumes of unstructured data. This, in turn, increases the infrastructure cost drastically. The initial costs for implementation will land on the higher side, caused by the investments in infrastructure that are specified by business partners and healthcare providers (Anmulwar et al., 2020).

Another challenge is that a large number of patients implies large data, therefore requires more storage, which can be overcome by integrating with the cloud. But integrating it with the cloud increases complexity. Some data such as body temperature, blood pressure, blood sugar levels and pulse require frequent updates, unlike contact information and geographic information, which need not be updated that often. Higher maintenance costs for these databases become an additional challenge.

11.2.3.5.2 Interoperability

One of the challenging factors in the large-scale implementation of IoMT is interoperability. Take the instance of a patient who requires the usage of multiple sensors that are sourced from different vendors. All these devices have to communicate with each other for the system to process and make a decision. As the sensors are from different vendors, they might have different communication protocols. Thus, there exists the possibility that sensors manufactured by different sources may not be able to communicate with each other.

An efficient and interoperable connected health system is characterised by the ability to flow data through one-to-many and one-to-one connections as well. This allows the exchange of necessary information between the multiple interfaces needed to let the systems cooperate.

11.2.3.5.3 Port Communication

Open ports are vulnerable to attacks when they have poor network security, unpatched or misconfigured. The services and networks that run on the open ports would continue to process the incoming traffic, irrespective of the request's validity. This leads to denial of service attacks. Attackers try to find vulnerabilities. To find the vulnerability, they try to identify those services which operate on that machine, any related protocols, the program implementing them, including the current program version as well. In order to execute this, attackers must utilize a publicly accessible port obtained through port scanning (Wu et al., 2019). Post the communication, termination ports must be closed to be safe.

11.2.3.5.4 Implementation

Even today, it remains quite an impossible task to automate the entire healthcare industry; there still exists the need for human intervention. It's quite obvious that there is a training process to help hospital staff and patients understand how to even handle these IoT devices. Any malfunction in the device may put the patient's life at risk.

11.3 Examples of Personalized Healthcare Devices (Application of IoT in Healthcare)

Some benefits of smart healthcare cannot be realized without the contributions of the variety of IoT powered devices that are delineated in this section. Smart healthcare helps by:

- Providing reduced waiting times for emergency rooms
- Patient, inventory and staff tracking
- Enhancing the manageability of drugs used.
- Guaranteeing the availability of essential hardware

The various devices that fall under the category of smart healthcare devices or IoMT devices are as follows:

11.3.1 Wearables

Smartwatches, activity trackers, belts, and ear-buds are a few examples of wearables that are developed in the market today. These wearable devices perform analysis on the collected data, and in some cases give an alert or make a smart decision. They are used for remote patient monitoring. These devices transmit the analyzed data to the cloud through connected smartphones.

The rehabilitation IoT devices assist patients with disabilities to maintain their physical health and improve it as well. Smart sticks for visually challenged people exist and are ultrasonic sensors that can detect obstacles and issue a warning to the person by a vibration or buzzer. Using a GPS module, the location of the person can be tracked using Android-based applications (APP). Using the emergency APP, the visually challenged person can immediately contact parents or friends in panic situations. The person needs to shake his/her smartphone or push the power button four times within a 5 second range (Sahoo et al., 2019).

QardioCore wireless Bluetooth ECG monitor continuously monitors the ECG data and possesses heart rate monitoring capabilities, as well as heart rate variability measuring, respiratory rate, skin temperature, and activity tracking. This can provide doctors a better insight into necessary factors influencing the patient's health (Walker and Muhlestein, 2018).

11.3.2 Ingestible Sensors

These sensors are the size of a capsule, made from biocompatible materials that make up a power source, microprocessor, sensors, etc. This application unfolds a new world of possibilities for remote patient monitoring. For example, Scripps Health is working on nano-sensors. These tiny sensors at the nano level, travel through the bloodstream, send messages to the user's smartphone, alerting any signs of infection and impending cardiovascular issues (Beardslee et al., 2020).

11.3.3 Moodables

Moodables are mood-enhancing devices that might help people overcome depression. These devices claim to elevate people's mood to help with stress disorder and ADD.

The devices read brainwaves and send low-intensity current to the brain. Thync has come up with feelzing. This is a wearable that sends electric stimulation programs which have been drafted for particular areas of the brain and peripheral nervous system that they have selected to launch the required positive effect (Moehringer and Knable, 2016).

11.3.4 Healthcare Charting

Healthcare charting reduces the need for human intervention and does not require the doctor to do the manual work. Various sensors can be used to monitor, record and analyze health related data like body temperature, blood pressure, etc., and use this data for charting on device connected apps. This reduces hours of manual work done by the doctor for charting.

11.4 Introduction to Machine Learning and its use in Personalized Healthcare

Machine learning helps us understand the structures/underlying patterns of data and fits them into models for easy decision-making. We use datasets with large amounts of information in multiple instances and fields. A set of columns known as features helps in determining the final column (labels). By identifying the patterns in data, we will be able to solve complex problems and improve decision-making. In ML, we input a dataset of past history, split them into training, validating, and testing sets.

11.4.1 Traditional vs ML Approach

In a traditional algorithm, a person creates a code and gives input. With the input received from the user, the compiler compiles the code and gives us the output, i.e., Input + program gives us the output.

But in ML, we train our input data with (Supervised learning) or without (Unsupervised learning) the output, understand the patterns, and test the new data against the pattern observed. In other words, it helps the software programmer to be more precise in prediction without being explicitly programmed. AI are playing important roles in the agriculture and healthcare fields to manage food supply chains, drug supply chains, traceability of products, smart contracts, monitoring the products, connected, and intelligent prediction.

An ML model helps us in connecting input features and labels. It also maps all decisions.

The basic 7 steps involved in the machine learning process are as follows:

1. Define objective
   The problem statement has to be defined along with a work plan on how one has planned to solve it.
2. Data gathering
   First, we need to decide the type of data we need for our project. Then there are many ways to extract data. Data can generally be created using any one of the three approaches:

- Data acquisition: Obtaining data from pre-existing sites and sources.
- Data entry: Manual entry of new data
- Data capture: Utilizing the captured data that are generated from devices.

Therefore, we can use websites like Kaggle, UCI, or collect data from surveys and/or focus groups. We can also use web scraping if the data is not publicly available. The web scraping software may directly access the World Wide Web (WWW) using Hypertext Transfer Protocol (HTTP) to extract data from websites and copy them into a central local database for further analysis (Saurkar et al., 2018).

3. Data Preparation
   At this stage, the data has to be checked for any errors, missing values, irrelevant data and duplicates. Then the data can be normalized and scaled if needed. The quality and quantity of the data play an important role in the prediction process. At this pre-processing stage, the data is prepared to be used in further analysis.

4. Exploratory Data Analysis (EDA)
   At this stage, we try to understand the underlying patterns in the data using data visualization. Some of the software used are KNIME, R, python, and tinkerplots. EDA is a way of visualizing, summarizing, and interpreting the information present in the dataset. This stage provides insight into the data, leading to new ideas.

5. Building a machine learning model
   Choose the suitable ML model for your problem statement. Some commonly used ML models include classification algorithms, like logistic regression, Support Vector Machine (SVM), k-nearest neighbours, and Naive Bayes and clustering algorithms like k-means.
   Next, the dataset has to be split into training, validating and testing sets as follows:
   - Training data: Identify the pattern in the data to predict output.
   - Validating data: Randomly divide the dataset into training and validation sets. The Machine Learning model fitting on the training set is used to predict the output for the observations in the validation set. The resulting error rate can be used to tune the parameters. It helps in choosing appropriate algorithms.
   - Testing data: After training, it is evaluated to check the performance of the algorithm over the dataset.

6. Parameter tuning
   If the testing set predictions did not meet the desired level of accuracy, then we may have overfitting or underfitting problems. So we can go back to the training stage and increase the number of iterations of our training data. We can also try varying the learning rate, which tries to bring the gradient closer to global or local minimal to minimize the cost function. All these hyperparameters are very sensitive and will have a significant change in accuracy.

7. Prediction
   The last stage of the process is to test the model for real life scenarios. This part is widely used in the healthcare industry, especially in personalized healthcare.

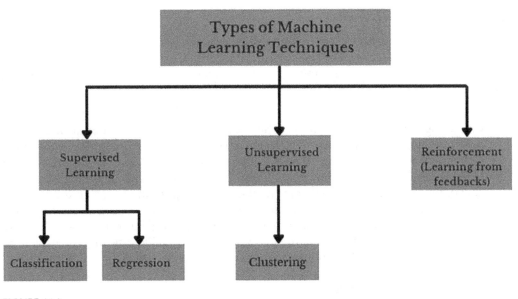

FIGURE 11.3
Types of machine learning.

11.4.2 Classification of Machine Learning Algorithms

11.4.2.1 Supervised Learning

In this type of learning, the input that is used to train the model is associated with an output. A comparison is made between the model's predicted output and the expected output to determine the error. Later, we can tune the parameters based on the error obtained. By doing so we can improve the accuracy of the model. For any new input data, supervised learning helps us to predict the label. Supervised learning can be considered as learning with a teacher.

- Classification

  We go for classification when the output data is a category. The given dataset is divided into training and testing data. The target/category is provided in the dataset. The whole dataset is categorized into labels/categories. The classification model predicts the category of the input data given for training. The aim of the classification algorithms is to predict the category of the input data. For example, in a COVID-19 patient dataset, only two categories are possible: either a COVID-19 positive patient or a COVID-19 negative patient. The various classification algorithms are logistic classification, Naive Bayes Classifier, stochastic gradient descent, k-nearest neighbor, and decision tree.

- Regression

  We go for regression when the output data is a continuous value. This model tries to fit the best hyper-plane passing through the data points. Paradigm regression algorithms include the basic linear regression, and extensions like logistic regression, method based approaches like stepwise regression, ridge regression, polynomial regression, elastic net regression, lasso regression, and Random forest regressors.

11.4.2.2 Unsupervised Learning

The environment of unsupervised learning is in such a way that the target (output data) is not presented to the network. The network learns on its own by discovering the patterns in the input data. There is a relatively better availability of unlabeled data existing today.

- Clustering

  Clustering is to organize the observations or things in a collection of uncategorized data into meaningful groups, so as to make comments about the group rather than individual objects. Therefore objects in the same cluster are more similar to each other in terms of their attributes than they are to the objects of different groups. The clustering algorithm aims to determine the intrinsic grouping based on the relationships existing in an unlabelled dataset. An example of a clustering-based approach is Netflix, where movie recommendations are based on the movies watched. A few more examples of clustering are document classification, identification of areas with high crime rates, detection of insurance fraud, and even data analytics on the public transport system. The various types of clustering are exclusive, overlapping, probabilistic, and agglomerative.

11.4.2.3 Reinforcement Learning

In this type of learning, the model learns based on its experience. Based on the nature of feedback, the behavior of the system is decided. If there is positive feedback, the system generating this action will strengthen the trend; otherwise, the system generating the action will diminish the trend (Qiang and Zhongli, 2011).

11.5 Predictive Analytics and Anomaly Detection

Predictive analytics is being used to make predictions about the upcoming events by analyzing data collected from past and present using various techniques like machine learning, data mining, artificial intelligence, etc. By extracting patterns from large datasets using ML algorithms, we can build a model to predict the output for a given input (Nithya and Ilango, 2017).

11.5.1 Predictive Analytics in Healthcare

In personalized healthcare, predictive analytics can be used to detect disease outbreaks, prepare consultation schedules, prevent patient health deterioration, etc.

For example, recently, an application called BlueDot located an aggregate of atypical pneumonia cases in Wuhan, China, predicting the outbreak of the coronavirus, nine days before the World Health Organisation (WHO) released its first statement on coronavirus. Thus, if we are able to predict the outbreak of communicable diseases such as COVID-19, it will become easy for medical and government employees to bring forward solutions with preventive and safety measures before an outbreak.

Another example is the Valuable predictive analytics tool, which was used to design a model based on the data gathered from several thousand prostate cancer treatments.

This model automatically detects the potential complications and success rate associated with the treatment plan, which aids doctors in deciding on which treatment option to use for a particular patient.

11.5.2 Anomaly Detection

Anomaly detection is a technique used to find abnormal patterns in normal data. We make an assumption while performing anomaly detection, i.e., the anomalies are distinct from normal data. In the healthcare sector, with the rapid growth of data, it will be utilitarian if an automated process is developed to find when the patient's vitals fall below or rise above the usual values. This will reduce the workload of both doctors and nurses or get them extra time to concentrate on a patient's treatment. To avoid medical errors due to the extensive workload, advanced algorithms can be put into use to completely automate the process of finding significantly different data in a real-time dataset and to alert the healthcare workers by highlighting the suspect parameters when needed. By using IoMT devices or applications or various other IoT platforms, we can present the results in interactive dashboards with a user interface of high standards. We can also send a message or set the alarm if there is a considerable drop or rise in a patient's vitals using IoT platforms. But, one of the main problems faced in anomaly detection is to bring down the number of false alerts sent to the doctor or official in charge of monitoring the patient's vitals,as this may affect the efficiency of the system (Šabić et al., 2021).

11.6 Research Issues and Future Directions of Modern Machine Learning and IoMT Applications for Personalized Healthcare

As mentioned above, various machine learning algorithms viz. supervised, unsupervised, and reinforcement learning methods have been employed for analysis of the different forms of data generated in the personalized healthcare sector. There is a range of fields where ML and IoT find applications in the healthcare industry. For instance, when sleep cycle and heart problems need to be monitored, the routine and sleep pattern may differ depending on the patient's age and health condition. Hence, a thorough list of sleep patterns cannot be consolidated. This might elicit inaccurate personal health calculations. In case IoT and Machine Learning are used to calculate the vitals, for anomaly detection, for prediction, and for alerting the patients and/or the doctors, an error may occur in the decision-making process involved. The important issue faced is how the machine's decisions are elucidated.

11.7 Conclusion

In this chapter, IoT applications for personalized healthcare systems are presented in detail. The classification and various machine learning algorithms are explained. Opportunities and challenges in implementation of IoT and machine learning algorithms for healthcare applications are discussed. Also, this chapter discusses the predictive analytics and anomaly detection applications to smart healthcare systems. Research challenges and the future direction of modern machine learning and IoMT applications for personalized healthcare is projected.

References

Alexopoulos, E.C. "Introduction to multivariate regression analysis." *Hippokratia* 14, Suppl. 1 (2010): 23.

Allam, Z., Dey, G., and Jones, D.S. "Artificial intelligence (AI) provided early detection of the coronavirus (COVID-19) in China and will influence future Urban health policy internationally." *AI* 1, no. 2 (2020): 156–165.

Al-Turjman, F., Nawaz, M.H., and Umit Deniz Ulusar, U.D. "Intelligence in the Internet of Medical Things era: A systematic review of current and future trends." *Computer Communications* 150 (2020): 644–660.

Amrane, M., Oukid, S., Gagaoua, I., and Ensari, T. "Breast cancer classification using machine learning." In *2018 Electric Electronics, Computer Science, Biomedical Engineerings' Meeting (EBBT)*, pp. 1–4. IEEE, 2018.

Anmulwar, S., Gupta, A.K., and Derawi, M. "Challenges of IoT in Healthcare." In *IoT and ICT for Healthcare Applications*, pp. 11–20. Springer, Cham, 2020.

Beardslee, L.A., Banis, G.E., Chu, S., Liu, S., Chapin, A.A., Stine, J.M., Pasricha, P.J., and Ghodssi, R. "Ingestible sensors and sensing systems for minimally invasive diagnosis and monitoring: The next frontier in minimally invasive screening." *ACS Sensors* 5, no. 4 (2020): 891–910.

Flore, J. "Ingestible sensors, data, and pharmaceuticals: Subjectivity in the era of digital mental health." *New Media & Society* 23, no. 7 (2020): 2034. doi:10.1177/1461444820931024.

Greco, L., Percannella, G., Ritrovato, P., Tortorella, F., and Vento, M. "Trends in IoT based solutions for health care: Moving AI to the edge." *Pattern Recognition Letters* 135 (2020): 346–353.

Groves, P., Kayyali, B., Knott, D., and Van Kuiken, S. "The 'big data' revolution in healthcare: Accelerating value and innovation." (2016).

Hamdan, S., Ayyash, M., and Almajali, S.. "Edge-computing architectures for Internet of Things applications: A survey." *Sensors* 20, no. 22 (2020): 6441.

Hassan, S.R., Ahmad, I., Ahmad, S., Alfaify, A., and Shafiq, M. "Remote pain monitoring using fog computing for e-healthcare: An efficient architecture." *Sensors* 20, no. 22 (2020): 6574.

Huda, N., Khan, S., Abid, R., Shuvo, S.B., Labib, M.M., and Hasan, T. "A low-cost, low-energy wearable ECG system with cloud-based arrhythmia detection." In *2020 IEEE Region 10 Symposium (TENSYMP)*, pp. 1840–1843. IEEE, 2020.

Klonoff, D.C. "Fog computing and edge computing architectures for processing data from diabetes devices connected to the medical internet of things." *Journal of Diabetes Science and Technology* 11, no. 4 (2017): 647–652.

Kotsiantis, S.B., Zaharakis, I.D., and Pintelas, P.E. "Machine learning: A review of classification and combining techniques." *Artificial Intelligence Review* 26, no. 3 (2006): 159–190.

Krotov, V., and Silva, S. *Legality and Ethics of Web Scraping*, Twenty-fourth Americas Conference on Information Systems, New Orleans, 2018.

Li, Z., Wang, Y., Wang, W., Chen, W., Ti Hoang, Greuter, S., and Mueller, F.F. "HeatCraft: Designing playful experiences with ingestible sensors via localized thermal stimuli." In *Proceedings of the 2019 CHI Conference on Human Factors in Computing Systems*, pp. 1–12. IEEE, 2019.

Lison, P. "An introduction to machine learning." *Language Technology Group (LTG)* 1, no. 35 (2015): 1–35.

Majumder, S., Aghayi, E., Noferesti, M., Memarzadeh-Tehran, H., Mondal, T., Pang, Z., and Deen, M.J. "Smart homes for elderly healthcare—Recent advances and research challenges." *Sensors* 17, no. 11 (2017): 2496.

Mathew, K., Tabassum, M., and Lu Ai Siok, M.V. "A study of open ports as security vulnerabilities in common user computers." In *2014 International Conference on Computational Science and Technology (ICCST)*, pp. 1–6. IEEE, 2014.

Moehringer, J., and Knable, M.B. "Transdermal electrical neurostimulation therapies in psychiatry: A review of the evidence." *Psychiatric Annals* 46, no. 10 (2016): 589–593.

Mohammed, C.M., and Askar, S. "Machine learning for IoT healthcare applications: A review." *International Journal of Science and Business* 5, no. 3 (2021): 42–51.

Mohiuddin, I., and Almogren, A. "Security challenges and strategies for the IoT in cloud computing." In *2020 11th International Conference on Information and Communication Systems (ICICS)*, pp. 367–372. IEEE, 2020.

Naranjo, D., Córdova, P., and Gordon, C. "Wearable electrocardiograph." In *2018 International Conference on eDemocracy & eGovernment (ICEDEG)*, pp. 201–205. IEEE, 2018.

Nithya, B., and Ilango, V. "Predictive analytics in health care using machine learning tools and techniques." In *2017 International Conference on Intelligent Computing and Control Systems (ICICCS)*, pp. 492–499. IEEE, 2017.

Osisanwo, F.Y., Akinsola, J.E.T., Awodele, O., Hinmikaiye, J.O., Olakanmi, O., and Akinjobi, J. "Supervised machine learning algorithms: Classification and comparison." *International Journal of Computer Trends and Technology (IJCTT)* 48, no. 3 (2017): 128–138.

Qiang, W., and Zhongli, Z. "Reinforcement learning model, algorithms and its application." In *2011 International Conference on Mechatronic Science, Electric Engineering and Computer (MEC)*, pp. 1143–1146. IEEE, 2011.

Randazzo, V., Pasero, E., and Navaretti, S. "VITAL-ECG: A portable wearable hospital." In *2018 IEEE Sensors Applications Symposium (SAS)*, pp. 1–6. IEEE, 2018.

Randazzo, V., Ferretti, J., and Pasero, E. "ECG WATCH: A real time wireless wearable ECG." In *2019 IEEE International Symposium on Medical Measurements and Applications (MeMeA)*, pp. 1–6. IEEE, 2019.

Reddy, A.R., and Suresh Kumar, P. "Predictive big data analytics in healthcare." In *2016 Second International Conference on Computational Intelligence & Communication Technology (CICT)*, pp. 623–626. IEEE, 2016.

Rich, E., and Miah, A. "Mobile, wearable and ingestible health technologies: Towards a critical research agenda." *Health Sociology Review* 26, no. 1 (2017): 84–97.

Šabić, E., Keeley, D., Henderson, B., and Nannemann, S. "Healthcare and anomaly detection: Using machine learning to predict anomalies in heart rate data." *AI & Society* 36, no. 1 (2021): 149–158.

Sahoo, N., Lin, H-W., and Chang, Y-H. "Design and implementation of a walking stick aid for visually challenged people." *Sensors* 19, no. 1 (2019): 130.

Saurkar, A.V., Pathare, K.G., and Gode, S.A. "An overview on web scraping techniques and tools." *International Journal on Future Revolution in Computer Science & Communication Engineering* 4, no. 4 (2018): 363–367.

Shehabat, I.M., and Al-Hussein, N. "Deploying internet of things in healthcare: Benefits, requirements, challenges and applications." *Journal of Communications* 13, no. 10 (2018): 574–580.

Simard, P.Y., Amershi, S., Chickering, D.M., Pelton, A.E., Soroush Ghorashi, S., Meek, C., Ramos, G., et al. "Machine teaching: A new paradigm for building machine learning systems." *arXiv preprint arXiv:1707.06742* (2017).

Simon, L.E., Rauchwerger, A.S., Chettipally, U.K., Babakhanian, L., Vinson, D.R., Warton, E.M., Reed, M.E., Kharbanda, A.B., Kharbanda, E.O., and Ballard, D.W. "Text message alerts to emergency physicians identifying potential study candidates increase clinical trial enrollment." *Journal of the American Medical Informatics Association* 26, no. 11 (2019): 1360–1363.

Singh, P., and Singh, N. "Blockchain with IoT and AI: A review of agriculture and healthcare." *International Journal of Applied Evolutionary Computation (IJAEC)* 11, no. 4 (2020): 13–27.

Singh, P., Singh, N., and Deka, G.C. "Prospects of machine learning with blockchain in healthcare and agriculture." In *Multidisciplinary Functions of Blockchain Technology in AI and IoT Applications*, pp. 178–208. IGI Global, 2021a.

Singh, P., Singh, N., Singh, K.K., and Singh, A. "Diagnosing of disease using machine learning." In *Machine Learning and the Internet of Medical Things in Healthcare*, pp. 89–111. Academic Press, 2021b.

Singh, S., and Singh, N. "Internet of Things (IoT): Security challenges, business opportunities & reference architecture for E-commerce." In *2015 International Conference on Green Computing and Internet of Things (ICGCIoT)*, pp. 1577–1581. IEEE, 2015.

Su, C.-R., Hajiyev, J., Fu, C.J., Kao, K.-C., Chang, C-H., and Chang, C-T. "A novel framework for a remote patient monitoring (RPM) system with abnormality detection." *Health Policy and Technology* 8, no. 2 (2019): 157–170.

Surya, L. "Security challenges and strategies for the IoT in cloud computing." *International Journal of Innovations in Engineering Research and Technology ISSN*: 3, no. 9, (September 2016): 2394–3696.

Thakor, A., Kher, R., and Patel, D.. "Wearable ECG recording and monitoring system based on MSP430 microcontroller." *International Journal of Computer Science and Telecommunications* 3, no. 10 (2012): 40–43.

Walker, A.L., and Muhlestein, J.B.. "Smartphone electrocardiogram monitoring: Current perspectives." *Advanced Health Care Technologies* 4 (2018): 15–24.

Wu, D., Gao, D., Chang, R.K.C., En He, E., Cheng, E.K.T., and Deng, R.H. "Understanding open ports in Android applications: Discovery, diagnosis, and security assessment." (2019): 1. Network and Distributed System Security Symposium 26th NDSS 2019: February 24-27, San Diego, CA: Proceedings. 1-14. Research Collection School Of Information Systems

Pointurier, Y., Benzaoui, N., Lautenschläger, W., and Dembeck, L. "End-to-end time-sensitive optical networking: Challenges and solutions." *Journal of Lightwave Technology* 37, no. 7 (April 1, 2019): 1732–1741. doi:10.1109/JLT.2019.2893543.

12

Blockchain Technology for Pharmaceutical Drug Supply Chain Management

Priti Rani Rajvanshi and Taranjeet Singh
GL Bajaj Institute of Management, Greater Noida, India

Deepa Gupta
GL Bajaj Institute of Management and Research, Greater Noida, India

Mukul Gupta
GL Bajaj Institute of Management, Greater Noida, India

CONTENTS

12.1 Introduction

Material providers, producers, merchants, drug stores, medical clinics, and patients are all important for the medical care store network, which is a co-founded organization of various separate associations. Due to the complexity of this network, tracking supply is difficult due to many reasons, such as insufficient data and a centralized system, with stakeholders competing and controling behavior. This level of complexity not only leads to inefficiencies, such as individuals who have been flagged by the COVID-19 epidemic (Omar et al., 2021), but who can also be exacerbating the problem of how to prevent counterfeiting. As a result, medicines like this can readily infiltrate the healthcare system. Examples of such medicines within the supply chain (Bellaj et al., 2018; Blanchard, 2021) are products with no active pharmaceutical ingredient (API) or with an erroneous API, a large number of APIs, a low-quality API, a bad API, pollutants, or outdated items that have been repackaged–and there are some fakes. It's also possible that medicines are designed improperlyand generated under unfavourable circumstances (Walter et al., 2012). The Health Research Funding Organization (HRFO) asserts that up to thirty percent of pre-scriptions showcased in poor nations are not as per guidelines. Furthermore, in new research of the World Health Organization, one of the primary problems identified by the World Health Organization (WHO) is counterfeit medications and fatalities in underdevel-oped nations, and in the majority of instances, children are the victims (Hulseapple, 2019; Corrado et al., 2013). In this regard, the yearly monetary misfortune to the US drug indus-try because of fake medication is assessed around $200 billion (Faisal et al., 2019; Khalid et al., 2013). An API provider is in charge of supplying the basic components needed to make medicines that the FDA has authorized; for example, the US Food and Drug Administration is a regulatory agency. The medicines are packaged by the manufacturer as a Great Deal or send to a repackage. The most important distributor gets a lot of the goods and is in charge of distributing them to drug stores dependent on the interest for the item or auxiliary wholesalers (if the quantity of medicine lots is huge) who is fit for moving these lots to drug stores. At last, contingent upon a specialist's solution, a drug store will apportion the prescription to patients (Kurki, 2016). The transmission of medicines is generally eased across the supply chain by UPS or FedEx, which are examples of third-party logistics ser-vice companies. The intricate nature of the healthcare supply chain is the major cause for counterfeit pharmaceuticals reaching the end-user market. Taking advantage of the distri-bution's intricacy, medication can readily flow through this mechanism with little or no difficulty (Jens et al., 2019). There is no information trail and no verifiable documentation. As a result, efficient management, monitoring, and tracking of the role of goods in the medical services store network are basic in the battle against irresistible illness fakes. The meaning of medication discernibility (following and following) couldn't possibly be more significant. A few countries are accentuating and commanding this trafficking from one side of the planet to the other. The DSCSA (Drug Supply Chain Security Act) in the United States of America made it necessary for the pharmaceutical organizations to create an auto-mated, interoperable system, a method for identifying and tracking prescription medicines as they are dispensed and are found all across the United States (Mettler, 2016). In a similar vein, China has demanded that all parties be involved over the past eight years to keep track of individual information in the medication supply chain any time pharmaceutical goods are stored in a committed IT framework, and medicines are moved to and from their storage spaces (Ahmad et al., 2021). Accordingly, drug traceability has become an impor-tant part of the drug business. Follow the inventory network, since it guarantees authentic-ity. The compelling sending of the information structure inside the Bitcoin application has made another worldview use of improvement dependent on blockchain innovation. The blockchain information construction's center thought is similar to a connected rundown in that it is shared by every one of the members, hubs in the organization, every one of which holds a neighbourhood duplicate of starting with every one of the squares (associated with the longest chain) (Nipun et al., 2021) its beginning square. Many genuine applications that have as of late been delivered, have been made in an assortment of fields, including the Internet, E-Government (Neetesh et al., 2020), Internet of Things (Pilkington, 2016), just an electronic record, the executives of these applications exploit blockchain's benefits (Manuela et al., 2017) on a shared organization (using hashes) and public accessibility of a circulated record of exchange records. Creating a chain of squares with cryptographic con-nections between them is incredibly difficult to temper the hashes in the recordings because rewriting the block from beginning would cost a lot of money. (Narendra et al., 2020). The most recent transaction in blocks with regards to blockchain-based detectability for monetary exchanges (Ganesan et al., 2021) shows one of the principal instances of drug inventory network endeavours. Regardless of the way that our answer is practically identical to this one as far as the attention on the drug production network and the use of blockchains, we adopt a more comprehensive strategy to the drug inventory network offering. Above all else, our procedure recognizes and draws in significant medication supply partners as the FDA, provider, maker, merchant, drug store, and so on are all important for the chain while it (Ganesan et al., 2021) is simply material to the provider, stakeholders to incorporate with the producer and distributor. Therefore, pharmacists are shown as a separate entity in a genuine drug supply chain; however, this is not the case. Secondly, we make a concerted effort to recognize and define relationships, smart contracts, on-chain resources among stakeholders. (Ganesan et al., 2021) does not mention decentralized storage systems. In addition, given the importance of contacts, we have provided detailed definitions among stakeholders to eliminate any uncertainty, but in (Zibin et al., 2018), such interactions were not defined. At last, we utilize shrewd agreement innovation to give ongoing ceaseless recognizability pop-up messages that are utilized to lessen human intercession. Therefore, there will be unwanted deferrals. Every medicine Lot, specifically, is given a unique shrewd agreement that triggers an occasion whenever there is a difference in proprietorship, and a timetable of events is shipped off the DApp's client. The brilliant agreements in (Ganesan et al., 2021) are, then again, intended for explicit jobs, like a provider and client. Every member needs to be a producer, distributor, and maker to affirm which medications have been received physically; such a system may cause irregularities and postponements in the changeless information kept in the record. Finally, we did an expense and advantage investigation security study to survey the proposed framework's presentation arrangement, as well as an explanation of how the suggested solution will be implemented. It's possible to apply it to different supply networks. The difficulty of obtaining traceability to combat counterfeit medications is well-known, and the pharmaceutical industry has made many attempts to solve it. However, a thorough study of the literature reveals numerous possibilities and gaps for a thorough implementation for medication traceability; blockchain technology is being used in this instance. This chapter's main contributions might be summed up as follows: a blockchain-based drug arrangement – A production network that guarantees security, recognizability, and responsibility in an unchanging nature, and information provenance available for medications made by drug organizations.

12.2 Blockchain Basics

Blockchain is a distributed ledger technology that has garnered a lot of traction recently. One of the most widely used cryptocurrencies, Bitcoin (Bellaj et al., 2018), has gained a lot of traction. It is possible to think of the blockchain as a system, a network of linked peers with the same state machinery information is exchanged between members of the blockchain network amongst themselves, and these transactions are grouped. A block is a construction made up of several pieces that fit together to form a whole. Each brick is unique and comprises several deals that have been put together, and Blockchain miners have added to the current list of blocks. Following a consensus process, blocks are mined and agreed upon among blockchain network members. Several procedures have been presented for the blockchain network's behavior (Blanchard, 2021). Various points of agreement protocols have many ways of reaching an agreement. This miner verifies transactions and combines them into another member of the group, then recognizes the block in the network. This block is sent out to the whole peer-to-peer network to keep a shared public key on the network and duplicated at all nodes as the blockchain's status. Depending on the use case, a blockchain can be public or private. Both private and public blockchains have grown in popularity because they applied for the right to this end, extensive study has been carried out to investigate the use of blockchain in the fields of IoT, as can be seen, AI, Supply Chain, and Fog Computing are all important areas. In the following articles (Walter et al., 2012; Yan et al., 2018) supply chain for pharmaceuticals is one of the most appropriate uses for blockchain. Using a distributed ledger to keep track of everything, there are numerous advantages of using medicines (Hulseapple, 2019). Because blockchain is an immutable record of transactions, all interactions documented are permanent, durable, and irreversible. Also, it is tamper-proof as a result, the medication delivery system will be secure if it makes use of blockchain technology. The level of service offered to patients must fulfil certain criteria. A set of criteria information access may be restricted using blockchain technology to a subset of the network's members (through permission access). The blockchain model protects the integrity of the data. Smart contracts are used in several blockchain networks by implementing business logic that may be customized. The term "smart contracts" refers to contracts in ethereum and other blockchains that employ passive components, but hyper ledger may be used to do a variety of tasks. Smart contracts are frequently used to make blockchain usage easier as back-end systems that connect with distributed networks. DApps are front-end apps, as it provides a practical solution with a user interface for interacting with the blockchain layer. During the process, DApps can be used to communicate data in the medication supply chain. Data regarding drug lots are shared between different entities, and medicines are sold to patients, with a straightforward logical system for returning unneeded medicines interface. Blockchain is most recognized for its use in the financial sector. The benefits of blockchain are numerous, and an unchangeable record is made up of a sequence of time-stamped data blocks linked together to contain transactions (Hulseapple, 2019). Miners first verify transactions before executing and confirming them. Then, at that point, there are exchanges and squares of mysterious personalities, and afterwards, there are exchanges and squares of unknown characters. It guarantees that assets are always accessible. Every block is associated with the other blocks of the system. The chain won't ever be broken, given the past block guarantee that the new square is saved endlessly. Contingent upon the agreement calculation and different elements of the framework, miners are, for the most part, made up for approving exchanges, making blocks, and adding them to the blockchain. The public trust model of blockchain is based on four columns: a common record, cryptographic strategies, and shrewd agreement agreements and sus conventions. It is comprised of a common and appropriated record that is not constrained by a solitary hub, by the by, by a gathering of hubs in a decentralized, shared organization way. The blockchain also utilizes encryption advancements, for example, SHA-2 and Elliptic-bend cryptography are utilized. The consensus strategies can be remembered for blockchain to give security, as it is safer due to the assent between different elements, just as shortcoming is open-minded. Furthermore, by agreeing, it is consistently conceivable to show up to a solitary truth. Proof-of-Work (PoW) and Proof-of-Stake (PoS) are two examples of such protocols. The PoW consensus protocol, for example, works by requiring miners to utilize the hash and nonce values from the block header to compete in a puzzle-solving competition. The puzzle's style is unique and asymmetric, which means it is difficult for miners to solve the puzzle. Nonetheless, the network may easily verify it. If you correctly solve it, you are the winner, and you will be paid. This protocol is effective because it prevents network attacks, and 51% of the peers in the network will be collaborative efforts were required. A separate consensus system, Proof of Stake, on the other hand, has 51% of the bitcoin accessible is required to be obtained by a single entity or a gathering of coordinating elements individuals to close the organization, it is conceivable, in any case. It was believed that assailants would be uninterested in an organization. At the point when they hold the greater part of the stock, thus, it is superfluous to have it (Khalid et al., 2013). The consistency of the squares in the Merkle tree is remembered for the blockchain to protect it. The hashes of the state root, exchange root, and header are put away in the header, just like the gathering root. A shrewd agreement is a PC component that empowers the execution of code on the blockchain and helps in the change of the blockchain into a computational structure. It empowers rationale execution, just as putting away state Smart agreement ability, but again is not accessible. All blockchain circulated processing frameworks are upheld. These fundamental thoughts add to the decentralized framework's prosperity. A blockchain network is a conveyed record that is consistently exceptional, a record that addresses a reliability because of these characteristics, the blockchain advances more straightforwardness, furthermore, examining potential, just as a lift in strength and the information's trustworthiness (Faisal et al., 2019; Kurki, 2016).

12.3 Need of Blockchain

This part traces blockchain technical feasibility of blockchain and requirements as is the most intelligent solution for our necessities. Blockchain is a type of computer science technology that provides a model for storing data, as it is made up of a series of blocks that carry information. It contains transactional data, is a decentralized system in which data is stored in several locations, can be efficiently exchanged over a network securely before a transaction can be added, it must first be approved, and it must be validated before it can be added to a blockchain. Nodes in the network use a consensus procedure to reach an agreement. The network agrees that the transaction should be completed. For any transactions that take place, it is impossible to change what has been recorded or obliterated, and the entire transactional history is lost at any point; you can look back in time. The block's hash, the preceding block's hash value, and the existing block's nonce, hashing is a technique for creating stacking integrity-protected blocks to build a safe chain for every piece of information. A unique identifier is assigned to each block on the blockchain, a digital signature that is one-of-a-kind matches the information contained in each block (Hashmark). On the off chance that the information in the square isn't right, the computerized mark of the record has been adjusted. The square will likewise change later on as it monitors exchanges as they occur and the blockchain fills in ubiquity. When more exchanges come in, the size of the information base develops and executes. At the point when the square is filled, it has a computerized signature doled out to it. The beginning square is the underlying connection in the square chain, and it does not allude to whatever else. To associate a square of the mark in the exchange information, the information of the principal block is added to the information of the subsequent square and. the square after that is advanced mark is a sort of electronic mark. The subsequent square is presently half-finished restrictive on the mark of the square going before it since it is important for the square's data. This is the way it works each time there are new exchanges that happen to frame the chain.

12.4 The Platforms of Blockchain

Ethereum is a decentralized blockchain network that allows users to send and receive money. Decentralized apps can only be deployed in the right environment. The smart contracts are managed by the platforms that the application has established ethereum, is a platform for developers is made up of several dispersed components like ethereum wallets and nodes dispersed. A node network has been built when miners or computers join the internet. The network isn't working possesses any rights to join, as well as any other permissions a node with sufficient computational power "I'm able to connect to the network."

AWS is a cloud computing platform provider as part of its services, and Amazon provides blockchain templates, a platform that offers customers with an easy-to-use interface a method for developing blockchain apps for companies. Amazon Web Services (AWS) supplies the infrastructure like the application's database as a ledger. As a result, the application is no longer required; the owner will develop the complex because the blockchain is a distributed ledger technology provided by this service. There are two sorts of use cases: tracking and verification. Centralized ownership transactions, as well as to complete deals and decentralized ownership contracts are ways to use the AWS blockchain. An Ethereum blockchain template is a network based on several nodes in cluster instances, with a loaded application, It is possible to make a balancer (ALB). We chose the AWS platform because its excellent service makes it simple to set up, deploy, and maintain scalable blockchain networks to manage. Oracle is a software company. Because it is so comparable to AWS, it is a supplier of blockchain-as-a-service. It enables companies to install apps across a nonchangeable electronic database with a distributed ledger.

12.5 The Blockchain-based Healthcare for Supply Chain Security Analysis

12.5.1 Integrity

The arranged task's primary objective is to keep up with its respectability. The reason for the blockchain framework is to monitor all exchanges, exercises that happen along with the medical services production network, ensuring ownership and recognizability of a lot of consignment, set of experiences transfers, and the containers in which they are put away. This is ensured since all occasions and logs are put away in the recommended arrangement, put away on the blockchain's changeless record. Furthermore, the utilization of IPFS to store pictures of delivered lots is another upgrade to the proposed arrangement's honesty. This will verify that guarantee that every single exchange in the medical care store network is secure, and it's feasible to track and follow it.

> **Accountability:** Every individual is answerable for their behavior. The Ethereum address of a capacity's execution of the guest's data is kept on the blockchain, taking into consideration the following: it is consistently conceivable to be the capacity guest. In this manner, everyone in the gathering is answerable for their lead. The maker in the medical care production network will be answerable for any medication

lot he makes, utilizing the capacity of lot details will be considered responsible, as will drug stores; they provide for a capacity to be for every remedy they give.

Authorization: Only allowed parties can use the modifier to execute the smart contract's essential functionalities. This provides defence against unrestricted access and the avoidance of any unwelcome intrusion entities from making use of the functionalities that have been implemented. This is because the healthcare supply chain is so crucial, the medication lot should only be manufactured in the United States, the prescription of medicines by a verified manufacturer, and only a verified pharmacist should do this procedure.

Availability: By their actual nature, blockchains are decentralized and scattered. Subsequently, after the savvy contract has been carried out on the blockchain, all records and exchanges will be erased and all members approach them rather than a unified administration. When it comes to exchanging information, there are a couple of alternatives. Accordingly, the passing of a hub has no impact, as exchange information is lost. The blockchain is a conveyed record innovation for the organization to work appropriately, it should be up and working consistently. To be successful, the medical services production network should be utilized. Any blackout may bring about pricey postponements in the field of medical services.

Non-Repudiation: Because transactions are cryptographically signed by their initiators' private keys, PKI's cryptographic characteristics ensure that private keys remain private. Public keys cannot be inferred as a result. For a transaction, it is possible to ascribe a signature signed by a certain private key to the person who has the key; this is comparable to the concept of accountability, where the blockchain-based participants are accounted. Since the healthcare supply chain cannot refute its conduct, they've already been signed using their private key that is inextricably linked to their identity.

MITM Attacks: Each exchange in the blockchain should be endorsed by the initiator's private key, so if an interloper attempts to change any of the first exchanges, it will fall flat. It won't be feasible to store information and data on the blockchain except if it is endorsed by the initiator's private mark key. Accordingly, MITM assaults are not possible in the climate, as climate dependents on the blockchain; so this usefulness is required due to the utilization of the medical services inventory network. It ensures that lone checked substances are permitted to perform exercises inside the inventory network, just as interlopers who enter the store network unlawfully attempt to make counterfeit prescriptions for the sake of a notable brand. This is something that the confirmed producer can presently not do. Figure 12.1 shows an illustration of the generic pharmaceutical supply chain

12.6 Case Study and Solution

SCM at Cisco: Cisco loses more than $500 million in sales each year as a result of these counterfeit items (much like the £218 million in losses for the United Kingdom every year due to phony wine and spirits[12]), It's apparent that this isn't merely a metaphor, a challenge that developing nations encounter as a result. Cisco is actively engaged in research and development on a distributed ledger technology (blockchain)

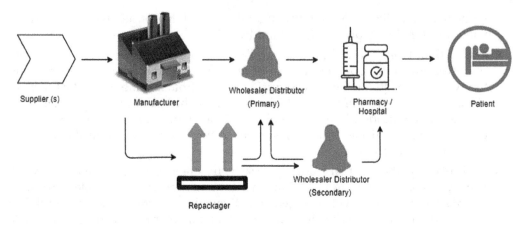

FIGURE 12.1
The pharmaceutical supply chain.

Source: Omar et al. (2021).

solution on the war against counterfeit goods in the company's supply chain, even though Cisco is working in a different field. Several additional blockchain-based businesses supplying chain management is an example of a use case. (IBM Food Trust) is a non-profit organization dedicated to the preservation of food. When examining the consensus process utilized, another restriction of blockchain emerges. Several options protocols for reaching an agreement are provided. It is feasible to create a private blockchain in a public blockchain that describes a single technique for reaching a consensus, even though it is a private company. It is not feasible to come up with a solution as a rigorous application. There is continuing situation research about how to reach an agreement as quickly as feasible and as pluggable as possible, for suppliers to appoint who they want to utilize as a consensus. For a while, consensus times are critical for a successful blockchain corporate application. Minutes or seconds are preferred. When deciding on a consensus method, we keep the following factors in mind, and the procedure must be followed.

12.7 Smart Contract Security Analysis

Notwithstanding the security study, the made Ethereum savvy contract for drug following was assessed utilizing expert instruments to uncover any code defects. Those apparatuses were used in rounds of code improvement to build the brilliant agreement's reliability. Remix the IDE was utilized to make the keen agreement, and it contains some code, Runtime blunder cautions and troubleshooting. Sometimes it lacks the ability to build confidence in the strength of keen agreements; therefore, SmartCheck was used to find imperfections at different seriousness levels in the code. After a few endeavours, the cunning code emphasizes that the smart code was changed. As indicated by the yield, there are no bugs. SmartCheck checked the shrewd agreement by investigating it and contrasting it with its information base, in that it was without threats that may deliver it defenseless, digital assaults, and abuse. Moreover, the oyente device was used to investigate the security of keen agreements. Oyente is a Linux-based application that completely inspects the code to preclude any secret perils or weaknesses. Its motivation is to protect the Ethereum keen agreement contract from notable attacks, for example, a profundity assault on the call stack just as re-emergence attacks. Following is a careful assessment of the shrewd agreement.

12.8 Issues Faced by Users in the Current Pharma Supply Chain

Notwithstanding the security study, the made Ethereum savvy contract for drug following was assessed utilizing the expert instrument. Several variables impact the ecumenical supply chain's fictitiously unauthentic medication. Figure 12.2 shows the issues in the existing pharmaceutical supply chain management system. These issues are already highlighted by (Ganesan et al., 2021).

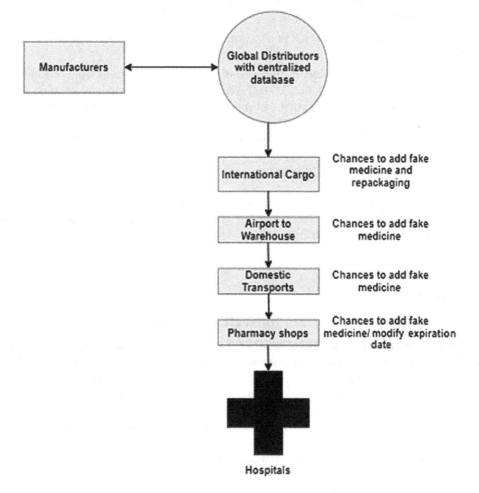

FIGURE 12.2
Issues in existing pharmaceutical supply chain.

Source: Ganesan et al. (2021).

Ethical concerns: Middle and Low countries account for most of the world's population, the rising entities that are in a conundrum of ethical concerns. It was immoral to oversee detecting bad medicine.

Regulations of the impotent regime: As a result, a variety of bogus medicine is available in the market.

Non-accessibility of the drug: Not many medicines are extremely expensive and are available to sick persons. As a result, individuals are compelled to put their faith in a third party. No one is sanctioned under the current system to verify the authorized drug distributors, as the mobile device that has been proposed where everyone is required to verify the distributor is under the terms of the application.

Lack of cognizance: The public in rural areas could not tell the difference between immaculate and phony medication. Medicos/Patients: The medico or the patient has access since they do not have direct access to the medication tracking system and we were unable to trace the beginning of the medication and its development logistics.

The poor economy of the society: Individuals trust the pharmacy shop and buy drugs due to a lack of mazuma (money).

Lack of lab facility: Due to a lack of mazuma, people trust the pharmaceutical shop and buy medicines.

Fake medicine: Fake medicine immensely affects individuals' lives from one side of the planet to the other (Jens et al., 2019). The drug store network doesn't provide straightforwardness. Patients, specialists, and drug specialists can't monitor their prescriptions while the medicines are in transport, and only a couple of meds are kept at a set temperature. If the emergency unit is utilized, there are alternatives to consider. Change the medication's assembling date to its lapse date; quite possibly, the impeccable repackaging will be finished due to medication of low quality.

The existing framework creates an opportunity to add destructive components to the generally flawless medication. The testing of the drug was directed in an unscrupulous way, and the outcomes were not distributed.

12.9 Limitations of Blockchain in Health Care Supply Chain

Albeit the recommended framework exploits the absolute most remarkable highlights of blockchain innovation, a couple of potential downsides need to be addressed to have a superior comprehension of what they could mean for the proposed framework. The healthcare industry has been significantly impacted by blockchain. It has tremendous promise in applications, such as supply chains for pharmaceuticals. This section contains the following information, as blockchain-based solutions face several significant difficulties.

Immutability: Blockchains are unchanging, implying that any information that is added to the record can't be changed or erased. While this might be profitable for information, Integrity is a major issue; it is impossible to get around it to fix errors on a blockchain because they are inconvenient and are unchangeable. The operators, for example, who are performing physical work in the pharmaceutical supply chain can still be done; people create mistakes when entering data into the ledger; as a result, even if the mistakes are discovered, they cannot be rectified. This can have a big impact on the healthcare supply chain with unwelcome consequences if the producer, for example, incorrectly enters medication information, and it has a lot of potential consequences. When it gets to the pharmacy, it starts to cause problems for a pharmacist.

Data Privacy: Even though the unchanging nature is viewed as one of the essential advantages of blockchains, it might struggle with new guidelines administering data issues with capacity, for example, the GDPR (General Data Protection Regulation). In Europe, the GDPR (General Data Protection Regulation) commands that organizations control where and how information is put away with exactness, since the individual from whom it is received has the legitimate right to change or remove it at any moment, and if no action is made, it will be deleted. The organization may be held responsible, based on its requirements from the patients, who have an important role in healthcare supply chains and may object to their data being retained indefinitely or they may lawfully sue the healthcare industry because of the blockchain center. Although the public availability of the source code compromises privacy, blockchain nevertheless protects the anonymity of all transactions. Its implication is that the vast majority of blockchain networks include ethereum has no rules to secure data privacy (Yan et al., 2018). All transactions are dispersed across the whole network system to guarantee that this did not happen; certain precautions were taken. Certain methods in the system can only be triggered by authorized entities. Smart contracts are a type of contract that may be used; however, all information is still available to the public. Anyone with access to the internet can see that having such knowledge is advantageous and is a violation of privacy that may hurt the people involved.

Scalability: Individual nodes on the blockchain must execute every transaction on the whole network, which ensures the system's security and variability. It has a limiting effect on scalability. There is, nevertheless, an ongoing study to deal with the problem; shading and slicing are two examples. Plasma and ethers scaling are the scaling choices that will get rid of the necessity for each ethereum hub to be refreshed to handle every single organization exchange (Swan, 2015). In the field of medication, if the inventory chains are set up, this may not be an issue as little to medium-scale creation is done. In any case, if the medicine is created on a major scale, the technique will be troublesome and tedious.

Interoperability: Other networks of blockchain operate in their unique fashion, resulting in interoperability difficulties across the various blockchains that are incapable of communicating with one another. This issue may be avoided by using data centers. However, if healthcare costs continue to rise, centers choose from a variety of blockchain-based solutions. It will be quite different if you combine solutions from different platforms. It will take a lot of work to achieve compatibility.

Efficiency: The effectiveness of a blockchain arrangement is intensely based on the brilliant agreement's code. The effectiveness of the blockchain arrangement is exceptionally subject to the coding of the shrewd agreement and furthermore the algorithimic coding used to check and affirm an exchange The execution and execution methodology will be costly. The last decides the level of energy use. There are a few exchanges in the medical services inventory network. Thus, the shrewd agreement must be secure. It is absolutelycoded to run quickly and effectively.

Smart contracts: When opposed to traditional centralized servers, programming blockchain smart contracts imposes various restrictions on the system (Bellaj et al., 2018). The high quality of smart contracts is a difficulty for developers for blockchain security, minimal debugging, and constraints on solidity. Furthermore, smart contract code must be very efficient by keeping just essential data and reducing the number of operations. The cost of completing the project and the complexity of a procedure determines how Ethereum operates. As a result, optimizing algorithms is essential to cut down on fuel use as much as possible.

Time delay: To collect transactions, store them, construct a block, validate them, and broadcast them requires a lot of electricity and time (Mazin et al., 2020), which results in the creation of other nodes. This process is conducted for each node separately until the network's miners achieve an agreement and choose a block to append. Ethereum is a distributed ledger system whose difficulty is adjusted with the help of consensus protocol. Approximately for 20 seconds, the nodes are assigned to this period as adequate time to digest information and communicate with others the presence of additional nodes, in addition to the time it takes for blocks to develop, for the block to be confirmed is sometimes set aside. If the block is followed, it is deemed confirmed by a certain number of bricks, so that there are no different parallels.

12.10 Conclusion and Future Work

In this chapter, we try to focus on the role of blockchain in the supply chain management of pharmaceutical drugs. A blockchain network in pharmaceutical drug supply chain management is consistently exceptional and reliable because of these characteristics: the blockchain advances with straightforwardness, examining potential threats, and the information is trustworthy. Various research challenges of blockchain in health care, several platforms used by researchers, and limitations are also addressed in this chapter. Future work will be implementing some new platforms of blockchain in the drug supply chain management process, based on the gaps of existing platforms.

References

Alkhoori, O., Hassan, A., Almansoori, O., et al. "Design and implementation of cryptocargo: A blockchain-powered smart shipping container for vaccine distribution." *IEEE Access* 9 (2021): 53786–53803.

Badr, B., Horrocks, R., and Wu, X.B. *Blockchain by Example: A developer's Guide to Creating Decentralized Applications Using Bitcoin, Ethereum, and Hyperledger.* Packt Publishing Ltd, 2018.

Blanchard, D. *Supply Chain Management Best Practices.* John Wiley & Sons, 2021.

Chambliss, W., Wesley, G.C., Daniel, A.K., et al. "Role of the pharmacist in preventing the distribution of counterfeit medications." *Journal of the American Pharmacists Association* 52, no. 2 (2012): 195–199.

Costa, C., Antonucci, F., Pallottino, F., et al. "A review on agri-food supply chain traceability by means of RFID technology." *Food and Bioprocess Technology* 6, no. 2 (2013): 353–366.

Debe, M., Salah, K., Raja, J., et al. "Blockchain-based verifiable tracking of resellable returned drugs." *IEEE Access* 8 (2020): 205848–205862.

Huang, Y., Wu, J., and Long, C.. "Drugledger: A practical blockchain system for drug traceability and regulation." In *2018 IEEE International Conference on Internet of Things (iThings) and IEEE Green Computing and Communications (GreenCom) and IEEE Cyber, Physical and Social Computing (CPSCom) and IEEE Smart Data (SmartData)*, pp. 1137–1144. IEEE, 2018.

Hulseapple, C. "Block verify uses blockchains to end counterfeiting and 'make world more honest'." (Online) (2019) (accessed April 12, 2015). https://cointelegraph.com/news/block-verify-uses-blockchains-to-end-counterfeiting-and-make-world-more-honest

Jamal, S.M.K., Omer, A., Qureshi, A., and Abdus, S. "Cloud computing solution and services for RFID based supply chain management." *Advances in Internet of Things* 3, no. 4 (2013): 79.

Jamil, F., Hang, L., Kim, K.H., et al. "A novel medical blockchain model for drug supply chain integrity management in a smart hospital." *Electronics* 8, no. 5 (2019): 505.

Kurki, J. "Benefits and guidelines for utilizing blockchain technology in pharmaceutical supply chains: Case Bayer Pharmaceuticals." Bachelor thesis, Dept. Inf. Service Econ., Aalto Univ., Espoo, Finland, (2016).

Mattke, J., Hund, A., Maier, C., et al. "How an enterprise blockchain application in the US pharmaceuticals supply chain is saving lives." *MIS Quarterly Executive* 18, no. 4 (2019).

Mettler, M. "Blockchain technology in healthcare: The revolution starts here." In *2016 IEEE 18th International Conference on e-Health Networking, Applications and Services (Healthcom)*, pp. 1–3. IEEE, 2016.

Musamih, A., Khaled, S., Raja, J., et al. "A blockchain-based approach for drug traceability in healthcare supply chain." *IEEE Access* 9 (2021): 9728–9743.

Navadia, N.R., Kaur, G., Bhardwaj, H., et al. "Applications of cloud-based Internet of Things." In *Integration and Implementation of the Internet of Things Through Cloud Computing*, pp. 65–84. IGI Global, 2021.

Pilkington, M. "Blockchain technology: Principles and applications." In *Research Handbook on Digital Transformations*. Edward Elgar Publishing, 2016. https://ssrn.com/abstract=2662660, [accessed 18 Jun 2017].

Saxena, N., Thomas, I., Gope, P., et al. "PharmaCrypt: Blockchain for the critical pharmaceutical industry to counterfeit drugs." *Computer* 53, no. 7 (2020): 29–44.

Schoner, M., Dimitris, M. K., Sandner, P., et al. *Blockchain Technology in the Pharmaceutical Industry*. Frankfurt, Germany: Frankfurt School Blockchain Center, 2017.

Singh, N., Tang, Y., and Ogunseitan, O. A. "Environmentally sustainable management of used personal protective equipment." *Environmental Science & Technology* 54, no. 14 (2020): 8500–8502.

Subramanian, G., Thampy, A., Sreekantan, U., Nnamdi, V., et al. "Crypto pharmacy – Digital medicine: A mobile application integrated with hybrid blockchain to tackle the issues in pharma supply chain." *IEEE Open Journal of the Computer Society* 2 (2021): 26–37.

Swan, M. *Blockchain: Blueprint for a New Economy*. O'Reilly Media, Inc, 2015.

Zheng, Z., Xie, S., Dai, H.-N., et al. "Blockchain challenges and opportunities: A survey." *International Journal of Web and Grid Services* 14, no. 4 (2018): 352–375.

13

IoT Based Vital Monitoring and Bed Availability System Using Arduino

Navneet Rajpoot, Shubham Bansal and Saru Dhir
Amity University, Greater Noida, India

CONTENTS

13.1 Introduction

In medicine, monitoring is the observation of several medical parameters over time. In today's world, medical technology has advanced in many cases such that loss of life that would be counted as normal 20 years ago is considered to be an exception. This advancement has been possible due to many factors, especially advancements in the field of patient monitoring. Due to these sophisticated systems, doctors have long been able to treat patients according to the statistics produced by constant monitoring of the patients themselves. This has resulted in more accurate treatment of the patients.

But, now the gaping holes present in the current iteration of technology need to be addressed to make the process of patient vital monitoring easy, reliable and efficient. In today's world, where highly contagious diseases have taken all of us by storm, the need of

DOI: 10.1201/9781003201960-13

the hour is to keep our medical professionals safe. The safety of our medical professionals can only be ensured by making smarter technological advancements, so as to reduce the chance of them being in the vicinity of the infected. This task is what the existing crop of patient vital monitoring systems have failed to address. As a result, our doctors, aid workers, nurses, and other front-line warrior professionals have fallen prey to diseases like COVID-19, that spread due to being in close proximity to the patient.

The system that we are proposing would not only keep our medical professionals safe but also make the system better by eliminating most of their vulnerabilities and adding some much-needed upgrades to the existing technology, as newer technology can monitor the patient much better than the technology currently used, and do so with as few risks as possible.

13.2 Literature Review

In today's world, an increasing amount of research on patient monitoring or physiologic monitoring is being conducted in the space of IoT (Internet of Things). The next generation of healthcare professionals is leaning heavily on the future benefits of this new internet-based technology to revolutionize the health monitoring industry. Recent studies at the University of Cordoba showed that the healthcare industry has been pushing M-healthcare (Mobile Healthcare) and E-Healthcare heavily onto newer incoming patients, believing that this sort of technology would advance in the near future and would assist in keeping these patients healthy (Gomez et al., 2016).

In the earlier stages, digital patient monitoring systems are mainly used to follow extreme situations, such as unusual or unsafe vital sign parameters. According to a patent research conducted by Mann Alfred E. Foundation for Scientific Research in 1996, the best connecting medium for the various components of the highly complex systems in the 1990s was cables connected individually to a monitor, which would then compute the reading and display results in a relatively understandable manner.

With the problem of connectivity solved, a new problem of data retention appeared due to increasing numbers of patients. In 2001, a publication from the Health Hero Network Inc.,showed the first traces of data being kept for future analysis; they connected servers to allow communication between machines. Even without a database, this system allowed efficient management of patient data (Stephen, 2001). Long before the advent of databases and communication servers, the healthcare industry had been trying to retain patient data. The first attempts in data retention were made in 1960, way before digitization occurred. The process was achieved by using magnetic tapes in a device called Dallon's Twin Beam Cardio scope, which allowed 15 seconds worth of data to be recorded for later analysis (Day, 2004).

Soon after, with the advent of the internet, the first usage of networking capable patient monitoring systems came to be, but despite of their obvious advantages over then existing technology, the medical community was still sceptical of the dependability of these new patient vital monitoring systems, one of the reasons being a lack of trust in the reliability of the internet itself. So, with hopes of countering these negative views against a newer generation of patient monitoring systems, the University of Oslo conducted a test for both the older systems and the newer systems in 2005, putting two wireless GSM-enabled systems up against the existing wired systems that used WLAN. These were set in twelve distinct stations on the same floor of the facility. When the results of the evaluation were disclosed, the wireless system proved to be slightly superior to the wired system. The only observed drawback was unnoticeable flickering on the wall-mounted display, while the wired system failed to deliver the data on two different occasions. Although the scientists believed that this test was hardly conclusive, it proved that the wireless system was advanced to such an extent that it was a strong contender to replace the nearly obsolete wired technology (Høgetveit et al., 2005).

These trials and calibrations have brought us to today, as the technology is now in urgent need of updates and a recent generation of vital monitoring systems is produced by Dutch manufacturer Phillips. The Phillips Intellivue MX 800 is the best all-around system for accomplishing the task of patient vital monitoring. It comes with a wall-mounted setup which reduces the portability, and it backs up the data for only a period of eight hours. Although the database is smaller, data is portable with the use of a cable that can be attached to any other Phillips monitor (Bracco and Backman, 2012). This system also comes with bedside alarms, with up to 12-Lead ST segment measurement analysis.

On account of the outbreak of COVID-19, flaws in the blueprint and usability of the current generation of monitoring systems were obvious. This indicates that the doctors, nurses, and other healthcare professionals were falling prey to the coronavirus while performing their duties in the hospitals (Burke et al., 2020). Many medical professionals lost their lives, in total 279 physicians died in the initial stages of the COVID-19 outbreaks (Ing et al., 2020).

To know the future implications for this technology, we can looks at Wi-COVID a blueprint to monitor respiratory rates of COVID-19 patients, using a non-intrusive, live-time, and personalized technology. The proposed blueprint uses the available WiFi signal made by commonly used equipment at home to monitor the respiratory vital signs of any COVID-19 patients.

13.3 Commercial History

The history of patient monitoring systems goes all the way back to the late 1950s and 1960s, back when the doctors were still working with relatively unreliable systems. This was before the age of data storage, and long before the advent of digitization (Engineering Staff of FCI, 2005).

13.3.1 1960s

The use of patient monitoring was beginning to proliferate in the healthcare industry in the 1960s. The intended function as well as the configuration of these systems was to serve the same tasks as the modern system of the 21st century. As seen in Figure 13.1, initially these systems were a staple of the operation room in order to obtain the immediate knowledge of any significant changes to the health of the patient. Some of the more integral parts of the PMS (Patent Monitoring Systems) from that point in time were the ECG, blood pressure and temperature sensors, and all of these different functions added more modules to the already highly complex system.

Furthermore, in the mid-60s, Dallons brought to market a new iteration of their existing PMS called the Twin-Beam Cardio Scope, as seen in Figure 13.2. The key difference between this new model and the older ones was the newer one's ability to record 15 seconds worth of data from the patients on a magnetic tape.

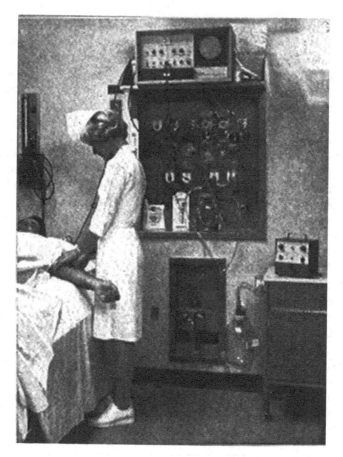

FIGURE 13.1
Wall Mounted P.M.S from 1960.

Source: Engineering Staff of FCI, 2005.

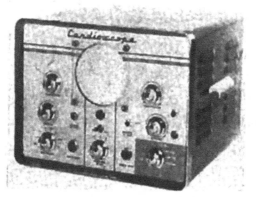

FIGURE 13.2
Twin-Beam Cardio Scope.

Source: Engineering Staff of FCI, 2005.

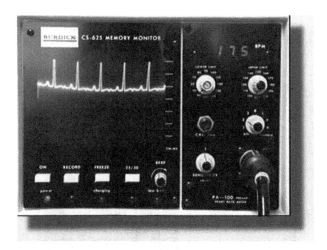

FIGURE 13.3
Burdick CS-625 Memory Monitor.

Source: Engineering Staff of FCI, 2005.

13.3.2 1970s

The first wave of digital PMS came to the market in the 1970s. These new systems came with monitors that could display both waveforms and other information. Moreover, this was the first time microprocessors were used in such a system. As seen in Figure 13.3, the appearance of the so called "Memory Monitor" occurred at the beginning of the decade. These monitors also contained analog to digital converters, as well as small memories to briefly store several seconds worth of incoming data. The stored data would later be displayed on the CRT displays.

Brands such as Westinghouse and General Electric also started putting ECGs into the PMS to ensure the electrical safety of the patient. In 1978, Siemens launched their best PMS up to that time, the Sirecust 300 DU.

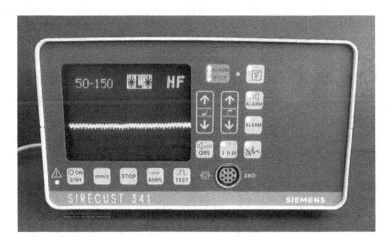

FIGURE 13.4
Siemens Sirecust 300 DU.

Source: Engineering Staff of FCI, 2005.

FIGURE 13.5
Abbott Life care 5000

Source: Engineering Staff of FCI, 2005.

13.3.3 1980s

The 80s brought even more advancements in these systems, Arrhythmia analysis became available at the bedside instead of centrally. As Figure 13.5 shows, the new monitors started coming with colored displays. At the same time, the computational power of monitors grew and the networking capabilities became more sophisticated. The sizes of the screens grew in the 80s, so now even more waveforms could be displayed on the monitors and the number of waveforms went from two to six.

In this decade, bed to bed viewing became the standard for patient monitoring systems. This new feature allowed the nurses and the attendants to view the waveform and vitals of any bed from any monitor connected within the network.

The newer trend at the end of the 80s was the new modular systems, which were heavily marketed by companies such as Siemens, Honeywell, and Westinghouse.

13.3.4 1990s

In the closing decade of the millennium, the need of the hour for patient monitoring systems was mobility and connectivity. Systems from this time became more accepting of outside data. This outside data could also be viewed on the monitors and was collected from other machines and other hospital departments.

It was at this time that portable monitors became more evolved, with an evolution in battery technology.

As Figure 13.7 shows, another trend started in the late 90s to establish vendor specific monitoring network connections at many bedside locations, so when network-compatible monitors could be connected into the monitoring network at patient bedsides wherever needed.

This was also when CRT became obsolete and flat screen LCD displays took hold of the patient vital monitoring system market.

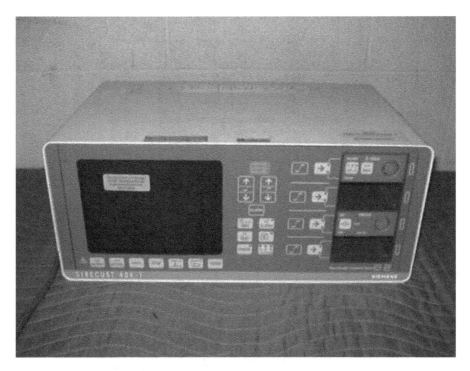

FIGURE 13.6
Siemens Sirecust 404-1.

Source: Engineering Staff of FCI, 2005.

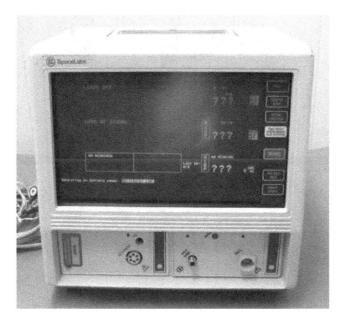

FIGURE 13.7
Spacelabs PC express.

Source: Engineering Staff of FCI, 2005.

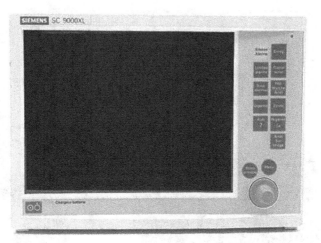

FIGURE 13.8
Siemens SC9000.

Source: Engineering Staff of FCI, 2005.

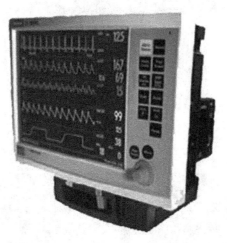

FIGURE 13.9
Siemens infinity SC 9000XL.

Source: Engineering Staff of FCI, 2005.

13.3.5 2000s

With the turn of the century, the systems became more flexible. These systems were flexible enough to go whereever the patient went, through any acuity, and all types of transformation.

As Figure 13.10 shows, Phillips is the market leader in the space of patient vital monitoring systems today. They have pushed the technology forward with the help of their Intellivue series of systems that has stayed the standard to beat in the market for the better part of two decades.

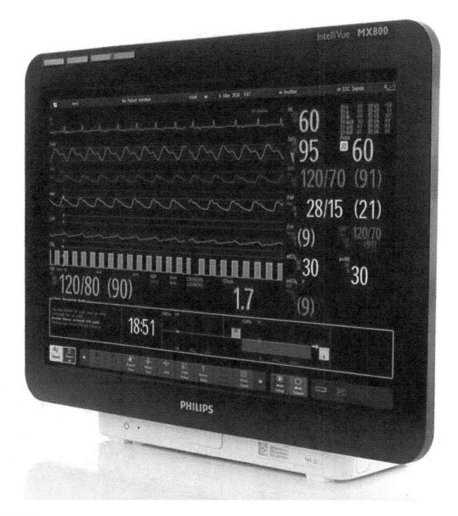

FIGURE 13.10
Phillips Intellivue MX800.

Source: Engineering Staff of FCI, 2005.

13.3.6 2010s

Wearable technology that makes use of Wi-Fi has started to flood the market, especially after the COVID-19 pandemic, as Figure 13.11 shows, companies such as Apple, Samsung, and Mi have all invested heavily in wearable technology, which has proven to have better chances of detecting Covid, due to the close proximity to the user's body.

13.4 Objective

This model is meant to forge an IoT system that would help doctors view patient's vitals data remotely. This would be accomplished by broadcasting the patient's vital signs in real time for the purpose of remote emergency consultancy or monitoring. This system would

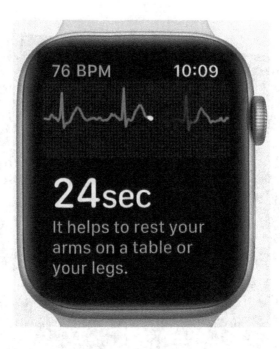

FIGURE 13.11
Apple Watch ECG.

also allow storage of an admitted patient's vitals via the net for further future analysis. Moreover, this system would halt the spread of these highly contagious diseases by reducing the number of people gathering at hospitals to inquire for availability of beds, as a live "available bed count" will be shown in real time on the net as well as on a LCD display. This would be accomplished by creating a system using Arduino and its various sensors.

13.5 Proposed Model FrameWork

As Figure 13.12 illustrates, in this model framework,

1. An Arduino board will be connected to all the components through cables.
2. The IR sensors will be placed on the bed moldings to detect whether the bed is occupied by a patient or not.
   - It will transmit the readings to the Arduino board, from where it will be shown on the display, and also can be viewed remotely on any device connected to the internet.
   - It will reduce the number of people coming to the hospitals to check for the availability of beds, and will save their time as well as save them from encountering a harmful infectious disease.
3. The LCD connected with the Arduino board will be placed at the reception desk, which will display the count of available beds in the hospital ward, saving people's time spent in queues to enquire about available beds, and will reduce crowds at the reception desk.

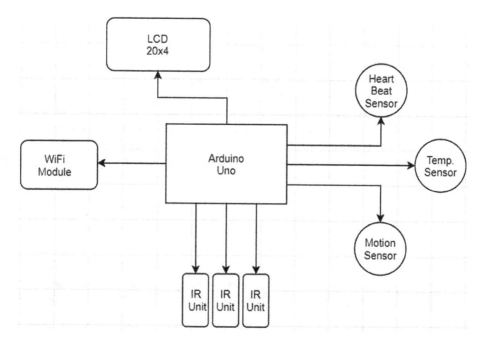

FIGURE 13.12
Model framework.

4. A Wi-Fi module will be connected to the Arduino board to connect the device to a hotspot and transmit the data over the internet, which can be accessed remotely on any handheld device.

5. A motion sensor is connected to the Arduino, to detect the motion of the patient which will let the staff know that the patient needs assistance so staff can help immediately. It will reduce the workload of healthcare professionals from continuously monitoring and keeping a check on the patient.

6. A temperature sensor will be used to measure the patient's body temperature, and the readings will be accessible on any device over the internet.

7. A heartbeat sensor will be used to keep a check on the patient's heartbeat and monitor any unusual changes in his/her breathing.

The model will be based on this framework and will be working as per the following steps:

Step 1: The various sensors send the data into the micro-controller.

Step 2: At the center, the data is processed in the micro-controller.

Step 3: The LCD display shows the information that is derived from the data from IR sensors.

Step 4: The rest of the data from the patient goes to the Wi-Fi module, which now transmits the data over internet to the application.

Step 5: The next step is not on the diagram, as now the relevant data is in the application and can be viewed remotely on any internet-surfing capable device, such as a smartphone, tablet, or personal computer.

13.5.1 Code

As Figure 13.13 shows, we see the heading as well as the included library for the LCD, Pulse Sensor, and others. At the bottom, we also see the API key for ThingSpeak app (this key is unique for every individual). It is this key that helps the system connect to the specific private channel on the ThingSpeak app.

Figure 13.14 shows the time required for the API to be updated by the chapter, in our system this time is 15 seconds, and this is done so the updates would require minimum amounts of computational power from the microcontroller. Another unseen benefit of setting a relatively larger window for updates is so that this system could perform reliably with a slower internet connection.

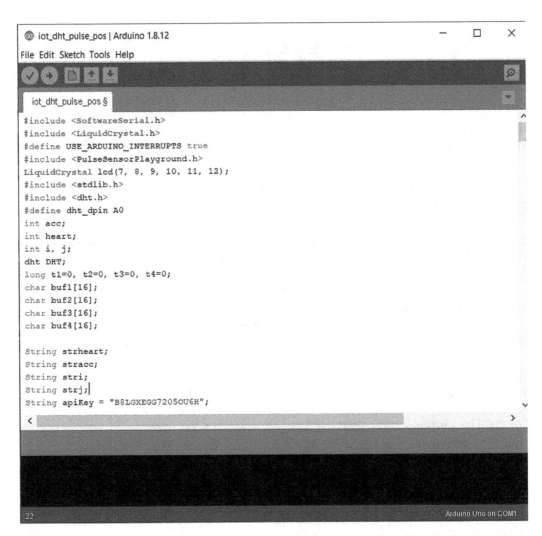

FIGURE 13.13
Code heading and ThingSpeak setup.

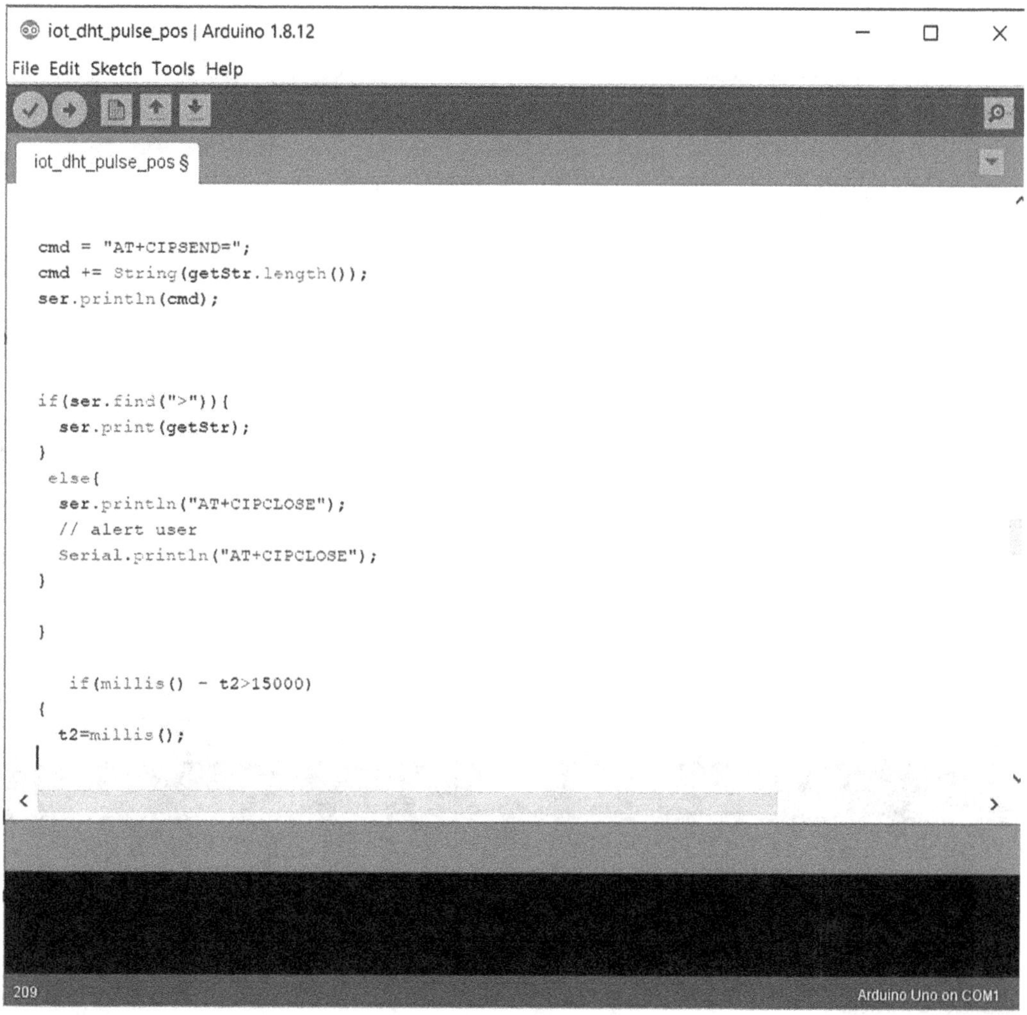
iot_dht_pulse_pos | Arduino 1.8.12
File Edit Sketch Tools Help
iot_dht_pulse_pos §
cmd = "AT+CIPSEND=";
cmd += String(getStr.length());
ser.println(cmd);
if(ser.find(">")){
ser.print(getStr);
}
else{
ser.println("AT+CIPCLOSE");
// alert user
Serial.println("AT+CIPCLOSE");
}
}
if(millis() - t2>15000)
{
t2=millis();
209
Arduino Uno on COM1

FIGURE 13.14
Delay time for update.

As Figure 13.15 illustrates, we see the setup of the Blynk app; this code is responsible for connecting the bed availability system to the Blynk API via the internet. First, we see the Node MCU library being included so the data from the IR sensors can be sent directly to the Wi-Fi module, bypassing the microcontroller.

The other thing we see is the authentication code, this is a 32 character authentication code that is sent by Blynk via an email, this is done to verify the account being used, and also to establish connection with the private channel on the Blynk API.

The last thing you see in the above window is the Wi-Fi setting for your Wi-Fi to connect to the system. The username and password are put in the code, so that the system can know clearly which network it is intended to connect to.

All of the above are important prerequisites for our Bed Availability System to work properly.

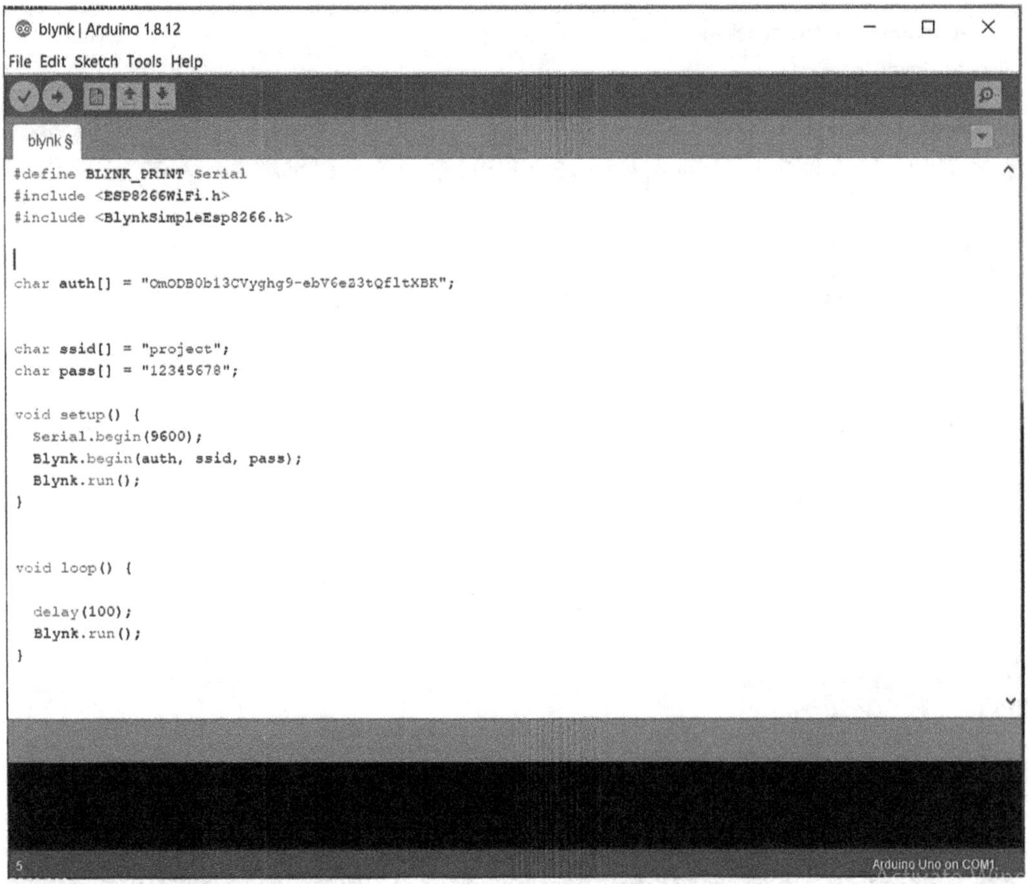

```
blynk | Arduino 1.8.12                                              —   □   ×
File  Edit  Sketch  Tools  Help

  blynk §

#define BLYNK_PRINT Serial
#include <ESP8266WiFi.h>
#include <BlynkSimpleEsp8266.h>

char auth[] = "OmODB0b13CVyghg9-ebV6eZ3tQfltXBK";


char ssid[] = "project";
char pass[] = "12345678";

void setup() {
  Serial.begin(9600);
  Blynk.begin(auth, ssid, pass);
  Blynk.run();
}


void loop() {

  delay(100);
  Blynk.run();
}




5                                              Arduino Uno on COM1
```

FIGURE 13.15
Blynk setup.

13.6 Comparison (Existing Technology vs. Proposed Model)

For this segment of this report, we will be put our model up against the industry leader Phillips Intellivue MX800, in order to see which system performs better under the new circumstances of 2020.

13.6.1 Existing Technology

As Figure 13.16 shows, for a comparison, we will be taking Philips IntelliVue MX800 and Philips M3001A Multi-Measurement Module, which is a widely used system for patient vital monitoring in the medical field today. Both of these machines are used in sync to do the work of vital monitoring.

Advantages

- Supports transferring patient data for flexible monitoring.
- Patient data (up to the last eight hours) is stored in the MMS, and can be transferred to a Philips IntelliVue or M-Series patient monitor.

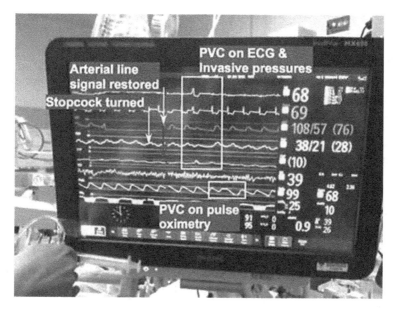

FIGURE 13.16
Philips IntelliVue MX800.

Source: Bracco and Backman (2012).

- Data can be transferred by disconnecting from a host monitor, and reconnecting to a new monitor.
- Bedside alarms with up to 12-Lead ST segment measurement analysis.

13.6.2 Proposed Model Technology

As Shown in Figure 13.17, this system would be created using Arduino and its various modules and sensors, such as Wi-Fi module, heart beat sensor, temperature sensor, motion sensor, etc. When in use, such a device would take in the patient's vital signs and broadcast

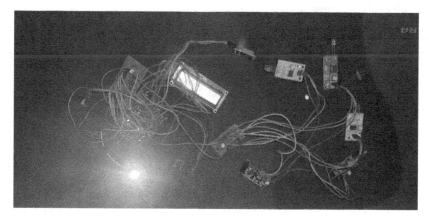

FIGURE 13.17
Proposed model.

TABLE 13.1

Comparison Table

Phillips Intellivue MX800	Proposed Model Work
1. Uses wire to connect the modules of the device.	1. Uses internet to connect the modules of the device.
2. The display is wall mounted.	2. The display is handheld.
3. Patient data backed up for eight hrs.	3. Patient data backed up for 30 days.
4. Multiple screens are needed for complete functional use.	4. All the needs for displays can be fulfilled by any handheld device, such as Tablets and smartphones.
5. Capabilities of the system are fixed at purchase.	5. New capabilities can be added by just adding new sensors.
6. No bed availability system.	6. Comes with bed availability system
7. Costs over $3,500.	7. Costs less than $50.

it live on the ThingSpeak App, the data would also be stored on an online database for the next 30 days. The bed availability updates will be done with IR sensors, feeding the data to the system and then displaying it live on the LCD display and the Internet.

Advantages

- This system would be deployed over the net and not use any wire to relay the statistics gathered from the patient, whereas existing systems rely heavily on the physical wires.
- All the results can be viewed on any handheld device, eliminating the need of bed mounted display panels.
- Because the internet is the connecting medium, the results and statistics can be viewed from remote locations, allowing remote consultation in case of an emergency.
- Patient data is backed up for further analysis over the internet for 30 days (90 times more than MX700's eight hrs.).
- The bed availability system solves the footfall problem hospitals face in times of major disease outbreaks.

13.6.3 Result of the Comparison

Using the findings of Table 13.1, we can reasonably conclude that this chapter has addressed many loop holes or shortcomings of the current iteration of the technology, and it is not only an upgrade but also makes economic sense to manufacture such systems that cost 20 times less and works reasonably well in many cases by comparison.

13.7 Conclusion

On the completion of our chapter, we would have a system that goes on to exhibit the transforming capabilities of the IoT technology. Another task for machines would be to serve as a substitute of the current technology, but also a prime contender to replace these old systems that are massively reliant on near obsolete technology.

Once completed, this system would effectively help the hospitals and numerous other healthcare establishments. The functionalities of this system would help keep diseases such as COVID-19 at bay and far away from our first line of defense. This system would also help reduce footfall in the hospitals by deploying the bed availability system, by which people coming to inquire about bed availability would get the information over the internet and from the display that would show the same information.

The USP would be that besides keeping the frontline aid workers safe, in times of emergencies the doctors will have the ability to get to the data of their patient and give them consultations remotely, which would save many lives all over the world.

Our concepts would help make the hospitals a safe place to work and to come to in an hour of need. This product, if mass produced would also come into use for elderly patients whose health needs to be constantly checked at home. Families won't have to set up a $3,500 system for the purpose of patient vital monitoring. The world and our own lives will benefit from such a product in the market.

References

Gomez, J., Byron, O., and Emilio, Z. 2016. Patient monitoring system based on internet of things. *Procedia Computer Science*, vol. 83, pp. 90–97.

Schulman, J.H., Ronald, J.L., Joseph, Y.L., Alfred, E.M., Orville, R.R., and David, I.W. 1998. *Patient Monitoring System*. U.S. Patent No. 5,791,344.

Stephen, J.B. 2001. *Multiple Patient Monitoring System for Proactive Health Management*. Health Hero Network Inc.

Day, H.W. 2004. *Trends in Physiologic Monitoring Systems*. ECRI Health Devices.

Høgetveit, J.O., Ilangko, B., Karl, O., and Oystein, J. 2005. Introducing multiple wireless connections to the operating room, interference or not. *IFMBE Proc*, vol. 11, no. 1, pp. 1727–1983.

Bracco, D., and Backman, S.B. 2012. Philips monitors: Catch the wave! *Canadian Journal of Anesthesia/Journal Canadien D'anesthésie*, vol. 59, no. 3, pp. 325–326.

Burke, R.M., Claire, M.M., Alissa, D., Marty, F., Thomas, H., Michelle, H., and Isaac, G. 2020. Active monitoring of persons exposed to patients with confirmed COVID-19—United States. *Morbidity and Mortality Weekly Report*, vol. 69, no. 9, p. 245.

Ing, E.B., Xu, Q., Salimi, A., and Torun, N. 2020. Physician deaths from corona virus (COVID-19) disease. *Occupational Medicine*, vol. 70, no. 5, pp. 370–374.

Prangshu, D.B., Saru, D., and Madhurima, H. Impact of IoT in current era. In *2019 International Conference on Machine Learning, Big Data, Cloud and Parallel Computing (COMITCon)*, pp. 334–339. IEEE.

Li, F., Maria, V., Hossain, S., Rumi, A.K., and Sheikh, I.A. 2021. Wi-COVID: A COVID-19 symptom detection and patient monitoring framework using WiFi. *Smart Health*, vol. 19, p. 100147.

Behera, S., Geetanjali, R., Subhadarshini, S., Meenakshee, M., Srimay, P., Manasa, K.P., Rina, N., Budhindra, N.H., and Yengkhom, D.S. 2020. Biosensors in diagnosing COVID-19 and recent development. *Sensors International*, p. 100054.

Engineering Staff of FCI. 2005. *Fifty Years of Physiologic Monitors*. Femtosim Clinical Inc.

Cechetti, N.P., Bellei, E.A., Biduski, D., Rodriguez, J.P.M., Roman, M.K., and De Marchi, A.C.B. 2019. Developing and implementing a gamification method to improve user engagement: A case study with an m-health application for hypertension monitoring. *Telematics Informat*, vol. 41, pp. 126–138.

Qudah, B., and Luetsch, K. 2019. The influence of mobile health applications on patient–healthcare provider relationships: A systematic narrative review. *Patient Educ. Counseling*, vol. 102, no. 6, pp. 1080–1089.

Sequeira, L., Perrotta, S., LaGrassa, J., Merikangas, K., Kreindler, D., Kundur, D., et al. 2020. Mobile and wearable technology for monitoring depressive symptoms in children and adolescents: A scoping review. *J. Affect. Disorders*, vol. 265, pp. 314–324.

Sisko, A.M., Keehan, S.P., Poisal, J.A., Cuckler, G.A., et al. 2019. National health expenditure projections 2018–27: Economic and demographic trends drive spending and enrollment growth. *Health Affairs*, vol. 38, no. 3, pp. 491–501.

Cristea, M., Noja, G.G., Stefea, P., and Sala, A.L. 2020. The impact of population aging and public health support on EU labor markets. *Int. J. Environ. Res. Public Health*, vol. 17, no. 4, p. 1439.

Khan, J.R., Awan, N., Islam, M.M., and Muurlink, O. 2020. Healthcare capacity health expenditure and civil society as predictors of COVID-19 case fatalities: A global analysis. *Frontiers Public Health*, vol. 8, p. 347.

Bashir, R.N., Bajwa, I.S., and Ali Shahid, M. 2020. Internet of Things and machine-learning-based leaching requirements estimation for saline soils. *IEEE Internet of Things*, vol. 7, no. 5, pp. 4464–4472.

Saad, W.H.M., Khoo, C.W., Ab Rahman, S.I., Ibrahim, M.M., and Saad, N.H.M. 2017. Development of sleep monitoring system for observing the effect of the room ambient toward the quality of sleep. *MS&E*, vol. 210, no. 1, article ID 012050.

Sattar, H., Bajwa, I.S., Amin, R.ul, et al. 2019a. Smart wound hydration monitoring using biosensors and fuzzy inference system. *Wireless Communication and Mobile Computing*, vol. 2019, article ID 8059629, pp. 1–15.

Sattar, H., Bajwa, I.S., and Shafi, U. 2019b. An IoT-based intelligent wound monitoring system. *IEEE Access*, vol. 2019, no. 7, pp. 144500–144515.

Sarwar, B., Bajwa, I., Jamil, S.N., Ramzan, S., and Sarwar, N. 2019. An intelligent fire warning application using IoT and an adaptive neuro-fuzzy inference system. *Sensors*, vol. 19, no. 14, article ID 3150.

14

Machine Learning for Designing a Mechanical Ventilator: An Approach

Jayant Giri, Shreya Dhapke, and Dhananjay Mutyarapwar

Yeshwantrao Chavan College of Engineering, Nagpur, India

CONTENTS

14.1 Introduction

Technology has changed a lot, and there is a growing need for fast and accurate systems to fulfill the needs of people. In today's world, there is the availability of large volumes of data in every domain. This has been possible due to the development of various hardware systems with vast storage capacity to store such a big amount of data. Due to these reasons Machine Learning (ML) and Artificial Intelligence (AI) emerged as the recent trends in technology. Mechanical ventilation is a procedure often implemented on patients with respiratory failure. It is a core therapy that is provided to the intensive care unit (ICU) patients suffering from critical illness. A ventilator delivers an air and oxygen mixture, with elevated oxygen content, to a patient's respiratory system through an endotracheal tube to facilitate the adequate exchange of oxygen and carbon dioxide, which reduces the patient's effort to breath and prevents the alveoli from collapsing. However, to use a mechanical ventilator, one needs to be aware of the modes and several control parameters of the ventilator. These are controls are managed by highly-trained medical professionals, who are specialized in the care of respiratory illnesses, the Respiratory Therapists. These therapists are essential for the appropriate care of mechanically ventilated patients. But the conventional way of manual monitoring of mechanical ventilators utilizes more time, human effort, and is not cost-effective.

There has been tremendous research in the field of critical care to date. Despite that, deciding an individualized ventilation strategy for patients with respiratory failure is still a major challenge. In ICU, the clinicians make decisions based on acquired data, the data available at the bedside, and their own experience. The ventilation strategy for an individual patient must be patient-specific and patient-interactive. It should be optimized. Sub-optimal ventilation strategies may lead to Ventilator Induced Lung Injury (VILI), toxic effects of oxygen, and hemodynamic instability [1]. Prolonged mechanical ventilation (MV) is prone to several medical complexities that increase the ICU stay period of the patient, which in turn increases the overall cost. It also stimulates ventilator-induced morbidities, increases mortality rate, and decreases the overall lifespan of the patient. Therefore, the complete optimization of MV treatment is significant in clinical as well as economic terms [2]. Several factors are considered before delivering an optimized and patient-specific MV treatment. Some of those factors are laboratory data, vitals, the severity of illness scores, various comorbidities, disease progression, etc. [1].

ML, AI, and DL are the promising technologies that are significant in achieving this goal. ML is a branch of computer science in which statistical methods are implemented to data to classify, predict, or optimize, based on previously gathered data [3]. ML techniques are well-defined computer algorithms that can learn (with the help of a tutor or self-extraction of features and form clusters of data) and update its knowledge by learning through errors (self-correction) without any explicit programming [4]. As discussed earlier, in the course of mechanical ventilation therapy, clinicians have to make decisions based on acquired data, various patient-specific factors, and their medical knowledge. These decisions can be made accurately and consistently with the help of machine learning models. The introduction of large volumes of past patient data to ML methods improved the results of statistical regression enormously, creating an opportunity for individualized patient-specific treatment [5]. A machine learning model uses various statistical methods to perform data analysis and keep improving its efficiency with the introduction of new data points. It can transform clinical care practice by helping clinicians interpret complex and diverse data types [6]. In addition to optimizing individual ventilation strategies, AI can reduce clinicians' workload and act as an alert system, as clinicians and nurses cannot always be present to monitor the patients with 100% efficiency. ML and AI also find their application in critical care to analyze data stored in electronic health records to predict mortality and length of stay in ICU [7]. Different DL algorithms help clinicians to successfully predict the tracheal intubation incorporation time, optimized allocation of resources and staff, and individual patient care strategy respectively [8]. Several ML and DL models were built for optimization of particular goals, like the selection of appropriate modes, prediction of asynchrony, prediction for successful extubation, etc. But these machine learning models were created to overcome a particular drawback and bring optimization in a particular domain of MV therapy. Thus, with the help of this study, we tried to present an overview to create optimization in the overall mechanical ventilation process.

14.2 Material and Methods

ICUs are extremely data-rich environments, where monitoring and therapeutic devices (for example mechanical ventilators) generate large volumes of data continuously [9]. Big Data is being utilized in a proper manner, which is producing a revolutionary optimization in the management of patients in critical care units [10]. It's been observed that several ML and DL methods have been used to create optimization in specific domains of critical care in ICU. Several models have been deployed for use in critical care systems. We provided a detailed overview regarding ML and DL methods applications in MV. The most successful and accurate ML and DL models are discussed below.

14.2.1 Convolutional Neural Network (CNN)

One of the most useful and significant applications of ML in critical care to date is that of analysis of visual imagery. Each image contains millions of pixels that need to be processed to be able to recognize patterns during the course of treatment. CNN more efficiently recognizes patterns by the process of segmentation of an image and thus preventing the processing of every individual pixel separately [3, 11]. A convolutional neural network (CNN) is a DL algorithm that takes an image as input data and can classify the images based on analysis of unique features of each image. CNN consists of multiple layers. With data progressing through each layer, basic to complex features of the image are recognized. When a patient is under the treatment of MV the physiology of his lungs is monitored with the help of pressure, flow, and volume waveforms. CNN finds its application in critical care in analyzing several unique features of these waveforms. As per changing respiratory mechanics of the patient corresponding changes take place in the waveforms. With the help of a ventilator waveform dataset, a DL model can be prepared, aided by CNN. A DL model was developed for detecting the patient-ventilator asynchrony (PVA) events [12]. PVA is caused due to a mismatch between ventilator breaths delivered and the patient respiratory requirements. The above-mentioned DL model was able to classify the breaths into normal breaths and asynchronous breaths. Thus, this type of DL model reduces the need for continuous monitoring and also reduces inefficiency caused due to false alarms. CNN can also provide predictions regarding the selection of an appropriate mode of ventilation as per the patient's respiratory needs. In addition, it needs a waveform dataset for model creation.

14.2.2 Long Short-Term Memory Neural Network (LSTM)

LSTM neural network is an advanced version of recurrent neural network (RNN). It gives output based on current input, but also takes into consideration any previous output stored in its memory to improve its efficiency and deliver accurate output. It can store previous outputs generated for a long period and can classify within which data to be stored for learning purposes and which data to be removed from its memory. LSTM neural networks also find their application in critical care in detecting the type of PVA introduced during the course of MV treatment. It also requires a ventilator waveform dataset consisting of pressure and flow waveforms of patients. A DL model using LSTM neural network was proposed which predicted the two most frequently occurring asynchronies during the course of MV [13]. The model was able to detect double triggering and ineffective inspiratory effort types of PVA. The proposed LSTM neural network consisted of two layers, and two DL models were created, one for double triggering asynchrony detection and the other for ineffective inspiratory effort detection [13]. Data screening was performed by a group of experienced critical care specialists and biomedical engineers. Thus, this type of model reduces the need for continuous monitoring of the patients and makes the process simple to handle.

One more DL model was proposed using LSTM neural network, which predicted alerts if the set tidal volume violates the safe tidal volume threshold value, which is calculated by tidal volume per ideal body weight [14]. These predictions were given one hour before the lung-protective tidal volume value is violated. The data set used for training the model consisted of tidal volume values for each patient, which was a set of N discrete observations recorded at per minute intervals [14]. Thus this model enabled lung-protective ventilation and provided an alert to the clinicians one hour before the potential damage is caused to the patient lungs.

14.2.3 Random-Forest Algorithm

A Random-Forest ML algorithm consists of multiple decision trees. The dataset for the creation of a Random-Forest ML model consists of several columns of features and corresponding labels and several rows of data. The training dataset is again divided into multiple row samples and features samples. The unique samples of row data and feature data are entered into each decision tree. Each decision tree provides an output. The output predicted by the majority of trees is taken as the final output. Random-Forest ML model can be efficient as it works effectively and predicts accurate results for large data sets, and can do the same if a large amount of data is missing. Random-Forest algorithm finds its application in critical care in creating both classifier and regression models. It is a supervised learning algorithm. A random-forest ML model was developed to predict the appropriate mode to be selected for MV treatment. Mode of the ventilator is an important ventilator setting. A ventilator waveform dataset was used. The data set consisted of pressure and flow waveforms. Several files containing breath cycles of a particular size were created. With the help of medical professionals, each breath was assigned one of these modes: pressure support (PS), proportional assist ventilation (PAV), pressure control (PC), continuous positive airway pressure (CPAP), and volume control (VC) [15]. Another ML model was proposed to detect the type of asynchrony using a random forest algorithm. The dataset used for the model creation consisted of flow waveforms, pressure waveforms, and volume waveforms. The group of medical professionals visually inspected each breath and assigned each of them a label: delayed termination, premature termination, or no asynchrony [16]. In preparation of both, the model's feature extraction was done manually by visual inspection of waveforms.

14.2.4 Gradient-Boosted Trees Algorithm

Gradient boosting is an ensemble method. It can act as a tool for both types of ML problems: classification and regression problems. The gradient boosting algorithm uses a boosting type of ensemble method in which predictions made are sequential and each leading predictor learns from the errors of the previous predictor. It's a combination of several decision trees that act as predictors and are connected. A gradient boosting ML algorithm finds its application in critical care in predicting several complex decisions. A gradient boosting ML classifier was developed for predicting prolonged mechanical ventilation and tracheostomy as outcomes. It used a dataset consisting of six severity of illness scores (SOIS), patient comorbidities, and the components of SOIS [17]. This classification is very significant in delivering optimized treatment and reducing the mortality rate. Sepsis is an infection that is linked with organ failure and is the major cause of disease in ICU [18]. An XGboost model was developed for predicting sepsis diagnosis for critically ill patients. Sepsis is still the cause of agonizing deaths in ICU [19]. An ML model using Light GBM (Light gradient boosting machine) algorithm was developed for predicting extubation success or failure. It outperformed all the previously developed ML models using ANN and SVM for the same purpose. The accuracy of the model was 80.23%. It made use of a dataset consisting of features such as patient demographics, vital signs, laboratory results, ventilator information, clinical intervention variables, and clinical scores [20].

14.2.5 Decision Tree Algorithm

A decision tree is one of the powerful tools of the ML library. It comes under the supervised ML algorithm category and uses a tree-shaped structure to process data. Each branch of the tree represents a possible decision. A decision tree can resolve both types of ML problems. In classification, the decision tree will determine a set of logical if-then conditions to classify output. A regression decision tree is used when the output to be predicted is a numerical value. It is preferably suitable for predicting target variables that are continuous in nature. Each of the independent variables is significant for fitting the resulting model on a target variable. An ML model was developed using a regression decision tree algorithm to predict the airway resistance (R) and lung compliance (C) values continuously and in real-time. They collected the data by connecting a pressure control ventilator to a test lung that stimulated several R and C values, and thus collected the sensor data [21]. This study was vital in developing an optimized lung protective ventilation strategy for patients.

14.2.6 Support Vector Machine (SVM) Algorithm

In SVM we assign labels according to each feature separately that are represented by individual data points on the plot of dependent variables against independent variables. Once all data points are plotted, the two classes of data are separated with the help of a hyperplane. Thus, SVM is mostly used for classification purposes. SVM finds its application in care in predicting extubation success or failure. Extubating a patient off the ventilator is a complex process. Delayed extubation increases the chances of ventilator-induced lung injury (VILI) and increased cost of ventilation. Premature extubation leads to increased chances of re-intubation within one or two months. An SVM ML was developed for predicting extubation success or failure. It utilized the patient demographics data, monitor data, time-series data, and laboratory data as features (predictors) for training the model. The dataset consisted of data in the form of comma-separated values. The model was accurate with 94.6% accuracy [22].

14.2.7 Unsupervised Machine Learning

Unsupervised machine learning is a data clustering technique. It doesn't require tagged data or any tutor to tag the data. It is the most unpredictable ML method in terms of deriving several relationships and patterns among data and can give unbelievable outcomes. Based on various relationships among the data, it forms several clusters of data. Thus, a cluster consists of similar data types. It can be used for feature extraction from any

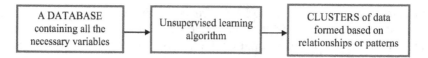

FIGURE 14.1
Conceptual block-diagram regarding data clusters formation in unsupervised learning.

complex database. It finds its application in care in analyzing the complex datasets and forming clusters of similar data, and thus, simplifies the process of model creation. An ML model was created using an unsupervised ML algorithm to identify the distinct subgroups of patients in an ICU [23]. Identifying distinct subgroups of patients having similar clinical morbidity enables more efficient delivery of critical care treatment.

14.2.8 A Conceptual Supervised Ml Model Creation for Critical Care

14.2.8.1 Model is ready to deploy

Figure 14.2 represents a generalizable conceptual supervised ML model for critical care applications. From introspection of previous studies, it is evident that most of the ML models developed to date used supervised ML algorithms. Firstly the database containing all the variables necessary for corresponding model creation is arranged. Then the relevant features for the preparation of a particular ML model are extracted from the database with the help of a suitable data extraction technique. Then the data is labelled or tagged with the help of a data scientist and a group of experienced medical professionals. Then the

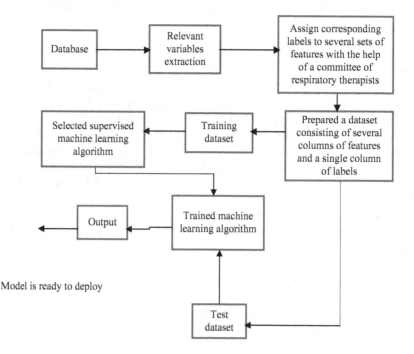

FIGURE 14.2
A conceptual model to create a supervised ML model for critical care.

TABLE 14.1

Comparison Table of Important Features of ML/DL Models [15, 17, 22]

Sr. No.	Important Features	Application Suitability	ML or DL Algorithms Can Be Used (Most Suitable)
1.	Ventilator waveform data (Pressure, flow and volume waveforms).	For creating an ML or DL model for selection of appropriate mode of ventilation (patient-specific).	Random Forest ML algorithm.
2.	Ventilator waveform data (Pressure, flow and volume waveforms).	For creating an ML or DL model for detection of the type of asynchrony encountered during the course of MV treatment.	Long Short-Term Memory Neural Network. Random Forest ML algorithm.
3.	Tidal volume dataset.	For creating an ML or DL model for predicting tidal volume behaviour and alerting if any violations were encountered.	Long Short-Term Memory Neural Network. Boosted trees ML algorithm.
4.	LODS pulmonary, SOFA, OASIS pre ICU LOS, APS III, OASIS heart rate, APS III PaO2/P(A-a)O2, Cardiac arrhythmias, Weight loss, APS III acid base.	For creating an ML or DL model for predicting the patient in requirement of prolonged mechanical ventilation and tracheostomy placement.	Gradient-boosted trees algorithm.
5.	SOFA score, infection (any site), LAB_BUN, APACHE score.	For creating an ML or DL model for predicting sepsis and non-sepsis status of a patient.	XGBOOST ML algorithm.
6.	Airway pressure and flow rate.	For creating an ML model for predicting airway resistance (R) and lung compliance (C) values.	Decision trees ML algorithm.
7.	DHMV, PaCO2, PAO2, Arterial PH, laboratory results, vital signs, clinical scores, patient demographics.	For creating an ML model for predicting extubation success or extubation failure.	Support vector machine ML algorithm. Light GBM ML algorithm.

tagged data is further divided into two datasets. This process is known as data splitting. Thus, the dataset is split into a training dataset and a testing dataset. The ML algorithm is then trained with the help of a training dataset. After training, the model is validated using a testing dataset. Once the model is confirmed to be accurate, the model is deployed for use. There are different terminologies, such as Area under Curve (AUC), sensitivity, and specificity, that determine the accuracy of the model.

14.3 Result and Discussion

A complete overview regarding the most accurate and successful ML and DL models developed for optimization of the MV process has been presented. MV therapy has three clinical goals to be accomplished: ensuring the adequate exchange of gases (oxygen delivery into lungs and carbon-dioxide removal from the body), enabling comfort to the patient, and preventing the patient from VILI, thereby reducing the cost of ventilation. The mentioned ML and DL models fulfill these clinical goals. ML and DL models for appropriate mode selection, asynchrony detection, prolonged mechanical ventilation or tracheostomy requirement prediction, and extubation success or failure prediction have been developed to date as necessary for designing an optimized mechanical ventilator. The most successful and widely applied ML and DL methods were: CNN, LSTM neural network, random-forest ML algorithm, decision tree algorithm, SVM, and the gradient boosting trees algorithm. ML and DL models can analyze complex patterns of data and predict an optimized ventilation strategy for clinicians to apply. An unsupervised ML algorithm can be used to create ML models predicting the most optimal patient-specific ventilation strategy. The ventilator waveform data is used to create ML models for asynchrony detection and appropriate mode selection. LSTM neural network is best suited for the creation of such models, as it can store previous outputs as per their requirement and for a long period. These characteristics help them in providing accurate outputs. The SVM ML algorithm is best suited for predicting accurate extubation strategy. The decision tree ML algorithm is best suited for creating repressor models for predicting accurate values of control parameters and ventilator settings according to the ventilator mode setting applied. A decision tree algorithm is best suited for predicting continuous output variables.

In the future, more ML and DL models will be developed to optimize the rest of the domains which have not been studied yet. Several regression models need to be developed to predict patient-specific values of control parameters, such as the fraction of inspired oxygen, positive end-expiratory pressure, inspiratory pressure, tidal volume, and I: E ratio. The values of these control parameters are needed to be updated continuously, as per

TABLE 14.2

ML and DL Methods for Designing an Optimized Mechanical Ventilator

Sr. No.	Author	DL or ML Method	Purpose/Outcome
1.	N. L. Loo et al.	CNN	Classifying whether a given breath is normal breath or asynchronous breath.
2.	Lingwei Zhang et al.	LSTM neural netrwork	Detecting the type of asynchrony: double triggering or ineffective inspiratory effort.
3.	Rachael Hagan et al.	LSTM neural netrwork	Predicted alerts if the set tidal volume violates the safe tidal volume threshold value which is calculated by tidal volume per ideal body weight.
4.	Gregory B. Rehm et al.	Random-Forest algorithm	Predicted the appropriate mode to be selected among: pressure support (PS), proportional assist ventilation (PAV), pressure control (PC), continuous positive airway pressure (CPAP), and volume control (VC).
5.	Behnood Gholami et al.	Random-Forest algorithm	Predicted the type of asynchrony encountoured: delayed termination, premature termination, no asynchrony.
6.	Tingting Chen et al.	Light GBM	Predicted extubation success or failure with accuracy of 80.23%.
7.	Joshua Parreco et al.	Gradient boosted decision trees algorithm	Classifiers for prediction of prolonged mechanical ventilation and tracheostomy placement.
8.	Kuo-Ching Yuana et al.	XGboost	Developed for predicting sepsis diagnosis for critically ill patients.
9.	Alexandre Fabregat et al.	Support vector machine algorithm	Predicted extubation success or failure with accuracy of 94.6%.
10.	N. Hezarjaribi et al.	Decision tree	Predicted air way resistance (R) and Lung compliance (C) values on a continuous basis and in real-time.

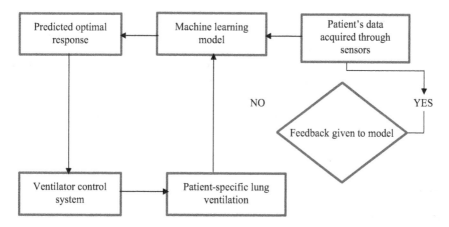

FIGURE 14.3
Conceptual block diagram representing automation in delivery of MV treatment.

feedback generated by sensors according to a patient's condition. Here, the regression decision tree algorithm can be used for model creation. To date, ML and DL models are developed to provide decision support to clinicians and reduce complexity and workload encountered during MV treatment, but the process is not completely automated. There is a need for clinicians to set the ventilator settings and monitor the patient's condition when specified by ML models. When ML and DL models for predicting each of the ventilator settings and control parameters are created, complete automation can be enabled. A basic conceptual model representing the idea of automation has been shown below.

Figure 14.3 represents a conceptual block diagram to create automation in delivering MV treatment. It is a closed-loop model. Every modern mechanical ventilator has default ventilator settings that are set when a patient is put on a ventilator. The dynamic data of patients gathered by the sensors will be input to the ML model deployed for use. Then the response generated by the ML the model will be input into the ventilator controller. Here we have to replace the physical setting of ventilator settings by clinicians with automatic settings of the same. Then, the respiratory requirements will be delivered to the patient. After delivery of the ventilation requirements as per the patient, the feedback generated by the patient will be sent to the ML model again. Now the new prediction will be dependent upon error and the patients' dynamic data provided by the sensors. ML models dependent on static variables are needed to be given input by clinical staff. Thus, in the future, a complete automated MV delivering system can be seen which will decrease the work-load of clinicians to almost negligible work. There will be fewer requirements of highly talented respiratory therapists in an ICU in terms of quantity.

14.4 Conclusion

The manual decision-making process regarding the patient-specific ventilation strategy is suboptimal. Optimization of conventional mechanical systems, with the use of recent technological trends like machine learning and artificial intelligence, is the solution to this problem. Artificial intelligence and machine learning enable the proper utilization of the large volumes of critical care data available in today's world to deliver the optimized MV treatment. Introducing machine learning concepts into mechanical ventilators for the decision-making process increases the accuracy, decreases the uncertainty factor, and decreases the utilization of human effort and time. The approach portrayed in the present investigation focused more on a different perspective of the application of machine learning and deep learning for mechanical ventilators. Further, actual patient data must be used with a suitable case study to explore all possible findings mentioned in the present investigation.

References

1. Peine, A., Hallawa, A., Bickenbach, J., et al. Development and validation of a reinforcement learning algorithm to dynamically optimize mechanical ventilation in critical care. *NPJ Digital Medicine*. 2021; 4(1): 1–12.
2. Kwong, M.T., Colopy, G.W., Weber, A.M., Ercole, A., Bergmann, J.H.M. The efficacy and effectiveness of machine learning for weaning in mechanically ventilated patients at the Intensive Care Unit: A systematic review. *Bio-Design and Manufacturing*. 2019; 2: 31–40.
3. Mlodzinski, E., Stone, D.J., Celi, L.A. Machine learning for pulmonary and critical care medicine: A narrative review. *Pulm Ther*. 2020; 6: 67–77.
4. Senders, J.T., Zaki, M.M., Karhade, A.V., et al. An introduction and overview of machine learning in neurosurgical care. *Actaneurochirurgica*. 2018; 160(1): 29–38.
5. Mekov, E., Miravitlles, M., Petkov, R. Artificial intelligence and machine learning in respiratory medicine. *Expert Review of Respiratory Medicine*. 2020; 14(6): 559–564.
6. Ben-Israel, D., Jacobs, W.B., Casha, S., Lang S., Ryu, W.H.A., de Lotbiniere-Bassetta, M., Cadotte, D.W. The impact of machine learning on patient care: A systematic review. *Artificial Intelligence in Medicine*. 2020; 103: 101785.
7. Gutierrez, G. Artificial Intelligence in the Intensive Care Unit. *Gutierrez Critical Care*. 2020; 24: 1–9.
8. Shashikumar, S.P., et al. Development and prospective validation of a deep learning algorithm for predicting need for mechanical ventilation. PhD diss., University of California, 2020.
9. Meyfroidt, G., Gu¨iza, F., Ramon, R., and Bruynooghe, M. Machine learning techniques to examine large patient databases. *Best Practice & Research Clinical Anaesthesiology*. 2009; 23: 127–143.
10. Heili-Frades, S., Minguez, P., Fernández, I.M., et al. Patient management assisted by a neural network reduces mortality in an intermediate care unit. *Arch Bronconeumol*. 2020; 56(9): 564–570.
11. Anwar, S.M., Majid, M., Qayyum, A., Awais, M., Alnowami, M., and Khan, M.K. Medical image analysis using convolutional neural networks: A review. *J Med Syst*. 2018; 42(11): 226.
12. Loo, N.L., Chiew, Y.S., Tan, C.P., Arunachalam, G., Ralib, A.M., et al. A machine learning model for real-time asynchronous breathing monitoring. *IFAC Papers OnLine*. 2018; 51–27: 378–383.
13. Zhang, L., Mao, K., Duan, K., et al. Detection of patient-ventilator asynchrony from mechanical ventilation waveforms using a two-layer long short-term memory neural network. *Computers in Biology and Medicine*. 2020; 120: 103721.
14. Hagan, R., Gillan, C.J., Spence, I., McAuley, D., and Shyamsundar, M. Comparing regression and neural network techniques for personalized predictive analytics to promote lung protective ventilation in Intensive Care Units. *Computers in Biology and Medicine*. 2020; 126: 104030.
15. Rehm, G.B., Kuhn, B.T., Nguyen, J., Anderson, N.R., Chuah, C-N., Adams, J.Y.. Improving mechanical ventilator clinical decision support systems with a machine learning classifier for determining ventilator mode [Google Books]. In *MEDINFO 2019: Health and Wellbeing e-Networks for All*, pp. 318–322, 2019.

16. Gholami, B., Phan, T.S., Haddad, W.M., Cason, A., Mullis, J., Price, L., Bailey, J.M. Replicating human expertise of mechanical ventilation waveform analysis in detecting patient-ventilator cycling asynchrony using machine learning. *Computers in Biology and Medicine.* 2018; 97: 137–144.

17. Parreco, J., Hidalgo, A., Parks, J.J., Kozol, R., and Rattan, R. Using artificial intelligence to predict prolonged mechanical ventilation and tracheostomy placement. *Journal of Surgical Research.* 2018; 228: 179–187.

18. Sakr, Y., Jaschinski, U., Wittebole, X., et al. Sepsis in Intensive Care Unit patients: Worldwide data from the Intensive Care over nations audit. *Open Forum Infectious Diseases.* 2018; 5(12): ofy313.

19. Yuana, K-C., Tsai, L-W., Lee, K-H., Cheng, Y-W., Hsu, S.-C., Lo, Y.-S., and Chen, R.-J.. The development an artificial intelligence algorithm for early sepsis diagnosis in the Intensive Care Unit. *International Journal of Medical Informatics.* 2020; 141: 104176.

20. Chen, T., Xu, J., Ying, H., Chen, C., Feng, R., Fang, X., Gao, H., and Wu, J. Prediction of extubation failure for Intensive Care Unit patients using light gradient boosting machine. *IEEE Access.* 2019; 7: 150960–150968.

21. Hezarjaribi, N., Dutta, R., Xing, T., et al. Monitoring lung mechanics during mechanical ventilation using machine learning algorithms. In *2018 40th Annual International Conference of the IEEE Engineering in Medicine and Biology Society (EMBC)*, pp. 1160–1163, 2018.

22. Fabregat, A., Magret, M., Ferre´, J.A., Vernet, A., Guasch, N., Rodriguez, A., Gomez, J., and Bodi, M. A machine learning decision-making tool for extubation in Intensive Care Unit patients. *Computer Methods and Programs in Biomedicine.* 2021; 200: 105689.

23. Vranas, K.C., Jopling, J.K., et al. Identifying distinct subgroups of Intensive Care Unit patients: A machine learning approach. *Critical Care Medicine.* 2017; 45(10): 1607–1615.

Appendix: Introduction to Machine Learning through Hands-on in Python

Ranjit Varma

Delhi Technical Campus, Greater Noida, India

Devendra Bharadwaj

Harman Connected Services, Bengaluru, India

CONTENTS

A.1 Introduction

AI or Artificial Intelligence is a field of engineering and science of making machines that can reason, learn, and act intelligently–a simple definition, though carrying the weight of the secrets of the next generation of human evolution. Most of us have been aware of AI recently when we got cameras tagging our smiling faces or phones with finger-print access or Alexa responding to our commands. However, AI's history dates to almost seven decades ago, when it was formally established in 1956 at a Dartmouth College, UK conference. It was also here that the term "Artificial Intelligence" was coined. For almost three decades afterward, universities and governments were developing AI, either as small projects or futuristic endeavours in their backyards. The major turning point for AI came in 1997, when IBM's Deep Blue became the first computer to beat a chess champion by defeating Russian grandmaster Garry Kasparov, though some projects like DARPA had covered initial milestones in implementing AI in the US. Since then, AI development has not turned back and has gained interest in almost every industry. Rather, it'd not be an exaggeration to say that it's disrupted industries to such a degree that the business models are experiencing major changes. For example, in the field of retail and ecommerce AI chatbots are helping retailers collect customer data, which they use to provide meaningful insights into retailers or help maintain CRM applications in retail stores with automated data entry, ad personalization, and account insights, etc. Likewise, AI has triggered major upheavals in manufacturing and production with Predictive Maintenance, telecommunication with AI-based cloud-based network management, supply chain and logistics by helping to forecast inventory, demand, and supply, and eventually revolutionizing the optimization and agility of supply chain decision making. However, two big industries that have gained significant AI and have utilized matured AI technologies are transportation and healthcare. Together, these two industries have started to revolutionize the economy and will be the frontier in applying cutting-edge AI research and solutions.

But from where did AI evolve to such a massive scale; was it a science miracle or engineering feat? The answer is, both. AI combines science and engineering to enable machine reason and perform like or better than a human. This encapsulates understanding the science behind capturing of sensory inputs (just like a human brain does) and applying the same through multi-disciplinary engineering techniques to determine the result. Take for example, the chatbot that we usually interact with while logging a ticket, etc. The chatbot is supposed to take inputs from a user and behave or respond like a human, with some rational output or results. Here, the inputs could either be a voice command or simple texts. These inputs are processed by a highly intelligent algorithm analyzing the characteristics of text/voice as well as the tone and the urgency. In order to build a system that could interact with humans on basic intelligence levels, the vocabulary, verbs, sentence structures, and contexts are augmented with Natural Language Processing algorithms. In summary, AI systems are no single example of only science or engineering, but utilize both in some form or the other.

With AI now taking the cornerstone of every major technical disruption, we need to understand various sub-disciplines of AI which are responsible for these changes. AI has been an umbrella terminology encapsulating multiple other facets, like Machine Learning and Deep Learning. These two terms have recently gained significance and have established a clear identity due to their distinct applications. Figure A.1 depicts the subsystems of Artificial Intelligence.

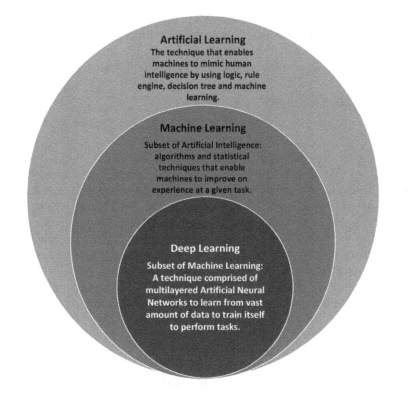

FIGURE A.1
Realms of AI.

Now that we know that Machine Learning and Deep Learning are two critical subsystems of AI let's dive into them to get a better understanding.

Machine Learning is an application of artificial intelligence (AI) that allows systems to learn and improve from experience without being explicitly programmed automatically. Machine learning focuses on developing computer programs that can access data and use it to learn for themselves. The learning process begins with observations or data, such as examples, direct experience, or instruction, to look for patterns in data and make better decisions in the future based on the examples that we provide. The primary aim is to enable machines to learn automatically without human intervention or assistance and take actions accordingly.

A mathematical definition for Machine Learning could be put as, "a computer program is said to learn from experience E with respect to some task T and some performance measure P, if its performance on T, as measured by P, improves with experience E" [1]. Let's try to understand this through an example. Let's say your email program watches which emails you do or do not mark as spam. So, in an email client like this, you might click the Spam button to report some email as spam, but not the other emails. Over a period, your email program will learn better how to filter spam from the hordes of email you receive every day. To derive the analogy, classifying emails is the task T, watching you label emails as spam or not spam would be the experience E, and the fraction of emails correctly classified might be a performance measure P.

Contrary to common perception, Machine Learning is not all about statistics. Rather, machine learning is a process of working with Data/Inputs, building the learning model, evaluating the model (using statistics) and optimizing the model to provide best predictions or actions. All the above steps could be represented [2] as:

$$Machine\ Learning : X \to X\ where\ X$$
$$\in (Exploration,\ Representation,\ Evaluation,\ Optimization)$$

To summarize, exploration is a process involving data collection, data cleaning, and data rebuilding, so that clean and unambiguous data is ready as an input. Representation is a process of transforming the data from one space to another so that it could be more easily interpreted or used by subsequent algorithms. Evaluation is where the heart of Machine Learning lies. It is where all the transformed data is processed or crunched by your algorithm or model to learn about data behavior or hidden trends and predictions thrown out by the model. And lastly, optimization is where the hyperparameters are tuned to improve the performance of the model.

As shown in the equation above, Learning is an iterative process where a model must constantly learn from new data and improve upon its performance and accuracy to predict. Sometimes, when the variety of data changes significantly over a period the old models will prove ineffective and will have to be replaced by entirely new models and tuning parameters.

Now that we've learned the innate working of Machine Learning, let's have a look at the primary techniques used. Figure A.2 shows the three broad categories of Machine Learning.

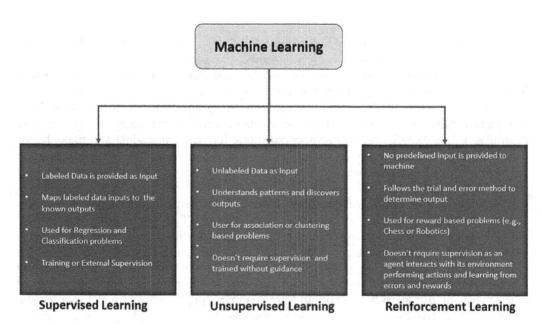

FIGURE A.2
Types of machine learning.

A.2 Supervised Learning

As the name suggests, this branch of Machine Learning involves training a machine to learn from already existing data and outcomes. Supervised Learning can handle two categories of problems, one that requires **Classification** or identification of categories, and second, **Regression**, which requires a discrete numerical output derived. Let's understand Classification first. Recall the previous example that we discussed for filtering a spam mail. In order to identify whether a mail is a spam or not, your program or machine will have to be trained to identify the characteristics of a spam mail. For this you may either pass some keywords which are usually a part of spam mail e.g., "lottery," "sale," "free credit", etc. With this you'll also have to tag or label the mails having these as either part of their body or headlines. Now, you train your machine with all these 'labeled' mails. Once your machine is trained with a certain degree of accuracy, you can now use it to classify an entire new set of mails as spam or not. This is how supervised learning is used for classification problems. Though the spam mail discussed is an example of binary classification, supervised learning also covers multi-classification problems, e.g., when used with animal images to identify fish, dog, or cat.

Regression on the other hand establishes a relation between various inputs and the desired output. For example, let's say you have a car data set containing year of manufacturing, horsepower, make, number of insurance claims, number of kilometers on the odometer, current condition, etc., the way KBB inputs resale value of these cars. Your regression program or model will determine an equation or relationship between all these independent inputs and the resale value. Once you get this relationship, you will be able to predict the resale value of any new input set.

Let's understand Supervised Learning with the help of the housing price determination Regression problem from Kaggle [3].

This problem attempts to build an ML model to estimate the price of the house. It provides information about other houses in the vicinity, such as area in sq-ft, number of rooms, age of house, number of bathrooms, etc., and current market price of these houses. We'll go over simple steps to build an ML model or algorithm by feeding all this data to our machine (algorithm) so that your machine learns how to utilize house features and what will be the prices. This exercise where all the house features are fed along with the target price is called Training. In machine learning terminology, the house attributes are called 'Input Features,' and the price of the house is known as 'Target Feature,' as shown in Figure A.3 below:

Learning Phase

Training data   Features vector   Algorithm   Model

FIGURE A.3
Training steps of ML model.

Image: Source [4].

Inference from Model

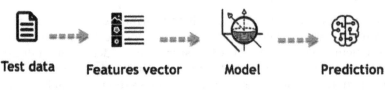

Test data   Features vector   Model   Prediction

FIGURE A.4
Testing steps of ML model.

Image: Source [4].

In the next step, we'll test this ML model for some more data sets of houses to ensure that our model has learned well and can predict with some threshold accuracy. Now your machine is ready, and you can feed in the features of the house you've identified to determine the suitable price (Figure A.4).

We'll be using Jupyter Notebook to develop code using Python v 3.7

A.2.1 Data Processing

A.2.1.1 Data Cleaning

In this step we address data quality issues such as missing values, outliers, data pollution, etc. Import the libraries. (Numpy, Pandas, and sklearn libraries are the primary ones.)

```python
# Numerical libraries
import numpy as np

# Import Linear Regression machine learning library
from sklearn.linear_model import LinearRegression

# to handle data in form of rows and columns
import pandas as pd

# importing ploting libraries
import matplotlib.pyplot as plt
import matplotlib.style
plt.style.use('classic')

#importing seaborn for statistical plots
import seaborn as sns
```

i. Download the housing data set from the Kaggle link and import the csv file in Jupyter Notebook to create a Dataframe

```python
# reading the CSV file into pandas dataframe
hprice_df = pd.read_csv("train.csv")
```

ii. Check for the features.

```
# Check top few records to get a feel of the data structure
hprice_df.head()
```

	Id	MSSubClass	MSZoning	LotFrontage	LotArea	Street	Alley	LotShape	LandContour	Utilities	...	PoolArea	PoolQC	Fence	MiscFeature	MiscVal
0	1	60	RL	65.0	8450	Pave	NaN	Reg	Lvl	AllPub	...	0	NaN	NaN	NaN	0
1	2	20	RL	80.0	9600	Pave	NaN	Reg	Lvl	AllPub	...	0	NaN	NaN	NaN	0
2	3	60	RL	68.0	11250	Pave	NaN	IR1	Lvl	AllPub	...	0	NaN	NaN	NaN	0
3	4	70	RL	60.0	9550	Pave	NaN	IR1	Lvl	AllPub	...	0	NaN	NaN	NaN	0
4	5	60	RL	84.0	14260	Pave	NaN	IR1	Lvl	AllPub	...	0	NaN	NaN	NaN	0

5 rows × 81 columns

The results show that the data set has 81 features, including house prices. As we observe, not all features have numerical values. The features 'Street', 'Utilities', etc., have categorical data that we'll discuss how to handle in the sections below.

iii. Remove unwarranted or irrelevant data.

Identify and Remove any null values or arbitrary characters (e.g., #, &, etc.) which intrinsically do not belong to a feature data type. This also includes removing any duplicate entries in rows or columns.

```
hprice_df.isnull().sum()

Id                    0
MSSubClass            0
MSZoning              0
LotFrontage         259
LotArea               0
                    ...
MoSold                0
YrSold                0
SaleType              0
SaleCondition         0
SalePrice             0
Length: 81, dtype: int64
```

In the snippet above we can clearly observe that the 'LotFrontage' feature has 259 rows with null values.

We need to treat all such scenarios of null, NaN, or random characteristics before we can use our data to build a model. Some techniques include replacing NaN values of a feature with either a median or mean value of that feature. Cases where entire rows have multiple NaN or null need to be removed, as they don't contribute to a data set. The approach depends upon how the data is distributed as well as the impact on the overall data volume if NaN or null are removed.

iv. Handling features with strings or 'object' data type.

As we observed, some features ('MSZoning', 'LotShape', etc.) have categorical data, i.e., non-numerical. This type of data must be either converted to numerical value or dropped from the data set before it can be processed further. Some well-known techniques that can be deployed are Label Encoding and One Hot Encoding.

A.2.1.2 Data Visualization

Once data is cleaned and pre-processed, an important step is to visualize how data in all the features is distributed and how features are correlated. Pairplot, Box plots, and Heatmap are the primary techniques to visualize your data. This will provide you with the information about outliers and how statistically your data is distributed (Figure A.5).

```
hsg_df.describe().transpose()
```

	count	mean	std	min	25%	50%	75%	max
MSSubClass	1460.0	56.897260	42.300571	20.0	20.0	50.0	70.00	190.0
MSZoning	1460.0	3.028767	0.632017	0.0	3.0	3.0	3.00	4.0
LotFrontage	1460.0	69.863699	22.027677	21.0	60.0	69.0	79.00	313.0
LotArea	1460.0	10516.828082	9981.264932	1300.0	7553.5	9478.5	11601.50	215245.0
Street	1460.0	0.995890	0.063996	0.0	1.0	1.0	1.00	1.0
...	...	...	...	...	...	...	...	...
SaleCondition	1460.0	3.770548	1.100854	0.0	4.0	4.0	4.00	5.0
HouseAge	1460.0	36.547945	30.250152	0.0	8.0	35.0	54.00	136.0
RemodellingAge	1460.0	22.950685	20.639875	0.0	4.0	14.0	41.00	60.0
GarageAge	1460.0	27.680137	24.950144	0.0	4.0	23.5	46.00	107.0
TotalHouseArea	1460.0	15256.408904	10541.462579	3423.0	11507.0	13953.5	17142.25	221966.0

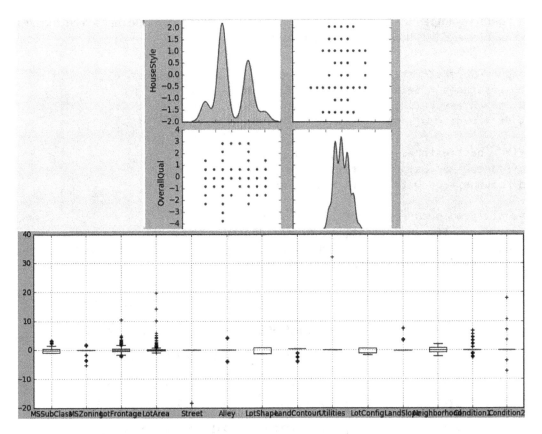

FIGURE A.5
Distribution plots (Pairplot and Boxplot) for a few features.

A.2.2 Feature Selection and Engineering

This step involves selecting the right attributes or features for building our model. The feature selection technique needs knowledge of the problem domain, as it helps identify the best set of features. For example, in case of a Housing problem, we may categorize area of the house, building material used, utilities, etc., as high priority, while Alley pavement, tilted tiling of the roof, etc., could be categorized as low priority features.

There are lots of feature selection techniques mainly categorized in filter, wrapper, embedded, and hybrid.

Feature selection techniques is a vast topic in itself and is not in the scope of this article.

Feature engineering is another technique that could be applied to create new and more meaningful features out of existing features. For example, we have summed up 'LotFrontageArea', 'LotArea', etc., to come up with a new feature, 'TotalHouseArea'.

For our example, we'll use a filter based feature selection technique that selects the best 15 features and lists them based on their scores:

```python
#Apply SelectKBest class to extract top 15 best features
bestfeatures = SelectKBest(score_func=chi2, k=30)
X_ft = X.astype(int)
y_ft = y.astype(int)

fit = bestfeatures.fit(X_ft,y_ft)
dfscores = pd.DataFrame(fit.scores_)
dfcolumns = pd.DataFrame(X_ft.columns)

#concat two dataframes for better visualization
featureScores = pd.concat([dfcolumns,dfscores],axis=1)
featureScores.columns = ['Specs','Score']  #naming the dataframe columns
print(featureScores.nlargest(15,'Score'))  #print 15 best features
```

```
           Specs          Score
82  TotalHouseArea  884892.928735
3          LotArea  753041.343964
43        2ndFlrSF  342553.084401
70        PoolArea  297844.826713
33       BsmtFinSF1  258010.879063
36        BsmtUnfSF  176081.545264
35       BsmtFinSF2  167794.384986
25       MasVnrArea  127574.505402
45        GrLivArea  106805.667616
37      TotalBsmtSF   80918.759294
65       WoodDeckSF   75832.432804
69      ScreenPorch   71808.261582
42         1stFlrSF   68340.348672
67    EnclosedPorch   64931.080747
61       GarageArea   49929.030814
```

A.2.3 Creating Training and Testing Data Sets

```python
from sklearn.model_selection import train_test_split

X_Train, X_Test, y_Train, y_Test = train_test_split(X, y, test_size=0.30, random_state=1)
```

Split entire data into training and test sets. As a rule of thumb, the data is split in a 70:30 ratio for training and test sets.

The other important step after creating training and test sets is normalizing or standardizing your data, so that all your data is at a common scale. Remember to normalize training and test sets separately to avoid data leakage from training to test data set and vice-versa. Z-score or Standard Scalar are the popular methods used for scaling.

```python
# Scaling training data set
from scipy.stats import zscore
X_Train_zscore = X_Train.apply(zscore)

X_Test_zscore = X_Test.apply(zscore)
```

```python
# Import `StandardScaler` from `sklearn.preprocessing`
from sklearn.preprocessing import StandardScaler

# Define the scaler
scaler = StandardScaler().fit(X_train)

# Scale the train set
X_train = scaler.transform(X_train)

# Scale the test set
X_test = scaler.transform(X_test)
```

A.2.4 Training Model

The model is now ready to be trained. As we have a regression problem at hand, we'll be using a simple grid search regression library to train our model. There are scores of other regression models, linear regression, random forest regressor, gradient booster regressor, etc., to name a few that could be applied.

A.2.4.1 Define the Hyperparameters (This is an Optional Step)

"Hyperparameters are parameters whose values are set prior to the commencement of the learning process" (*wiki*).

```python
# use a full grid over all parameters
param_grid = {"max_depth": [5,6,7,8],
              "max_features": ['auto'],
              "min_samples_split": [6,7,8,9],
              "min_samples_leaf": [2,3,4],
              "bootstrap": [True],
              'n_estimators': [180,200,220,240]
              }
```

A.2.4.2 Fit the Model

```
# run grid search
grid_search = GridSearchCV(clf, param_grid=param_grid)

grid_search.fit(X_Train, y_Train)
```

```
GridSearchCV(cv=None, error_score=nan,
             estimator=RandomForestRegressor(bootstrap=True, ccp_alpha=0.0,
                                             criterion='mse', max_depth=None,
                                             max_features='auto',
                                             max_leaf_nodes=None,
                                             max_samples=None,
                                             min_impurity_decrease=0.0,
                                             min_impurity_split=None,
                                             min_samples_leaf=1,
                                             min_samples_split=2,
                                             min_weight_fraction_leaf=0.0,
                                             n_estimators=100, n_jobs=None,
                                             oob_score=False, random_state=None,
                                             verbose=0, warm_start=False),
             iid='deprecated', n_jobs=None,
             param_grid={'bootstrap': [True], 'max_depth': [5, 6, 7, 8],
                         'max_features': ['auto'],
                         'min_samples_leaf': [2, 3, 4],
                         'min_samples_split': [6, 7, 8, 9],
                         'n_estimators': [180, 200, 220, 240]},
             pre_dispatch='2*n_jobs', refit=True, return_train_score=False,
             scoring=None, verbose=0)
```

A.2.4.3 Find Best Parameters for Higher Performance of the Model

```
best_random1 = grid_search.best_estimator_
```

```
print(grid_search.best_params_)
```

```
{'bootstrap': True, 'max_depth': 8, 'max_features': 'auto', 'min_samples_leaf': 3, 'min_samples_split': 6, 'n_estimators': 200}
```

A.2.4.4 Check Training Model Performance

```
random_accurac2 = evaluate(best_random1, X_Train, y_Train)
```

```
Model Performance
Average Error: 10442.5703 degrees.
Accuracy = 93.90%.
```

Training performance is quite high. This means our features and training data set are fitting very well through grid search algorithm.

A.2.4.5 Testing Model

```
random_accuracy = evaluate(best_random1, X_Test, y_Test)

Model Performance
Average Error: 17338.5444 degrees.
Accuracy = 88.42%.
```

The model shows very high accuracy for test data as well. However, it seems our model has a bias issue, which roughly means it's an underfit and needs more features or *less regularization*. Another issue which test models usually face is high variance or over-fitting. Finding a balance between bias-variance for your model needs a careful selection of features, feature engineering, and the right split of training and testing data.

A.3 Unsupervised Learning

This type of learning is mostly used identifying clusters or groups among a huge set of data. Unsupervised Learning fits well to those problems where you have raw, unlabeled data and you must segregate data as a first step to your problem. For instance, consider you are leading a technical support center and at the end of the month you analyze all the categories of incidences/tickets that your team has handled. One major issue at hand is the huge time taken to resolve all these incidences. In this scenario, you would use unsupervised learning to identify what kind of incidences fall in one group. Are they technically complex or FAQ, which is consuming your team's bandwidth. This way unsupervised learning provides you the clusters, and you can then prioritize which one to address first.

One major difference with supervised learning is that the data used for unsupervised learning is not labeled. This makes an easy starting point for unsupervised learning problems, as there is no dependency on label data.

To understand how unsupervised algorithms work, we'll use an example of bank data. This data contains various banking parameters of commercial entities, like industrial risk, management risk, credibility, and competitiveness, and in which class do they belong, bankruptcy or non-bankruptcy.

The rating system used for input features is P = positive, A = average and N = negative, while B = bankruptcy, NB = non-bankruptcy are used for Target Feature, i.e., class.

Let's understand the working of unsupervised learning through python code. There are primarily three techniques used in unsupervised learning, clustering, anomaly detection and neural networks. We'll be using the K-Means Clustering technique.

A.3.1 Data Processing

```python
import numpy as np
import pandas as pd
import seaborn as sns
import matplotlib.pyplot as plt
%matplotlib inline
```

```python
from sklearn.preprocessing import LabelEncoder
from sklearn.cluster import KMeans
from scipy.spatial.distance import cdist
from sklearn.model_selection  import train_test_split
```

```python
bank_df = pd.read_csv('banking.csv')
```

```python
bank_df.info()
```

```
<class 'pandas.core.frame.DataFrame'>
RangeIndex: 250 entries, 0 to 249
Data columns (total 7 columns):
 #   Column                 Non-Null Count   Dtype
---  ------                 --------------   -----
 0   Industrial Risk        250 non-null     object
 1   Management Risk        250 non-null     object
 2   Financial Flexibility  250 non-null     object
 3   Credibility            250 non-null     object
 4   Competitiveness        250 non-null     object
 5   Operating Risk         250 non-null     object
 6   Class                  250 non-null     object
dtypes: object(7)
memory usage: 13.8+ KB
```

```python
bank_df.head()
```

	Industrial Risk	Management Risk	Financial Flexibility	Credibility	Competitiveness	Operating Risk	Class
0	P	P	A	A	A	P	NB
1	N	N	A	A	A	N	NB
2	A	A	A	A	A	A	NB
3	P	P	P	P	P	P	NB
4	N	N	P	P	P	N	NB

Encode categorical values with numerical values. Though label encoding could have been used here we are using another technique to replace the values directly with custom discrete value.

```
# Encoding 6 Features and 1 Target Var

encode_feat = {"Industrial Risk":      {"P": 10, "N": 1,"A":5},
               "Management Risk": {"P": 10, "N": 1,"A":5},
               "Financial Flexibility": {"P": 10, "N": 1,"A":5},
               "Credibility": {"P": 10, "N": 1,"A":5},
               "Competitiveness": {"P": 10, "N": 1,"A":5},
               "Operating Risk": {"P": 10, "N": 1,"A":5},
               "Class": {"B": 1, "NB": 0}}

bank_df.replace(encode_feat,inplace=True)

## Encoding with Highest value for P =10, Average value for A = 5 and Low value for N = 1. Other similar set of values
## could be 1,0,-1 etc
```

	Industrial Risk	Management Risk	Financial Flexibility	Credibility	Competitiveness	Operating Risk	Class
0	10	10	5	5	5	10	0
1	1	1	5	5	5	1	0
2	5	5	5	5	5	5	0
3	10	10	10	10	10	10	0
4	1	1	10	10	10	1	0

Next, we visualize the statistical distribution of data

```
bank_df.describe().transpose()
```

	count	mean	std	min	25%	50%	75%	max
Industrial Risk	250.0	5.176	3.704039	1.0	1.0	5.0	10.0	10.0
Management Risk	250.0	4.336	3.664535	1.0	1.0	5.0	5.0	10.0
Financial Flexibility	250.0	4.236	3.575393	1.0	1.0	5.0	5.0	10.0
Credibility	250.0	5.076	3.737123	1.0	1.0	5.0	10.0	10.0
Competitiveness	250.0	5.172	3.965516	1.0	1.0	5.0	10.0	10.0
Operating Risk	250.0	4.756	3.898365	1.0	1.0	5.0	10.0	10.0
Class	250.0	0.428	0.495781	0.0	0.0	0.0	1.0	1.0

A.3.2 Normalize Data

```
from scipy.stats import zscore
```

```
# Normalizing the data before applying K - means
X = X.apply(zscore)
```

	Industrial Risk	Management Risk	Financial Flexibility	Credibility	Competitiveness	Operating Risk
0	1.304975	1.548726	0.214111	-0.020377	-0.043461	1.347878
1	-1.129680	-0.912174	0.214111	-0.020377	-0.043461	-0.965413
2	-0.047611	0.181560	0.214111	-0.020377	-0.043461	0.062716
3	1.304975	1.548726	1.615364	1.320234	1.219938	1.347878
4	-1.129680	-0.912174	1.615364	1.320234	1.219938	-0.965413

A.3.3 Group Data into Similar Clusters

```
distortion = []
K = range(1,10)
for k in K:
    kmeanModel = KMeans(n_clusters=k).fit(X)
    kmeanModel.fit(X)
    distortion.append(
        sum(np.min(cdist(X, kmeanModel.cluster_centers_, 'euclidean'), axis=1)) / X.shape[0])
```

```
import matplotlib.pyplot as plt
plt.plot(K, distortion, 'bx-')
plt.xlabel('k')
plt.ylabel('Distortion')
plt.title('The Elbow Method showing the optimal k')
plt.show()
```

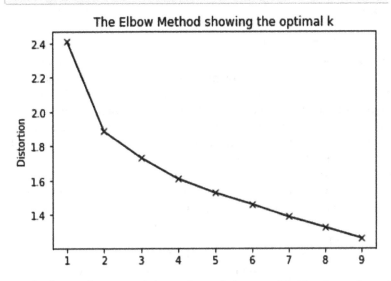

The elbow graph shows the potential number of clusters. The best number of clusters is obtained when the error or distortion decreases maximum with increasing number of clusters. In the example above we find the best case with two clusters.

A.3.4 Label Each Data with Cluster Number

```
bank_df['labels']=kmeanModel.labels_
```

```
bank_df.shape
```

```
(250, 7)
```

```
bank_df.head(10)
```

	Industrial Risk	Management Risk	Financial Flexibility	Credibility	Competitiveness	Operating Risk	labels
0	10	10	5	5	5	10	1
1	1	1	5	5	5	1	1
2	5	5	5	5	5	5	0
3	10	10	10	10	10	10	1
4	1	1	10	10	10	1	1
5	5	5	10	10	10	5	1
6	10	10	5	10	10	10	1
7	10	10	10	5	5	10	1
8	10	10	5	10	5	10	1
9	10	10	5	5	10	10	1

Now our data is ready to be analyzed further for each cluster. For example, we observe that industrial risk, management risk with positive ratings (10) always belong to cluster one, i.e., non-bankruptcy, and can draw inference that entities with positive ratings on various parameters will have less chance for bankruptcy.

A.4 Reinforcement Learning

This technique employs a system of rewards and penalties to compel the computer to solve a problem by itself. Human involvement is limited to changing the environment and tweaking the system of rewards and penalties. As the computer maximizes the reward, it is prone to seeking unexpected ways of doing it. Reinforcement learning is useful when there is no "proper way" to perform a task, yet there are rules the model must follow to perform its duties correctly. Moreover, just like unsupervised learning, reinforcement learning also doesn't take any labeled inputs to plan its actions.

The best way to understand how reinforcement learning works is to visualize playing chess where your opponent is AI based reinforcement learning program, and it calculates the rewards and penalties for every move, then takes an action. This way, every time it makes a move in the white or black square, it will not only calculate the probabilities of winning, i.e., reaching the opposite side, but also rewards and penalties. Reinforcement learning has so far been successfully implemented in simulation games, rather Go or Atari Games have popularized reinforcement implementation [5]. However, there is still a long way to go for reinforcement learning, especially in mission critical applications like autonomous driving.

Code implementation for reinforcement learning is usually complex and requires understand of complex mathematics (Q Functions or Bellman's Theorem). If you are interested in understand primary coding, I encourage you to visit the Freecodecamp article [10].

A.5 Deep Learning

Deep Learning is a type of machine learning (ML) and artificial intelligence (AI) that imitates the way humans gain certain types of knowledge. Deep Learning is an important element of data science, which includes statistics and predictive modeling. It is extremely beneficial to data scientists who are tasked with collecting, analyzing, and interpreting large amounts of data; deep learning makes this process faster and easier.

At its simplest, deep learning can be thought of as a way to automate predictive analytics. While traditional machine learning algorithms are linear, deep learning algorithms are stacked in a hierarchy of increasing complexity and abstraction.

To understand deep learning consider you are building a machine to identify a car. Initially you will pass a huge data set with car images. What deep learning will do is start identifying the features of a car, like door, tire, windshield, head lamps, etc. This it does using Neural Networks, which is an algorithm mimicking the human brain. Just like human brains have millions of neurons, the Neural network contains nodes and layers to build a complex algorithm for feature extraction. Finally, this neural network, when supplied with images of vehicles, will be able to differentiate cars from truck or vans or bicycles because of unique features it has stored in its memory.

We'll be using Google Colab to implement the deep learning model for MNIST data. The MNIST database (Modified National Institute of Standards and Technology database) is a large database of handwritten digits that is commonly used for training various image processing systems. Our problem is to design a deep learning model using Neural Networks to identify handwritten digits (from 0 to 9).

A.5.1 Install Tensorflow and Load Libraries

```
#!pip3 install -U tensorflow --quiet

import numpy as np

import tensorflow as tf
```

A.5.2 Collect or Load the Data

Tensor flow comes pre-loaded with the MNIST database. The database contains 70,000 images of handwritten digits. After loading, we simultaneously split the data set into Train and Test sets.

The train and test input sets (trainX and testX) contain the bitmap values (0–255) of the image, while the output sets (trainY, testY) contain the digit number.

```
(trainX, trainY),(testX, testY) = tf.keras.datasets.mnist.load_data()

Downloading data from https://storage.googleapis.com/tensorflow/tf-keras-datasets/mnist.npz
11493376/11490434 [==============================] - 0s 0us/step

trainX.shape

(60000, 28, 28)

testX.shape

(10000, 28, 28)
```

As we observe below the first image is a handwritten digit '5

```
plt.imshow(trainX[0],cmap='gray')
```

```
<matplotlib.image.AxesImage at 0x7f9a8b74aeb8>
```

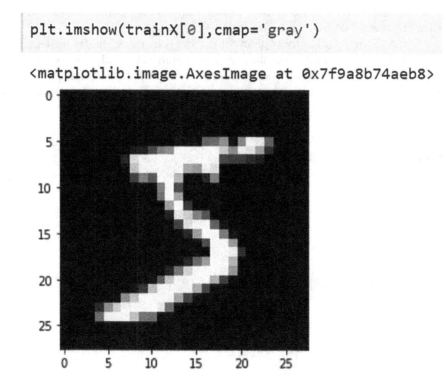

A.5.3 Convert Output Labels to Binary Classes

The output labels train Y and test Y can have multiple values (from 0 to 9) for an input row. Since we are building a categorical neural network, we'll have to convert the output labels to multi-class format.

We'll be using Keras Neural Network library for our example.

```
trainY = tf.keras.utils.to_categorical(trainY, num_classes=10)
testY = tf.keras.utils.to_categorical(testY, num_classes=10)
```

```
testY[0]
```

```
array([0., 0., 0., 0., 0., 0., 0., 1., 0., 0.], dtype=float32)
```

A.5.4 Prepare Inputs for Model

Keras Neural Network Model can be Sequential or Functional. We'll be using sequential API, as it adds Neural network layers linearly while building a model.

```python
#Initialize Sequential model
model = tf.keras.models.Sequential()

#Reshape data from 2D to 1D -> 28x28 to 784
model.add(tf.keras.layers.Reshape((784,),input_shape=(28,28,)))

#Normalize the data
model.add(tf.keras.layers.BatchNormalization())
```

A.5.5 Build and Compile Model

We've built a four-layer model with 'sigmoid' activation. The more layers we add, the more complex the neural network will become, and hence, more computationally expensive. Apart from sigmoid, we could also use the "relu" activation function. Observe the last layer (output layer) has "softmax" as an activation function, the reason being that we are building a multi class neural network.

```python
#Add 1st hidden layer
model.add(tf.keras.layers.Dense(200, activation='sigmoid'))

#Add 2nd hidden layer
model.add(tf.keras.layers.Dense(100, activation='sigmoid'))

#Add 3rd hidden layer
model.add(tf.keras.layers.Dense(60, activation='sigmoid'))

#Add 4th hidden layer
model.add(tf.keras.layers.Dense(30, activation='sigmoid'))

#Add OUTPUT layer
model.add(tf.keras.layers.Dense(10, activation='softmax'))

#Compile the model
model.compile(optimizer='sgd', loss='categorical_crossentropy',
              metrics=['accuracy'])
```

A.5.6 Review Model (Optional)

```
model.summary()

Model: "sequential"
```

Layer (type)	Output Shape	Param #
reshape (Reshape)	(None, 784)	0
batch_normalization (BatchNo	(None, 784)	3136
dense (Dense)	(None, 200)	157000
dense_1 (Dense)	(None, 100)	20100
dense_2 (Dense)	(None, 60)	6060
dense_3 (Dense)	(None, 30)	1830
dense_4 (Dense)	(None, 10)	310

```
Total params: 188,436
Trainable params: 186,868
Non-trainable params: 1,568
```

A.5.7 Training the Model

```
model.fit(trainX,trainY,
          validation_data=(testX,testY),
          epochs=20,
          batch_size=32) ## Run 20 ephocs

Epoch 1/20
1875/1875 [==============================] - 6s 3ms/step - loss: 2.3064 - accuracy: 0.1117 - val_loss: 2.2968 - val_accuracy: 0.1135
Epoch 2/20
1875/1875 [==============================] - 5s 3ms/step - loss: 2.2946 - accuracy: 0.1196 - val_loss: 2.2905 - val_accuracy: 0.1135
Epoch 3/20
1875/1875 [==============================] - 5s 3ms/step - loss: 2.2872 - accuracy: 0.1244 - val_loss: 2.2817 - val_accuracy: 0.2090
Epoch 4/20
1875/1875 [==============================] - 6s 3ms/step - loss: 2.2730 - accuracy: 0.1667 - val_loss: 2.2604 - val_accuracy: 0.3158
Epoch 5/20
1875/1875 [==============================] - 5s 3ms/step - loss: 2.2337 - accuracy: 0.2997 - val_loss: 2.1877 - val_accuracy: 0.3545
Epoch 6/20
1875/1875 [==============================] - 6s 3ms/step - loss: 2.0694 - accuracy: 0.3899 - val_loss: 1.8786 - val_accuracy: 0.4080
Epoch 7/20
1875/1875 [==============================] - 5s 3ms/step - loss: 1.6703 - accuracy: 0.4528 - val_loss: 1.4523 - val_accuracy: 0.4842
Epoch 8/20
1875/1875 [==============================] - 5s 3ms/step - loss: 1.3518 - accuracy: 0.5219 - val_loss: 1.2213 - val_accuracy: 0.5444
Epoch 9/20
1875/1875 [==============================] - 5s 3ms/step - loss: 1.1668 - accuracy: 0.5892 - val_loss: 1.0458 - val_accuracy: 0.6443
Epoch 10/20
1875/1875 [==============================] - 5s 3ms/step - loss: 1.0134 - accuracy: 0.6538 - val_loss: 0.9117 - val_accuracy: 0.7029
```

```
Epoch 11/20
1875/1875 [==============================] - 5s 3ms/step - loss: 0.9048 - accuracy: 0.7003 - val_loss: 0.8065 - val_accuracy: 0.7527
Epoch 12/20
1875/1875 [==============================] - 5s 3ms/step - loss: 0.8195 - accuracy: 0.7410 - val_loss: 0.7253 - val_accuracy: 0.7895
Epoch 13/20
1875/1875 [==============================] - 5s 3ms/step - loss: 0.7495 - accuracy: 0.7694 - val_loss: 0.6651 - val_accuracy: 0.8097
Epoch 14/20
1875/1875 [==============================] - 5s 3ms/step - loss: 0.6961 - accuracy: 0.7898 - val_loss: 0.6130 - val_accuracy: 0.8288
Epoch 15/20
1875/1875 [==============================] - 6s 3ms/step - loss: 0.6452 - accuracy: 0.8119 - val_loss: 0.5643 - val_accuracy: 0.8457
Epoch 16/20
1875/1875 [==============================] - 6s 3ms/step - loss: 0.6001 - accuracy: 0.8302 - val_loss: 0.5218 - val_accuracy: 0.8600
Epoch 17/20
1875/1875 [==============================] - 5s 3ms/step - loss: 0.5529 - accuracy: 0.8463 - val_loss: 0.4795 - val_accuracy: 0.8745
Epoch 18/20
1875/1875 [==============================] - 6s 3ms/step - loss: 0.5134 - accuracy: 0.8576 - val_loss: 0.4465 - val_accuracy: 0.8837
Epoch 19/20
1875/1875 [==============================] - 6s 3ms/step - loss: 0.4807 - accuracy: 0.8676 - val_loss: 0.4189 - val_accuracy: 0.8902
Epoch 20/20
1875/1875 [==============================] - 5s 3ms/step - loss: 0.4507 - accuracy: 0.8754 - val_loss: 0.3918 - val_accuracy: 0.8965
<tensorflow.python.keras.callbacks.History at 0x7f9a966b6080>
```

As can be observed, the final accuracy of this model after 20 epochs in 89.65

A.5.8 Validate Results

i. Input image for first data set.

```
#Lets print the image as well
import matplotlib.pyplot as plt

plt.imshow(testX[0],cmap='gray')

<matplotlib.image.AxesImage at 0x7f9a92f0e588>
```

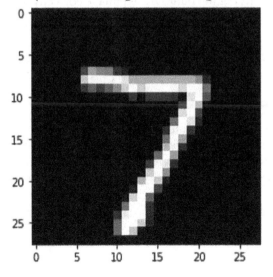

ii. Model prediction.

```
input_data = np.expand_dims(testX[0], axis=0)
input_data.shape
```

```
(1, 28, 28)
```

```
pred = model.predict(input_data)
pred
```

```
array([[3.0697035e-07, 2.8398163e-03, 3.5578771e-05, 1.1195106e-02,
        5.1953211e-05, 3.7976503e-04, 7.8133908e-08, 9.5068020e-01,
        3.3185240e-03, 3.1498645e-02]], dtype=float32)
```

```
pred.shape
```

```
(1, 10)
```

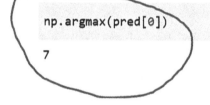

```
np.argmax(pred[0])
```

```
7
```

As we can see, our model is identifying the handwritten image correctly as "7".

A.6 Conclusion

It'll not be an exaggeration to say that the 22nd century will be the century of technological breakthroughs, with the help of AI. Be it automotive, retail, logistics, genetics or any other field, AI will become a vital component and will be all-pervasive at the grassroots levels. The next wave of the AI revolution will ride on a more human-centric AI, though humans ought to be the key beneficiaries of AI. Undoubtedly then, AI will aid human intelligence and evolution to the next level.

References

1. "Machine Learning | Coursera." *Coursera*, https://www.coursera.org/learn/machine-learning.
2. Davison, J. "No, Machine Learning Is Not Just Glorified Statistics." *Towards Data Science*, June 27, 2018, https://towardsdatascience.com/no-machine-learning-is-not-just-glorified-statistics-26d3952234e3.
3. "Housing Prices Competition for Kaggle Learn Users." *Kaggle: Your Machine Learning and Data Science Community*, https://www.kaggle.com/c/home-data-for-ml-course/overview.
4. "Machine Learning Tutorial for Beginners: What Is Basics of ML." *Meet Guru99 – Free Training Tutorials & Video for IT Courses*.
5. Osiński, B. "What Is Reinforcement Learning? The Complete Guide – Deepsense Ai." *Deepsense. Ai*, July 5, 2018, https://deepsense.ai/what-is-reinforcement-learning-the-complete-guide/.
6. https://expertsystem.com/machine-learning-definition/.
7. "Notes-from-the-ai-frontier-insights-from-hundreds-of-use-cases-discussion-paper.pdf." *Mckinsey.com*, https://mckinsey.com.
8. "Supervised vs Unsupervised vs Reinforcement Learning | Intellipaat." *Intellipaat Blog*, December 26, 2019, https://www.facebook.com/intellipaatonline/; https://intellipaat.com/blog/supervised-learning-vs-unsupervised-learning-vs-reinforcement-learning/.
9. "What Is Deep Learning? | How It Works, Techniques & Applications – MATLAB & Simulink." *MathWorks – Makers of MATLAB and Simulink – MATLAB & Simulink*, https://in.mathworks.com/discovery/deep-learning.html.
10. "A Brief Introduction to Reinforcement Learning." *FreeCodeCamp.Org*, August 27, 2018, https://www.freecodecamp.org/news/a-brief-introduction-to-reinforcement-learning-7799af5840db.

Index

Taylor & Francis Group
an **informa** business

Taylor & Francis eBooks

www.taylorfrancis.com

A single destination for eBooks from Taylor & Francis
with increased functionality and an improved user
experience to meet the needs of our customers.

90,000+ eBooks of award-winning academic content in
Humanities, Social Science, Science, Technology, Engineering,
and Medical written by a global network of editors and authors.

TAYLOR & FRANCIS EBOOKS OFFERS:

A streamlined
experience for
our library
customers

A single point
of discovery
for all of our
eBook content

Improved
search and
discovery of
content at both
book and
chapter level

REQUEST A FREE TRIAL
support@taylorfrancis.com

Routledge
Taylor & Francis Group

CRC Press
Taylor & Francis Group